Evangelical Foundations

American University Studies

Series VII
Theology and Religion

Vol. 33

PETER LANG
New York · Bern · Frankfurt am Main · Paris

Marvin W. Anderson

Evangelical Foundations

Religion in England, 1378–1683

PETER LANG
New York · Bern · Frankfurt am Main · Paris

Library of Congress Cataloging-in-Publication Data

Anderson, Marvin Walter.
Evangelical foundations.

(American university studies. Series VII, Theology and religion ; vol. 33)
Bibliography: p.
Includes index.
1. England—Church history. 2. Evangelicalism—England—History. 3. Bible. English—Versions. I. Title. II. Series: American university studies. Series VII, Theology and religion ; v. 33.
BR747.A53 1988 274.2 87-3558
ISBN 0-8204-0486-1
ISSN 0740-0446

CIP-Kurztitelaufnahme der Deutschen Bibliothek

Anderson, Marvin W.:
Evangelical foundations : religion in England, 1378–1683 / Marvin W. Anderson. – New York; Bern; Frankfurt am Main; Paris: Lang, 1987.
(American University Studies: Ser. 7 Theology and Religion; Vol. 33)
ISBN 0-8204-0486-1

NE: American University Studies / 07

Printed by Weihert-Druck GmbH, Darmstadt, West Germany

To My Sons

STUART BRUCE

CHAD MARTIN

In Memory of Cambridge Days:

Twenty-Seven Months In All

1970/71 and 1977/78

I will pack, and take a train,
And get me to England once again!
For England's the one land, I know,
Where men with Splended Hearts may go:
And Cambridgeshire, of all England,
The shire for Men who Understand...
Say, do the elm-clumps greatly stand.
Still guardians of that holy land?

-- Rupert Brooke

TABLE OF CONTENTS

FOREWORD ix-x

AUTHOR PREFACE xi-xiv

PROLOGUE: "WORKS OF TIME" 1-12

SECTION I: BIBLICAL VISION 13-67

Chapter 1) Oxford: Reform & Reaction 13-39

Chapter 2) Wycliffite Bible: First in English 39-55

End Notes 56-67

SECTION II: PRINT AND PROTEST 69-138

Chapter 3) Tyndale's Testament 75-93

Chapter 4) "With Eagles' Wings..." 93-111

Chapter 5) Politician, Primate and Printers 111-125

End Notes 126-138

SECTION III: EXEGESIS IN EXILE 139-214

Chapter 6) John Knox: Pastor to the English 142-152

Chapter 7) Geneva Bible 152-171

Chapter 8) Beza in England 171-188

Chapter 9) Catholics and Controversy 189-200

End Notes 201-214

SECTION IV: PURITANS AND PASTORS 215-306

Chapter 10) Mitres and Ministry 222-244

Chapter 11) Presbyterian Protest 245-260

Chapter 12) A Rustie Talent 260-276

Chapter 13) Thomas Shepard: Colonial Pastor 276-290

End Notes 291-306

SECTION V: SCRIPTURE AND SOCIETY 307-361

Chapter 14) Pre-Critical Biblical Commentaries 307-321

Chapter 15) Sermons and Society 321-346

End Notes 347-361

SECTION VI: TRANSCONTINENTAL PROTESTANTS 363-450
Chapter 16) The Shadow of Servetus 363-386
Chapter 17) Radical Puritans 387-402
Chapter 18) Pilgrim Existence 402-419
Chapter 19) The Moral Minority 419-433
End Notes 434-450

EPILOGUE: WILDERNESS EXPERIENCES 451-459

SELECT BIBLIOGRAPHY 461-468

INDEX OF PERSONS 469-488

FOREWORD

This admirable learned volume is addressed to what the author believes is an identity crisis within contemporary American religion, and it is with diffidence that an English student of the sixteenth and seventeenth centuries dare comment on its importance and relevance. But while an English scholar must ask his own rather different questions in evaluating the continuity of an English evangelical tradition (he would for example also be very interested to evaluate the evangelical tradition not dissenting, still less separatist, but continuously and loyally within the Church of England) and while he would have his own techniques for survival during the infiltration of those perilous minefields labelled "Protestant" and "Puritan", it is all important to relate the American Protestant tradition to its origins in Europe. Certainly this comes to the heart of Dr. Anderson's splendidly erudite treatise. It is important to see the English Protestant and dissenting tradition as itself at all points coloured and refracted by the Continental reformation.

What Dr. Anderson has finely done, is to sketch the solid religious content of this evangelical tradition, in the Bible, in preaching, in the witness of Christian men and Christian communities from the time of John Wyclif to that of Roger Williams, and he has done this in continuous awareness of the continuing ferment of scholarship concerned with this period, as with the most recent Wyclif studies associated with Dr. Anne Hudson, or with the most recent studies, monographs and dissertations such as those of Dr. Kinder and the Spanish exiles in London, and Dr. C. J. Clements' recent illuminating discussion of the English radicals and Anabaptists. Dr. Anderson's account is up-to-date, well written and well worth the reading.

The result is a score of related essays in depth, rooted in the particularity of men, books and movements, so that all students of this intricate period, whether English or American cannot but find profitable material for study and for reflection in these pages. If the ground bases of the work are the principles enunciated in its opening pages, and summed up in his conclusion, it is the sound historical method and the constant reference to up-to-date historical scholarship which make this book an important contribution to the solution of the immense and timely questions which he has raised.

Gordon Rupp
Cambridge
September, 1985

AUTHOR PREFACE

Evangelical Foundations is an in-depth survey of renewal in the English Church from Wyclif (1378) to Roger Williams (1683). This three-hundred year account explores the European roots of Evangelicalism which was planted in North American soil. The purpose is to show how, by use of an English Bible, a national church was renewed through the centrality of preaching. This book is designed for adult readers who wish to understand the dynamic of that multi-million member group. Readers will find documentation of topics raised in the text which will assist them to understand how such a program of Biblical renewal is not sectarian but stands at the center of the English church. Catholic readers should especially profit from this analysis of renewal which originated in medieval times. The book may be useful as a compass pointing the direction to a renewal of congregational life. Any parish which will adjust its priorities to place Scripture and preaching at the center will understand what it means to be evangelical.

John Wyclif died six-hundred years ago on December 31, 1384 at Lutterworth. By that time a vernacular Bible circulated among his followers and sat on the library shelves of the English aristocracy. As archbishops burned those copies and in turn were themselves burned, such as Cranmer at Oxford, one is unsure which event is more startling -- the burning of Bibles and their readers or the penetration of Biblical narrative into every level of English society over the three centuries, from Wyclif's demise to John Bunyan's Pilgrim's Progress of 1678. Our account, begun while this author helped to celebrate Martin Luther's quincentenary in 1983, commemorates the six-hundreth anniversary of the first complete English Bible.

I am grateful to those individuals who made this study possible by their encouragement, permission and concern. My son, Stuart Bruce, typed the entire manuscript into the computer during June to August of 1984, editing several drafts in the process. Mrs. Gloria Metz, Bethel Seminary faculty secretary, keyboarded the computer text while adding in some dozen pages of narrative during August-December 1985 and again in October of 1986. Her transferral of copy from one computer system and pitch to another improved the final copy. Errors which remain are my entire responsibility, whether typographical or otherwise.

The Board of Regents of Bethel College and Seminary granted two quarters' sabbatical leave during 1983-1984 to write this book and the Bethel Alumni Council granted research funds for a stint at London-Oxford-Cambridge in July/August of 1982. I am grateful for institutional support of this project which permitted three separate visits to England.

Hirofumi Horie, now a doctoral student under Professor Sir Geoffrey Elton at Cambridge, kindly permitted me to use material from his 1980 Bethel Th.M. thesis prepared under my supervision. Stephen Brachlow released a portion of his 1978 Oxford D.Phil. thesis now published in the Journal of Ecclesiastical History. These former students helped me to understand John Knox and Henry Jacob, respectively. Two other Bethel students have contributed data in the past five years for this study. I am grateful to David Henly and Clifford Christensen for their respective research on Thomas Cartwright and Thomas Shepard. Ian McPhee permitted me to summarize and update his paper on "Beza in England" written in 1976 for G.R. Elton's doctoral seminar at Cambridge. Its alterations are based on Beza literature published over the last decade.

Special thanks must go to Vivian Nuttall, Associate Director of the Wellcome Library for the History of Medicine, London, who guided me through the plague literature in that superb collection during July/August of 1982. The following libraries granted access to printed primary sources for this study:

I. London

1. British Library
2. Guildhall Library
3. Lambeth Palace Library
4. Society of Antiquaries

5. Wellcome Library
6. Dr. Williams's Library

II. Oxford

1. Balliol College
2. Bodleian Library
3. Merton College
4. Regent's Park College

III. Cambridge

1. Cambridge University Library
2. Emmanuel College Library
3. Jesus College Library
4. Pembroke College Library
5. Trinity College Library

IV. Other

1. Center For Reformation Research, St. Louis MO
2. Huntington Library, San Marino CA
3. J.E. Klingberg Puritan Collection, New Britain CT
4. Luther/Northwestern Seminary, St. Paul MN

Christopher Clement was kind enough to discuss English religious radicals during the Cambridge "long vacation" of 1979. His Cambridge thesis is quoted by permission. Dr. Peter Newman Brooks, Fellow of Robinson College, Cambridge, read Sections II and III in 1984, especially commending the quotations. Dr. Barrington White, Principal of Regent's Park College, Oxford, listened to my concerns about English Separatism. His oral comments on recent and current literature were most helpful. Professor A.G. Dickens kindly invited me to London where his help on the English Reformation, 1525-1558 was greatly appreciated. His forthcoming article in the *Archiv für Reformationsgeschichte* (1987) was crucial to that visit and this study. I treasure the counsel of these English mentors whose religious history is the subject matter of an American's narrative.

John Augustine, instructor in English Composition at Yale University and Fulbright Scholar in Seventeenth Century English studies at Merton College, Oxford, read the third draft. I appreciate his perception and literary analysis of the entire document. Special commendation must go to my Old Testament colleague at Bethel, Dr. Gary Smith, who answered all of my Quaestionae Hebraicae. A revised portion of the section on Tyndale has appeared in the Sixteenth Century Journal XVII (1986): 331-51.

This study would not have been completed without the encouragement of Ernest Gordon Rupp, Fellow of the British Academy and Emeritus Professor in Ecclesiastical History at Cambridge University, who gave me several sixteenth century books for my research. His Cambridge seminar, "The Continental Impact on the English Church, 1540-1580," spurred me on to write up what we discussed during the three academic terms of 1977-1978. His guidance through the intricacies of sixteenth century literature and critique of the penultimate draft balanced my American account with sensitivity to the continuous and loyal evangelical tradition which survives in the English Church. Our lengthy discussions on that score in May and again in December of 1984 were most helpful as was his detailed critique of the third draft in September of 1985. His own account of Religion In England: 1688-1781 will appear in the Oxford History of the Christian Church late in 1986.

Dr. Peter Newman Brooks wrote in his introduction to Christian Spirituality (S.C.M.: 1975): "E.G.R.'s many-sided achievements and interests effectively mirror his depth of character and pastoral genius." The section on "Romans VIII in Peter Martyr Vermigli" is added as a special tribute to this mentor of Reformation Studies. It is done in gratitude for two memorable sabbaticals spent at Cambridge University in the 1970s under his supervision and four annual visits to Cambridge in the 1980s. This scholar-pastor is an extraordinary person whose care for texts and their authors taught me at first-hand the meaning of the ancient episcopal expression: Reverend Father-in-God.

> "A generous man will prosper;
> he who refreshes others will himself
> be refreshed." Proverbs 11:25 (N.I.V.)

St. Paul, Minnesota
December 1, 1986

PROLOGUE: "WORKS OF TIME"

Ralph Waldo Emerson spoke a refreshing word to the famine of the heart which the pulpit spread in the early decades of nineteenth century America. Emerson's Divinity School Address describes the specter of a preacher who had not learned to convert life into truth. Outside the church his eye could see the silent snow, its beauty wiser than the discourse of vain words. Emerson went on to lament:

> This man had ploughed and planted and talked and bought and sold; he had read books; he had eaten and drunken; his head aches, his heart throbs; he smiles and suffers; yet was there not a surmise, a hint, in all the discourse, that he had ever lived at all.[1]

Emerson's wider glance caught a glimpse of transcendental beauty which the narrow pulpit focus missed in 1838.

American religious studies fall prey to that narrow spirit when they ignore the European setting of American religious history. "How American is Religion in America?" asked Winthrop Hudson in a now famous essay of 1968.[2] Hudson deplores the concentration on the unique American experience which all too often leads to a provincial understanding. To remember that we are Englishmen and Europeans as well as Americans in our religious life "guards us against cultural and intellectual isolationism, and serves to restrain messianic impulses."[3] American religious historians as well as ministers can restrict their vision to the extreme when they appeal to their North American tradition independent of the ecclesiastical world from which their protestant ancesters came. When one's eyes are opened to a vision of that historical continuity, a sense of identity emerges to replace the narrow vision of a grim provincial pulpit.

Patrick Collinson uses the language of a narrowed vision in his classic essay on the dissenting tradition. Denominational historians are a step ahead of their secular counterparts and "have much the better chance of getting it right."[4] None the less, even those who explore the Free Church setting of English

Puritanism must learn to appreciate the impressive world of the early seventeenth century shared by moderate puritans, separatists and 'parish anglicans' alike. A common core of sermonic material lies at the heart of that religious world.[5] Collinson's thesis of a "broader understanding" will be explored in this study as its central theme is tested through three centuries of English/European renewal in which preaching is central, from John Wyclif in the 14th century to Roger Williams in the 17th.

Laurence Duggan traces the failure of the late medieval church to respond to perceptions of clerical decay.[6] Whether or not the clergy were immoral, the more germane question which Duggan raises is whether they ministered to the needs of their flock in spite of preaching which filled five thousand volumes of printed sermonic literature before 1500. Pastoral work did not always suffer as plural offices were held without obligations. When pluralism and absenteeism were practiced together over the long haul, that posed a dilemma for pastoral care which the Council of Trent resolved by mandating episcopal residency. "Major Catholic reformers from Eck to Canisius also singled out the clergy as the leading source of the church's troubles."[7] They became the source of renewal as well when clerics such as John Wyclif, Desiderius Erasmus and Martin Luther responded to the responsibilities in which the Church had trained them. The hierarchy which neglected preaching struggled to control the biblical cadences of its lower clergy. This pastoral crisis of the late medieval church formed a Catholic as well as Protestant response.

Erasmus (1469-1536) troubled the church by his prolific writings. From the Book of Antibarbarians (1494/95-1520) to the Ecclesiastes (1535) Erasmus left an imprint on European Christianity. His paraphrases on the New Testament were placed together with the Great Bible in every English parish church.[8] His view of preaching is central to his reforming concern. The Ecclesiastes mirrors that care for a church more responsive to biblical and patristic models of vital pastoral care.[9] Erasmus began his manual on preaching in 1525 which is in fact a collection of three books. First of all, Erasmus in this manual gave a theological treatise on the importance of preaching, then a textbook in homiletics and finally an outline of sermon topics. Self-discipline and sincerity of heart must mark the preacher. "If sincerity of heart is lacking, the rest are nothing but wine mixed with poison."[10] Sincerity mingled with piety would characterize the sacred orator whose teaching office would coordinate all the functions of scriptural discourse. Instruction and persuasion are the twin goals of the Christian preacher.[11]

> The role of the priest is not to kill, but to make souls alive. It is far easier to compel by force than to persuade by speech, much simpler to destroy the body than to convert the mind.12

A century and a half earlier in Central Europe a native tradition emerged in Prague where regular sermons were a feature of reform. Conrad Waldhauser operated from the chief church in Prague. By his death in 1369 this Czech preacher set the tone for his successors. Jan Milic became a preacher in 1364 at St. Giles in Prague where his success led to accusations nine years later. Milic died in 1373 before he could return from the Papal Court in Avignon. His fiery denunciation of clerical sins made him the father of Czech reform.[13]

John Hus preached some three thousand sermons at the endowed Bethlehem chapel during twelve years, twice on every Sunday as a rule and as well on Saints' days. The chapel was decorated with pairs of pictures on opposite walls where, as Hus spoke in Czech only, the audience could see the pope on horseback opposite Christ carrying his cross.[14] While in exile Hus wrote to the Pragers about his preaching. Hus deplored the authorities who decided to pull down the Bethlehem chapel in 1412:

> Bishops, priests, masters and scribes... condemned the Truth, put Him to death and buried Him in the grave., But He rose again and conquered them all. In place of one preacher, that is Himself, He gave them twelve and more. That same Truth in place of one faint-hearted goose, gave Prague many eagles and falcons, who have keen sight, soar high by grace, and skillfully catch birds for the king, Lord Jesus.15

Hus' name means 'goose' in the Czech language!

Several years before his exile, Hus defended biblical preaching in a letter of 1408. He complained to Archbishop Zbynek of Prague that true preachers of the gospel are jailed while criminal priests freely walk the streets of Prague.

> 'love grew cold' among the clergy and 'iniquity increased among the people' for lack of love among the clergy, who desist from devout preaching of the gospel and from true following of Christ.16

In Prague preaching was the vehicle of evangelical renewal. A true priest in this native reform was one who gave himself to devout preaching as well as truly following Christ.

In fourteenth century England John Wyclif cited a medieval bishop for his support of biblical preaching. John Wyclif often used Robert Grosseteste, scholar/bishop of Lincoln from 1235 to 1253, as a bridge over which to link the church of fourteenth century England with the scholar/bishops of Patristic times. Wyclif refers to Lincoln's support of scripture since the proper cure of souls rests on a right use of sacred scripture.[17]

As an administrator of the Diocese of Lincoln, Bishop Grosseteste rooted out abuses with the help of the two new Orders, the Dominicans and Franciscans. He asks for help from the Master General of the Dominicans, requesting one John of St. Giles, whose understanding of the Scriptures can help administer the largest diocese in England.[18] Regular visitation of his diocese made Grosseteste famous as a medieval bishop. The visitation procedure is given in his <u>Proposition On Visitation of One's Diocese</u>, in which the clergy are to hear the bishop preach and friars will be chosen to preach to the people. In his constitutions Grosseteste endorsed daily bible study.

> All pastors after reciting the offices in church are to give themselves diligently to prayer and reading of Holy Scripture, that by understanding of the Scriptures they may give satisfaction to any who demand a reason concerning hope and faith. They should be so versed in the teaching of Scripture that by reading of it their prayer may be nourished, as it were, by daily food.19

Small wonder that Wyclif saw a model in this English bishop whose famous 'sermon' at the Council of Lyons in 1250 obligated those in a pastoral charge to teach the living truth, "in the awe-inspiring condemnation of vice"[20] Wyclif early on found a close affinity to Grosseteste while he was lecturing on logic from 1361 and before he became a theologian. In his De Logica Wyclif placed him with "those more subtle thinkers like Pythagoras, Democritus, Plato, Epicurus, and, among the moderns, Lincolniensis and others."[21] By the time Wyclif started his lectures on theology, Grosseteste was indeed his advocate for a clerical pastoral office sensitive to plausable conditions for the decline of Christendom. Richard Southern asks whether Wyclif was justified in his use of Grosseteste, especially since his citations were partial and extensions of his great speech of 1250 on papal weakness were distorted.[22]

As Wyclif turned from one subject to another, from the sufficiency of the Bible and the primacy of pastoral care to the essential nature of preaching and the need for new translations from the Greek, "he found that Grosseteste had been there before him."[23] Though Wyclif was more shrill than Lincoln, he was the first person after Roger Bacon to read Grosseteste so widely and with so broad an understanding.[24] A broader vision sees Wyclif as a national reformer, applying scripture to the wounds of a church which he loved. Dom David Knowles comments on the monastic ideal at the close of his narrative of the English Religious Orders. Knowles notes four factors which contributed to monastic decline, from great wealth and external activity of Abbots, to the lack of satisfaction in daily work and lack of a spiritual doctrine. They became in the end works of time rather than of eternity.[25] Wyclif was the Evening Star of scholastic theology as well as the Morning Star of the English Reformation. He chose a different path for the foundation of his theology than the interminable Scotist speculation about the absolute power of God. He did not argue from the analogy of being in the Thomistic sense in which there is nothing in the intellect which is not first in the senses. Biblical reality for Wyclif precluded analogies based on the identity of man with God, which was idolatry in its corporate form of claims to papal dominion over the created order. He chose rather the law of Christ to rescue the church from its philosophical heresies which taught in effect that God can be known in Himself apart from biblical revelation centered in the law of Christ.

Evangelical Foundations, 1378-1683 is a title used to describe Wyclif's response as Doctor Evangelicus to the pastoral crisis which the double papal election of 1378 created for the Western Church. His dissemination of biblical knowledge in textual commentary and Latin sermon was matched by the Lollards in their vernacular translation of scripture and the sermon cycle. However dimly at times, that mirror of eternity which was scripture reflected the pain and promise of the Ecclesia Anglicana. As the decades passed on, the Good Shepherd of St. John's account, so treasured in the Sermon Cycle, was seen as the chief shepherd and bishop of the church. The Godly added to these Johannine and Petrine concerns that the foundation of St. Paul, on which they wished to rebuild the English Church, had already been laid in apostolic times. It was none other than Jesus Christ, the good and chief shepherd. (John 10:14/I Peter 2:21/I Cor. 3:11)

When we travel into the past from Williams' New England of 1683 to Wyclif's England of 1378, those three centuries give Americans a wider perspective than is possible from a solitary analysis of American religious history. Indeed, past the rubble of European religious wars and the bare ruined choirs of English monasteries one finds in the centrality of scripture the hoped for renewal of national churches. To paraphrase Emerson, these persons were ones whose heads ached and whose hearts throbbed. There is the hint in the historical discourse which follows that on several occasions the church lived by the preaching of the gospel. An example would be Sundays in the 1580s when the godly of Eastern England would convene to hear the gospel, as in the vivid account at Ramsey where in 1581 a dozen villagers gathered in a clearing "to eat roast beef and goose while listening to one

William Collett, who expounded St. John's Gospel from a ladder."[26]

Several concerns emerge as one traces the renewal of the English Church over three centuries from its late medieval setting to the early modern scene. The term **Evangelical Foundations** means attention to much held in common during those centuries. The narrative is described in the six sections which follow:

I. Biblical Vision
II. Print and Protest
III. Exegesis in Exile
IV. Puritans and Pastors
V. Scripture and Society
VI. Transcontinental Protestants

This study seeks to provide a sense of identity created by more careful attention to the religious heritage of those European centuries from Wyclif to Williams. Renewal of the Corpus Christianorum over these three centuries came from within the national or state church. To focus on the genealogy of these concerns in American religious history at the expense of their genesis in the European setting would seem to foster sectarian attitudes. Marsden, for example, suggests that fundamentalism appealed to a number of immigrant groups, "especially those who shared a northern European Protestant heritage."[27] The concern of this study is to show that such an assumption lacks coherence for contemporary evangelical christians whose ethnic roots and religious heritage is European. One possible antidote for that narrow vision is to explore a wider European tradition reflected in conservative Protestantism whose reading of John Wesley[28] and Charles Haddon Spurgeon[29] made these household words in twentieth century congregations who were sustained by hymns of Charles Wesley.

American evangelical circles need a recognition of this English and European heritage in order to establish their historical continuity.[30] One could view what follows as an essay on Evangelicalism in European Culture from 1378 to 1683. As the American heirs of Wyclif and Williams do their own ploughing and planting, aching and throbbing, smiling and suffering, may they avoid too narrow a focus on American religious history. A wider vista of evangelical renewal in the thirty decades from John Wyclif to Roger Williams, reflected as it was for them in the mirror of scripture, can reorient American Christianity in the twenty-first century and provide a fresh vision for its evangelical character in the third Christian millenium.

Marvin W. Anderson
St. Paul, Minnesota
All Saints Day, 1986

END NOTES to PROLOGUE

[1]Brooks Atkinson, The Selected Writings of Ralph Waldo Emerson (New York: Modern Library, 1968): 77.

[2]Winthrop S. Hudson, "How American is Religion in America?" Reinterpretation in American Church History, edited by Jerald C. Brauer (Chicago: Univ. of Chicago Press, 1968): 167.

[3]loc.cit.

[4]Patrick Collinson, "Towards a Broader Understanding of the Dissenting Tradition". The Dissenting Tradition, edited by C. Robert Cole and Michael E. Moody (Athens: Ohio Univ. Press, 1975): 26.

[5]Ibid., p. 12. Now see Patrick Collinson, "Lectures by Combination: Structures and Characteristics of Church Life in 17th Century England," Bulletin of the Institute of Historical Research XLVIII (1975): 182-213.

[6]Lawrence G. Duggan, "The Unresponsiveness of the Late Medieval Church: A Reconsideration," Sixteenth Century Journal IX (1978): 3-26.

[7]Ibid., p.25.

[8]Roland Bainton, "The Paraphrases of Erasmus," Archiv für Reformationsgeschichte 57 (1966): 67-76.

[9]John C. Olin, "Eramus and the Church Fathers," Six Essays on Erasmus (New York: Fordham Univ. Press, 1979), pp.33-37.

[10]Opera Omnia (Leiden: 1703) 5: 783.

[11]James Michael Weiss, "Ecclesiastes and Erasmus The Mirror and the Image," Archiv für Reformationsgeschichte 65 (1974), pp.98-99. See John W. O'Malley, S.J., "Erasmus and the History of Sacred Rhetoric: The Ecclesiastes of 1535," Erasmus of Rotterdam Society Yearbook Five (1985): 1-29.

[12]Roland Bainton, Erasmus of Christendom (New York: Charles Scribner's Sons, 1969), p.268.

[13]Howard Kaminsky, A History of the Hussite Revolution (Berkeley: Univ. of California Press, 1967), pp.8-13.

[14]Mathew Spinka, John Hus, A Biography (Princeton: Princeton Univ. Press, 1968), pp.47-48.

[15]Mathew Spinka, The Letters of John Hus (Manchester: Manchester Univ. Press, 1972), p.83.

[16]Ibid., p.23 cf. Matthew (24:12) and Philippians (2:21).

[17]Edith C. Tatnall, "John Wyclif and Ecclesia Anglicana," Journal of Ecclesiastical History XX (1969), p.39.

[18]J.H. Srawley, "Grosseteste's Administration of the Diocese of Lincoln," Robert Grosseteste Scholar and Bishop, edited by D.A. Callus (Oxford: At the Clarendon Press, 1955), p.148.

[19]Ibid., p.168-169. See Beryl Smalley, "The Biblical Scholar," in Callus, Robert Grosseteste, p.95.

[20]Ibid., p.170.

[21]Cited in R. W. Southern, Robert Grosseteste, The Growth of an English Mind in Medieval Europe (Oxford: Clarendon Press, 1986): 218.

[22]Ibid., pp. 302-303.

[23]Ibid., p. 306. See the brilliant sketch by Anthony Kenny, Wyclif (Oxford: Oxford University Press, 1985): 56-79, "The truth of scripture" and "Church, King and Pope."

[24]Ibid., p. 307.

[25]Dom David Knowles, The Religious Orders in England Volume III. The Tudor Age (Cambridge: At the Univ. Press, 1961), pp.460-463.

[26]Cited from Patrick Collinson, "The Godly: Aspects of Popular Protestantism in Elizabethan England," Papers Presented to the Past and Present Conference on Popular Religion (1960):16 in Margaret Spufford, Contrasting Communities English Villagers in the Sixteenth and Seventeenth Centuries (Cambridge: At the Univ. Press, 1974), p.258.

[27]George Marsden, Fundamentalism and American Culture The Shaping of Twentieth-Century Evangelicalism 1870-1925 (Oxford: Oxford Univ. Press, 1980), p.205.

[28]V.H.H. Green, The Young Mr. Wesley, A Study of John Wesley and Oxford (London: The Epworth Press, 1963) pp.289-302.

[29]The Spurgeon Collection. A List of the Books in the Charles Haddon Spurgeon Library in William Jewell College Library, Liberty, Missouri. See pp.32-34 on Calvin, p.122 on Jewel, p.195 on Richard and John Rogers and p.53 on Edward Dering as examples.

[30]Richard Lovelace, "A Call to Historical Roots and Continuity," pp.61-62 in Robert Webber and Donald Bloesch, The Orthodox Evangelicals (Nashville: Thomas Nelson Inc., 1978), pp.61-62. See also Robert T. Handy's discussion of the permanence of that European influx which he sees translated from geographical to other wilderness experiences. These are a wilderness of sects, of war, of urban life and of conflicting ideas. "Wilderness experiences of Religion in America" in F.F. Church and T. George, editors, Continuity and Discontinuity in Church History (Leiden: E.J. Brill, 1979), pp.301-314.

SECTION I. BIBLICAL VISION

Chapter 1) Oxford: Reform & Reaction

A. Archbishops and Bibles

The Papacy obliged the Archbishop of Canterbury to bring John Wyclif to trial in 1377. Four years later Wyclif retired from Oxford to the parish of Lutterworth. Not until 1409 and two primates later did the English Church prohibit circulation of an English Bible. Several dynamics of English society fill that quarter century with support and suspicion of Wyclif and his followers known as Lollards. Political support continued for Wyclif's followers until Sir John Oldcastle's rebellion in 1413. Several factors other than political support are germane to this delay. It took great effort to staunch the wounds inflicted on the proprietary church by these disciples of the Evangelical Doctor.

Moves were made early on to secure Oxford against Wyclif, such as the refutation drawn up in 1397 based on his Trialogus and the death penalty passed against such adherents in 1401. Even so, Wyclif had support within the precincts of those Oxford spires. Peter Payne, who spent forty years abroad interpreting Wyclif to the Hussites, had arranged for regent masters at Oxford in 1406 to send a letter which testified to Wyclif's reputation and exemplary life.[1]

Literature of the past decade points to a mixed reception of the Doctor Evangelicus between his death (in 1384) and 1409. Anne Hudson explores why these ideas became so explosive when in the hands of his predecessors they were not. Could the new ingredient be the vernacular, she asks, and goes on to answer in the affirmative. It was not the citation of the English ecclesiastical tradition as such, nor the setting of canon law against civil law that was crucial so much as it was the use of English to spread these ideas.[2] "We must always remember that books themselves become voices,"[3] writes Margaret Aston, who quotes the ordinances at St. Albans in 1426-7 that heresy was caused by "the possession and reading of books which are written in our vernacular tongue."[4]

It is necessary then to inquire into the content and form of Wyclif's several teachings as circulated by his supporters in that quarter century after his demise. That inquiry involves a glimpse at the activities of three Archbishops of Canterbury as well as Wyclif's life and lore. In all of this the biblicism of his early supporters emerges. Recent publications of Wycliffite writings help one to reconstruct this period in ways that demonstrate the centrality of Wyclif's position in English society and the rejection of his vernacular biblical vision.

Aston's most recent account reflects on the poverty and politics of that early period. She points to a crucial distinction which Wyclif made between able-bodied alms takers such as members of the wandering monastic orders and all other categories of beggars. In little noted expositions of the great supper in Luke 14, Lollard exegesis altered the Vulgate reading of four classes. Instead of inviting those who were poor, crippled, blind and lame, Lollards saw three classes invited to the royal banquet, all of whom were poor. There were the "poor feble, poor blynde and poor crokid."[5] The Lollard sermon cycle renders this as: "And bring into this feast these three manner of men: poor feeble men, poor blind men and poor lame men -- these three are God's prisoners that both God and man help with alms."[6] Alms should go to the poor rather than to line the pockets of story-telling wandering preachers. Wyclif calculated the social consequences of exempting such friars from taxation as costing the realm some £40,000 English pounds _per annum_.[7]

One Lollard alternative was the disendowment bill of 1410 which would net all the revenues of the English bishops, archbishops and some seventy-five abbeys and religious houses for the poor and needy. This triple proposal would first of all link the creation of new earls, knights and squires for national defence with a second proposal to establish 100 almshouses for the poor. In the third place the number of universities would increase (to fifteen) and new clerks be secured. The fifteen thousand priests and clerks would fill their offices by being as one glossed version has it "good priests and perfect clerks to preach the word of god without flattering or begging or worldly reward."[8] What remains is to link the particularities of this renewal of the Ecclesia Anglicana within the time frame of late medieval English life.

Three Archbishops are linked with the public career of Wyclif and attempts to prohibit an English Bible. Simon Sudbury (1375-81), William Courtenay (1381-1396), and Thomas Arundel (1396-97, 1399-1414) are involved with the first English Bible which was translated by 1395.

When John of Gaunt, Duke of Lancaster, forced Bishop Wykeham of Winchester out of political office in 1371, clerical privilege was under attack. Gaunt retained the services of John Wyclif to present a case against the clerical ownership of property. When the papacy obliged Archbishop Sudbury to bring Wyclif to trial in 1377, he let him off with a mild caution. Was Sudbury Gaunt's partisan or recipient of his favour? Some have mistaken his lethargy for weakness.[9]

The chronicler Thomas Walsingham is responsible for a low evaluation of Sudbury.[10] Sudbury sought to avoid trouble wherever possible, as in the affair of Bishop Wykeham. In arousing the clergy to Gaunt's humiliation of the bishop, which forbade Wykeham to approach within twenty miles of the King, leaving him unable to attend the Westminster parliament of January 1377 or the Convocation following it at St. Paul's, Sudbury led the ecclesiastics to refuse a subsidy to the duke's government. Such resolute action is helpful to understand Sudbury's lenient treatment of Wyclif.

> Wyclif was still not a heretic when brought before Sudbury, and the archbishop perhaps felt that he was dangerous only because of the men who patronized him. In letting him off with a caution he was refusing to provoke his patrons...11

Sudbury became chancellor in January 1380 but had only eighteen months until he was murdered in the Peasants' Revolt of 1381.[12]

In the mid-afternoon of February 19, 1377 John Wyclif appeared before the convocation of bishops assembled at St. Paul's. Wyclif did not come alone but with him was the duke and Lord Henry Percy, the marshal of England. Convocation broke up in a row between the duke and the Bishop of London, William Courtenay.[13] Mob action threatened at the doors of Percy's residence as well as the duke's home.

The Lambeth trial nine months later responded to the five papal bulls issued against Wyclif. Courtenay and Sudbury were named in the third bull to secure scholars well versed in the scriptures who could refute Wyclif's heretical propositions. Dahmus claims that Wyclif responded to the bulls by circulating a pamphlet.[14] No official report exists in the episcopal registers. The subsequent Blackfriars council took action against Oxford dissidents. On November 24, 1377 Repingdon formally retracted his errors.

John Aston had been in prison since his defiance before the archbishop on June 20. His Confessio aroused controversy for its orthodox assertions. In a second Confessio for Courtenay in October, Aston admitted his crime of imprudent answers. Aston procrastinated at the Oxford encounter but finally submitted on November 24. Courtenay treated the Oxford disciples of Wyclif as scholars who had momentarily erred. It was a delicate problem well handled by Courtenay. Hereford remained unrepentant in a Roman jail. He was not to recant until 1390. The three became vigorous opponents of Lollardy at Oxford.

During this time Bishop Buckingham had his hands full with Lollards in Lincoln diocese. It began on March 5, 1382 with the trial of William Swinderby. Sentence was passed on July 11.[15] When Courtenay visited Northampton on November 5-6, 1389, he heard of no heresy. By 1393 the town had Lollard demonstrations with sermons preached by the laity. In August Buckingham set up a commissary to seek out heresy by September 8. The commissars fled for their lives from the Lollards to All Saints' Church. One Anna Palmer received the Lollards in her house by night. Anna charged the bishop with being anti-Christ.[16] The fifteen charges are attached to the bishop's report. The members held among other tenets that

> It is lawful to inform his christian brother about the ten commandments and the holy gospels inorder that he may know and preach, and respond as head of the family for him and his set family.17

Thomas Arundel earned his hostile reputation amongst his opponents by the constitutions of 1407-09 which forbade the Bible in English. The Lanterne of Light, a contemporary Lollard tract, called the Archbishop Antichrist "bi whos strengthe anticrist enterditith chirchis, soumneth prechours...cursith heerars, & takith away the goodis of hem."[18] Arundel was not present at the 1382 Blackfriars council when he was bishop of Ely near Cambridge. Suspicion of heresy emerged in 1384. At William Thorpe's trial in 1407 Arundel said that he well knew that for twenty winters and more Thorpe had sown false doctrine.[19] John Purvey reports that Arundel preached at the funeral of Queen Anne who had the Glossed Gospels. The Queen "hadde sent hem unto him, and he seide thei weren goode and trewe."20

According to the alarmist chronicler Walsingham, some time early in 1395 the Archbishop of York and others visited the king in Ireland to urge his sudden return to defend the English church from "the unbelievable affliction of the Lollards and their supporters."[21] The two churchmen were Arundel and Braybrooke. Because Oxford was the focus of attention that summer, the account is credible. That February a manifesto was drawn up by the southern convocation "against the sect of Lollards and to their confusion."[22]

On February 27, 1397 various Oxford doctors and scholars denounced the presence of Wyclif errors at the University. Eighteen passages from the Trialogus including a denial of transubstantiation became the basis of a lengthy refutation drawn up by William Wodeford. As a result of such widespread increase of sordid sectarian teaching, the two Archbishops urged parliament to establish the death penalty in 1397 for such persons.[23] Such did indeed happen two years after Arundel's return from exile in 1399.

> So the believers in these doctrines grew in number... and they became so bold... that in public places they shamelessly barked like dogs with unwearying voices... They were everywhere called Wyclif's disciples, and the name was not insuited to them.... These Wycliffites proclaimed how commendable was their sect, and uncited men and women everywhere to reject the teachings and preachings of others... and vociferously proclaimed themselves true and evangelical preachers, in that they had the gospel in the English tongue.24

Thomas Arundel, Archbishop of Canterbury, closed off debate about a national bible translation which the English hierarchy could support. Arundel's Constitutions of 1407/9 came after the 1401 decree that heretics must be burned at the stake. The end of the fourteenth and beginning of the fifteenth century mark a sharp struggle for a national Bible in European Christianity. In the Czech, Dutch and English debates the apologetics came from England.[25]

The primary document in the debate is a Latin manuscript found in Vienna. It is of Bohemian origin but originated in England and is the source of the Lollard English tract reprinted in the sixteenth century under the title A Compendious olde treatyse Shewynge Howe that we ought to have the scripture in Englysshe.[26] The surprise is that Richard Ullerston composed the Latin treatise. That Ullerston was not a Wyclif disciple means that an open debate over the issues raised by Wyclif continued at Oxford up to 1401,[27] even though authorities searched out and seized Wyclif books from 1382.[28] Aston concludes that this new evidence is important beyond the fresh ascription of an individual text. It has implications "that the hardening of attitudes, and definitions of the bounds of orthodoxy, took place, not at the departure of Wyclif for Lutterworth in 1382, but nearly twenty-five years later under the zeal of Arundel."[29] Retrospective interpretation that possession of an English Bible was prima facie evidence that its owners were 'Wycliffistes' can not be sustained. The seventh conclusion to Ullerston's text reads that "just as the exercise of preaching God's word... is to be controlled by the wise planning of bishops, so also should be the practice of translation."[30] The English version of this tract on translation exists in at least seven extant manuscripts. John Foxe used the 1530 printed edition when he included the tract in his 1563 Actes and Monuments.[31] A comparison of the Luft edition with Foxe and the Trinity College, Cambridge manuscript indicates that Luft/Foxe are based on a later transcription. Aston's "Debate" shows that this tract is a translation of the Vienna Latin text dated to 1401. The text quotes from Bede, Grosseteste, Fitzralph, Hampole and Thoresby. Biblical quotations are not taken from the Wycliffite Bible but are independent translations.[32]

The tract cites several scriptural reasons for a vernacular translation, one of which is to II Corinthians (4:3) at lines 144-146:

> Also Seint Paule Seith: if oure Gospel is hid, it is to hem that schal be dampned: & eft he seith: he that knoweth not, schal not be knowen of God.33

Equally intriguing are the references to English writers. Bede is quoted from the Ecclesiastical History that King Oswald of Northumbria asked Bishop Aidan

> to preche his puple, and the kynge of him-self interpreted it on Engliche to pe puple. If this blessed dede be aloued to the kynge of all hooli chirche, how not now as wel aughte it to be alowed a man to rede the Gospel on Engliche and do ther-after.34

Bede not only put the liberal arts into English to ward off barbarism, but also translated the Gospel of John.[35] Two favorite Lollard episcopal illustrations are William Thoresby, Archbishop of York (1351-1373) and Robert Grosseteste, bishop of Lincoln (1235-1253). Thoresby commissioned an English version of the Ten Commandments.[36] Several extant manuscripts of Middle English versions indicate that Wyclif's own Ten Commandments ties into Episcopal endorsed English versions. John Foxe knew of several manuscript versions of the Ten Commandments in English circulating in the sixteenth century. The Grosseteste reference will repay careful scrutiny. The text says that in a sermon *scriptum est de leuitis* Grosseteste urges that a priest who can not preach should resign his benefice. "If it is lawful to preach the naked text to the people, it is also lawful to write it to them and consequently, by process of time, so all the Bible."[37] That conclusion is precisely the point in the struggle over Wyclif's legacy from 1382 to 1407.

A recent study endorses the pastoral concern in the *Cura Pastoralis* in which Grosseteste connected the knowledge of revealed truth with active ministry.[38] McEvoy concludes that both were pre-conditions set by the bishop of Lincoln for ecclesiastical office.

> "The very substance of hierarchy is the Scriptures and its sole end is the salvation of souls. Knowledge of revealed truth, therefore, and active involvement in ministry are the chief conditions for office in the church."39

B. John Wyclif (1329-1384): Life and Lore

John Wyclif inspired a reform of the English Church. Wyclif in England and Hus in Bohemia elevated scriptural reform to a national and, in Wyclif's case, an international level.

> His agitation never went beyond the lecture hall and the pulpit; his media were words, thousands upon thousands, not action; his audience was the kingdom of England not a clandestine group.40

1. Realist Philosopher

Wyclif was a schoolman who spent the greater part of his adult life at Oxford where he was fellow of Merton in 1356, master of arts at Balliol in 1360 and doctor of divinity in 1372.[41] He lived except for two years in hired rooms at Queen's College until 1381. To graduate bachelor in theology an M.A. must attend lectures for four years on set books, three of which were spent hearing the Bible read. In the fifth year he could oppose and in the seventh, respond. Then the scholar was admitted to read the Sentences of Peter Lombard and for two more years preach in public and lecture on a Biblical book.[42]

For a quarter of a century, from his going up to Oxford before 1350 until his controversial career began in 1374, John Wyclif participated in the philosophical debates of the Oxford Schools. His metaphysical works such as the Summa de Ente mark him as a realist indebted to his teachers Thomas Bradwardine and Richard Fitzralph. Wyclif was devoted to the memory of Grosseteste.[43] It is there that one can appreciate the shaping of realist categories in Wyclif's philosophical works. Wyclif often cited the Commentary on the Posterior Analytics. Matter is perfected by form while cognition employs the sense faculties as the medium but never the cause of knowledge. The intellect elicits the universal from sense data with three characteristics: 1) it must be free from material phantasms, 2) involve the experience of many singulars and 3) actualize the potential to know first principles.[44] These universals conform to the unchangeable prototypes which exist in God's mind. Therefore one can know God, for in a state of grace the mind is subject to the First Cause that illumines things, clarifies understanding and imparts infallibility proportionate to its penetration. Thomas Bradwardine and Richard Fitzralph upheld a conservative interpretation of Duns Scotus, whose moderate realism could insist on the priority of the divine intellect to the divine will.

Fitzralph's Armenian Questions on free will are cited by Wyclif who was interested in their philosophical conclusions. Fitzralph went to the heart of the matter when he sought to reconcile the vision of God with a person's denial of it. He rejected Scotus who said the will could deny the clear vision and Aquinas who declared that, once seen, one must enjoy God's love. Was the intellect or the will more significant in attaining that clear vision of God? "If we have seen with complete clarity the end to which God has directed us, we are not free to will any other; but if our vision is only partial, we retain the freedom

...which belongs to imperfection."[45] Fitzralph refused to blur distinctions between willing and knowing, and by showing that men often act in ways that show they can enjoy what they will not and will what they do not like, he opposed the Modernists. In 1356 the implications of how God reveals the future were spelled out in the De Pauperie Salvatoris to which Wyclif would turn when later he wrote on lordship.[46]

This particular writing stems from the lengthy controversy over whether the Friars Minor or Christ owned property. The preface to On Poverty of the Saviour tells us that Pope Clement VI before May of 1350 appointed Fitzralph to a commission which would investigate this long standing issue between the Franciscans and the Dominicans. They reached no conclusion, though Fitzralph began to work on a major treatise which would investigate apostolic poverty. Fitzralph composed the long dialogue between 1351 and 1356.

Human lordship (dominium) is natural or civil. Original dominium is that which God exercised over all his creation, an inalienable lordship. If Adam had not sinned, argues Fitzralph, his descendants would have shared in that exercise equally. After the fall man can only control the earth by coercion. Civil or political lordship is the result of sin; it includes possession and use. Political lordship introduces property which is an acquired right of possessing and using the things subject to positive law. It involves the exclusion of others from this right or use over things and would not exist without sin. Natural lordship excludes no just man from its use, i.e., it is dependant upon grace. Therefore true lordship, whether original or political, is held only by those in a state of grace. In practice this doctrine meant "not that the friars should lose civil lordship because they abused it; it is rather that the friars are supposed to live by natural lordship."[47]

Though Fitzralph is on the Franciscan side of strict poverty, scholars argue that such distinctions had little practical effect so long as one could not know who was damned and who was saved. Yet Wyclif does seem to know who was heretical in his treatise On Simony. If Wyclif uses that definition as coterminous with signs of apostasy, then indeed the doctrine of dominion had practical effect in renewal of the church. Those guilty of simony are also guilty of heresy; those guilty of heresy are apostate; such have forfeited their civil lordship over property and of course their sovereignty over souls.

Wyclif's philosophical works are the De ente (1365-75); the De compositione hominis (1365-75); the De Actibus animae (1365-75); the De logica (1365-75); and the De materia et forma (1365-75). The dating is so complicated that one does best to view these works on academic subjects, except for the biblical commentary, as prior to 1373 and to date all others on theological subjects after that date.[48] The polemical political writings belong to that later period as well.[49]

The earliest Wyclif writing is the De logica from about 1363. Thomson has located an Italian copy of a fourteenth century English manuscript, superior to the printed edition based on two incomplete Bohemian manuscripts. A second English copy is in the Escorial.[50] Quite early in his Oxford career Wyclif built up a philosophical system extensive in its metaphysical rejection of Roman teaching. In fact, Wyclif composed a double Summa, the first on philosophical questions and the second on theological. Both were integrated about a biblical vision as can be seen from the introductory sentence in De logica I:

> "I have been urged by some friends of God's law to compile a treatise to demonstrate the logic of Sacred Scripture... I am putting forward, in order to sharpen the minds of the faithful, proofs of propositions which may be deduced from the Scriptures."51

Thomson indicates that Wyclif's grand design was to produce a "Christian focused logic" in a formal substructure on which his theology would be built. The Summa de ente would implement that plan in thirteen tractates "On Being". The first part concerns itself with man (universals) and the second with God (ideas).[52]

"Certain friends of God's law" wanted Wyclif to expound the logic of Holy Scripture.[53] This interpenetration of reason and faith occupies the first period of his public activity, a time from 1358-1372 in which Wyclif covered all the philosophical questions commonly lectured on in the schools. Since these questions also impinge on the second period from 1373-1379 and the third from 1379 to his death in 1384, it would be well to understand the philosophical utterances of the early period. The political/theological questions of the second period as well as the unorthodox sacramental views and program of scriptural education for the common people in the vernacular depend on Wyclif's realist metaphysics.

Wyclif held it certain that universals exist apart from the thing, that the archetypical world of divine ideas is real and that these are the patterns by which God Himself knows his creatures.[54] At this point Wyclif defined the essence of universal ideas by turning to Grosseteste's <u>Posteriorum</u> VII. Nominalists distain universals because they misunderstand the nature of predication, holding that they are not parts of the real world inasmuch as nothing in the real world is a part of a sentence. So universals are terms only and as such signify nothing. Wyclif distances himself from this denial of real predication in which species depend on the thinking mind.

> All envy or actual sin is caused by the lack of an ordered love of universals ... because every such sin consists in a will preferring a lesser good to a greater good .... Beyond doubt, intellectual and emotional error about universals is the cause of all the sin that reigns in the world.55

Distinct archetypes make up the divine mind for Wyclif. They are created by, are coeternal with, yet are inferior to God. They are real because they partake of His being; they communicate their content to God's other creatures who then possess being to that self-same degree. Aquinas had not seen the whole truth because universals are held by him as an abstraction of the mind. The other issue for Wyclif is the doctrine of the possibles. For something to be, it must have existed, now exist, or will exist at some future time.

> If everything to be possible has to be really possible, and have a real existence in God's mind, God's mind is then the present and permanent measure of all things, singular and universal. What is apparently infinite to our minds, is finite to God's, to whom nothing is infinite, in number, space, or time, not even his own power or existence.56

What is capable of thought is really possible. Since it is of God it can not be annihilated. What is possible to God is infinity to us, for He unites possibility and reality in space as well as time. The universe is fixed and its content unchangeable. Necessity follows from this doctrine of universals and the possibles.

> If the possible includes that which has been, that which is, and that which shall be... then it follows that everything which is to take place is already known to God.57

Since God's knowledge and action are one and the same, all things that are possible are decreed and thus necessary.[58]

This mental training, as Thomson observes, equipped Wyclif to enter the second period which was a theological/political query of Rome and ultimately the final period in which he provided scriptural education for the common folk. Wyclif's realism is the foundation of his radicalism. By 1372-3 Wyclif applied this to the text of Scripture, holding that the word of God was the material form of the eternal Word and a divine emanation in historic times of a divine exemplar.[59]

2. Augustinian Theologian

The earliest printed edition of Wyclif's Trialogus appeared at Worms in 1525. This began the legend of John Wyclif's Reformation reputation, which John Foxe put as "the greatest clerke that they then knew living."[60] John Bale in his 1548 catalogue of British writers described Wyclif as the Morning Star (stella matutina). Bale went on to say:

> Apart from the true apostolic life which he led, he far excelled all his fellows in England by his ability, eloquence, and erudition.... He was roused by the spirit of the eternal father to stand for His truth in the midst of the darkness of impious locusts, as the magnanimous warrior of Jesus Christ, and he became the most invincible organ of his day against Antichrists.61

Such rhetoric aside, most recent work points to Wyclif as the latest in a line of disciples of St. Augustine. His De Trinitate follows that of St. Augustine but also draws on contemporary thinkers in viewing reason as a positive aid to faith.[62] The theological writings range from the early 1370s to 1382. The second period opens with Wyclif involved in a diplomatic mission to Bruge in July of 1374. In 1376 he took part in John of Gaunt's persecution of William of Wykeham by preaching in London pulpits.[63] By February 1377 William Courtenay, bishop of London, summoned Wyclif to St. Paul's in London to answer for his political writing and activities. The Summa Theologica was written in twelve parts between 1375 and 1380/81. Thomson gives a helpful summary of their contents which are introduced by a strong theological statement on divine dominion preparatory to all twelve sections.[64]

a. Summa Theologica

Treatise I: On The Ten Commandments. The old law is the necessary basis for the "new law" which perfects the old.

Treatise II: On the State of Innocence. Civil power controls the church for God alone possesses dominion, while man only uses it. Without grace, even that use is forfeit.

Treatises III-V: On Civil Dominion i,ii,iii: "Whoever abuses his power is in unjust possession of the goods of God without license ... the Almighty by that very fact deprives him of his right."

Treatise VI: On The Truth of Sacred Scripture: "All law, all philosophy, all logic and all ethics are in Sacred Scripture." Literal sense of scripture is prior to the other three. Common folk should have scripture in English.

Treatise VII: On The Church. A polemical work somewhat repetitious in which the church is defined as the "corporation of the predestined." If the elect are known only to God, then the elaborate establishment of the visible church collapses.

Treatise VIII: On the Office of the King. Canon law often cited in this the most erudite of Wyclif's works. The King is subject to the law which the people should obey. Scripture contains God's law which if the ruler violates may be used to depose him.

Treatise IX: On Papal Power. Papacy is an historical phenomenon which should return to the simpler days of the church before Constantine.

Treatise X: On Simony. Papacy easily guilty of selling spiritual offices for material profit.

Treatise XI: On Apostasy. Philosophers use scholastic modes to cover human sin and failure.

Treatise XII: On Blasphemy. Practical expression of his philosophical and theoretical thought, now re-stated in lay language as the avenue of his anger.

To appreciate the impact of Wyclif's theological opinion on contemporary English life it seems helpful to linger over his arguments in several of these treatises in the Summa Theologica. On Civil Dominion appeared between 1376 and 1378 in which Wyclif gave full expression to his critique of lordship and church wealth. Wyclif turned to Fitzralph's De pauperie salvatoris for his doctrine of dominion and grace. Only if one was 'graced' by God could one rule on God's behalf. Only God could confer the right to lordship which for that reason was not transferable. Possessions were not property.[65] Wyclif demonstrated in his treatise that grace alone conferred the right to civil dominion.[66] The eighteen errors singled out by Pope Gregory XI are summarized in a papal bull of May 22, 1377 sent to Archbishop Sudbury and the Bishop of London. Wyclif has so

> rashly broken forth into such detestable madness that he does not fear to assert, profess and publically proclaim ... certain propositions and conclusions, erroneous and

> false, and discordant with the faith, which endeavour to subvert and weaken the stability of the entire Church ...67

Wyclif argues in effect that the clergy enjoy evangelical dominion as a grant of God's lordship in imitation of Christ. Civil dominion is enjoyed by secular powers, "whose very existence is rooted in man's sinfulness."[68] One important corollary of secular power lies in its regulation of the clergy. As Kaminsky points out, Wyclif destroys the papal right to tax or govern the English clergy by transferring all public and religious functions to royal regulation. When the law of Christ is identified with the law of the realm, "sin becomes crime."[69]

The model is the Primitive Church which enjoyed direct conversation with God. The law of God coerces those who rebel against God's order. The civil order is thereby reduced to the divine order as it, the civil order, has been the instrument to control the clerical order. The gospel is that which conveys the lex evangelicus - thus Wyclif's title of Doctor Evangelicus.

> The temporal lords, can, by the grace of God, study Christ's gospel in the language known to them, and reduce the church to the order that Christ instituted; this would be the supreme work of caritas.70

King Edward II died on June 21, 1377. The papal bulls against Wyclif were published on December 18. Pope Gregory died on March 27, 1378, which precipitated a schism over the double papal election which followed on April 8 and September 30, 1378. This gave Wyclif some time to summarize his De Civili Dominio in a Latin/English tract called Thirty-Three Conclusions on the Poverty of Christ. The ensuing papal struggle helped to turn Wyclif from a critic into a rebel.[71]

The tractate On The Church appeared in 1378, though in his inaugural doctoral lecture Wyclif already in 1372 questioned the prevalent papal ecclesiology.[72] 1378 was also the year in which Wyclif's Truth of the Holy Scripture appeared, which John Hus cited in 1411:

> My conviction was confimed by his writing in which he seeks with every effort to return all the people, and

> especially the clergy, to Christ's law, that they might relinguish worldly splendor and rule, and might live with the Apostles a Christlike life.73

The De Officio Regis, which follows the treatise On The Church, is the most complete of Wyclif's tracts on Church and State. It summarizes the direction in which De Ecclesia articulates Wyclif's maturing thought. The King's dignity was derived immediately from God, representing the glorified hence ruling Christ. The priest represents the suffering and submissive Christ; the king represents the will; the priest the love of God.[74] The De Ecclesia builds on the evangelical law of the Scriptures and Thomas Bradwardine's De Causa Dei. The church is the corporation of the predestinate, past, present and future - the whole body of the elect. Neither of the two popes mattered because the true church is independant of the papal institution. "O that happy schism that teaches fully so many, beautiful, catholic truths."[75] One of those truths would be to obey popes only as they follow Christ:

> This division of these popes may turn to good of many realms, that men believe to none of them but, for love of Jesus Christ, in as much as they see Christ in their life and in their lore.76

Wyclif gave the attributes of divinity to his definition of the church as the congregation [universitas] of the predestinate. The church is one of those archetypal universals which was eternal and perfect. Wyclif's church which is independent of space and time stands in opposition to the papal church. Christ is the head of the whole church.[77] The Church Militant is a political community with a real existence in both time and space. As a blemished human form, however, certain orders must function in that human society, i.e., clergy, temporal lords and the commoners.[78] The prayers, fighters and laborers must so work as to overcome those wrinkles and stains through love.

The particular teaching which struck home in every English parish would be Wyclif's denial of transubstantiation. Arguing from his realist philosophy, Wyclif could not accept the annihilation of bread and wine in order for them to become the blood and body of Christ. His withdrawal from Oxford in 1381 was the direct result of his eucharistic doctrine. McFarlane has well written:

> His objections to transubstantiation were that... it exposed Christ's body to the chances of daily accident and indignity, and that its grossness encouraged men to become idolatrous.[79]

Wyclif denied both the Thomistic explanation that only quantity remained and the Scotist view that bread and wine were annihilated to become Christ. There could be no accident without a substance, no being without archetypal essence. Leff provides a helpful summary of that teaching on the Lord's Supper from Wyclif's three tracts on Eucharist, Apostasy and the Trialogus. Bread and wine have an independent existence after consecration. The whiteness of the consecrated host represents the whiteness of the bread. To stop at the appearance would negate knowledge by placing men at the mercy of their sense impressions. Men need a means to attain to the reality beyond them.[80]

Chapter Four of De Papa (c.1380) summarizes Wyclif's eucharistic concerns. There one reads that the pope should clarify the nature of the host by teaching the gospel. Four sects hold the papal teaching that the host is not God's body, but is an accident without a subject.[81] The Lords should give no alms to priests who do not teach well, since there is no harm in discussing the truth. It is idolatry to bow down before an accident.[82]

The most recent analysis of Wyclif and the Eucharist shows how his Confessio of May 10, 1381 before the Oxford schools was the crisis point. Even John of Gaunt was reported to be outraged. J.I. Catto argues that the intellectual answer to this question outlined above is inadequate because it is based on eucharistic theory and not its cultic practice. In this view the social unity of the rite was threatened by an individualistic practice outside of the Mass. Surely, however, the point is that the new community which followed Christ's law celebrated His meal as a genuine spiritual/social group more authentic than the one it replaced.

Wyclif uses the image of a mirror to explain how the image of Christ in heaven was present on the altar. It seems he borrows this language of optics from Robert Grosseteste. Thus in a sermon of April 18, 1378 he preaches (at Easter?):

> To understand how the Body of Christ is sacramentally, not dimensionally, present in this venerable sacrament, consider the view of the optical philosophers who tell us that when a clean mirror is placed proportionately opposite a shape, a full likeness of that shape is present in every point of that mirror, although one man may see it in one point and another man in another point, depending on where the mirror falls and reflects. [J.I. Catto, "John Wyclif and the Cult of the Eucharist" in Katharine Walsh and Diana Wood, eds. The Bible In the Medieval World (Oxford: Basil Blackwell, 1985): 269, 273.]

This was his attempt to endow the Eucharist with a higher mode of real presence than the material accidents of bread and wine alone.

b. Biblical Scholar

Wyclif's inaugural doctoral lecture known as the Principium was given in 1372. It became the preface to the Song of Solomon in his as yet unpublished Postilla super totam Bibliam.[83]

Wyclif acknowledges three debts to scripture. First of all there is the moral inclination which assists the affections to exclude the triple threat of I John (2): "All that is in the world, the lust of the flesh and eyes and the pride of life." Secondly is that attitude of mind which reorients the natural and moral learning about wisdom. Finally Wyclif argues for that which produces a soul made knowledgable by understanding true wisdom and true theology.[84]

> There is no ecclesiastic who is excused from receiving the gift of understanding which obliges him to illuminate through his office by preaching or engaging in honest conversation or providing scholastic information ... one in school, another in the church; one in public, another in his closet, one like Mary in exalted contemplation, another like Martha in sincere conversation...

> that they might perfect the mystical body of Christ... by being taught and knowing the fulness of sacred scripture.85

The Postilla has recently come to light in four Oxford manuscripts which preserve five-eights of the total, whereas continental manuscripts at Prague and Vienna contain incomplete postills on the New Testament. Only part one on the Pentateuch and part two on the Historical Books of the Old Testament are now missing. Job to the Apocalypse is now complete, with manuscripts making cross references possible from one part to another. The eight fold division comes from Peter of Auriol's Compendium written in 1319 which Wyclif cites along with Nicholas of Lyra.[86]

The last chapters of the Opus Evangelicum, written when Wyclif was a dying man in 1384, quotes from the Postilla. Wyclif reproduces almost word for word the postil at John (13:1-15) on footwashing in his Opus Evangelicum. He goes on to comment on the state of the pope so fixed in greed that Peter's word seems certain; he will never be washed clean. Only these foolish words of Peter can be the foundation of papal authority which aspires to worldly honor whilst it is stained by the sin of greed and ambition. This addition to the Postilla means either Wyclif expands the early copy or becomes more radical after the Great Schism of 1378.[87] The monks of Bury on the otherhand treasured their copy of the Postilla, erasing Wyclif's name to preserve a precious volume. These manuscripts written before 1378 show Wyclif at the crossroads of ecclesiastical reform.[88]

Benrath points to the three strands in Wyclif's approach to contemporary problems of church and society. His chapter on "Realism, Biblicism and Criticism of the Church" weaves these into an unbroken strand as no one has done before.[89] Benrath notices how Lyra's phrase "Omnis Christi actio est nostra informatio" took in Wyclif the form "Omnis Christi accio est nostra instruccio." The natural law, Mosaic law and evangelical law are the grounds for discipleship.90 In the Postilla Wyclif was careful to employ the primary sense of scripture "without adding on the human traditions for ordering the universal militant church."[91] One place where Wyclif pressed this point was in his treatise, Of Feigned Contemplative Life.

> Also the Ordinal of Salisbury hinders much preaching of the Gospel; for fools value that more than the commandment of God, and to study and teach Christ's Gospel. For if a man fail in his Ordinal, men hold that a great sin, and reprove him for it sharply; but if priests say their matins, mass, and evensong according to the Sarum use they themselves and other men deem that is enough, though they neither preach nor teach the behests of God and of His Gospel. And thus they think that it is enough to fulfil sinful man's ordinance, and to neglect the rightful ordinance of God, that He charged priests to perform. Oh lord, if all the study and travail that men have now about Sarum use, with a multitude of new costly portable breviaries, antiphons, grails, and all other books, were turned into the making of Bibles and into studying and teaching thereof, how much would God's law be furthered and known and kept![92]

Those Scriptures were not only true, but were themselves a mirror of eternity. In this mirror Christianity had to look to see the instruction of Christ:

> The Scriptures are a mirror in which eternal truths are reflected, the way by which the traveler passes on to the goal of salvation and the consolation in which a sad soul is revitalized.[93]

When William Courtenay was elevated to Canterbury he waited until the pallium or symbol of his office arrived in England before performing any official acts. After May 2, 1382 he moved swiftly against Wyclif by summoning a Blackfriars Council to meet in London on May 17.[94] Wyclif was not invited! The council condemned twenty-four articles divided into ten heretical and fourteen erroneous conclusions. The first heretical proposition read,"That the substance of material bread and wine remains after consecration in the sacrament of the altar."[95] The fifth erroneous conclusion attacked unlicensed preaching.

At Oxford a scholar named Nicholas Hereford took his doctorate and then "began to magnify Wyclif and his doctrine in his first lecture."[96] The Archbishop sent a commission or permission to the Carmelite friar Peter Stokes to publish the London conclusions before another defender of Wyclif named Philip Repingdon could preach at Oxford on the feast of Corpus Christi. The chancellor stirred up the university against Stokes with the result that Courtenay crushed the opposition after both Stokes and the chancellor had travelled to London's Lambeth Palace. Chancellor Rigg on pain of excommunication was told not to let these doctrines be taught or preached at the university; as well, the twenty-four conclusions were to be published at St Mary's church "in English and in Latin, and also in the schools, and to enquire throughout the students' halls for adherents of Wyclif."[97] By May 21 of 1382 Courtenay had the Blackfriars formal statement to bolster his attack on Wyclif. On May 26 a parliamentary statute required the chancellor to issue orders that unauthorized preachers be imprisoned. On June 26 King Richard issued a patent which corroborated the statute. None the less, Repington's sermon described Wyclif as a "doctor eminently catholic."[98] That sermon in the first week of June 1382 marks an incendiary situation at Oxford.

On July 1 the Blackfriars council reconvened at Canterbury after Courtenay had interviewed both Hereford and Repingdon at Otford. Courtenay then excomunicated the two and urged on July 13 that the bann be proclaimed at St. Paul's and published in Oxford. A royal patent on July 13 to Chancellor Rigg was the heaviest blow of all. It instructed him to search the entire university community for those who favored the Blackfriars theses or befriended Wyclif and his company. The royal patent said that any book or tract by Wyclif or Hereford must be seized and handed over to the Archbishop within a month's time.[99] Wyclif had left Oxford for retirement due to illness in the Summer of 1381.

c. Biblical Sermons

In addition to the formal treatise On The Truth of Sacred Scripture (1378) and the Commentary on the Whole Bible (1382), Wyclif prepared sermons in a simple and plain style. He complained of the friars who preached flashy discourses:

> For some by rhyming, and others by preaching poems and fables, adulterate in many ways the word of God;... the poor priests preach purely and freely the word of God: but the friars preach feigned words and poems in rhyme, and therefore the friars' preaching is acceptable to the people.100

One of these tracts urging all Christians to acquaint themselves with the biblical text is called The holy prophet David saith.[101] It outlines six steps which lead to a reading of the text of the New Testament, a following of Christ's holy life and a trust in "the goodness of the Holy Ghost, which is special teacher of well willed men...."[102] Wyclif in several places answers the charge that since the letter kills, it is harmful to provide simple men with the Scriptures.[103] He quotes from Amos "I shall send hungyr on the herthe: not hungir of breed neither thourst of watir, but to heer the word of God." It is greater cruelty to withhold ghostly than bodily meat from "christene men that hungryn and thoursten therafter."[104]

Forty Latin sermons from the early period show Wyclif in his prime at Oxford.[105] Benrath dates sermon 59 to October 19, 1376 and sermon 51 to August 28, 1379. In between sermons 55, 56, 57, 62, 60 and 23 are dated to 1376 and 61 and 24 to 1377. All seem to come prior to 1378.

Corresponding sermons after this date attack the abuses of the Church, as in the Twenty Four Mixed Sermons. English sermons were made as well as the Latin models. Wyclif prepared plain sermons in English for the people.

The plain style is a rhetoric based on evangelical precepts in which two themes capture Wyclif's imagination. One theme is the imitation of Christ and the other is the reduction of outward ornamentation by the life of the spirit which defines the activities of a true Christian.[106] The reduction according to Auski is responsible for the plain style. Its components urge that the power of Christ's words reside in his spiritual followers.

The Latin sermons were models for others including Hus in Bohemia. Those imitating the plain style were to eschew love of excellence practiced by the friars who spoke with rhetorical tricks and exuberant worldly examples. Simplicity meant imitation of Christ who spoke bluntly. It must be "bare and appropriate with a clear intent."[107] Such muted eloquence builds upon evangelical imagery all the while it distrusts more extravagant literary modes. Wyclif would learn this evangelical eloquence from Augustine whose De Doctrina Christiana rejects the grand style since it often leads to pride.[108]

When these English Sermons cite Scripture they often telescope the text. For example, the Early and Late Versions of the Lollard Bible read at Matthew (25:31):

> When saw we thee hungary, and we fed thee; thirsty, and we gave to thee drink? And when saw we thee shelterless and we sheltered thee; or naked and we covered thee? Or when saw we thee sick, or in prison, and we came to thee?

The English Sermon summarizes the passage as "When saw we thee in these states, hungary, or thirsty, shelterless, or naked in body, sick or in prison, and we did this to thee, Lord?"[109]

The English Sermons are divided into five distinct groups. The Sunday Sermons, one set each on the gospels and the epistles, appear in parallel columns in one manuscript. The gospel series commences with the first Sunday after Trinity Sunday and the epistle series with the first Sunday in Advent.

The thirty-one sermons called "Commune Sanctorum" are based on texts for special feast days. The thirty-eight which make up the "Proprium Sanctorum" series bear the names of special events. The Ferial Gospels are for weekday services, one hundred sixteen in all. Ferias was an ecclesiastical term for all days except Saturday at first but then it excluded Sunday as well.[110]

Talbert dates these sermons as follows:

1. Sunday Gospel:	1376/77-1412
2. Proprium Sanctorum:	1377 -1383
3. Sunday Epistle:	1377 -1384
4. Commune Sanctorum:	1381 -1395
5. Ferial Group:	1382 -1395.[111]

Talbert does not accept Wyclif as the author of these 294 sermons which Hudson has now related more carefully to the extant manuscript tradition,[112] virtually complete in eleven manuscripts and altogether in thirty one copies.[113] Hudson dates the sermon-cycle no later than 1400 and would prefer an earlier dating such as 1389/90.[114] In any event they were models which gave preachers examples for Sundays, Feast Days and Weekdays according to the Sarum Use, a Latin Mass in use at Winchester. If not all by Wyclif, these sermons are yet compiled in imitation of his plain style and within five years of his death. References to events after Wyclif's death make him unlikely to be the author of such a closeknit enterprise.[115] Unlike later preachers such as John Donne and Jonathan Edwards, whose non-scriptural metaphors all too often soar beyond the boundary of a strict scriptural sense, the figures in these sermons strengthen the literal point. The only metaphors which go beyond a sentence in length are terms taken from scripture.[116]

Hudson's fresh edition gives the biblical texts for each of these 294 Sermons. The five sets are readily scanned in her tables.[117] The Sermon for the Second Sunday after Trinity describes the excuses made by those invited to share in the joys of heaven. This second sermon of set one concludes with a call to obedience.

> But God's servants, both of men and angels, seen after this second manner of calling, "Lord, it is done as thou commandest, and yet here is a void place for men that should sup with thee." For this manner of calling of men to the joy of heaven filleth not heaven of men that God hath ordained to bliss; and herefore the lord of heaven, in his bride calling that shall be in time near the day of doom, biddeth his servant [to] go out into ways and hedges and constrain men to enter 'that my house be filled.'
>
> For now in the last days when priests be turned to avarice, stones should cry and contrain priests that make them a private religion as a hedge and other men that see them in the brood way towards hell -- these stones, that be mighty men in the world, should constrain both priests and people to enter into heaven by holding of God's law. For fear of taking of their goods and pun-

ishing of their bodies shall constrain them by dread to keep this straight way to heaven. And so the number of men that God hath ordained to bliss/must need be fulfilled magrey antichrist.

But Christ saith to his apostles that none of the first men that God called to the feast [meat] and would not come shall taste his supper in the bliss of heaven. For God hath ordained which men shall be saved and which shall be damned, and both these numbers must need be fulfilled. And instruction for their advantage must need help as well, and antichrist's feigning must also be known.

Here may men touch of all manner of sin and especially of false priests, traitors to God that should truly call men to bliss and tell them the way of the law of Christ, and make known to the people the tricks of antichrist.118

Sermon 3 for the third Sunday in Advent takes its text from I Corinthians (4:1-5). This third sermon from set five on the Sunday Epistles sets out the agenda for clerical reform. The text says that men ought to regard the apostles as servants of Christ for it is required of a servant that he be faithful to his trust. It is a matter of conscience, for no human court can judge but only the Lord himself. The sermon distinguishes between God's day and man's day. The former is doomsday.[119] The day of man judges by human law, that of secular judges and worse yet that of antichrist.[120]

Popes and cardinals "take on often foal judgments" which if never questioned whether they be against the judgement of God become the judgement of antichrist.[121] If one heeds popes and prelates, one falls afoul of belief since their pride and covetousness is the smoke of beasts whose judgement stretches only to man's day. Since doomsday is the judge of belief, their word is void.[122]

A third example of this preaching is the fourth sermon for Sunday Epistles, based on Philippians (4:47): Rejoice always in the Lord. The worldly person is known by joy in winning worldly goods or coveting fleshly lusts[123], while the spiritual person is known by four special gifts. These are subtilty, agility, clarity and immortality. True men who are so gifted by God "clerly see the opon resoun of Godis wille" and therefore rejoice at all times.[124]

Chapter 2) Wycliffite Bible: First in English

> General opinion from his own day onwards had considered the translation of the Bible Wyclif's most important literary achievement, and this verdict, though it needs interpretation, may still stand. Two complete versions made from the Vulgate are associated with his name. One is a literal version, reproducing as nearly as may be the Latin idiom, often almost unreadable and sometimes obscure. The other is a free translation into running English, far more intelligible to readers who were unfamiliar with the construction of Latin sentences; this has also orthodox prefaces translated from the Vulgate and a more tendencious general prologue specially written.125

A. Wyclif's Role

In the fifty years since Manning penned that traditional account, scholars have questioned the nineteenth century editors Forshall and Madden and their view of Wyclif's bible based on observation of Ms. Bodley 959 at Baruch (3:20). Ms.Bodley Dauche 369 also breaks at Baruch (3:20) with the note: "Explicit translacom Nicholay de herford." Cambridge University Library Ms. El 1.10, an abridgement of the latter part of the Old Testament, notes at Baruch (3:20): "Here endeth the translaciun of N and now beginneth the translaciun of J and of othere men."[126] 'N' seems to be Hereford, while 'J' could be John Purvey, John Wyclif or even somone else. Margaret Deanesly in 1951 supports 'Lollard Bible' as a fair name "because manuscript evidence forbides us to believe that they were the work of Master John Wycliffe personally, and shows that they were the work of his followers."127

Hargreaves cites unanimous evidence from friend and foe that Wyclif was responsible for the translation.[128] Michael Wilks summarizes the opinion of the Swedish scholars S. L. Fristedt and C. Lindberg that Ms. Bodley 959 can not be the original by the first translator and that John of Trevisa was the leader of the translation team at Queen's College, Oxford early in the 1370s.[129] Lindberg thinks Wyclif translated the New Testament first about 1380, leaving Hereford to do the Old Testament after 1384. Purvey needed to step in where Hereford left off at Baruch (3:20) and complete a better version by 1390. Fristedt thinks Wyclif himself supervised the work of a first revision by 1384 with Purvey doing a second revision in the mid 1390s.[130] Further complication is introduced when Knapp and Wilks insist on Wyclif's authorship of the English sermons.[131] Hudson convinces this author that they are wrong in that ascription.[132]

Reconstruction of current opinion about the various attempts to provide an English Bible between 1378 and 1395 must not let one forget in that process that such a Bible exists in more than 230 manuscripts from the fourteenth and fifteenth centuries. Five items need to be considered in this complicated process: 1) 1378 is the earliest date by which John of Trevisa could have seen a New Testament at least in circulation, while 1395 is the date which Hargreaves assigns to the General Prologue affixed to the full late version ascribed to John Purvey.[133] 2) John Wyclif wrote that codices of an English New Testament were being burned in 1384. "The devil held a burning of codices of the law of the Lord. The languages which contain the laws of the Lord are Hebrew, Greek, Latin and English."[134] 3) Ms. Bodley 959 need not be assigned to 1382 when Hereford failed to answer the Blackfriars Council at London. Hereford went to Rome to appeal in person to Pope Urban VI who imprisoned him. Hereford returned to England after a Roman mob released him in 1385. Hereford was named in a 1387 proclamation issued by Bishop Wakefield of Worcester though already in custody at Nottingham.[135] Thus by 1387 a draft of the original is available because it was revised by Hereford who was the editor of the Glossed Gospels. 4) The Earlier Version had appeared in revised form in the Glossed Gospels, based on a commentary by Thomas Aquinas, the _Catena Aurea_, which permits the learned commentator to cite from Scripture, canon law, and favorite Wyclif authors such as Grosseteste. Because the compiler uses Purvey's favorite designation as "a sinful caytiff", Hargreaves assigns these to Purvey.

In 1394 Archbishop Arundel said he had approved for the use of Anne of Bohemia (Richard II's Queen) "Al the foure gospeleris on Engliche with the doctouris upon hem."[136] Aston dates this between 1387 and 1394.[137] This is an intermediate version as in Cambridge University Library MS. El 1.10. Therefore the Earlier Version seems complete before the Glossed Gospels revision of 1387-1394. Neither the original of the Early Version nor that of the Glossed Gospels has survived. 5) With the General Prologue dated on internal evidence to 1395, the time frame of seventeen years saw several translation efforts underway. John of Trevisa in 1378 might have seen an English New Testament which Wyclif saw burned in 1384. Nicholas Hereford revised a draft of the original translation in 1387 while the Glossed Gospels revise this between 1387 and 1394. The General Prologue completed this process of revision by 1395 so that between 1384 and 1395 there were at least three revisions of a now missing original version.

Wyclif's Pastoral Office (1378), as it turns from holy living to holy teaching, inserts into its Middle English Version a section advocating knowledge of God's law in English. Purvey or another lollard may be responsible for this insertion.[138] In this tract written for knights and secular lords Wyclif wrote:

> Christ and His apostles converted much people by uncovering of scripture, and this in the tongue which was most known to them... why then may not the modern disciples of Christ gather up the fragments of that same bread? The faith of Christ ought therefore to be recounted to the people in both languages.139

Archbishop Arundel wrote John XXIII in 1411 that Wyclif out of malice instigated the translation of scripture into his maternal language.[140] Wyclif bears the responsibility of these English Versions even if his relationship to them is still a puzzle.[141]

B. First English New Testament (1384-1395)

Wyclif witnesses to an English New Testament burnt by the authorities in 1384. Nicholas Hereford is mentioned in Ms. Bodley 959 as the translator up to Baruch (3:20) of the Old Testament by 1387. Independent translations show up in the English Sermons by 1390. By 1395 the General Prologue introduces a Later Version. It seems plausible that the Glossed Gospels which Anne of Bohemia treasured were part of the process by which the literal Early Version became the Later Version with one or more intermediate stages between 1384 and 1395.

One naturally is first interested in the translators of the English Bible, then in its text and finally in its transmission among the followers of Wyclif. Since several recensions exist of two principal versions, a brief comparison will be made based on the differences in vocabulary, sentence length and sentence structure used to translate the underlying Latin clauses.

Because the Early Version was so literal, Deanesly thinks it was made as the basis for a new Magisterium, a new authority, to set over against the canon law.[142] Since for him scripture was 'Goddis law' and the gospels were 'Christis law', Wyclif desired a literal accurate translation of the Latin to replace the 'Fiend's law'. The Later Version was done for the people to acquaint them with the scriptural story of man's redemption. One must remember when citing the Forshall/Madden edition that the first column is not the original! None the less, one would expect to know what the text said, what differences exist between the later and earlier recensions, and the use to which each was put. Since Hargreaves has given fresh examples from manuscript sources as does Hudson, one should begin with their examples.

Hudson gives John (10:11-12) in the Early Version and in the Later Version as follows:[143]

Early Version (Christ Church Oxford MS. 145)	Later Version (Lincoln College Oxford MS Latin 119)
I am a good shepherde.	I am a good shepperde.
A good shephearde giveth	A good shepperde giveth

his soule for his shep.	his life for his sheep.
Forsoothe a marchaunt,	But an hyrid hyne,
and that is not shepherde,	and that is not the shepperde,
whos the shep be not his owne,	whos ben not the sheep his owne,
seeth a wlf comende,	seeth a wolf comynge,
and he lefeth the shep	and he leeuith the sheep
and fleeth,	and fleeth,
and the wlf raueshith	and the wolf rauissheth
and disparplith the shep.	and disparplith the sheep.

The Glossed Gospels' comment on verse eleven says that Christ would not add "good" to "shepherd" except that there are evil shepherds.

> The evil shepherds be night thieves and day thieves, or hired hands. Christ is the door, shepherd, doorkeeper, sheep, lion and precious stone by some likeness, not by properties: for by property he is God, and son of God without beginning... Christ is door by himself and enters by himself, and we enter by him for we preach him.144

The Sermon on John (10:11) says the greatest peril in the church is the default of priests, but Christ cannot so fail for he is both God and man.[145] The glossed commentary goes on to cite Grosseteste that "if curates preach not the word of God they should be condemned."[146]

Hargreaves prints specimens from the two groups of manuscripts, observing that the Gospel of Matthew is extant in eighteen copies of the smaller group and nearly one hundred in the larger.[147] These correspond to the Early and Later Versions printed by Hudson. Luke (1:7) is a good example of literal versus idiomatic sentence structure:[148]

Luke (1:7)

Smaller Group (B.M. Royal MS I Bvi)	Larger Group (Lambeth Palace Ms.369)
And a sone was not to hem	And thei hadden no child,
for that Elizabet waş bareyn;	for Elizabeth was bareyne,
and bothe hadden gon forth fer	and bothe weren of great age
in her dayes.	in her daies.

It is obvious that the smaller group of manuscripts is more complex in its sentence structure which opens with a passive voice of the verb and closes with a past participle.

Forshall and Madden were correct in noticing the two groupings of manuscripts and printing in the left hand column the earlier version. Their text for the early New Testament conflates the two given by Hudson for John (10:11-12). Hargreaves shows how some mixed texts survive which contaminate the original.[149]

The Prologue of John is given in four versions from Forshall and Madden's New Testament.[150] The first prologue seems to be printed from G (Brit. Mus. Egerton 618) about 1420. The second is from M (Brit Mus. I.B.G) about 1400. The two additional prologues to John are p and y. It is difficult to use the printed edition because the editors mislead the reader in their critical apparatus.[152] In any event one can compare four versions of this prologue.

Prolog of John	Prologue on Joon
This is John euangelist, oon of the disciplis of God, the which a mayde of God was chosun, whom fro the sposailis willinge be weddid, God clepide; to whom double witness of maydenhod in the gospel is geue;	This is Joon euangelist, oon of the disciplis of the Lord, the which is a virgyn chosen of God, whom God clepide fro the sposeilis whanne he wolde be weddid; and double witnesse of virginyte is gouun to huym in the gospel.

The additional prologues vary from the one above and from each other. One can see from all the above that fresh editions of these manuscripts are necessary.

One more example must suffice, taken this time from chapter two of James. In the entire chapter there are only vocabulary changes in verses 2 (white/feir), 3 (habit/clothing), and 8 (up/by). A further glance at the entire text of James confirms the identical vocabulary. Even the sentence structure is parallel as in verse eleven. The main difference is spelling.

Early Text	Late Text
For he that seide Thou shalt not do leccherie,	For he that seide Thou schalt do no letcherie,

seide and, Thou shalt not sle;	seide also, Thou schalt not sle;
that if thou shalt not do	that if thou doist not
leccherie,	letcherie,
but thou sleest,	but thou sleest,
thou art maad trespassour	thou art maad trespassour
of the lawe.	of the lawe.

One wonders if the oral transmission or memorization of these chapters did not preclude vocabulary or rhythmic changes for the revisors when they reached the text of James. The possibility remains that since James was so little changed in the texts which survive, here perhaps one can come closest to the text of the missing original.

Forshall and Madden printed a full set of marginal glosses to the Wycliffite Bible. It is convenient to distinguish systematic from sporadic glosses. The systematic glosses are confined to two manuscripts which Forshall and Madden failed to distinguish.[153] The later version is uniform in all copies while the earlier version admits of such variety that a number of revisions seem to be represented.[154] They are composed in the New Testament to accompany the most revised form.

The glosses partly come from the _Ordinary Gloss_, some from Augustine, and almost all from Nicholas of Lyra, a fourteenth century commentator.[155] The author of the Old Testament glosses is the same as that of the General Prologue often thought to be John Purvey. One might assume that Purvey authored the New Testament glosses as well as the Old Testament.[156] Such an assumption is based on weak evidence.[157] The surprise is that only two of the more than one hundred manuscripts have glosses to the Gospels. Laud MS 36 and Longleat MS 5 differ from the glosses to the rest of the New Testament by being alternate suggestions for translating individual words.

Longleat MS. 5 was not available to Forshall and Madden so that it represents fresh data on these gospel glosses. Hargreaves finds that the gospel glosses here are taken from the _Glossed Gospels_, a work in which sections of the text from one to ten verses have a commentary as long as or much longer than the text.

For Mark, Luke and John there are two forms, one a summary from the other. For Matthew there are two distinct commentaries. The Catena Aurea of Thomas Aquinas was the starting point and in the longest form one finds extended citation from Robert Grosseteste. Lukan glosses in Longleat MS.5 derive by summary from the longer Glossed Gospel.[158] Hargreaves points out that spiritual exposition is found here unlike the literal stress from Lyra in the remainder of the New Testament. He concludes that more study is needed of the Glossed Gospels. Whoever prepared the late version of the Wycliffite New Testament used extensive expository notes to the Gospels and briefer ones to the rest of the books. This intermediate stage is not the same as the final revision most common in the manuscripts.

> Anyone literate only in English had available to him in marginal gloss and Gospel commentary a wide enough range of orthodox exposition, literal and spiritual, to enable him to make that serious study of the Bible in the vernacular which... it was the intention of Wyclif and his associates to encourage.159

The General Prologue has fifteen chapters, the last of which refers to the translation. Authorship questions do not affect its evidence about the translation process between the early and late versions. The translator is called "this simple creature (who) has translated the Bible out of Latin into English."[160] First of all the Latin text needed to be clarified and then grammarians would be consulted "to translate as clearly as he could to the sentence, and to have many good acquaintance and cunning at the correcting of the translation."[161]

Hudson clarifies two important issues in her notes to chapter fifteen of the General Prologue. To translate after the sentence and not after the words only so that the sentence is as "opin" in English as in Latin is not a debate between a close and free rendering. She reads these lines to suggest a debate between a transposition of Latin into English and a "close translation into English word order and vocabulary." The debate arose because a straight translation of a Latin absolute participle introduces ambiguity into English. Mark (6:20) is an instance of this where the EV has "Thei... prechiden everywhere, the Lord worchinge with" while the LV interprets a causal relationship between the two clauses, i.e., "thei... prechiden everywhere, for the Lord wroughte with hem."[162]

Whoever the author might be, this General Prologue of the 1390s describes the Wycliffite translation activity. From the earliest reference to English Lollard works by William Smith, i.e. 1383, to this text of 1395/96, great care was taken to present the English Church with its first complete English Bible. Only the careful reader can now understand the prophetic words in the final lines:

> God graunte to us alle to kunne wel and kepe wel holi writ, and suffre ioiefulli sum peyne for it at thlaste! Amen.163

C. Biblical Vision

1. Early Lollards (1384-1414)

An influential group of Lollard knights were not molested by either the secular or the spiritual arm for thirty years between Wyclif's death and Oldcastle's trial. That the 1401 On Burning of Heretics passed into law midway between those events requires some exploration.[164] Thomas Latimer who was born and baptized at Braybrooke comes from the center of Lollard activity.

In May of 1388 the Council ordered Latimer to appear before them "with certain books and schedules existing in his custody concerning errors and perversions of the catholic faith."[165] Bishop Buckingham's register supports this anxiety of 1388. John Warden had been preaching at the village of Chipping Warden in Northamptonshire. Sir Thomas Latimer was the lord of that small town with the privilege of holding a Tuesday market. Attempts to serve a writ against Warden led to consecutive weeks of disorder. Warden was arrested in March of 1389 on complaint of the bishop that he led forty-five supporters into error.[166]

Heresy continues at Braybrooke, Latimer's residence, throughout the early fifteenth century. The rector presented to the living in 1402 was a notorious Lollard. It was he who in 1407 provided two Czech scholars with a copy of Wyclif's De Domino to transcribe for dispatch to Prague. Knighton's story is essentially true that a Lollard knight forced his neighbors to hear the preacher even in the parish church, all the while standing by to protect the heretic from their hostility. McFarlane thinks the Lollard knight in question was Latimer himself.[167]

Sir John Clanvow, though less well known than Latimer, can be proven the author of an evangelical tract. It is the only known religious statement attributed to one of the Lollard knights by a contemporary. It is an exposition of the two ways to salvation described in Luke (13:22-24) conflated with Matthew (7:13-14). The treatise of almost ten thousand words returns again and again to the theme of the broad way to loss and the narrow gate to life.[168] Clanvow was a trusted counsellor of Richard II. Though a man of war he became a lay preacher who said nothing about sacraments, confession, veneration of saints or the Church as an institution. Passing over these functions he put together a mosaic of biblical quotations asserting direct access to God. At one point Clanvow defends the meek and patient folk whom the world despises:

> Such folk the world scorneth and holdeth them lollers and losels (good-for-nothing) fools and shameful wretches. But surely God holdeth them most wise and most worshipful... For the world scorned Christ and held him a fool... And therefore follow we his traces and suffer we patiently the scorns of the world as he did.[169]

McFarlane goes on to examine the wills of these knights which by comparison with the great series proved at York, Lincoln and Norwich were remarkable for their denigration of the flesh, sense of unworthiness and rejection of funeral pomp.[170] McFarlane finds the significance of such sentiments so overwhelming that it seems to reverse the interpretation of his 1952 book.

Three Lollard preachers emerge in the early records. They are William Swinderby, William Brute and William Thorpe. On August 10, 1387 Bishop Wakefield of Worcester prohibited five

Lollards by name from preaching. One of these was Swinderby, a lapsed heretic, who preached widely in the diocese during the next two years. In June of 1391 Bishop Trefnant summoned Swinderby to hear fifteen articles which accused him of heresy. Among the counts against him are a denial of transubstantiation and the view that sin excommunicates a sinner without the need for a prelate.

In October Swinderby offered a written defense of his views in a lively composition which denied papal power to grant indulgences. After his excommunication Swinderby appealed to the knights in parliament. The open letter was eloquent:

> This land is full of ghostly cowardice, in ghostly battle few do stand. But Christ the comforter of all... barks for our love against the fiend. That daughty Duke comforteth us thus: 'Be ye strong in battle', He says, 'And fight ye with the old adder.' Awake, ye that be righteous men![171]

Soon after all this Swinderby took a literate lay companion, Stephen Bell, into Wales. In 1392 Bishop Trefnant applied for a royal petition which Richard II granted to arrest the fugitives. They were never given up. On Palm Sunday of 1382 at Leicester, Swinderby attacked the begging friars.[172]

Walter Brute was brought to justice, a Lollard who called himself a "sinner, layman, husbandman and Christian." Brute was caught in 1391. At Hereford he asserted that the pope was antichrist and Swinderby's opinions were true and catholic. Cross-examination by Bishop Trefnant led to a set trial in which Brute replied in Latin essays. He called the pope an "idol of desolation sitting in the temple of God" and Rome "the great whore sitting upon many waters." Judgment came in October of 1393 when Brute made his submission by reading an English obeisance to Trefnant.[173]

William Thorpe from the north of England studied at Oxford. After taking priest's orders he was tried for heresy in 1397 and imprisoned. After his release Thorpe became a wandering preacher only to be arrested again and brought before Archbishop Arundel in 1407. William Tyndale a century later published a manuscript of Thorpe's examination which had been popular among Lollards. Thorpe says he penned the account in 1460. Arundel claimed that Thorpe for more than twenty years had spread these concerns, marking this trial and narrative a valuable account of early Lollardy. When Arundel asked Thorpe about those holy and wise men who were the source of his information, he answered:

> And I said, 'Sir, Master John Wyclif was held by full many men to be the greatest clerk that they knew then living... and loved so much his learning that they wrote it, and busily enforced themselves to be guided according to his learning....' And with all these men (John Aston, Philip Repingdon, Nicholas Hereford, John Purvey) I was quite often at home, and communed with them long and often; and so, before all other men, I chose deliberately to be informed of them and by them, and especially of Wyclif himself...174

Thorpe quotes from Scripture fifty-two times and from other works twenty-five times. Seven of these are from St. Gregory and three each from Sts. Augustine, Jerome and Chrysostom.[175]

Thorpe preached that pilgrimages were a waste of money better spent on mercy, since men and women who travel to long distant shrines sing along with wanton songs and such loud bagpipes that dogs bark after them. The noise is louder than if the king passed that way with all his minstrels. Many pilgrims after the trip are "great janglers, tale-tellers, and liars."[176] Arundel defended the singers and pipers because, if a pilgrim were to strike his toe on a stone and to bleed, "it is well done that he or his fellow should begin then a song or else take out of his bosom a bagpipe to drive away with such mirth the hurt of his fellow." Lollards like Thorpe were spoilsports in the Archbishop's eyes.[177]

Arundel's Constitutions of 1409 single out several items for condemnation after thirty years of struggle. The first constitution prohibited unlicensed preaching, while the sixth forbade the use of Wyclif's writings without examination. The seventh constitution made English tracts *prima facie* cause for excommunication unless the translator had prior approval. By March of

1411 Wyclif's views were condemned and Oxford gave up its papal exemption from archiepiscopal visitation.[178] The first phase of Lollardy ended when Sir John Oldcastle had been tried for heresy in September 1413, escaped from the Tower in October and was executed for leading a plot to seize the king in January 1414.

2. Later Lollards (1414-1512)

a. Official Books

The statute On Burning of Heretics (1401) drew attention to Lollard literacy as a vehicle of their heresy. "They make unlawful conventicles and confederacies, they hold and exercise schools, they make and write books, they do wickedly instruct and inform people...."[179] Margaret Aston who cites this reference chronicles the literature of Lollardy as it moved outside the Oxford collegiate circle. She goes on to translate a 1437 admission from Bishop Neville's register at Salisbury which parallels the 1401 statute. One William Wakeham three years before said: "I with other heretics and Lollards was acustomed and used to hear in secret places, in nooks and corners, the reading of the Bible in English...."[180]

In 1511/12 some Midlands heretics owned and used several books. Among these were a complete Old Testament, a copy of St. Paul's Epistles, Tobit, Epistle of James and Acts. Only Matthew and John are mentioned of the Gospels.[181] John Foxe reports that the Colyns family owned a considerable library of English books: Wycliffe's Wicket, Gospel of John, Epistles of Paul, James and Peter, Pricke of Conscience, Book of Solomon and others.[182] The most popular book in these trials at Coventry and Litchfield was the Ten Commandments.[183] This would be either the Wycliffite version, the Lay Folks' Catechism or the orthodox Dives and Pauper. A list of questions is preserved in the register of Bishop Thomas Polton of Worcester (1426-33) which includes one about possession of books in English.[184]

Anne Hudson has demonstrated that it is impossible from the existing printed editions to gain any accurate picture of Lollard views.[185] Eighty per cent of the material exists in manuscript form. Apart from the Bible Lollard books can be seen in three forms: 1) scedula such as the Twelve Conclusions of 1395 or documents nailed to St. Paul's door in 1382. 2) Quaterni which were lists of biblical and patristic texts on subjects such as images and the Eucharist.[186] The only surviving quaternion is a dialogue between a knight and a clerk from about 1400.[187] 3) Libri or books which are of greater interest than either scedula or quaterni.

Official books are the Bible itself, the Gospel commentaries which are not yet edited[188], the sermon cycle and some shorter tracts. The peripheral group are each preserved in less than six manuscripts and difficult to date. The Lantern of Light is one of these peripheral documents. The Sermon Cycle draws from Wyclif's Latin sermons and was a tightly knit unit of 294 sermons. One manuscript preserves the order of Sunday Gospels, Commune and Proprium Sanctorum, Ferial Gospels and the Sunday Epistles. Two reorganizations are extant, one of which intercalates the Sunday Gospel and Epistle sermons into a complete dominical cycle, and the other which puts together the Sunday Epistle, Sunday Gospel and Ferial Gospel to form a single cycle for the liturgical year.[189] The basis is clearly the Sarum use of the Latin mass at Winchester. Two columns are often used to facilitate public reading.[190]

There are no random groupings of the sermon-cycle, nor, with a single exception, did the scribes tamper with the text. All the manuscripts were carefully corrected with supervision.

> Taking the two aspects together, the variety in the ordering of the sets on the one hand, the close regularity of the texts themselves on the other, it seems clear that we must suppose that the manuscripts were made under tight control in a limited period of time and within a small number of centres.191

If all the sermons were used within a year, the Lollard would hear two sermons every Sunday as well as weekday sermons. There is no parallel outside of Lollard circles for such regular circulation of sermons in Medieval Europe.

One now knows thanks to Hudson's work that dissemination of Lollard thought went beyond poor preachers giving extemporaneous summaries of Wyclif's moral agenda for reform of the English Church. Some of Wyclif's material was collected into a commonplace book known as the Floretum or Rosarium. Manuscripts reveal that the Floretum was in its full version a compilation of quotations under 509 entries, in its intermediate version a shortened text for all entries and a reduced version of 303 items called the Rosarium. All three versions quote a number of passages from D. E., i.e., Doctor Evangelicus (Wyclif). The entry for "fastyng" [Ieiunium] in the Rosarium cites Ambrose, Augustine, Pope Gregory I, Chrysostom and Jerome.

In the Floretum some 170 passages have Wyclif's authority attached by means of the letters D.E.In some instances more than an equivalent page from the modern printed edition is given.[192] Even more interesting are the quotations from the Latin sermons, the Sunday Gospel and Epistle sets and the Proprium and Commune Sanctorum sermons. The number of a sermon and its series is correctly given.[193] The dating comes from the Opus Evangelicum finished in 1384 and used in all redactions. Copies of all three versions were taken to Prague. Hudson thinks that the compilation comes from a center near Oxford in which university men entirely in agreement with Wyclif provide these precise handbooks for Lollard preachers.[194] Thus were the Latin writings of the Evangelical Doctor used to spread Lollard teachings between 1396 and 1414.

b. Lantern of Light

The Lantern of Light is the best know of the peripheral works. The Londoner John Claydon, who died for his stubborn adherance to Lollardy, had owned the Lantern of Light which he had copied and bound. He could not read so his servant John

Fuller read it aloud.[195] It thereafter figures prominently in heresy trials.

Even though Christ is the only means of salvation, because Antichrist leads men astray, true believers like the Psalmist (119:105) must seek the Lantern of Light in God's Word . The Fiend's church is rejected with its gluttony and loose living.

> This church, when it is beaten, it waxes the harder; when it is blamed, it waxes the duller; when it is taught, it is the more ignorant; when it is done well to, it is the more oppossed. And it falls down and comes to naught, when in man's eyes it seems most strongly to stand.196

God's Church of the predestined is called a little flock as in Luke (12).

> Readers in Christ's church read holy lessons and attend to their reading with mindful devotion as St. Jerome says. But readers in the fiend's church chatter their lessons like jays that chatter in a cage and know not what they mean...197

The lesson of holy writ is that of a clean mirror of life which reflects the good that it may become better and the evil that it be amended.[198] The tone of Lollardy which can be documented from its manuscript books grew more and more anticlerical as it held up the mirror of scripture to the clerical foibles of the Fiend's church. Dedicated laity using collections of Wyclif quotations, patristic references and the sermon cycle set the tone for another century after 1414 of what Lambert calls "one of the underestimated forces in medieval Church history."[199]

A powerful contribution to that force for renewal was the involvement of Lollard women.[200] That women should become priests was an indefinite conclusion of Wycliffite theology,[201] though their sociological function in the Lollard movement as teachers and educators of biblical reality is well documented.[202] That same realist metaphysics which denied transubstantiation to a male priesthood through declaring a miracle in the Eucharist, elevated all the godly laity to a teaching and preaching function.

These were persons who not only possessed English versions of the scriptures but also sought an _Ecclesia Anglicana_ renewed by the mirror of God's Word. For that John Wyclif was responsible. Their hopes and faith circulated in hundreds of manuscripts, more often memorized to avoid burning. Their own later version of I Corinthians (13) is surely at the heart of their biblical vision:

> If I speke with tungis of men and of aungels, and I have not charite, I am maad as bras sownynge, or a cymbal tynkynge. And if I haue prophecie, and knowe alle mysteries, and all kunnynge, and if I have al feith, so that I meue hillis fro her place, and I have not charite, I am nought.... And we see now bi a myrour in derknesse, but thanne face to face; now I knowe of parti, but thanne I schal knowe, as I am knowun.203

END NOTES to SECTION I

[1]D. Wilkins, ed., Concilia Magnae Brittaniae et Hiberniae (London: 1737) 3:202. Translated in John Foxe, Acts and Monuments, ed. S. R. Cattley. 4th ed., rev. by J. Pratt (London: 1877) 3:57-58.

[2]Anne Hudson, "Lollardy: The English Heresy?" Studies In Church History 18: Religion and National Identity, ed. Stuart Mews, (Oxford: Basil Blackwell, 1982): 263-67.

[3]Margaret Aston, "Lollardy and Literacy," History 62 (1977): 369-70.

[4]Ibid., pp. 362-63.

[5]Margaret Aston, "'Caim's Castles': Poverty, Politics, and Disendowment" in The Church, Politics and Patronage, ed. R.B. Dobson (Gloucester/New York: Alan Sutton/St. Martins Press, 1984): 49.

[6]Ibid., p. 70 note 22 from Hudson, English Wycliffite Sermons I (Oxford: 1983): 230.

[7]Ibid., p. 73 note 48.

[8]Ibid., p. 55.

[9]W. L. Warren, "A Reappraisal of Simon Sudbury, bishop of London (1361-75) and archbishop of Canterbury (1375-81)," Journal of Ecclesiastical History X (1959), p.141.

[10]Ibid., p.142: Chronicon Anglia.

[11]Ibid., p.147.

[12]Ibid., p.151.

[13]Joseph Dahmus, William Courtenay Archbishop of Canterbury 1381-1396 (Univ. Park: Pennsylvania State Univ. Press, 1966), pp.35-38.

[14]Ibid., p.51.

[15]A. K. McHardy, "Bishop Buckingham and the Lollards of Lincoln Diocese," Schism, Heresy and Religious Protest, edited by Derek Baker (Cambridge: At the Univ. Press, 1972), p.131. For Salisbury in 1389 see Anne Hudson, "A Lollard Mass," Journal of Theological Studies XXIII (1972), pp.407-419.

[16]Ibid., pp.137-138.

[17]Ibid., p.144. See also Metropolitan Visitations of William Courtenay (Champaign: Univ. of Illinois, 1950), p.164.

[18]Cited in Margaret Aston, Thomas Arundel (Oxford: At the Clarendon Press, 1967), p.320.

[19]Ibid., p.326.

[20]Margaret Deansely, The Lollard Bible (Cambridge: At the Univ. Press, 1920/1966 reprint), p.45.

[21]Aston, op.cit., p.328.

[22]Ibid., p.329.

[23]H. G. Richardson, "Heresy and the Lay Power under Richard II," English Historical Review LI (1936), p.22.

[24]Chronicon Henrici Knighton C. 1382: in English Historical Documents 1327-1485, pp.843-844.

[25]F. M. Bartos, "Hus, Lollardism and Devotio Moderna in the Fight for a National Bible," Communio Viatorum (1963): 247-254.

[26]Margaret Aston, "The Debate on Bible Translation, Oxford 1401," English Historical Review XC (1975), pp.2-4.

[27]Ibid., pp.9-11.

[28]Calendar of Patent Rolls Richard II, 1381-5 (London: 1897), p.153.

[29]Aston, op.cit., p.17.

[30]Anne Hudson, Selections From English Wycliffite Writings (Cambridge: At the Univ. Press, 1978), p.190.

[31]London: John Day, 1563, I 452-455. Trinity College, Cambridge MS. B.1.26, f.146.

[32]Curt F. Buhler, "A Lollard Tract: On Translating the Bible into English," Medium Aevum VII (1938), p.169.

[33]Ibid., p.174.

[34]Ibid., p.173, lines 117-124.

[35]Ibid., p.174, lines 161-162 and 135-140.

[36]Ibid., p.175, lines 188-195. Published in George G. Parry, Religious Pieces in Prose and Verse, Early English Text Society, Old Series 26, pp.1-15. On the relation of these Middle English versions to Wyclif see Anthony Martin, "The Middle

English Versions of The Ten Commandments, With Special Reference to Rylands English MS. 85," Bulletin of the John Rylands Library 64 (1981), 191-217. On the Lollard use see A. L. Kellogg and E. W. Talbert, "The Wycliffite Pater Noster and Ten Commandments," Bulletin of the John Rylands Library XLII (1960), 363-377.

[37] Ibid., p.175, lines 166-168 and lines 179-182. See S. Harison Thomson, The Writings of Robert Grosseteste, Bishop of Lincoln, 1235-1253 (Cambridge: At the Univ. Press, 1940).

[38] James McEvoy, The Philosophy of Robert Grosseteste (Oxford: The Clarendon Press, 1982), pp.419-441. See Leonard Boyle, "Robert Grosseteste and the Pastoral Care," Medieval and Renaissance Studies VIII (1979):3-51.

[39] Ibid., p.433.

[40] Gordon Leff, Heresy in the Later Middle Ages Vol.II (Manchester: Manchester Univ. Press, 1967), p.494.

[41] J. A. Robson, Wyclif and the Oxford Schools (Cambridge: At the Univ. Press, 1961), pp.9-17 describes the years to 1374.

[42] Ibid., p.15.

[43] S. Harrison Thompson, "The Philosophical Basis of Wyclif's Theology," Journal of Religion XI (1931), pp.96 and 106.

[44] Robson, op.cit., p.28.

[45] Ibid., p.80.

[46] Ibid., p.96.

[47] James D. Dawson, "Richard Fitzralph and the fourteenth-century poverty controversies, "Journal of Ecclesiastical History 34 (1983), pp.330-338.

[48] Robson, op.cit., p.115.

[49] Bernard Manning, "Wyclif," Cambridge Medieval History VII Decline of Empire and Papacy (Cambridge: At the Univ. Press, 1932), pp.900-904 discusses the printed sources. On manuscripts see S. Harrison Thomson, "Unnoticed MSS. and Works of Wyclif," Journal of Theological Studies XXXVIII (1937), 24-36 and 139-148. Structure of Summa in Robson, op.cit., pp.118-122.

[50] S. Harrison Thomson, "Unnoticed MSS," pp.25-27.

[51]S. Harrison Thomson, "John Wyclif," in B. A. Gerrish, editor, Reformers In Profile (Philadelphia: Fortress Press, 1967), p. 22.

[52]loc.cit. Now see G. R. Evans, "Wyclif's Logic and Wyclif's Exegesis: The Context" in Katharine Walsh and Diana Wood, editors, The Bible in the Medieval World, Essays in Memory of Beryl Smalley (Oxford: Basil Blackwell, 1985): 287-300. This arrived after the final revision of this chapter. On page 299 Evans points to Wyclif's principle of consonantia between a gloss or interpretation, Scripture and reason.

[53]S. Harrison Thomson, "The Philosophical Basis of Wyclif's Theology," p.91.

[54]Trialogus (Oxford: 1869), p.66. De Ydeis is the most copied and cited of Wyclif's works: Robson, op.cit., p.133.

[55]Thomson, op.cit., p.98. In De Logica Wyclif uses this five-fold classification to relate universals to particular propositions. Citation from De Universalibus in Anthony Kenny, Wyclif (Oxford/New York: Oxford Univ. Press, 1985): 10-11.

[56]Ibid., p.111.

[57]Ibid., p.113.

[58]De logica, III, 34-35; De ente, 52-57.

[59]Robson, op.cit., p.163.

[60]Cited by John Stacy, John Wyclif and Reform (Philadelphia: Westminster Press, 1964), p.13.

[61]Margaret Aston, "John Wycliffe's Reformation Reputation," Past and Present 30 (April 1965), p.25. Reference to Ecclesiasticus (1:6-7) repeated by John Foxe in 1563/1570 Acts and Monuments.

[62]Gordon Leff, "Wyclif and the Augustinian Tradition," Medievalia et Humanistica I (1970), pp.29-31.

[63]K. B. McFarlane, John Wycliffe and the Beginnings of English Nonconformity (London: MacMillan, 1952), pp.63-70. Gaunt was the Duke of Leicester.

[64]Thomson, "John Wyclif," pp. 26-31.

[65]Gordon Leff, Heresy in the Later Middle Ages II, p.547.

[66] *loc.cit.*

[67] Henry Gee and William John Hardy, *Documents Illustrative of English Church History* (London: MacMillan and Co., Ltd., 1896), p.106. See Joseph H. Dahmus, *The Prosecution of John Wyclif* (New Haven: Yale Univ. Press, 1952/Archon reprint 1970), pp.38-49 for a translation of all five bulls.

[68] Howard Kaminsky, "Wyclifism as Ideology of Revolution," *Church History* XXXII (1963), pp.64-65.

[69] *Ibid.*, p.67.

[70] *Opera Minora*, edited J. Loserth, 1907, p.378. Translation by Kaminsky, *op.cit.*, p.68. See the discussion of property rights in Michael Wilks, "Predestination, Property, and Power: Wyclif's Theory of Dominion and Grace," *Studies In Church History* II, edited G. J. Cuming (London: Nelson, 1965), p.233. Wilks concludes that Wyclif was the reverse of a revolutionary (p.235).

[71] Bernard Manning, *op.cit.*, pp.491-492.

[72] This became the second prologue to the Song of Solomon in the *Postilla super Totam Bibliam*.

[73] F. M. Bartos, *Husitstvi a cizina* (Praha: 1931), p.25 translated by Amedeo Molnar, "Recent Literature on Wyclif's Theology," *Communio Viatorum* VII (1964), p.186.

[74] Thomas Arnold, *The Select English Works of John Wyclif* (Oxford: Oxford Univ. Press, 1869-71), p.362.

[75] *Tractatus de Potestate Papae*, edited Johann Loserth (London: The Wyclif Society, 1907), p.353. Translated in William Farr, *John Wyclif as Legal Reformer* (Leiden: E.J. Brill, 1974), p.27.

[76] *De Papa*, Capitulum III, *The English Works of Wyclif hitherto Unprinted*, edited F. D. Matthew (London: Trubner & Co., 1880), p.463. Most of these are of doubtful authenticity. See Workman, *John Wyclif* I, 331: "To Wyclif we may definitely assign de Papa."

[77] Farr, *op.cit.*, pp.28-33.

[78] *De Papa*, Capitulum XI, p.478: "Here it has been said often by witness of true men that there must needs be an order of three

parts of the church, that there be clerks, lords and commons, and in each of them is order."

[79]McFarlane, op.cit., pp.102-103.

[80]Leff, Heresy II, p.552.

[81]De Papa IV, p.465.

[82]Ibid, p.466.

[83]Printed in Gustav Adolf Benrath, Wyclifs Bibelkommentar (Berlin: Walter De Gruyter, 1966), pp.338-346.

[84]Ibid., pp.338-339.

[85]Ibid., p.346.

[86]Beryl Smalley, "Wyclif's Postilla on the Old Testament and His Principium," Oxford Studies Presented to Daniel Callus, O.P. (Oxford: Oxford Univ. Press, 1964), pp.253-96.

[87]Beryl Smalley, "John Wyclif's Postilla Super Totam Bibliam," Bodleian Library Record VIII (1953), pp.186-205.

[88]Ibid., pp.204-205.

[89]Beryl Smalley's review of Benrath in Zeitschrift für Kirchengeschichte 1967, p.175.

[90]Benrath, op.cit., pp.324-325. "Genau genommen ist dieser Satz das heuristische Prinzip fur die Lehre von der Nachfolge Christi."

[91]Ibid., p.327.

[92]English Historical Documents IV. 1327-1485, Edited by A. R. Meyers (New York: Oxford Univ. Press, 1969), p.840. Compare this with the De Mandatis Divinis, p.402 ff. which cites Dictum 35 of Grosseteste: "Exemplum esto fidelium" (Responsibility of Priests and Prelates toward their parishioners). Thomson, The Writings of Robert Grosseteste, p.219.

[93]Benrath, op.cit., p.345.

[94]Joseph H. Dahmus, op.cit., p.89, n.9.

[95]English Historical Documents IV, 1327-1485, p.844.

[96]Ibid., p.846.

[97]Ibid., p.848.

[98]Dahmus, op.cit., p.107.

[99]Ibid., p.123.

[100]Exposition on Matthew (23), translated in Margaret Deansley, The Lollard Bible (Cambridge: At the Univ. Press, 1920/1966 reprint), p.244.

[101]Deansley. op.cit., pp.445-56. Workman also accepts this as Wyclif's own work.

[102]Ibid., p.269.

[103]Ibid., pp.452-454.

[104]Ibid., p.454.

[105]Benrath, op.cit., pp.378-386, i.e., nos. 23-62 in Sermones Band IV, edited J. Loserth.

[106]Peter Auski, "Wyclif's Sermons and the Plain Style," Archiv für Reformationsgeschichte 66 (1975), pp.7-8.

[107]Ibid., p.14. Sermones IV. 268: "in clara intencione nude et apte."

[108]Ibid., p.18.

[109]Peggy Ann Knapp, The Style of John Wyclif's English Sermons (Hague-Paris: Mouton, 1977), pp.40-41.

[110]Ibid., p.23. This totals 289!

[111]Ernest William Talbert, "The Date of the Composition of the English Wyclifite Collection of Sermons," Speculum XII (1937), p.473.

[112]Anne Hudson, "A Lollard Sermon-Cycle and Its Implications," Medium Aevum XL (1971), 142-156.

[113]Anne Hudson, Selections from English Wycliffite Writings (Cambridge: At the Univ. Press, 1977), p.11.

[114]Anne Hudson, "Contributions to a Bibliography of Wycliffite Writings," Notes and Queries NS XX (1973), p.448.

[115]Anne Hudson, "Some Aspects of Lollard Book Production," Schism, Heresy and Religious Protest, edited by Derek Baker (Cambridge: At the Univ. Press, 1972), p.152.

[116]Loc.cit.

[117]Anne Hudson, English Wycliffite Sermons I (Oxford: At the Clarendon Press, 1983), pp.215-222.

[118]Ibid., pp.230-231.

[119]Ibid., p.488, lines 47-51.

[120]*Ibid.*, p.489, lines 75-76

[121]*Ibid.*, p.489, lines 82-86.

[122]*Ibid.*, p.490.

[123]*Ibid.*, p.492, lines 21-22.

[124]*Ibid.*, p.494, lines 102-125.

[125]Manning, *op.cit.*, pp.504-505.

[126]Henry Hargreaves, "The Wycliffite Versions," *Cambridge History of the Bible* II (Cambridge: At the Univ. Press, 1969), p.400.

[127]Margaret Deanesly, *The Significance of the Lollard Bible* (London: The Athlone Press, 1951), p.3.

[128]Hargreaves, *op.cit.*, p.388.

[129]Michael Wilks, "Misleading Manuscripts: Wyclif and the Non-Wycliffite Bible," *The Materials Sources and Methods of Ecclesiastical History*, edited by Derek Baker (Oxford: Basil Blackwell, 1975), pp.150-152.

[130]*Ibid.*, pp.152-153.

[131]*Ibid.*, p.159. Peggy Ann Knapp, "John Wyclif as Bible Translator," *Speculum* XLVI (1971), p.715: "Six centuries of tradition ascribe these sermons to Wyclif, and only one or two possible topical references cast any doubt on that ascription."

[132]*Supra*, note 80.

[133]Hargreaves, *op.cit.*, p.410.

[134]Latin text of *De contrarietate duorum dominarum*, 2, p.700 in Wilks, *op.cit.*, p.155. William Smith of Leicester at his 1391 trial confessed to copying translations of the Gospels and Epistles for eight years. These works of 1383 can not be the Bible because they are requested by Doctors and Bishops.

[135]Hargreaves, *op.cit.*, p.400. Under special protection by Sir William Nevill, constable of Nottingham Castle on petition to the King. See K. B. McFarlane, *Lancastrian Kings and Lollard Knights* (Oxford: At the Clarendon Press, 1972), p.199.

[136]*Ibid.*, pp.408-409. See Hudson, *English Wycliffite Writings*, pp. 167-168 who shows that this account is questionable and may be part of later Lollard rhetoric.

[137]Margaret Aston, Thomas Arundel (Oxford: At the Clarendon Press, 1967), p.327. See also Richard G. Davies, "Thomas Arundel as Archbishop of Canterbury, 1396-1414," Journal of Ecclesiastical History XXIV (1973): 9-22. Aston's story is detailed only to 1397/8.

[138]Margaret Deanesly, The Lollard Bible, p.378. See for text Matthew Spinka editor, Advocates of Reform (Philadelphia: Westminster Press, 1953), pp.49-51.

[139]Ibid., p.246.

[140]Wilkins III, p.350 cited in Wilkes, op.cit., p.148 n.7.

[141]Hargreaves, op.cit., p.404.

[142]Deanesly, The Significance of the Lollard Bible, p.8.

[143]Hudson, English Wycliffite Writings, pp.58-59. The later is identical to Forshall and Madden; the earlier is not.

[144]Ibid., p.60. MS. Bodley 243.

[145]Ibid., p.64. British Library Royal 18 B. This sermon overlaps with Wyclif's own sermon on the same text.

[146]Ibid., p.62.

[147]Hargreaves, op.cit., p.395.

[148]Ibid., p.398. Both texts identical to Forshall and Madden.

[149]Ibid., p.403.

[150]Josiah Forshall and Frederick Madden, The Holy Bible, containing The Old and New Testaments...in the earliest English Versions...by John Wycliffe and His Followers, Volume IV (Oxford: At the Univ. Press, MDCCCL), pp. 233-234 and 685-686.

[151]Sven L. Fristedt, The Wycliffe Bible Part I The Principal Problems connected with Forshall and Madden's Edition. Stockholm Studies in English IV (Stockholm: Almquist/Wiksells Boktryckeri-A.B., 1953), p.13.

[152]Forshall and Madden IV, p.598.

[153]Henry Hargreaves, "The Marginal Glosses to the Wycliffite New Testament," Studia Neophilologica XXXIII (1961), p.285.

[154]Ibid., p. 186. Hargreaves uses this data on the Old Testament to argue for an intermediate version. See H.

Hargreaves, "An intermediate version of the Wycliffite Old Testament," Studia Neophilologica XXVIII (1965), 130-147.

[155] Ibid., p.292. See Beryl Smalley, "Postills and Postillators," Study of the Bible in the Middle Ages, (Notre Dame: Univ. of Notre Dame, 1970), pp.264-280.

[156] Ibid., p.293.

[157] Anne Hudson, English Wycliffite Writings, pp.173-174.

[158] Ibid., p.296. As in Cambridge Univ. Library MS. Kk.2.9. but not Bodley MSS. 143 and 243 of similar derivation.

[159] Ibid., p.300.

[160] Hudson, op.cit., p.67.

[161] Ibid., p.68.

[162] Ibid., pp.174-175.

[163] Ibid., p.72.

[164] K. B. McFarlane, Lancastrian Kings and Lollard Knights, p.144.

[165] Ibid., p.193.

[166] Ibid., pp.194-195.

[167] Ibid., p.196.

[168] Ibid., p.202. Printed in V. J. Scattergood, "'The Two Ways': An Unpublished Religious Treatise by Sir John Clanvowe," English Philological Studies X (1967), pp.33-56.

[169] Ibid., p.206. Univ. College Oxford MS. (Coxe) 97, fols. 114r-124v.

[170] Ibid., p.211.

[171] K. B. McFarlane, The Origins of Religious Dissent in England (New York: MacMillan, Collier reprint 1966), p.144.

[172] J. Crompton, "Leicestershire Lollards," Transactions of the Leicestershire Archaeological and Historical Society XLIV (1968-69), pp. 20-22.

[173] Ibid., pp.145-148.

[174] English Historical Documents 1327-1485, pp.851-852.

[175] John Fines, "William Thorpe: An early Lollard," History Today (1968), p.497.

[176] Ibid., p.853.

[177] *loc.cit.*

[178] *Ibid.*, pp.856-857.

[179] *English Historical Documents 1327-1485*, p.850.

[180] Margaret Aston, "Lollards and Literacy," *History* 62 (1977), p.353.

[181] John A. F. Thomson, *The Later Lollards 1414-1520* (Oxford: Oxford Univ. Press, 1967), p.113. The General Prolog to the Later Version of the Lollard Bible urges reading of Tobit for its teaching of patience in adversity.

[182] Aston, *op.cit.*, p.355.

[183] John Fines, "Heresy Trials in the Diocese of Coventry and Litchfield," *Journal of Ecclesiastical History* XIV (1963), p.164.

[184] Anne Hudson, "The Examination of Lollards," *Bulletin of the Institute of Historical Research* XLVI (1973), p.154: "34 Item an iurare super librum sit licitum." Hudson thinks the list was drawn up for a Lollard scribe. The *Opus Arduum* drawn up in 1389/1390 refers to persecution of "those who possess and read evangelical writings in English": Anne Hudson, "Lollardy: the English Heresy," *Religion and National Identity*, edited by Stuart Mews (Oxford: Basil Blackwell, 1982), p.277.

[185] Anne Hudson, "Some Aspects of Lollard Book Production," *Schism, Heresy and Religious Protest*, edited by Derek Baker (Cambridge: At the Univ. Press, 1972), p.147.

[186] Anne Hudson, "A Lollard Quaternion," *Review of English Studies* XXII (1971), pp.435-42.

[187] Hudson, *English Wycliffite Writings*, pp.131-134.

[188] Henry Hargreaves, "The Marginal Glosses to the Wycliffite New Testament," *Studia Neophilologica* XXIII (1961), pp.285-300.

[189] Hudson, "Lollard Book Production," p.153.

[190] Anne Hudson, "A Lollard Sermon Cycle," p.145.

[191] *Ibid.*, p.150.

[192] Anne Hudson, "The Dissemination of Wycliffite Thought," *Journal of Theological Studies* XXIII (1972), pp.66-67.

[193] *Ibid.*, p.71.

[194] *Ibid.*, p.75.

[195]Register of Henry Chichele, IV, 132-8. Reported in Aston, "Lollardy and Literacy," p.356.

[196]David Herlihy editor, Medieval Culture and Society (New York: Harper and Row, 1968), p.407. From Chapter 13.

[197]English Historical Documents 1327-1485, p.855.

[198]Hudson, English Wycliffite Writings, p.118.

[199]M.D. Lambert, Medieval Heresy (London: Edward Arnold Ltd., 1977), p.271.

[200]Clair Cross, "'Great Reasoners in Scripture': the activities of women Lollards 1380-1530," Medieval Women, edited by Derek Baker (Oxford: Oxford Univ. Press, 1978), pp.359-380.

[201]Margaret Aston, "Lollard Women Priests?," Journal of Ecclesiastical History XXXI (1980), p.461.

[202]John Fines, "Heresy Trials," pp.161-162.

[203]Forshall and Madden IV, pp.362-363.

SECTION II. PRINT AND PROTEST

In 1409 the English Church prohibited vernacular translations of the Bible. For a dozen decades oral transmission became the safest way to pass on the New Testament, whose English text many Lollards memorized in large sections. Eleven decades later Luther's writings began to circulate in England. The authorities quite naturally feared the links between the Lollards and Luther's evangelical views. The bishops burned books and bibles to prevent the disease of private religious judgment from spreading.

They could as soon stop the sun from shining. Lollards and Lutherans were in contact as early as 1520 when John Hacker of Coleman Street in London distributed heretical books at Burford. John Stacey and Lawrence Maxwell in the adjacent London parish of Aldermanbury also become distributers of imported Lutheran books. Essex seems to have been a center where the numerous Lollards recognized a kindred spirit in continental complaints. An example would be Tyndale's translation of Luther's 1522 _Ein sermon von dem unrechten Mammon_ which appeared in 1528 and which the leather-merchant John Tewkesbury sold in the late 1520s. Tewkesbury was a disciple of Hacker.[1] John Foxe writes of these common folk that, "few or none were learned, being simple laborours and artificers, but as it pleased the Lord to work in them knowledge and understanding by reading a few English books such as they could get in corners."[2] By October 1526 London civic authorities were alarmed enough to commence an examination of every parson in each alderman's ward to find unspecified books of heresy.[3]

As early as March of 1518 Erasmus sent Luther's _Conclusions on Pontifical Vanity_ to Thomas More. A year later John Froben, printer of Basel, reported to Luther that his books had been exported to England.[4] Late in 1518 Luther's works were circulating in England. By the end of 1520 Luther was suspect no doubt because of his three great treatises of that year. At Oxford during 1520 John Dorne sold six or more copies of Luther's tract on papal power, a copy of the early Galatian commentary, two copies of his complete works and some other pieces.[5] The bonfire at St. Paul's Cross in London on May 12, 1521 reflects the misgivings about Luther in English circles since "he terribly thonderyth agaynst the poopes authorite...."[6]

John Skelton described popular anticlerical attitudes in his poem of late 1521/early 1522. In Colyn Clout he linked up Lollard with Luther in the popular mind.

> And som have a smacke
> Of Luthers sacke,
> And a brennynge sparke
> Of Luthers warke,
> And are somewhat suspecte
> In Luthers secte;
> And some of them barke,
> Clatter and carpe
> Of that heresy arte
> Called Wytclyfista,
> The devylyshe dagmatista;[7]

This poem went through seven printings by 1558(?).[8] Christopher Haigh finds this and other anticlerical expressions inconclusive since "the need to explain the Protestant outcome of the English Reformation imposes a perspective which finds in 'anticlericalism' both a cause of religious change and a reason for its acceptance."[9] Skelton's poems become for Haigh part of the attack mounted by his patrons, the Howards, against the dominance of Cardinal Wolsey rather than the clergy.[10] Lines 75-177 of the Clarendon edition seem to contradict that impression, for they sustain an attack on bishops in general rather than Wolsey in particular, i.e.:

> What trowe ye they say more
> Of the bysshoppes lore?
> Howe in matters they ben rawe,
> They luber forth the lawe
> To herken Jacke and Gyll,
> Whan they put up a byll;
> And judge it as they wyll,
> For other mens skyll,[11]

Skelton's satire is now seen to stand in continuity with similar denunciations of clerical crimes since the writings of Walter Map in the thirteenth and William Langland of the fourteenth century. The Plowman's Tale of 1393/95, for example, is a Lollard refutation which includes a debate between the Christ-bird Pelican and a Griffon who was "on the Popes syde." Like Colyn Cloute of a century later, the Pelican's homily attacks the secular clergy who "shuld for ne cattel plede ... Nor to no batail shuld men lede."[12]

Colin Cloute (the person in Colyn Cloute) in 1522 delivers his anti-clerical warning in long familiar plebian terms when he stresses episcopal extravagance. These bishops:

"hunt in parkes,
And hawke on hobby larkes,
And [do] other wanton warkes,
Whan the nyght darkes"13

Recent analysis finds that Skelton patterned his poem on John Colet's convocation sermon of 1511/12. The Dean of St. Paul preached from Romans (xii:2) when he urged the English clergy not to conform to the world.[14]

In a brilliant article Susan Brigden of Oxford has traced the spread of these anti-clerical sentiments in London to the social consequence of London's growth from a city of some 60,000 inhabitants in 1500 to one of almost 200,000 by 1600. "Adolescents were the most restless," comments Brigden, who then goes on to describe the impact of delayed adulthood on apprentices who after the 1550s could not marry until age 24. That was the age for completing this pathway to membership in a guild and hence freedom of the city and civic privileges.[15] In fact the total English population excluding Wales expanded from 2.3 million in 1522/25 to 2.85 million by 1545 and 3.75 million in 1603. It fluctuated as the rate of increase was 1% per annum from 1576 to 1586 but slowed to 0.5% each year of the next decade. The population as a whole rose some 35% during Elizabeth's reign.[16]

Back in London these young people intensified their attacks on the London clergy as the reformation progressed. These irreverent young radicals jeered at Catholic clerics while the Protestant "hot-gospellers" became their heroes. Preaching campaigns in the capital seized the minds of these youth by the "brabbling of the New Testament."[17] All sermons were halted in London during December of 1548 so that the Mercers' Company could order every householder to "loke to his apprentices... that they do not ronne to Paules a gasynge or gapynge as they have been wonte to do..."[18]

Skelton himself seems to have anticipated such activity when he attacked the young Cambridge Lutherans Thomas Bilney and Thomas Arthur in 1528. Their abjuration of heresy the prior September 27 at St. Paul's led Skelton to versify his revulsion. In the _Replication_ he again links Wyclif with Luther whose lute they so stringed," that ye dance all in a suit."[19] The complete title should be noted, which is a _Replication against Certain Young Scholars Abjured of Late_. Skelton's anti-clerical comments no doubt were part of the tinder which helped to fan the flames of gospel preaching in the social context and conflagration which Ms. Brigden describes. One can sense the pain in lines 222-227 of the _Replication_:

"Ye cobble and ye clout
Holy Scripture so about
That people are in great dout
And feare leeste they be out
Of all good Christen order,
Thus all thyng ye disorder."[20]

Two centuries of clerical complaint found an audience among the Lollards and these bachelor London apprentices of the mid-sixteenth century.[21]

The theological content of that dispute was boldly stated by contemporary Londoners who took transubstantiation seriously, telling the priest as he lifted up the Host:

"'Hold up, sir John, hold up; heave it a little higher'. And one will say to another: 'Stoop down, thou fellow afore, that I may see my Maker: for I cannot be merry except I see my Lord God once in a day'."[22]

Such sentiments of the ancient church were swiftly answered by the rhetoric of the gospellers when they countered the visual with the verbal, i.e.:

> "And that men ought to put their trust in goddes worde and to have better regarde to good sermons and preaching than to the sacrament of the alter, masse, matins, and evensonge".23

John Longland, bishop of Lincoln, was particularly concerned about Luther because Oxford University lay within his jurisdiction. When he became bishop in May 1521 his diocese covered an area of 7,265 square miles and by 1536 had 1736 parishes. By 1532 Longland became chancellor of the University.[24] Within a week of Longland's consecration as bishop, Luther's books were burned at St. Paul's Cross London. Longland wasted little time in obtaining a royal proclamation in October 1521 for the diocese of Lincoln which required mayors, bailiffs and other officers to assist the bishop in bringing heretics to trial.[25] Longland then alerted his commissary in Oxford to turn the bookshops upside down. Longland's register has the following entry:

> I commanded Dr. London my commissary to call the booksellers of your university and to make search for these corrupt works as Luther and other(s) have caused to be printed and sent into this realm, he sayeth you promised you would within fourteen days make search and send such books to me... Wherefore in other wise such great danger and slander as might insue unto your university by such-books, which young indiscreet persons will desirously read and talk of, I sent my commissary purposely to Oxford to stay all occasion of selling, bringing or buying such books whereof some he brought unto me.26

Longland wrote to Cardinal Wolsey on January 5, 1526 about secret book searches and in November of 1526 and in 1527 reported Lutheran opinions from Lincolnshire pulpits.[27] 1528 brought the bad news that a heretic bought Lutheran books in London only to sell them to students at both Oxford and Cambridge. Then a known Lutheran named Thomas Garrett had been apprehended in Oxford. Books and other documents linked Garrett to the parson of Honey Lane in London, and a bookseller named Nicholas in the churchyard of St. Paul's in London. When Longland's commissary, one Dr.

London, wrote the bishop in alarm in February 1528, it was because Garrett had been in Oxford since Easter. Garrett "sowght owt all siche whiche were gevyn to greke ebrew and the polyt latyn tonge....he procured a great numbre of corrupt bokes and secretly dydd destribute them amonge his new acquayntans in sondry colleges and hallys...."[28]

Luther's works circulated in English after 1528 in several translations. The first to appear after Tyndale's Parable of the Wycked Mammon was William Roye's An exposition in to the/seventh chaptre of the first pistle to the Corinthians. This work printed by Hoochstraten at Antwerp is a complete translation of Luther's 1523 Das siebente Kapital S. Pauli zu den Corinthern without Luther's prefaces.[29] This work of June 20, 1529 comes between Tyndale's translation of the Wycked Mammon and John Frith's rendering of July 12, 1529 from Luther's attack on Ambrosius Catherinus. This concluded with a commentary on Daniel which Frith translated as The Revelation of Antichrist.[30] Tyndale's translation called The Parable of the Wycked Mammon was printed in 1528, 1536, 1537, 1547, 1548, 1549 and 1561(?).[31]

John Frith (1503-1533) was educated at Eton and King's College, Cambridge. Wolsey made Frith a junior canon of his new 'Cardinal College' (Christ Church), Oxford in 1525. The authorities arrested him for heresy in 1528, but Frith escaped to Marburg where he helped Tyndale with his Bible translation. On his return to England Frith was arrested in 1532 and condemned to death for denying both purgatory and transubstantiation. He was burned at Smithfield on July 4, 1533.[32]

When Frith translated Luther's Offonbarung des Endchrists (1524) in his Antwerp book, A pistle to the Christen reader. The Revelation of Antichrist (1529), he placed himself in jeopardy. More's letter against Frith is dated from Chelsea on December 7, 1532 and goes on to complain about Frith's language.

> "A wors than this is, though the wordes be smoth and fayre, the deuyll, I trow, can not make. For herin he ronneth a great way beyond Luther, and techeth in a few leuys shortely, all the poyson that Wycliffe, Huskyn [Oecalompadius], Tyndale and Zwingluis haue taught..."33

More goes on to call all these persons "bestes".

William Tolwyn of St. Atholin's Church, London, recanted on December 18, 1541 at St. Paul's Cross. The recantation repudiates the contents of several books. These included Thorpe and Oldcastle, The Old God and the New, (Vadian: 1534), Ridley's Commentary on Ephesians, Zwingli, On The Book of Prayer (final leaves of Roman's Prologue?), Door of Holy Scripture, Catechism of Melanchthon and of Hubmaier and "one from Fryth". Since Frith wrote five works while in the Tower after October 1532, John Bale speculates on the Frith repudiation.[34]

That work which Tolwyn renounced in 1541 could have been one on purgatory, an answer to More, articles, exhortation to Christ's followers of the gospel or A bulwork against Rashtell. Bale singles out the sacramental issue as did More, only to call contemporary eucharistic practice, "the holye sygne of an heape of bryckes".[35] Bale concludes as only he could with a reference to the brick altars of Isaiah (65:3).

> "Moche better yt was wyth vs whan christ was our onlye aulter, and we the lyuynge sacrifyce offred ther vpon in a syncere faythe vnto god the father, than now hauynge your brycke aulters amonge dead mennys graues (as Esaye telleth your tale and yow to stande vpp there as newe redemers and sauers for moneye, with touche me not for I am holyar than thu."36

In the 1530s Richard Taverner translated Melanchthon into English as 1536 saw the printing of the Augsburg Confession and the Apology.[37] Richard Morison translated Luther's lecture on Psalm 127 though it was never published.

It seems to be part of Cromwell's attempt to promote reform.[38] In 1537 Coverdale translated Luther's Psalm 22 as well as Osiander's sermon on the plague based on Psalm 91, which was printed once in 1537, twice in 1538 and reset in 1603.[39] Luther's Psalm 23 was printed in 1537 and twice in 1538.

Chapter 3) William Tyndale (d. 1536): A Martyr for All Seasons

The earliest circulation of Luther in English was in the margins of Tyndale's 1525 Cologne fragment of Matthew where the marginal comments are virtual translations from Luther's 1522/1524 New Testament annotations. That Tyndale put into circulation a quarto edition of Matthew/Mark with notes in 1526 is significant.[40] The Cologne fragment of ten sheets was printed in 1525 with one extant copy of eight sheets now in the British Library. Robert Ridley, chaplain to the Bishop of London, wrote in 1527 about a printing with "comentares & annotations in Mathew & Marcum."[41] It seems that Tyndale completed a printing at Worms of Matthew and part of Mark with annotations from Luther before the printer reset a complete octavo edition of the New Testament without the notes.

In 1527 John Tyball of Steeple Bumpstead, who was an Essex Lollard, told the court how that he and a friend visited the Augustinian friar Robert Barnes at Cambridge. They produced their Lollard manuscript version of the Four Gospels as well as certain Pauline and Petrine epistles.

> Which books the said friar did little regard, and made a twit of it, and said, 'A point for them, for that they be not to be regarded toward the new printed Testament in English, for it is of more cleaner English![42]

By cleaner English Barnes would have in mind such passages as Matthew (6:24-30).

> ye cannot serve god and mamon. There fore y saye unto you/be not carefull for youre lyfe what ye shall eate/or what ye shall dryncke/nor yet for youre boddy/what rayment ye shall weare. Ys not the lyfe more worth then rayment? Beholde the foules of the aier: for they serve not nether reepe/nor yet cary into the barnes/and yett youre hevenly father fedeth them. Are ye nott better then they?
>
> Whiche of you (though he take thought there fore) could put one cubit unto his stature? And why care ye then for rayment? Be holde the lyles of the felde/howe they growe/They labour nott/nether spyn. And yet for all

> that I saye unto you/that even Solomon in all his royalte/was not arayed lyke unto one of these. Wherefore yf god so clothe the grasse/which ys to daye in the felde/& to morrowe shalbe cast into the fournace: shall he not moche more do the same unto you/o ye of lyttle fayth?

A. Tutor

The Tyndale family carried a second name of Hutchins/ Hitchins. Edward, the brother of William Tyndale, dwelt in the manor of Berkeley in Glouchestershire in 1519. Since a family of Tyndales lived there from 1478, it has been usual to claim that Tyndale was a Gloucestershire man. New evidence cited by Canon Mozley points to William Hychens and John Hychens ordained in June 1514 in Herefordshire. This 1514 entry of his ordination coupled with the June 1515 date of his Oxford master's degree places William Tyndale's birth in 1493 or 1494.[44]

Tyndale entered Magdalen Hall as a child in the University of Oxford, taking his B.A. on July 4, 1512. Since the whole arts course took seven years, Tyndale went up to Oxford in 1508. Magdalen college statutes laid down a minimum age of twelve on entry. If the birth were fixed at 1494 and entry to Magdalen Hall took place in 1506, then William studied first in the grammar-school before he entered the college.[45] John Foxe records that Tyndale increased in learning, was especially addicted to a knowledge of the scriptures and "ripened in the knowledge of God's word" at Cambridge before he left that university to become a tutor to a knight's family in Gloucestershire. He seems to have come to Cambridge in 1519 and to Little Sodbury perhaps as late as the summer of 1522.[46]

Tyndale's patron was Sir John Walsh who had been at Henry VIII's court and twice would be high sheriff of Gloustershire. Foxe describes his teaching as well as his preaching "about the town of Bristol" some fifteen miles from the manor. In the _Acts and Monuments_ (1563) Foxe gives a graphic account from one who heard from Tyndale's own lips the conversations at Sir John's dining-table.

> Master Tyndall, it runs, being in good favour with his master, sat most commonly at his own table, which kept a good ordinary (liberal board), having resort to him many times divers great beneficed men, as abbots, deans, archdeacons, and other divers doctors and learned men. Amongst whom commonly was talk of learning, as well of Luther and Erasmus Roterodamus as of opinions in the scripture. The said Master Tyndall, being learned, and which had been a student of divinity in Cambridge, and had therein taken degree of school, did many times therein show his mind and learning; wherein as those men and Tyndall did vary in opinions and judgments, then Master Tyndall would show them on the book the places, by open and manifest scripture: the which continued for a certain season... until... those great beneficed doctors waxed weary, and bare a secret grudge in their hearts against Master Tyndall.47

Tyndale then shifted his argument from table conversation to translation. The great Erasmus himself would cinch the argument over biblical living.

> Then did he translate into English a book called, as I remember, Enchiridion militis Christiani. The which being translated, he delivered to his master and lady; and after they had read that book, those great prelates were no more so often called to the house, nor when they came, had the cheer nor countenance as they were wont to have: the which they did well perceive, and that it was by the means and incensing of Master Tyndall, and at the last came no more there.48

This treatise by Erasmus gained enormous popularity after the 1515 edition. Between 1519 and 1542 it appeared in translation in eight different languages. The 1533 English version is now thought to be Tyndale's translation in print.[49] Gee goes on to cite Henry Monmouth's petition of May 19, 1528 from the Tower of London in which he mentions Tyndale's translation as well as the Pater Noster and On Christian Liberty both in English. At least two copies of Tyndale's translation are in circulation. Based on its diction Gee confidently assigns the 1533 text to Tyndale. The ten words and their combination which with one exception appear first in Tyndale's undisputed writings and the 1533 Enchiridion are beautiful, excommunicate, filthy lucre, godliness, jot or tittle, pick-quarrel, sackcloth and ashes, schoolmen, self-minded and tropes.[50]

Tyndale saw that the laity were ignorant of the Latin scriptures and that they had no English version in print. The hostility at Little Sodbury needed more direct attention than even a fine translation of Erasmus. Only a fresh translation of the New Testament into English could fill that gap. In spite of Arundel's 1408 Oxford prohibition against translation, Tyndale was determined to proceed. Foxe again tells the tale.

> Soon after, Master Tyndall happened to be in the company of a learned man, and in communing and disputing with him drove him to that issue, that the learned man said: We were better be without God's law than the pope's. Master Tyndall, hearing that, answered him: I defy the pope and all his laws; and said: If God spare my life, ere many years I will cause a boy that driveth the plough shall know more of the scripture than thou dost.51

In the preface to his Pentateuch of 1530, Tyndale tells why he sought to translate the New Testament.

> A thousand bokes had they lever to be put forth agenste their abhominable doynges and doctrine, then that the scripture shulde come to light. For as longe as they maye kepe that doune, they will so darken the ryght way with the...miste of their sophistrye, and so tangle them that ether rebuke or despyse their abhominations with argumentes of philosophye & with wordly symylitudes and apparent reasons of naturall wisdom. And with wrestinge the scripture unto their awne purpose clene contrarye unto y processe, order and meaninge of the texte, and so delude them in descantynge vppon it with alligoryes, and amase them expoundinge it in manye senses before the vnlerned laye people, (when it hath but one symple litterall sense whose light the owles can not abyde) that though thou feale in thyne harte and arte sure how that all is salfe yt they saye, yet coudeste thou not solve their sotle rydles.
>
> Which thinge onlye moved me to translate the new testament. Because I had perceaved by experyence, how that it was impossible to stablysh the laye people in any truth, excepte ye scripture were playnly layde before their eyes in their mother tonge, that they might se the processe, ordre and meaninge of the texte.52

B. Theologian

William Tyndale contributed several theological comments both in the context of his translation and in the turmoil which swept over his literary encounter with Sir Thomas More. Apart from the biblical translations themselves a good bit of Tyndale's theology emerges as early as 1526 in the _Compendious Introduccion/prologe or preface vn to the pistle off Paul to the Romayns_.[53]

This Roman's preface from Luther's September Testament of 1522 circulated in many translations, including the Swedish New Testament of 1526. Though Tyndale translates Luther's famous preface, he also introduces some real differences. Trinterud interprets these differences as an attempt on Tyndale's part to substitute a Reformed understanding of obedience to the law through the Spirit for Luther's strict law/gospel dialectic which precludes such a compulsive attitude toward keeping of the law.[54] Trinterud then traces a similar development in Tyndale's translation of Luther's sermon on the Wicked Mammon (May 1528).[55] There Tyndale wrote that "The promises when the are beleved/are they that iustifie/for they bringe the spirite which loesith the hert giveth lust to the law and certifieth vs of the good will of god vnto vs worde."[56]

By the time of Tyndale's 1530 _Pentateuch_ the reader was given a clear motif of promise.

> Every man must worke godly and truly to the vttmoste of the power that god hath geven him: and yet not truste therein: but in goddes worde or promisse and god will worke with vs and bringe that we do to good effecte. And the when oure power will extend no further goddes promesses wyll worke all alone.57

Tyndale adopts the language of covenant in his _Sermon on the Mount_ published in 1532/33. Here a moralistic tone emerges which has led some to view Tyndale as the parent of Puritanism.[58] The revised prologue to Matthew produced the extraordinary affirmation that "the general covenant, wherein all other are comprehended and included, is this: if we meek ourselves to God, to keep all his laws after the example of Christ, then God hath bound himself vnto us, to keep and make good all the mercies promised in Christ...."[59]

Trinterud concludes that by 1530 Tyndale had worked a scheme of compact or covenant into his understanding of biblical history which followed the thinking of men such as Oecolampadius, Zwingli and Bucer. "Tyndale had learned more from Basel than from Wittenberg."[60] Trinterud goes on to the apparatus of the 1534 New Testament which he reads through the continental lenses of Switzerland and South Germany. There the opening preface of "W.T. unto the reader" repeats the identification of promise with covenant. Møller concludes from all of this that Tyndale focused his theology through the twin lenses of faith and deeds. The separate edition of the Pathway into the Holy Scripture inserts passages on the necessity of deeds, that they "certify us that we are heirs of everlasting life," that "we kill the sin that remaineth yet in us" and that "we do our duty unto our neighbor therewith." Such a theology, claims Møller, is no longer Lutheran but stands in the Zurich line.[61]

More recently Robert Williams has noted Tyndale's lack of connection between outward baptism and salvation, a 'sign and badge' of the consent to God's covenant. This concept of baptism as a covenant is in Erasmus. In fact, Tyndale surely saw it in the Enchiridion which is the first work which he translated. Tyndale's break with the covenants of baptism and that of the Lord's Supper "are not evidence for his passing away from Luther to come under the influence of the Swiss."[62] Nonetheless, Tyndale's views are similar to the Swiss. Robert Williams admits that covenant appears more frequently in Tyndale after 1530. Tyndale, however, uses the term as a synonym for testament. The 1534 preface to the New Testament claims that "the new testament is as much to say as a new covenant... But the new testament is an everlasting covenant made unto the children of God through faith in Christ, upon the deservings of Christ."[63]

McGiffert insists on the "evangelical impulse and experiential reference of Tyndale's teaching because previous studies have given little heed to them and for that reason have missed the heart of the matter."[64] McGiffert blames Clebsch for perpetuating this legalistic interpretation of Tyndale.[65] The mutuality of the covenant bond is not in question, whereby God offers hope and happiness to men, but what McGiffert finds naive is the "signification of conditionality in Tyndale's thought."[66]

> Conditionality thus was crucial to the practice of piety: by the conditions of the covenant God secured the tribute of trust from the elect. Consequently, the promissory if/then was, at the deepest level, spiritually affiliative. It represented not a contractual transaction, not a bargain over salvation, not a quid pro quo of any kind, but a way of articulating the mutuality of God and man in a communion of commitment. Piety, not legality, supplies the key.
>
> To underscore the evangelical impetus of Tyndale's thought is not at all to minimise its moral stress. But if his covenantal writings verge on identifying the profession of faith with the pursuit of practical godliness, far more fundamentally they put morality to the service of piety, making good deeds the chief means for experiencing and evincing grace. Far from inciting Tyndale to bound into works-righteousness, at grave risk to his protestant credentials, covenant expressed the spiritual salience of his thought. The proper test of this proposition will be found in his teaching on the subject of works. The question is whether his use of covenant to enjoin morality on the part of the elect can correctly be called legalistic in substance, tenor or intent.67

There is another Tyndale text overlooked by everyone except Trinterud who mentions it but does not cite from it. This is Tyndale's translation and introduction to Luther's Pater Noster which filled out signature c of the 1526 Compendious Introduccion...to the Romans. Tyndale comments on the sinner who prays these petitions, only to see them answered by the law "as though he (God) wolde putt hym from hys desyre."[68] Tyndale makes an important distinction about God's response.

> Marke this well and take it for a sure conclusion/when god commaundeth vs in the lawe to doo any thinge/he commaundeth not therefore/that we are able to do yt/but to bryng vs vnto the knowlege of oure selues/that we might se what we are and in what miserable state we are in/and to knowe oure lack/that thereby we shuld torne to god and to knowledge oure wretchednes vn to hym...69

Tyndale notes as well that prayer is a longing after health in the heart which requires the "law and also the gospel, that is to say, the promises of God." This preface is a clear articulation of law and gospel.

> Fayth ys the ancre of all health ad kepeth vs fast vn to the promyses of God which are the sure haven or porte of all quietnes of the conscience. Nothyng/nether the lawe nether workes nether yet any other thynge can quiette a mans conscience save only fayth and trust in the promyses of God.70

C. Captain of Englyshe Heretickes

Sir Thomas More complained that William Tyndale was the "captain of our Englyshe heretickes"[71] In the battle of books which followed, More's first salvo was the Dialogue of June 1529. Its full title concluded with the phrase, "with many other things touching the pestilent sect of Luther and Tyndale by the one begun in Saxony and by the other laboured to be brought to England." Tyndale's response in July of 1531 makes use of at least the Parable of the Wicked Mammon among his earlier writings.[72]

More's encounter with Luther began as early as 1518 when Erasmus sent him a copy of the Ninety-Five Theses.[73] In a letter of 1520 More connected Luther's writings with heresy that conveys evil.[74] It was his response to the royal exchange between the German reformer and Henry VIII which documents More's bitterness toward Luther. More was drawn into this debate when Luther retorted to Henry's Assertion of the Seven Sacraments written against his 1520 Babylonian Captivity of the Church. Luther proceeded to pelt and plaster Henry's crown with muck and dung.[75] In 1523 More's rambling Response to Luther appeared in two issues, the second of which inserted a lengthy defense of the Church. It was the first of More's polemical works, was written in Latin for an international audience and responded to six of Luther's writings.[76]

In 1526 More directed a literary attack on Johann Bugenhagen, Luther's pastor, whose 1525 Letter to the English sought in Pauline style to convert that nation to the Reformation. For this More had access to the Strasbourg collections of Luther's sermons published in March and August of 1526. The primary sermon was Vom hailigen Creutz in den Kirchen. (On The Holy Cross in the Church).[77]

More reminded Bugenhagen how Luther discarded the scholastics for the patristic theologians, only to abandon a thousand Augustines in favour of his own beliefs. Likewise his fornicating Bishop Bugenhagen presides over the moral laxity rampant at Wittenberg. More recovered his composure in time to invite Bugenhagen to forsake that sect, abandon his mistress (wife) and return to the Catholic Church.

> It is not therefore true, Pomeranus, that faith alone suffices, and whoever has faith, necessarily produces the fruite of good works.But why should I adduce Christ to you? Why not rather Luther to a Lutheran? Hear therefore what he says, whose authority with you is incontestable. 'Nothing', he says, 'can damn a man except incredulity. For all other things, if faith remains or returns, are absorbed by faith.'78

More then asks Bugenhagen to consider whether the man who neglects good works and commits evil does not close heaven and open hell to himself. "If you deny this, you leave no one in doubt... that you are he, who provokes the whole world to sin, having offered impunity for such deeds. But if you concede the value of good works, which you must, then you can never deny that if the evil of our works plunges us to hell, the goodness of those which we do with the divine aid, helps us from hell and renders us to some degree suitable for the promised reward of heaven. It would be absurd... if God, who is so merciful, did not reward virtue, when he punishes wickedness."[79]

Tyndale for his part argued in 1528 that royal supremacy ought to settle the authority of scripture. Both the title and the prologue are quite explicit, i.e., The Obedience of a Christen man and how Christen rulers ought to governe, where in also (yf thou marke diligently) thou shalt fynde eyes to perceave the crafty conveyaunce of all iugglers (Antwerp: Johannes Hoochestraten, October 2, 1528).

> For as moch as oure holy prelates and oure gostly religious, which ought to defend Gods worde, speake evyll of it and doo all ye thaine they can to it, and royle on it and bere their captives in honde ye it causeth insurrection and teacheth the people to disobeye their heeds and governers, and moveth them to ryse agenst their princes and to make all comen and to make havoke of other mens goodes. Therefore have I made this litle treatyse....80

Henry's comment about this book is well known, that "this book is for me and all kings to read." Henry did not catch the heart's cry of Tyndale who skewered the catholic clergy while clarifying the scriptures. The problem lay with those who like Origen draw all the scripture in allegories. They say "the litteral sence kylleth and the spirituall sence geveth lyfe. We must therfore, saye they, seke out some choplogicall sence."[81] After all the invective, Tyndale argues for a literal sense of scripture "where with God draweth us unto him and not where with we shuld be leade from him. The scriptures springe out of God and flow unto Christe... Thou must therfore goo alonge by the scripture as by a lyne, untyll thou come at Christ, which is the wayes ende and restynge place."[82]

More's 1529 Dialogue adopts an apocalyptic mood when it excoriates the reformed barbarians whose Lutheran heresy would "runne (London) to ryot." Tyndale and his ilk would "tourne the world up so down, and defende theyr foly and false heresye by force."[83] What is more to the point after such rhetoric is the charge that Tyndale's New Testament was burnt in haste. More heads chapter VIII of book III, "The Author sheweth why the new Testament of Tyndale's translation was burned..." More claims that "the good and wholesome doctrine of Christ", was corrupted and changed to a devilish heresy.

> For he hath mistranslated three words of great weight, and every one of them is, as I suppose, more than trice three times repeated and rehearsed in the books... The one is, quoth I, this word Priests; the other, the Church; the third, Charity.84

Tyndale chose elder, congregation and love as translations which he defended in his answer to Sir Thomas More. In early editions Tyndale used senior which he changed to elder. The Answer begins with a definition of the church and a defense of these terms. Church once meant a place or house where people resorted at convenient times "to hear the word of doctrine, the law of God, and the faith of our Saviour Jesus Christ, and how and what to pray, and whence to ask power and strength to live godly."[85] Now prayer "is nothing else but to say pater noster unto a post" and that in a church only![86] That church is not as though God sets one place more than another as More argued in his Dialogue at chapter four. God loves no church so much, responded Tyndale, but that the parish can take it down. "It is the heart, and not the place, that worshippeth God. The kitchen-page, turning the spit, may have a purer heart to God than his master at church; and therefore worship God better in the kitchen than his master at church."[87] Tyndale's tintinabulation rang out the evangelical notes in response to his perception of More's mouldering piety.

More wrote to Erasmus on June 14, 1532 that one or two of his fellow countrymen have been sending a steady stream of heretical books in the vernacular from Belgium into England. He has written replies to several of those books because novel ideas evoke a sort of superficial curiosity "and to dangerous ideas out of deviltry."[88] One will never satisfy "that breed of humans who have a passion for wickedness." A second letter of June 14 congratulated Cochlaeus for his fighting heart which did battle with Luther. More was glad to hear that both Zwingli and Oecolampadius were dead.

> Still it is right for us to rejoice that such savage enemies of the Christian faith have been removed from our midst, enemies that were so fully equipped for the destruction of the Church and so eager for every opportunity to uproot piety.89

In an earlier letter to Roper of 1526 More commented on the futility of converting such persons.

> Troth it is indeed, sonne Roper, I pray God, that some of vs, as highe as we seeme to sitt uppon the mountaynes, treading heretikes vnder our feete like antes, live not the day that we gladly wold wishe to be at a league and composition with them, to let them have their churches quietly to themselves, so that they wold be contente to let vs have ours quietly to ourselves. Roper replied, By my troth, sir, it is very desperately spoken.... More, by thes wordes perceiuinge me in a fume, said merily vnto me: Well, well, sonne Roper, It shall not be so, It shall not be so.90

Professor Rupp's response to this passage is apropos of More's true feeling toward Tyndale and his fellows: "Under our feet. Like ants. But they were men" - as indeed was More himself.[91]

D. Toleration

A brief account of those other responses will set More's retort to Tyndale in context. Henry Brinkelow in The lamentacyon of a Christen against the Citye of London (1542) defended the Lutherans Robert Barnes and John Frith.

> "Well, the poore well feleth the bournynge of Docter Barnes and hys fellowes, which laboured in the Lorde. For, accordynge to their office, they barked uppon you to loke uppon the poore, so that then some relefe they had... Though they be gone, considre it was not theyr commandement, but Goddes, whose Testament ye haue euen nowe in youre very mother tonge, thankes be to the Lorde therefore."92

Brinkelow, whose comments were reprinted in 1545 and again in 1548, urged that Frith had written invincibly on the Lord's Supper, whose eating is with "fayth", not with "teth".[93]

> "And I exhorte you in Gods name, yf there be anie Christian printer in London, to print moo of these workes, for there can never be to many of them."94

John Rastell was one such printer whom Frith converted in 1532 when he visited the Tower of London to confute Frith's denial of purgatory. An other boke against Rastel was published in 1537/38. That Rastell was More's brother-in-law may lend some personal point to More's refutation of Tyndale.[95]

Christopher St. German explained the religious divisions in 1530 as a triple problem. First of all, the religious are exalted in their "ghostly pryde" and their opponents accuse them as "lovers of worldely delytes."[96] In the second place, such diversity of opinions violate the honor of God.[97] In the third place, spiritual men who know that these abuses exist, yet persist in these indecencies and punish those who call them to public accountability amidst the murmurs from the people, should alter their conduct. This would "brynge a new lyght of grace in to the worlde, and brynge the people to perfecte love and obedience to theyr superyours."[98] In his seventh section St. German attacks the law on heresy where the accuser can remain unknown even though the accused must purge himself. A man may be suspect without actual guilt. "This is a daungerous lawe," wrote St. German, "and more lyke to cause vntrewe and vnlawfulle men to condempne innocentes, than to condempne offenders."[99]

What animated More was the concern that "the great archheretyke" Wyclif, who himself had revived the ancient heresies of patristic times, had perverted scripture itself. This fundamental perversity could again lead to violence or destruction as with the Donatists in North Africa.[100] Professor Greenslade questions More's knowledge of church history on this point.

> Eager to brand Luther and Tyndale as Donatist heretics, he seriously misunderstands Donatism itself... did More seriously try to understand Luther and Tyndale? I fear the answer is no.[101]

More argues that biblical history teaches that when Christ abrogated the old law, He thereby expected that the new law offered greater assistance to meet increased moral responsibility.[102] Such obedience to the new law requires harder things to believe than before. "And therfore are we bounden", argues More, "not onely to byleue agaynste oure owne reason/the poyntes that god sheweth vs in scrypture/but also that god techeth his chyrche without scrypture and agaynste our owne mynde also."[103]

The essense of More's ecclesiology, which denies the scriptural arguments of Tyndale, may be found in an extensive passage in the Dialogue where More establishes the point that what Peter preached was later written down in inspired canonical scripture. Since not everything was written, those scriptures can not be the unique source of revelation. The ongoing life and preaching of the church means that she will never be deceived in taking any book for holy scripture that is not scripture. Tradition and scripture together transmit the divine will for God's people in the church. That is the Christian law, which is called:

> the lawe of Crystes faythe/the law of hys holy gospell. I mene not onely the wordes wrytten in the bookes of hys euangelystes/But moche more specyally the substaunce of our fayth it selfe/whiche oure lorde sayd he wolde wryte in mennes hartes/.... But also for that he fyrste without wrytynge reueled those heuenly mysteryes by hys blessyd mouth/ thorowe the eres of his appostles and dyscyples in to theyr holy hartes/or rather as it semeth it was inwardely infused in to saynt Peter his harte/by the secrete inspyracyon of god/without eyther wrytynge or any outwarde worde.... And so was it conuenyent for the lawe of lyfe/rather to be wrytten in the lyuely myndes of men/than in the dede skynnes of bestes. And I nothynge doubte/but all had it so ben/that neuer gospell hadde ben wrytten/yet sholde the substaunce of this fayth neuer haue fallen out of crysten folkes hartes/but the same spyryte that planted it/the same sholde haue watered it/the same shold haue kepte it/the same shold haue encreased it.104

More goes on in his Confutation of Tyndale's Answer (1532) to develop this argument in several directions. The first complains that by Tyndale's translation of "church" as "congregation" he has left out the signification of church as a parliament which may draft laws that "heretikes shall not be suffered to preach."[105] Then More laments that prayer at church is nothing else "but to saye a pater noster to a post...."[106] Then comes the response to evangelical preaching which More calls into question.

> I must wyt of Tyndale whyther he meane the word wryten or unwryten or bothe. If he say they preched the worde of god bothe wryten and vnwriten and onely that: then I saye so do we now to... For we be very sure that yt is his worde when we se that all the holy doctours that spent theyr lyfe in the studye of his worde, and in the kepynge of his worde, and the prechynge of his worde:

> do testifye from age to age by theyr holy wrytynge, that those wordes vnwriten which ye chyrch beleueth, were and be his wordes, as well and as veryly as those that be wryten in any parte of scrypture.[107]

More then elaborates upon this distinction between written and unwritten matters of faith. He will give Tyndale "respyte tyll domes daye" to prove that all the words which the Savior and his apostles taught without writing are "wryten, preserued, and kepte, in playne and euident scripture."[108] Luther, Tyndale, Zwingli and friar Barnes and his fellows are not only contentious about the meaning of the written text, but in the end they interpret it against the "comen fayth of all trewe crysten people. xv. hundred yere before them."[109] More's parting volley must surely be his reference to II Peter (3:16) that Paul's letters have things hard and difficult which unlearned and unsutable persons misconstrue to their own perdition. More suggests that Barnes understood this text to mean the opposite of Tyndale's concern, that this text denies the clarity of scripture. More concludes that Tyndale was wise to leave II Peter (3:16) out of his argument.[110]

Louis Martz defends the style of More's <u>Confutation</u> when he argues that More's repetition has a triple function in his digressions against Tyndale. If the reader has but time to sample one section, he will locate all the main points of the argument. If he reads on, then the refutation is reinforced through a full reading. Martz discovers that all the component essays are bound together gradually as one reads on in More past one digression after another.[111] More's repetitive essays in this view knock Tyndale's logic off stride by answering the primary concern, that Tyndale's doctrine "diminishes hope and changes that gracious word <u>charity</u> to a dubious, highly fallible word <u>love</u> -- a word that, as More sees it, can as well turn to lechery as to the love of God."[112] Thus More exhorts his reader:

> "Let not therfore Tyndall (good reader) wyth his gay gloryouse wordes carye you so fast & so far away, but that you remember to pull hym bakke/by the sleve a lytle."[113]

Gordon Rupp forty years ago called attention to the "tardy justice" which the fourth centenary of the English Bible has done to Tyndale. Rupp calls attention to "the depth of his intuitive regard for truth, so that... what he wrote was coloured by his own rich feeling." At times its purity "differs from the cumbrous Latinity of Sir Thomas More as the prose of Bunyan differs from the conceits of Donne."[114] C.S. Lewis added his reservations about More in his 1954 English Literature In The Sixteenth Century (pp.175-176) where Lewis faults More because he fails to rebuke magnificently. More "loses himself in a wilderness of opprobrious adjectives. He cannot denounce like a prophet; he can only scold and grumble like a father in an old fashioned comedy."

Then one is reminded that modern studies of More are shaded by Roper's contemporary account which portrays More as the King's good servant, but God's even more. Such historical shading needs to be noted whilst one reads the lengthy introductions to the Yale edition of More or takes Chamber's twentieth century biography without several grains of salt.[115]

Tyndale's defense was to argue against More's tearing at the scriptures with distinctions confirmed from Aristotle. As the Scribes and Pharisees blinded the Jews with false interpretations, so have "popyshe doctours of dunces darcke learninge, which with their sophistrye, sarved vs...."[116]

G.R. Elton has now published his extemporaneous anniversary lecture on "The Real Thomas More?" given at Cambridge University in the Spring of 1978. Is the traditional More the real More?, asks Professor Elton, who reminds us that Roper's Life was written out of affection and a desire to prove his father-in-law worthy of canonization.[117] More lost all sense of proportion in his "highpitched scream of rage and disgust which at times borders on hysteria", a stance which mars his Confutation of Tyndale's Answer. Elton argues that More is as passionate as Luther in his pessimistic view of human nature. He faulted Luther and his English disciples like Tyndale for cracking the crust of civilization over that boiling cauldron of human depravity, a crust which the Catholic Church sought to toughen with its moral controls over human souls. The only equal among More's contemporaries to share such a pessimism was the Augustinian Luther himself.[118]

Man's disobedience to God had condemned More to a life which was itself a prison, with death at the end its only certainty. The Tower was his tonsure and monk's cell alike, which granted him passage to "his only possible cloister, out of the world."[119] Tyndale, on the other hand, took the reality of human sin to be the opportunity for God himself clothed in Jesus Christ to open the cloister of the heart so that he might walk a life of faith. As Luther put the matter in 1531, that faith was a source of hope not despair, comments which came from the Galatian Commentary at chapter five and verse five: "by faith we wait for the hope of righteousness."

> faith is a theologian and a judge, battling against errors and heresies, and judging spirits and doctrines. On the other hand, hope is a captain, battling against feelings such as tribulation, the cross, impatience, sadness, faintheartedness, despair, and blasphemy; and it battles with joy and courage, etc., in opposition to those great evils....Therefore when I take hold of Christ as I have been taught by faith in the Word of God, and when I believe in Him with the full confidence of my heart - something that cannot happen without the will - then I am righteous through this knowledge. When I have been thus justified by faith or by this knowledge, then immediately the devil comes and exerts himself to extinguish my faith with his tricks, his lies, errors and heresies, violence, tyranny, and murder. Then my battling hope grasps what faith has commanded; it becomes vigorous and conquers the devil, who attacks faith. When he has been conquered, there follow peace and joy in the Holy Spirit.[120]

Tyndale himself would strike that cord of trust when he translated Hebrews (XI:I) that "Fayth is a sure confidence of thynges which are hoped for, and a certayntie of thynges which are not sene."[121]

The Obedience of A Christian Man contains a passage which explains Tyndale's persistance under persecution to translate the New Testament into English. This will set the tone for the careful textual work over which he labored for a dozen years from 1524 to his death in 1536.

> Christ is the cause why I love thee, why I am ready to do the utmost of my power for thee, and why I pray for thee. And as long as the cause abideth, so long lasteth the effect: even as it is always day so long as the sun shineth. Do therefore the worst thou canst unto me, take away my goods, take away my good name; yet as long as Christ remaineth in my heart, so long I love thee not a whit the less, and so long art thou as dear unto me as mine own soul, and so long am I ready to do thee good for thine evil, and so long I pray for thee with all my heart: for Christ desireth it of me, and hath deserved it of me. Thine unkindness compared unto his kindness is nothing at all; yea, it is swallowed up as a little smoke of a mighty wind, and is no more seen or thought upon. Moreover that evil which thou didst to me, I receive not of thy hand, but of the hand of God, and as God's scourge to teach me patience, and to nurture me: and therefore have no cause to be angry with thee, more than the child hath to be angry with his father's rod; or a sick man with a sour or bitter medicine that healeth him or a prisoner with his fetters, or he that is punished lawfully with the officer that punisheth him. Thus is Christ all, and the whole cause why I love thee.122

Chapter 4) "With Eagles' Wings..."

A. Miles Coverdale: Scholar

John Tyball, the Lollard from Bumpstead, confessed his heresy on April 28, 1528. Tyball had the Four Gospels in English as well as some of the

> Epistoles of Peter and Paule... Futhermore, he saythe, that abowght ij yeres agon he companyed with Sir Richard Fox, curate of Bumstede, and shewid him al his bookys that he had; that is to say the New Testamente in Englishe, the Gospel of Matthew and Mark in Englishe; which he had of John Pykas, of Colchester...123

The New Testament had been sold to him by Robert Barnes,[124] which would be the Worms octavo, whereas the Matthew and Mark with notes would be the Cologne/Worms quarto of which only the Grenville fragment to Matthew (22:12) is extant. Tyball delivered the New Testament to Gardiner in the fall of 1527.[125]

Thomas Topley, an Augustinian from Stoke Clare in Suffolk, was serving in Bumpstead when Coverdale preached during Lent of 1528. Topley describes the impact of that preaching which taught him that the blessed sacrament was but the remembrance of Christ's body.

> Furthermore, he said and confessed, that in the Lent last past, as he was walking in the field at Bumstead, with sir Miles Coverdale, late friar of the same order, going in the habit of a secular priest, who had preached the fourth Sunday in Lent at Bumstead, they did commune together of Erasmus's works, and also upon confession. This sir Miles said, and did hold, that it was sufficient for a man to be contrite for his sins betwixt God and his conscience, without confession made to a priest; which opinion this respondent thought to be true, and did affirm and hold the same at that time. Also he saith, that at the said sermon, made by the said sir Miles Coverdale at Bumstead, he heard him preach against worshipping of images in the church, saying and preaching, that men in no wise should honour or worship them; which likewise he thought to be true, because he had no learning to defend it.126

Late in 1528 Miles Coverdale crossed to the continent. He was forty-two years old and would spend the next eighteen years on the continent. He went first of all to Hamburg where the Hanseatic merchants were in control of the sea lanes. One need think only of the contacts between the Hanse and Kings Lynn on the Norfolk coast or Norwich in East Anglia as examples of open commerce between England and the Northern rim of Germany. On February 8, 1526 the English bishops had forced several Hanse merchants to bear faggots as penance for marketing forbidden books and to do so on the same day in London when the Lutheran Robert Barnes bore his unlit torch and John Fisher used the occasion to warn the crowd against heresy by attacking Luther in his sermon.[127] Tyndale reappeared at Hamburg in 1529 to publish his Pentateuch translation. Foxe describes the disaster and Coverdale's help.

> For at what time Tyndale had translated the fifth book of Moses called Deuteronomy, minding to print the same at Hamburgh, he sailed thitherward; where by the way, upon the coast of Holland, he suffered shipwreck, by which he lost all his books, writings, and copies, and

> so was compelled to begin all again anew, to his hinderance, and doubling of his labours. Thus, having lost by that ship, both money, his copies, and his time, he came in another ship to Hamburgh, where, at his appointment, Master Coverdale tarried for him, and helped him in the translating of the whole five books of Moses, from Easter till December, in the house of a worshipful widow, Mistress Margaret Van Emmerson, A.D. 1529; a great sweating sickness being at the same time in the town. So, having dispatched his business at Hamburgh, he returned afterwards to Antwerp again.128

Miles Coverdale (1487-1569) was born at York in the north of England. His early life is obscure to the biographer until at age thirty-two he entered the Augustinian House at Cambridge in 1519. Robert Barnes returned from Louvain in 1520 to become the Austin prior and to lecture on Terence, Plautus, Cicero and the Pauline letters, lectures which Foxe records that Coverdale attended.[129] Several of these reformers attended "Little Germany", the inn called the White Horse where they discussed and read Luther. Among the several dozen attending these sessions were the future prominent reformers Cranmer, Ridley and Latimer as well as Barnes and Coverdale.

After his apprenticeship to Tyndale between 1528-1534, Coverdale was commissioned by an Antwerp merchant to translate the whole of the Bible into English. Shortly after its appearance in 1535, Coverdale returned to England where he produced a Concordance of the New Testament, a New Testament Diglot in Latin/English and two new 1537 editions of the English Bible which James Nycholson published in folio and quarto at Southwark. These were the first English Bibles printed in England. Coverdale then revised Matthew's Bible for official use which took him to Paris to supervise the printing. From 1535 to 1539 Cromwell supported the project to place a Great Bible in every English parish church.

During the 1530s Coverdale translated short works by Luther (Psalm 22) and Osiander (Psalm 91 on the Plague), a Latin paraphrase of the Psalms by John Campensis, and ten other works.[130] Among these are the unique copies at Gonville and

Caius College, Cambridge of the 1537 Causes and Ursachen why the evangelical princes would not go to the Mantua Council of Pope Paul III, and the faithful and true pronostication upon the year 1536.

The most important work of Coverdale apart from the Biblical translations is the 1539 Ghostly Psalms and Spiritual Songs which is the first English hymn book. Nine out of the twenty-four hymns are English versions of Luther. "Like Luther, Coverdale makes each stanza of his hymns self-contained, because this helps people to memorize and to understand."[131] Be Glad Now, All Ye Christian Men is a case in point, whose first lines read as follows:

> Be glad now, all ye christen men, And let us rejoyce unfaynedly. The kyndnesse cannot be written with penne, That we have receaved of God's mercy; Whose love towarde us hath never ende: He hath done for us as a frende; Now let us thanke him hartely.132

B. Bible Translator

1. Proclamations & Parliament (1530/31)

Miles Coverdale was an Henrician migrant who translated Protestant literature and the Bible into English, a Marian exile who joined the trek to civic safety on the Continent and became an Elizabethan bishop upon the restoration of Protestantism in 1559. Both Haaland and Hughes are concerned about that other identity after 1540. This narrative will return to the biblical translation from 1530 to 1539. In June of 1530 a royal proclamation was issued against erroneous books and heresies. "Pestiferous English books" were singled out as seditious agents of perversity and blasphemy.[133] Among these books were Tyndale's Obedience of A Christian Man (1528) and Simon Fish's Supplication of Beggars (1529). The king commanded that henceforth "any of the books before named, or any other book, being in the English tongue, and printed beyond the sea...." must be delivered within fifteen days to the bishop of the diocese or his representatives.[134] Then came the comments on the English Bible.

And furthermore, forasmuch as it is come to the hearing of our said sovereign lord the King, that report is made by divers and many of his subjects, that it were to all men not only expedient, but also necessary, to have in the English tongue both the New Testament and the Old: and that his highness, his noblemen, and prelates were bound to suffer them so to have it, His highness hath therefore similarly thereupon consulted with the said primates, and virtuous, discreet, and well learned personages in divinity aforesaid, and by them all it is thought that it is not necessary, the said scripture to be in the English tongue, and in the hands of the common people, but that the distribution of the said scripture, and the permitting or denying thereof, dependeth only upon the discretion of the superiors, as they shall think it convenient. And that having respect to the malignity of this present time, with the inclination of people to erroneous opinions, the translation of the New Testament and the Old into the vulgar tongue of English, should rather be the occasion of continuance or increase of errors among the said people, than any benefit or commodity toward the weal of their souls. And that it shall now be more convenient that the same people have the Holy Scripture expounded to them, by preachers in their sermons, according as it hath been of old time accustomed before this time. Albeit if it shall hereafter appear to the King's highness, that his said people do utterly abandon and forsake all perverse, erroneous, and seditious opinions, with the New Testament and the Old, corruptly translated into the English tongue now being in print: And that the same books and all other books of heresy, as well in the French tongue as in the Dutch tongue, be clearly exterminate and exiled out of this realm of England for ever: his highness intendeth to provide that the Holy Scripture shall be by great learned and catholic persons, translated into the English tongue, if it shall then seem to his grace convenient so to be. Wherefore his highness at this time, by the whole advice and full determination of all the said primates and other discreet and substantial learned personages, of both universities, and other before expressed and by the assent of his nobles and others of his most honourable Council, willeth and straitly commandeth, that all and every person and persons, of what estate, degree, or condition soever he or they be, which hath the New Testament or the Old translated into English, or any other book of Holy Scripture so translated, being in print, or copied out of the books now being in print, that he or they do immediately bring the same book or books, or cause the same to be brought to the bishop of the diocese, where he dwelleth, or to the hands of other the said persons.135

A year later in the Parliamentary sessions of 1531 proposals were advanced which called for a vernacular Bible. The extant document found among Thomas Cromwell's papers is now assigned to Christopher St. German.[136] It would seem to be a piece begun in 1530 and reworked for the 1531 session of Parliament. A "great standing council" of bishops and laity were to review the rationale for an English New Testament. If that rationale sprang from "meekness and charity," then the king would allow the council to "have such a part thereof translated into the mother tongue as shall be thought convenient."[137]

St. German's corrections in his own hand and the famous phrase 'some say' which was a distinctive mark of his style indicate formidable support for a vernacular translation from the source which More himself rejected. St. German was one of the most learned jurists of his day who took his training at the Middle Temple. His reputation rests on his Latin work _A Dialogue concerning the fundamental law of England and about the Conscience_ (1528), better known as Doctor and Student.[138] This book assumes that the King in Parliament has power to make laws binding on both clergy and laity.

Christopher St. German wrote several anticlerical tracts between 1532 and 1535. The first of these was _A Treatise concernynge the Diuision betwene the Spiritualitie and Temporaltie_. After More responded, St. German retorted with _Salem and Byzance_ (1533) in which the plight of Jerusalem (Salem) and Constantinople (Bizance) becomes the setting for an attack on ecclesiastical internal dissension. When More fired his salvo in _The Debellacyon of Salem and Bizance_ (1533), St. German added four more retorts in two years. More's _Apology_ (1533) answered St. German's _Diuision_ point by point. More nicknames him "Sir John Some-say." The _Diuision_ went through five printings in 1532![139]

Guy thinks that St. German was working for Henry VIII, who met him at Hampton Court in October 1530. The printer of _New Additions_ and the _Diuision_ was Thomas Berthelet, the king's printer. Cromwell may have obtained the 1530 Draft because he was sympathetic to its ideas.[140]

2. Translation (1534/35)

The Coverdale Bible is a small folio edition, printed in Schwabacher black letter type with two columns and 57 lines to a full page. It was "prynted in the yeare of oure Lorde M.DXXXV. and fynished the fourth daye of October."[141] All the recorded copies which numbered 65 in the census of 1974 are incomplete. Possible continental copies may some day clear up current confusion between extant copies. The title page is a case in point, with some copies reading seven lines of title and others only six. The six line or London (?) title page has the more complete citation from Joshua (1), i.e., "yt thou mayest kepe and do euery thynge accordynge to it that is wrytten therin."

Zurich? Title-Page	London? Title-Page
BIBLIA The Bible/that is, the holy Scripture of the Olde and New Testament faithfully and truly translated out of Douche and Latyn in to Englishe.142	BIBLIA The Byble: that is/the holy Scrypture of the Olde and New Testament, faythfully translated in to Englyshe.143

The first printers were Eucharius Cervicorn and Johannes Sater, though the place of publication is uncertain. Perhaps, as Greenslade speculates, Peter Quentel of Cologne was consulted or cooperated with Cervicorn and Soter. Nycholson of Southwork dropped the "Douche and Latyn" from the second title page.

One major bibliographical problem relates to the preliminary leaves. The first and last leaves are extant in the Holkham-British Library copy, just enough with a fragmentary title from another copy to prove that the original had a title-page, index of books, prologue and a summary of Genesis. "Was there also a dedication?", asks Professor Greenslade.[144] The answer revolves around an assumption of four preliminary leaves (eight pages in a folio) or eight. A preliminary section can have six leaves or twelve pages of material. Greenslade refers to Nycholson's letter of August 1535 sent to Thomas Cromwell which proves that there was a dedicatory epistle for the king's bible which Nycholson asks Cromwell to "visit (inspect)."[145] The dedication is reproduced in the 1974 Facsimile from another copy which Nycholson reprinted in 1537 with the change from 'Quene Anne' to 'Queen Jane'.[146] This other copy has 54 lines whereas the original continental edition had 58 lines of text. It is clear that something akin to the dedication inserted at the front of the 1974 Facsimile edition accompanied the first printing. This reads in part as follows:

> The ryght & iust administracyon of the lawes that God gaue unto Moses and unto Josua: the testimonye of faythfulnes that God gaue of Dauid: the plenteous abundaunce of wysdome that God gaue unto Salomon: the lucky and prosperous age with the multiplicacyon of sede whiche God gaue unto Abraham and Sara his wyfe, he geue unto you most gracyous Prynce, with your Dearest iust wyfe, and most vertuous Pryncesse, Quene Anne, Amen.147

The main argument of the dedication includes Coverdale's purpose for translation.

> What is now the cause of all these untollerable and nomore to be suffred abhominacions? Truely euen the ignoraunce of the scripture of God. For how had it els ben possyble, that such blyndnes shulde haue come in to ye worlde, had not ye lyghte of Gods worde bene extyncte? How coulde men (I saye) haue bene so farre from the true seruyce of God, and from the due obedience of theyr prynce, had not the lawe of God bene clene shut up, depresed, cast asyde, and put out of remembraunce? As it was afore the tyme of that noble kynge Josias, and as it hath bene also amonge us unto youre graces tyme: by whose most ryghteous admynistracyon (thorowe the mercyfull goodnes of God) it is now founde agayne, as it was in the dayes of that most vertuous kynge Josias. And praysed be the father, the sonne, and the holy goost worlde without ende, which so excellently hath endewed youre Pryncely hert with such feruentnes to his honoure, and to the welth of youre louying subjectes, that I maye ryghtuously (by iust occasyons in youre persone) copare youre hyghnes unto that noble and gracyous kynge, ye lanterne of lyghte amonge prynces, that feruent protectour and defender of the lawes of God: which comaunded straytly (as youre grace doth) that the lawe of God shulde be redde and taught unto all ye people: set the prestes to theyr office in the worde of god: destroyed Idolatry and false ydols: put downe all euell customes and abusyons: set up the true honoure of God: applyed all his studye and endeuoure to the ryghtuous admynistracyon of the most uncorrupte lawe of God, etc. O what

> felicite was amonge ye people of Jerusalem in his dayes? And what prosperous health both of soule & body foloweth the lyke mynistracion in youre hyghnes, we begynne now (praysed be God) to haue experience. for as false doctryne is the origenall cause of all euell plages and destruccyon, so is ye true executynge of the law of God ad the preachyng of the same, the mother of all godly prosperite. The onely worde of god (I saye) is the cause of all felicite, it bryngeth all goodnes with it, it bryngeth lernynge, it gendreth understondynge, it causeth good workes, itmaketh chyldren of obedience, breuely, it teacheth all estates theyr office and duety. Seynge then that the scripture of God teacheth us euery thynge sufficiently, both what we ought to do, and what we oughte to leaue undone: whome we are bounde to obey, and whome we shulde not obeye: therfore (I saye) it causeth all prosperite, and setteth euery thyng in frame: and where it is taught and knowen, it lygteneth all darkenesses, comyforteth all sory hertes, leaueth no poore man unhelped, suffreth nothynge amysse unamended, letteth no prynce be disobeyed, permytteth no heresie to be preached: but refourmeth all thinges, amendeth that is amysse, and setteth euery thynge in order. And why? because it is geuen by the inspiracyon of God, therfore is it euer bryngynge profyte and frute, by teachynge, by improuynge, by amendynge and refourmyng all them yt (who) wyl receaue it, to make them parfecte & mete unto all good workes.148

The list of New Testament books parallels that of Luther as imitated by Tyndale, with the exception that I and II Peter, and John's three letters are in the third part with Hebrews, James, Jude and Revelation. That would seem to suggest an integration of those four books into the New Testament list of twenty-seven. The Old Testament order requires a brief discussion of patterns available. Luther had a separate section of unusual order when he came to the Apocryphal works. The eleven excluded the Prayer of Manasseh and I-II Esdras (Wittenberg: Hans Luft, 1535). Coverdale grouped the books after Malachi for the most part, but put I-II Ezdras at the head of the list with the number III-IV. Baruch follows Lamentations. The Three Children are put after Daniel (3:23) and the Prayer of Manasseh is omitted. In 1539 he places all fourteen together after Malachi.[149]

Mozley has demonstrated that the "Douche and Latyn" refer to Tyndale, Luther, the Vulgate, Pagninus and the Zurich Bible of

1531. The Zurich version is his chief guide. Mozley gives the following examples:

1) Vulgate: Jeremiah (40:12). All the Jews (I say) returned. "I say" only in Vulgate.

2) Pagninus: Job (4:11) The great lion peresheth because he can get no prey. Only Luther has "lion." Others have "tiger."

3) Luther: Zechariah (4:7) So that men shall cry unto him: Good luck, good luck. Luther has gluck zu, gluck zu.

4) Zurich: II Corinthians (12:7). There is a warning given unto my flesh.150

Coverdale leans heavily on the German versions, less so on the Latin and freely chooses Tyndale to revise. The use of the German would have a stylistic impact as well in leading Coverdale away from Latinisms to an Anglo-Saxon idiom. Four Old Testament excerpts must suffice for the modern reader whom Professor Greenslade graciously invites to read on in this handsome volume.

a) Deuteronomy (32)

Vengeaunce is myne, and I wyll rewarde in due season. Their fote shall slyde, for the tyme of their destruccion is at honde, and the thinge that is to come upon them, maketh haiste. For the LORDE shall iudge his people, and shal haue compassion on his seruauntes. For he shal considre that their power is awaie, and that it is gone with them, which were shut up and remayned ouer. And he shal saye: Where are their goddes, their rocke wherin they trusted? Of whose sacrifices they ate ye fatt, and dranke the wyne of their drynk offeringes? Let them ryse up and helpe you, and be youre proteccion. Se now that I I am, and that there is none other God but I. I can kyll and make alyue: what I haue smytten, that can I heale: and there is noman able to delyuer out of my hande. For I wil lifte up my hande to heauen, I wyl saye: I lyue euer. Yf I whet ye edge of my swerde, and my hande take holde of iudgment, then wyll I auenge me on myne enemies, and rewarde them that hate me. I wil make myne arowes dronken with bloude, and my swerde shal eate flesh ouer ye bloude of the slayne, and ouer the captyuite, and in that the enemies heade shall be discouered.

b) Proverbs (9)

Reproue not a scorner, lest he owe the euell wil: but rebuke a wyse man, and he wil loue the. Geue a discrete man but an occasion, & he wilbe the wyser: teach a rightuous man, and he wil increase. The feare of the LORDE is the begynnynge of wysdome, & the knowlege of holy thinges is understondinge. For thorow me ye dayes shalbe prolonged, and the yeares of thy life shal be many. If thou be wyse, ytwysdome shal do ye selfe good: but yf thou thynkest scorne therof, it shalbe thine owne harme. A foolish restlesse woman, full of wordes, and soch one as hath no knowlege, sytteth in the dores of hir house upo a stole aboue in the cite, to call soch as go by and walke straight in their wayes. Who so is ignoraunt (sayeth She) let him come hither, and to the unwyse She sayeth: stollen waters are swete, & the bred that is preuely eaten, hath a good taist. But they cosider not that death is there, and that hir gestes go downe to hell.

c) Isaiah (40)

The same voyce spake: Now crie. And I sayde: what shal I crie? Then spake it: that, all flesh is grasse, and that all the bewtie therof, is as the floure of the felde. When the grasse is wytthered, the floure falleth awaye. Euen so is the people as grasse, when the breath of the LORD bloweth upon them. Neuerthelesse whether the grasse wyther, or the floure fade awaye: Yet the worde of oure God endureth for euer. Morouer the voyce cried thus: Go up unto the hill (o Sion) thou that bringest good tidinges, lift up thy voyce with power, o thou preacher Jerusalem. Lift it up without feare, and say unto the cities of Juda: Beholde, youre God:.... hast thou not herde, that the euerlastinge God, the LORDE which made all the corners of the earth, is nether weery nor faynt, and that his wisdome can not be comprehended: but that he geueth strength unto the weery, and power unto the faynte? Children are weery and faynt, and the strongest men fall: Bvut unto them that haue the LORDE before their eyes, shal strength be encreased, Aegles wynges shal growe upon them: When they runne, they shal not fall: and when they go, they shal not be weery.

d) Job (39)

Hast thou geuen the horse strength, or lerned him to bowe downe his neck with feare: that he letteth him self be dryuen forth like a greshopper, where as the stoute neyenge that he maketh, is fearfull? he breaketh ye grounde with the hoffes of his fete chearfully in his strength, and runneth to mete the harnest men. He layeth asyde all feare, his stomack is not abated, nether starteth he a back for eny swerde. Though the quyuers rattle upon him, though the speare and shilde glistre: yet russheth he in fearfly, and beateth upon the

> grounde. He feareth not the noyse of the trompettes, but as soone as he heareth the shawmes blowe, tush (sayeth he) for he smelleth the batell afarre of, ye noyse, the captaynes and the shoutinge.
>
> Commeth it thorow thy wysdome, that the goshauke flyeth towarde the south. Doth the Aegle mounte up & make his nest on hye at thy commaundement? He abydeth in the stony rockes, and upon the hye toppes of harde mountaynes, where no man can come. From thence maye he beholde his praye, and loke farre aboute with his eyes. His yonge ones are fed with bloude, and where eny deed body lyeth, there is he immediately.

3. Matthew's Bible (1537)

Among the reprints of Coverdale's bible one finds both a quarto edition and a folio printed by Nycholson in 1537. These are the first such Bibles printed in England. The folio is a close reprint of the 1535 Bible. There are two forms of the prayer to be said before and after reading holy scripture. In the Psalter the first line of Latin is given at the head of each Psalm. "Quene Jane" replaces "Quene Anne" in the Dedication. It is important to note that this Bible is printed in six parts, i.e., 1) Genesis - Ruth, 2) I Samuel - Esther, 3) Job - Salomons Ballettes, 4) Isaiah - Malachi, 5) Apocrypha (includes Baruch), 6) New Testament.[151] The quarto has a special feature, for on the title page are the words, "Set forth with the Kynges moost gracious licence."[152]

William Fulke tells the story that King Henry VIII called his bishops to decide the merits of Coverdale's translation. When they carped at several flaws in the translated text the King asked the crucial question, "but are there any heresies maintained thereby?" When the bishops could specify none, the king retorted: "If there be no heresies then in God's name let it go abroad among our people."[153] Mozley takes this to refer to Coverdale's 1535 Bible. In all of this one detects the influence of Thomas Cromwell, architect of the state instrument which translated a social/humanistic programme into parliamentary statutes. As early as 1532 Cromwell employed Richard Taverner to translate Continental literature useful to the Tudor state.[154]

From 1535 Taverner was the special agent to disseminate Protestant humanism.[155]

Professor Elton has recently challenged the older, political and cynical view that Cromwell "had not heart and no conscience and no religious faith; no man was more completedly blighted by the sixteenth century's worship of the state."[156] The state which Pollard thought Cromwell seemed to worship was "a commonwealth reformed in body and soul... a state devoted to true religion as well as to secular renewal...."[157] Cromwell sought secular safeguards for spiritual reasons, proof of which was to pursue those policies to the point of giving his life on the block. His support of Taverner will demonstrate that spiritual core of service to the Tudor cause.

Richard Taverner (1505-1575) translated Erasmus, Melanchthon, Capito and others. He had joined the Cambridge White Horse group in the 1520s, and was drafted from Cambridge for the foundation of Cardinal's College, Oxford in 1527 as one of Cardinal Wolsey's seventeen young scholars. He was accused in 1528 of spreading Lutheranism there. Around 1532 after completing an Oxford A.B. and a Cambridge M.A., Taverner wrote to Cromwell from the Continent sending along his translation of Erasmus's Encomium Matromonii. The preface states his public debt to Cromwell. Taverner translated the Augsburg Confession and Melanchthon's Apology in 1536 as well as Sarcerius, Common Places (1538).

Cromwell appointed Taverner as Clerk of the Privy Seal in 1536. In the last two years of Cromwell's era before his downfall in June of 1540, Taverner controlled the small press of Richard Bankes which issued edition after edition of official translations. Yost points to the last major project which was The Epistles and Gospelles with a brief Postyl upon the same. Taverner wrote some of these sermons and drew others from Continental sources. Coverdale wrote to Cromwell in 1539 that Henry VIII had read this and Nycholson should receive Cromwell's aid for the royal privilege to print this work.[158] This translation went through five editions in 1540 as well as reprints in 1542 and 1545. The preface to Taverner's Bible of 1539 put the entire context in perspective when it stated Henry's support of vernacular scripture for the English people.

> your highnes never did thing more acceptable unto God, more profitable to the avancement of true christianitie, more displeasant to the enemies of the same, & also to your graces enemies then when your majestie lycenced and wylled the most sacred Byble conteynyng the unspotted and lyvely worde of God to be in the English tong set forth to your hyghnes subjectes.[159]

Matthew's Bible (1537) was printed for Robert Grafton and Edward Whitchurch perhaps at Antwerp. The text of the Pentateuch follows Tyndale while the New Testament follows the G.H. version (1535). The section from Ezra to the end of the Apocrypha, which includes Jonah, is essentially Coverdale. The text from Joshua to Chronicles is a very different matter, which Mozley demonstrates to be Tyndale's manuscript translation now first printed. Based on vocabulary study Mozley finds the same firm hand, direct style, rhythm and dignity as in the Pentateuch. Colorful phrases are 'troounced' (Judges 4:15), 'starched her eyes' (II Kings 9:30), 'a fool's paradise' (II Kings 4:28) and 'stripped' (II Samuel 6:20).[160]

Thomas Matthew is now viewed as a pseudonym for John Rogers (1500?-1555), close friend of Tyndale and first Protestant martyr under Mary Tudor.[161] The Dictionary of National Biography summarises what is known about Rogers. During 1536 he prepared the English version, using Tyndale in the Old Testament completed by Coverdale minus that portion from Joshua to Chronicles which Rogers supplied from Tyndale's manuscript with the exception of Jonah. Rogers contributed the Prayer of Manasses drawn from Pierre de Vingle's Neuchatel French Bible of 1535. This was the first English version of this Prayer.[162]

This second complete printed version in English is important for two additional reasons than those just mentioned. First of all, Rogers by providing notes for use with this version, contributed to its selection as the basis of the future revisions via the Great Bible of 1539. Secondly, it became the vehicle for preserving Tyndale's prose in that literary tradition of the English Bible.

The first letter of 4 August 1537 will be reproduced in its entirety. The fifth is a clear example of a printer concerned about his competition which at the time was James Nycholson.

Cranmer to Cromwell
4 August (1537)

My especial good Lorde after moost hartie commendacions unto your Lordeship. Theis shalbe to signifie vnto the same, that you shall receyure by the bringer herof, a Bible in Englishe, both of a new translacion and of a new prynte, dedicated vnto the Kinges Majestie, as farther apperith by a pistle vnto his grace in the begynnyng of the boke, which, in myn opinion is very well done, and therefore I pray your Lordeship to rede the same. And as for the translacion, so farre as I haue redde therof I like it better than any other translacion hertofore made; yet not doubting but that ther may, and wilbe founde some fawtes therin, as you know no man euer did or can do so well, but it may be from tyme to tyme amendid. And forasmoche as the boke is dedicated vnto the kinges grace, and also great paynes and labour taken in setting forth the same, I pray you my Lorde, that you woll exhibite the boke unto the kinges highnes; and to obteign of his Grace, if you can, a license that the same may be sold and redde of euery person, withoute danger of an acte, proclamacion, or ordinaunce hertofore graunted to the contrary, vntill such tyme that we, the Bishops shall set forth a better translacion, which I thinke will not be till a day after domesday. And if you contynew to take such paynes for the setting forth of goddes wourde, as you do, although in the meane season you suffre some snubbes, many sclandres, lyes, and reproches for the same, yet one day he will requite altogether; and the same wourde (as Saincte John saieth) Whiche shall judge every man at the last daye must nedes shewe favour to theym, that now do favour it. Thus my Lorde, right hartely faire you well.

At Forde the 4th of August,

Your assured ever,

T. Cantuarien To the Right Honourable and my especiall good Lorde my Lorde Pryvye Seale.163

The fifth letter printed by Pollard introduces the reader to Richard Grafton.

Richard Grafton to Cromwell
after 28 August 1537

> Moost humbly besechynge your lordshippe to vnderstand that accordynge as your comyssyon was by my servaunt to sende you certen bybles, so have I now done, desyrynge your lordship to accept them as though they were well done.
>
> And where as I wryt vnto your lordship for a preuye seale to be a defence vnto the enemyes of this byble I vnderstonde that your lordshipes mynde is that I shall not nede it. But now moost gracyous lorde, for as moche as this worke hath bene brought forthe to our moost great and costly laboures and charges, which charges amount aboue the same of v c li., and I have caused of these same to be prynted to the same of xv c bookes complete. Which now by reason that of many this worke is commended, there are that will and dothe go aboute the pryntynge of thesame worke againe in a lesser letter, to the entent that they maye sell their lytle bookes better chepe then I can sell these gret, and so to make that I shall sell none at all, or elles verye fewe, to the vtter vndoynge of me your orator and of all those my credytors that hath bene my comforters and helpers therin... Therfore by your moost godly fauor if I maye obtayne the kynges moost gracyous priuiledge that noen shall prynt them tyll these be solde, which at the least shall not be this iij yere, your lordship shall not fynde me vnthankfull, but that to the vtter most of my power I wyll consyder yet, and I dare sye that so will my lorde of Cantorbury with other my moost speciall frendes. And at the least, god will loke vpon your mercifull heart that consydereth the vndoynge of a pore yonge man. For truly my whole lyuynge lyeth hervpon, which if I maye have sale of them, not beynge hyndered by any other man, yt shalbe my mkyng and welthe, and the contrary is my vndoynge. Therfore most humbly I beseche your lordship to be my helper herin that I maye obtayne this my request.164

The 1500 copies were soon insufficient to meet the demand.

4. Taverner's Bible (1539)

Taverner revised Matthew's Bible which John Byddell printed for Thomas Berthelet in 1539. Tyndale's prologue to Romans is omitted as well as many of the notes of Matthew's Bible. The Old Testament changes are dictated by the Vulgate with some attention to Pagninus. Mozley finds that Taverner used Coverdale in the New

Testament alterations but on occasion did strike a fine phrase as in "express image" at Hebrews (1:3).[165]

Hutson and Willoughby dispute the general opinion created by the Great Bible that Matthew's text rather than Taverner contributes directly to the Authorized Version of 1611. So they observe that Pollard has no Taverner documents in his valuable Records nor did the English Hexapla include it with Wyclif, Tyndale, Cranmer, Geneva, Rheims and King James.[166]

Signature K is missing between Acts and Romans in all Taverner first editions. This perhaps was meant to contain Tyndale's prologue at Romans.[167] At I John (5:7-8) the doubtful clauses about the three heavenly witnesses are set off in parentheses and smaller type. The order of New Testament books is Luther/Tyndale/Coverdale and Rogers.[168] The Moulton collation of fourteen chapters in the Gospel of Matthew shows about one hundred separate readings when Taverner is compared to Tyndale (G.H. 1534). Ninety-five percent of these were also in the Matthew Bible.

An example of separate readings in Taverner's version would be the use of 'parables' for 'similituds' at Matthew (13:35) and 'prophecye' for 'tell' at Matthew (26:68).[169] One extended example is given below from I John (4):

> God is loue/and he that dwelleth in loue, dwelleth in God, and God in hym. Herein is the loue perfecte in us, that we should haue trust in the daye of iudgement: for as he is, euen so are we in this worlde. There is no feare in loue, but perfecte loue casteth oute all feare, for feare hathe vexacion. He that feareth, is not perfecte in loue. We loue hym, for he loued us fyrste. Yf a man saye, I loue God, and yet hate his brother, he is a lyar. for howe can he that loueth not his brother, whome he hath sene, loue God whome he hath not sene? And this commaundemente haue we of hym: that he whyche loueth God woulde loue his brother also.[170]

One additional reading which the 1611 Version retained is Matthew (16:24): "If any man will come after me, let him denie himselfe, and take up his crosse, and follow me."![171]

The Taverner Bible was printed in folio (1539) and the New Testament in quarto and octavo (1539) by Petyt for Berthelet. Taverner's dedication is given below.

TO THE MOST NOBLE, MOST MYGHTYE, AND MOST redoubted prysnte kynge HENRY the VIII. kinge of Englande and of Fraunce,defendour of the fayth, Lorde of Ireland, and in erth supreme heed immediatly under Chryst of the churche of England, his humble Seruaunt RYCHARDTAVERNER desireth all Joye, felycite, and longe lyfe.

How hyghly all England is bounde to your incomparable majestie for the infinite and manifolde benefites receyued at your most gracious handes from tyme to time without ceasing, euem from the begynning of your most noble raigne: truly no mortal tonge is hable with wordes sufficiently to expresse, or with secret thoughtes of hert worthely to contriue: Certes, it far passeth bothe the sklender capacitie of my wyt and also ye rude infancy of my tong to do either thone or thother: yea an other Cicero & Demosthenes wer not ynough here unto. Wherfore omittinge or rather leauinge to some other the iust Encomye and commendation of your graces most ample dedes, worthy of eternall memorie, yet this one thing I dare full well affirme, that amonge us all your maiesties deseruinges upon the christen religion (then which surely nothing can be greater) your highnes neuer did thing more acceptable unto god, more profitable to ye auauncement of true christianitie, more displeasaunt to the enemies of the same, & also to your graces enemies then whern your maiestuie lycenced and wylled the moost sacred Byble conteynyng the unspotted and lyuely worde of God to be in the Englysh tong le forth to your hyghnes subiectes.

To the setting forth wherof (most gracious & moost redoubted soueraigne lorde) lyke as certeyn men haue neither undiltgently nor yet unlernedly tmueied: So agayn it cannot be denied, but yt some faultes haue escaped their hades. Neither speke I this to depraue or maligne their industrie & paynes taken in this behalf: no rather I think them worthy of no litle praise & thankes for the same, considering what great utilitie & profit hath redounded to your graces hole realme by the publysshyng and setting forth therof, although it were not finisshed to the ful absolucion and perfection of the same. For assuredly it is a work of so great difficultie. I meane so absolutely to translate the hole bible that it be faultles, thhat I feare it can scarce be donne or one or two persons but rather requyreth bothe a deper confarrynge of many lerned wittes togyther, and also a iuster tyme and longer leysure.

Wherfore the premisies wel considered, for asmoch as ye printers herof were very desirous to haue this most sacred volume of the bible comforth as faultlesse & emendatly, as the shortnes of time for the recognising of yt same wold require, they desired me your most humble servant for default of a better lerned, diligently to ouerloke & peruse the hole copy: and in case I shold fynd any nowtable default yt neded correction, to amend the same, according to ye true replars Which thynge accordying to my talent I have gladly done.

These therfore my simple lucubrations & labours to who might I better dedicate them unto ywour moost excellent & noble maiestie, ye only anthour & grounde nexte God of this so hghe a benefite unto your graces people, I meane that the holy scripture is communicate unto the same.But now though many faultes prchance be yet left behind uncastigat, either for lacke of lerning sufficient to so great an enterprise, for default of leasure. I trust your maistie & all other yt shal rede the same wyll pardon me, consyderynge (as I haue already declared) how harde & difficult a thinge it is so to set forth this worke, as shal be in al pointes faultles & without reprehension. And thus I commit your most gracious & excellent maiestie to ye instrucion ye highest to who be al honour, glory & prayse, worlde without ende. amen

Chapter 5) The Politician, Primate and Printers

A. Thomas Cromwell

In November of 1538 a Royal injunction forbade printing or sale of English Bibles with notes or prologues apart from Royal approval.[172] Thomas Cromwell prepared another injunction to the clergy of September 1538, set forth by the authority of the King. The third and fourth injunctions read in part as follows:

> Item, that ye shall provyde on this side the feast of... next commyng, one boke of the whole Bible of the largest volume in Englyshe, and the same sett up in summe convenyent place within the said churche that ye have cure of, whereas your parishners may most commodiouslye resort to the same, and rede it... Item, that ye discorage no man pryuely or apertly from the readinge or hearing of the same Bible, but shall expresslye provoke, stere, and exhorte every parsone to rede the same, as that whyche ys the verye lively worde of God, that every christen man ys bownde to embrace, beleve, and followe, yf he loke to be saved...173

Thomas Cromwell was a man devoted to detail. He helped to guide Wolsey's project of founding colleges at Oxford and Ipswich which required the suppression of twenty-nine monasteries.[174] Cromwell survived Wolsey's demise to become a superb professional politican. He is thought to have drafted the Supplication of the Commons against the Ordinaries (1529?) on behalf of the House of Commons. As redrafted in 1532 it linked together the legislative action of the Church with the practices of the ecclesiastical courts. The King wanted to control the former while the laity with memories burned deeply into their consciousness by the Hunne case wished freedom from the latter. Discord and heresy are blamed on these activities by which ecclesiastical lawyers lay subtile traps for people unlucky enough to be accused of heresy.

The complicated challenge which the Supplication represented came as Thomas Audley presented it to the King on 18 March 1532. Crown policy can only be understood if one views Thomas Cromwell as more than a smart lawyer who solved the King's matrimonial problem.[175] As Professor Elton concludes in 1977, "Perhaps those who condemn him for his uses of power because they think him irreligious and cynical will be willing to overlook those same deeds once they are persuaded that Cromwell committed them in the service of a spiritual cause."[176] Professor Slavin has joined the revisionist chorus in favour of Cromwell's Christian humanism. In the preface to his 1969 edition of Selected Letters, 1523-1540, Slavin assesses Foxe's account from the Acts and Monuments (1583), which is the bright end of the spectrum, with Merriman's Life and Letters of Thomas Cromwell (1902), which is the dark end.[177] Foxe's "valiant soldier and captain of Christ" has been inserted into the central argument of A.G. Dicken's The English Reformation (1964).[178] Among Cromwell's concerns was the promotion of order as in Thomas Starkey's Dialogue Between Master Lupset and Cardinal Pole, which Cromwell urged Starkey to write. William Marshall redirected poor relief between 1531 and 1536 while Richard Morison actually submitted reform programs to Henry VIII in 1535.[179] Educational reform was also promoted under Cromwell's aegis during the decade of the 1530s.[180] Central to this was the translation of Erasmus which Cromwell promoted through the support of Taverner and the publisher John Bydell.[181]

As early as 1527 Coverdale wrote to Cromwell mentioning their godly communication at the home of Sir Thomas More. Coverdale hints about the lack of necessary books to study the scriptures.[182] From this mention of preparatory study to some correspondance of 1531 is a fascinating journey, for Henry VIII after 1528 considered employing William Tyndale. Cromwell wrote Stephen Vaughn to find Tyndale and encourage him to return to England. The Practice of Prelates (1530) with its seditious opinions put aside that prospect.[183] A letter of June 1538 to an unknown bishop returns to Cromwell's concern for circulation of an English Bible.

> for as much as it is come to his grace's knowledge that his said ordinances, commandments and injunctions have been very remissly hitherto observed, kept and obeyed within your diocese, and his highness' people there for want of the sincere and true teaching of the Word of God suffered to live and dwell continually in their old ignorance and blindness, his grace's pleasure and express commandment is that you, having a more vigilant eye and better respect to his highness' said commandments and ordinances, cause the same and every of them to be duly published and observed... And further, his grace's pleasure and high commandment is that you with no less circumspection and diligence cause the Bible in English to be laid forth openly in your own houses and that the same be in like manner openly laid forth in every parish church, at the charge and costs of the parsons and vicars; that every man having free access to it, by reading of the same may both be the more apt to understand the declaration of it at the preacher's mouth and also the more able to teach and instruct his wife, children and family at home; commanding nevertheless all curates and other preachers within that your diocese that they at all times, and specially now at the beginning, exhort and require the people to use and read the Bible so left amongst them according to the tenor of my instructions, which you shall receive herein enclosed, to be sent to every curate within a certain day by you to be appointed, within the which the Bible in English be as aforesaid laid forth in every church. Draft, William Petre's hand; corrected by T. Cromwell.184

What was the labour involved in reprinting sufficient copies of the "largest volume in Englyshe" for every parish to possess a whole Bible? To print 8500 copies was a mammoth enterprise which could only be done in Paris. Some bishops like Saxton of Salisbury had already ordered beneficed priests to have at least a Latin-English New Testament and read a chapter in it every day. Archbishops Lee of York and Cranmer of Canterbury made similar orders. When Cromwell received a copy of Matthew's Bible from Grafton, he immediately showed it to the king who granted a license for distribution. In spite of the notes which met conservative resistance, Cromwell encouraged wide distribution. Early in 1538 he required the Justices of the Peace to supervise parish priests to make certain that the people had an English Bible.[185] The copies were in such demand that Nycholson ran off his 1537 reprints as well as the 1538 Latin English New Testament in collaboration with Coverdale. Regnault in Paris printed an improved diglot. So steady was the demand that Nycholson reprinted this with the name of John Hollybush substituted for Coverdale.[186] The only printer with the resources to produce sufficient copies to meet Cromwell's injunctions was Francois Regnault in Paris.

Francois Regnault had been in London before 1500 to supervise the family's English enterprise. When the elder Francois died in 1518, Regnault produced many English service books between 1519 and 1535. Regnault even wrote to Cromwell when the 1534 acts forbade importation of religious books printed abroad unless they were licensed.[187] Among those profitable earlier works were the Liturgies of the Latin English rite. There are fifty-eight extant liturgical editions from Regnault's press, comprised of Breviaries (10), Graduals (1), Hours of the Blessed Virgin (15), Ortolus Animae (Garden of the soule or englishe primers) (18), Manuals (3), Missals (10) and Processionals (1) all printed between 1519 and 1538.[188] There were 25 editions between 1530 and 1534 printed by and for Regnault for use in England. Regnault seems to have slipped some editions into England after 1534, since S.T.C.2 records three printings in 1535, two in 1537 and five in 1538 of which four were English/ Latin diglots of the Ortolus Animae (Garden of the soule or englisshe primer).[189]

When John Day (1522-1584) obtained a monopoly to print the Psalms and the A.B.C. it was quite profitable. Oastler has estimated the costs involved in the fourth edition of John Foxe's Actes and Monuments. This cost Day seven shillings per ream of paper and each copy cost seven shillings. His press could handle one corrected sheet a day and two presses required a year to print a book of 2000 pages.[190] The labor to operate each press required two compositors, two pressmen, and an apprentice to run errands as well as a corrector. The compositors did well to set up two or three forms a day, depending on the difficulty of the text, beginning by candle-light at 5:00 A.M. and ending at 8:00 P.M. In the narrow Paris streets such lighting was needed even at mid-day.

The outlay to produce a book of 2000 pages in a year's time would require £500 in wages and £350 in paper. Often the printer would provide £250 of his own money and borrow £600. At 24 shillings per 1000 copies (1/2 penny per sheet retail) the profit would be as follows if the edition were sold out in two years:

1. Retail Sales: 1000 X 24s. = £2200
2. Printer's Costs: £500 (wages) + £350 (paper) = £850
3. Interest Charge: £600 @ 20% X 2 years = £240
4. Profit if 1000 copies sold in 2 years = £1100

The profit would be 50.45% on sales or 277.5% per annum after expenses on a capital outlay of £200. There were profits in printing, bibles included, as these figures for John Day suggest. The Plantin Press in Antwerp and Giolito at Venice each reached the 50% profit level.[191]

Richard Grafton feared piracy by his rivals. He pestered Cromwell to license the Matthew Bible under his privy seal, and to forbid any other reprint for three years. If that were not possible, would Cromwell please require every parish priest to buy a copy and every abbey six? Nycholson solicited Cromwell to sanction the Coverdale Bible which he twice reprinted in 1537. After licensing both versions in 1537, Cromwell turned to Coverdale as editor and Grafton with his partner Whitchurch as printers. Cromwell chose Paris as the site since "printing is finer there than elsewhere, and with the great number of printers and abundance of paper, books are dispatched sooner than in any other country."[192]

On June 23, 1538 Grafton and Whitchurch wrote from Paris to Cromwell that the work had begun as he could see from the first printed sheets. Henry VIII wrote to King Francis I who then licensed the English printers for Latin and English Bibles with any French printer, if it contained no "private or unlawful opinions." Two vellum copies survive, one at St. John's College, Cambridge, and another in the National Library of Wales.[193]

On December 17, 1538 Regnault was cited by Henry Garvais, Inquisitor general of all France, for "printing a bible in British in the vulgar tongue, by occasion of which scandals and errors might arise in the church...."[194] The French Ambassador in England reported on December 31 that Cromwell had invested 600 marks, intended to give away the copies and urged the French King to permit its printing in Paris. If not, would the King allow the sheets to be sent to London? The Imperial Ambassador in England summarizes the same conversation, giving the cost to Cromwell as 2000 crowns.[195]

The September 12 letter encouraged Cromwell to issue his clerical circular on display of the Great Bible. Now a complex series of events revolve around this printing project. Cromwell heard from Bishop Bonner that Francis would release the books. In the month after that letter of January 1, 1539, Montmorency, who was the Constable of France, railed against the version, though he apparently relented enough to rid France "of the type, printers and even the paper."[196]

Foxe records that when Grafton and Whitchurch went to Paris to search for the sheets, a French official had sold four vats full of unbound copies to a haberdasher who intended to wrap hats with the printed paper. Only a few copies were recovered, which by April were back in London with the craftsmen, type, paper stock and salvaged sheets.[197] Now Cromwell brought pressure to release the remaining sheets. One press run took place at Grafton's Grey Friars shop in April of 1539, another was in progress when the Royal injunction of December 14 appeared, but this printing would not be ready until April of 1540. These two runs of 3000 copies each, even with the mix of rescued Paris sheets, were 2500 copies short of Cromwell's goal that every English parish must provide a copy of "one boke of the whole Bible of the largest volume in Englyshe." Grafton's account of the Paris seizure mentions 2500 copies.[198]

The Rochepot Affair enters into this scene when on August 4 of 1537 three German merchantmen were raided by three French ships in the English Channel. The French sailed under letters issued to Rochepot, whose brother Montmorency was constable of France. After the French killed the most severely wounded Germans and set the German captain of the flagship adrift in the Channel in a small boat, they made for France with the prize. Two English ships out of Newcastle set upon the French prize ship which had been isolated by a storm. They escorted it back to Whitby on the East coast of England where a jurisdictional fight broke out as the English captain claimed his prize before the Duke of Norfolk.[199]

Cromwell hardened his attitude toward this Rochepot affair as soon as sale of the Great Bible began. On December 9, 1539 he informed Montmorency that the case could not be settled. Montmorency wanted the ship. Cromwell wanted his bibles. Francis had written directly to Henry VIII for the honour of France was at stake in this Rochepot affair. He also wrote to Cromwell.[200] A trade seemed in the works until on June 10, 1540 Cromwell was arrested on charges of heresy and treason. He was beheaded at the Tower of London on July 28. Neither the ship nor any of its cargo were released. The second printing with Cranmer's preface appeared in April. The five printings after Cromwell's fall suggest that the confiscated sheets remained in France.

The Byble in Englyshe... translated after the veryte of the Hebrue and Greke textes was a revision by Coverdale of Matthew's

Bible. Coverdale corrected that 1537 text by Sebastian Munster's Latin translation of the Hebrew Old Testament (1534/35), the Vulgate and Erasmus' Latin versions of the New Testament and the Complutensian Polyglot (c.1520). It was printed in five parts with part four using the title, The volume of the bokes called Hagiagrapha. The text was printed in bold black letter with 62 lines to a full double column on the page. Words not found in the original are printed in smaller type, while many signs for notes are inserted but the notes are absent.[201] The familiar title page represents Henry VIII, Cranmer and Cromwell distributing Bibles to the people, who are shouting "vivat Rex" and "God save the King." Cranmer and Cromwell have their coats of arms inscribed, though the second edition erases Cromwell's. A reprint of 1540 in smaller size inserts the admonition which Bishop Bonner issued when in May 1540 he set up six copies in St. Paul's Cathedral after the Royal Proclamation. It reads in part as follows:

> It shall therfore be very expedyent that whosoeuer repayreth hether to reade thys booke (or any soche lyke in any other place) he prepare hym selfe chefelye and principally wyth all deuocion, humilite and quyetnes, to be edefyed and made the better therby. Adioynynge thervnto his perfect and most bounden duetye of obedyence to the Kynges maiestye our moost gracious and drad soueraygne Lorde & supreme heade: especiallye in accomplysshynge hys graces moost honorable iniunctions and comaundementes geuen and made in that behalfe.
>
> And ryght expedient, yee, necessarye it shalbe also that leauynge behynde hym vayne glorye, hypocresie, and all other carnall and corrupt affeccyons: he brynge with hym discrecion, honest intent, charyte, reuerence & quyet behaueour: to and for the edifycacyon of hys awne soule, wythout the hineraunce, let, or disturbaunce of any other his christen brother. Euermore forseynge, that no nombre of people be specyallye congregate therfore, to make a multitude. And that no exposition be made thervpon, otherwyse then it is declared in ye boke it selfe. And that especiall regarde be had, that no readinge therof be vsed (alowde & wyth noyes) in the tyme of any deuyne seruice or sermonde; or that in the same there be vsed any disputacion, contencion, or any other mysdemeanour. Or finallye that any man iustlye maye reken him selfe to be offended therby, or take occasyon to grudge or maligne therat.
>
> God saue the Kynge[202]

B. Cranmer's Bible (1540)

The first edition of the Great Bible was finished in April of 1539. The second printing and the second edition both appeared in April of 1540. This has been called Cranmer's Bible from the preface which the Archbishop contributed to the Whytchurche edition (John Rylands Library, Manchester has Richard Grafton on the title page). Apart from Cranmer's preface, the text is similar to the 1539 edition in signatures, borders on the general and New Testament title pages and five parts in printing with separate foliation. A special feature is the large initial letter (86 x 87 mm) before Romans with the initials E.W. One block on the Apocrypha title-page represents a madman astride a hobbyhorse.[203] The title page was printed in alternating lines of red and black type with the final two lines reading:

> This is the Byble apoynted/
> to the use of the churches.

More significant than all of the above was the prologue made by the "Prymate of Englande, Thomas Archbiyshop of Canturbury." The opening paragraph affirms the ancient English custom to read the Scriptures in a common-speech translation. Cranmer quotes from John Chrysostom, the great preacher of Antioch and Constantinople, who urged his hearers to study the Bible between sermons. After references to English custom and Patristic precedent, the prologue concludes its first half with a sweeping lesson for several classes of society. The last half warns against misuse of Scripture by citing from Gregory of Nazianzus how not every man nor audience should address high questions of divinity. "Let us keep us in our boundes," wrote Cranmer, "and nether let us go farre on thone syde, lest we retorne into Egypte, ne-/ther to farre over ye other, leste we be caried awaye to Babylon."[204] What follows are selected portions of this prologue from a modernized version sufficient in length to convey the flavour of Cranmer's lively prose.[205]

> For two sundry sorts of people, it seemeth much necessary that something be said in the entry of this book by the way of a preface or prologue; whereby

hereafter it may be both the better accepted of them which hitherto could not well bear it, and also the better used of them which heretofore have misused it. For truly some there are that be too slow and need the spur, some other seem too quick and need more of the bridle; some lose their game by short shooting, some by over shooting; some walk too much on the left hand, some too much on the right. In the former sort be all they that refuse to read, or to hear read, the Scripture in their vulgar tongues; much worse, they that also let (hinder) or discourage the other from the reading or hearing thereof. In the latter sort be they which by their inordinate reading, indiscreet speaking, contentious disputing, or otherwise by their licentious living, slander and hinder the Word of God most of all other, whereof they would seem to be greatest furtherers. These two sorts, albeit they be most far unlike the one to the other, yet they both deserve in effect like reproach. Neither can I well tell whither (which) of them I may judge the more offender; him that doth obstinately refuse so godly and goodly knowledge, or him that so ungodly and so ungoodly doth abuse the same.

Thy wife provoketh thee to anger, thy child giveth thee occasion to take sorrow and pensiveness, thine enemies lieth in wait for thee, thy friend (as thou takest him) sometime envieth thee ... poverty is painful to thee, the loss of thy dear and well-beloved causeth thee to mourn; prosperity exalteth thee, adversity bringeth thee low:... Where canst thou have armour or fortress against thine assaults? Where canst thou have salve for thy sores, but of Holy Scripture?... Let us read and seek all the remedies that we can and all shall be little enough.

"How shall we then do, if we suffer and take daily wounds, and when we have done, will sit still and search for no medicines? Doest thou not mark and consider how much the smith, mason, or carpenter, or any other handy craftsman, what need so ever he be in, what other shift so ever he make, he will not sell or lay to pledge the tools of his occupation; for then how should he work his feat, or get his living thereby? Of like mind and affection ought we to be towards Holy Scripture; for as mallets, hammers, saws, chisels, axes, and hatchets be the tools of their occupation, so been the books of the prophets and apostles, and all holy writ inspired by the Holy Ghost, the instruments of our salvation. Wherefore, let us not stick to buy and provide us the Bible, that is to say, the books of Holy Scripture. And let us think that to be a better jewel in our house than either gold or silver...

> The reading of Scriptures is a great and strong bulwark or fortress against sin; the ignorance of the same is the greater ruin and destruction of them that will not know it.

Cranmer includes in his preface a summary statement about the benefits of a vernacular Scripture for those who neither ignore the Word of God nor bury it with misplaced speculations about its primary Author and Giver of Life.

> In the Scriptures be the fat pastures of the soul; therein is no venomous meat, no unwholesome thing; they be the very dainty and pure feeding. He that is ignorant shall find there what he should learn. He that is a perverse sinner shall there find his damnation to make him to tremble for fear. He that laboureth to serve God shall find there his glory and the promises of eternal life, exhorting him more diligently to labour. Herein may princes learn how to govern their subjects; subjects obedience, love, and dread to their princes: husbands how they should behave them unto their wives, how to educate their children and servants; and contrary, the wives, children, and servants may know their duty to their husbands, parents, and masters. Here may all manner of persons, men, women, young, old, learned, unlearned, rich, poor, priests, laymen, lords, ladies, officers, tenants, and mean men, virgins, wives, widows, lawyers, merchants, artificers, husbandmen, and all manner of persons, of what estate or condition soever they be, may in this book learn all things what they ought to believe, what they ought to do, and what they should not do, as well concerning Almighty God as also concerning themselves and all other(s). Briefly, to the reading of the Scripture none can be enemy, but that either be so sick that they love not to hear of any medicine, or else that be so ignorant that they know not Scripture to be the most healthful medicine.206

The third Great Bible appeared in July 1540 with Cranmer's Prologue. The fourth was printed in November 1540 though its publication was delayed until 1541. The title page says it is "oversene and perused" by Bishops Tunstall and Heath.[207] There is no sign of such revision. The title page shows Cromwell's arms chisled out of the woodcut. Again, it is not surprising to find some copies with Whitchurch on the title page instead of Grafton.

The fifth Great Bible comes from May 1541 with slight revisions of the text. That very month a royal proclamation provided stiff fiscal penalties for each parish which did not have a copy in its church by November of 1542. The sixth Great Bible is dated to November and the seventh to December of 1541.[208]

Coverdale's revisions have been the special concern of Mozley's study, who lists some textual varients as Francis Fry did the bibliographical varients.[209] The ecclesiastical words which Tyndale substituted for church, priest, charity and penance are retained by Coverdale. The Psalms passed into the Book of Common Prayer which meant that generations of English parishioners read Coverdale rather than any future revision of the Psalms.

The second edition has only one deliberate revision at Sirach 35:5. The third edition returns to the first at two places only, i.e., in Joshua 5:3 (in the top) and Song of Songs 4:16 ("my" garden). The solid emendations are four in number with the only New Testament change at Ephesians (5:16): "redeeming the time," where G.B. had "Avoiding occasion" and G.B. read "winning occasion".[210] The fourth edition was carelessly edited, whereas Mozley concludes that the sixth follows the fourth and the fifth and seventh depend upon the second or the third.[211]

Circulation of licensed and authorized versions of the English Bible did not guarantee their use in the English church after Cromwell's fall. Enemies were active, as can be seen at the third session of the convocation of Canterbury on Friday, February 3, 1542. When Archbishop Cranmer asked each prelate whether the English Bible could be retained "without scandal and error and open offense", the majority said it could not without corrections from the Vulgate. The New Testament was then divided into fifteen portions with each assigned to a bishop. The three 'protestant' bishops took Matthew (Cranmer), John (Goodrich of Ely) and four short Pauline letters (Barlow of St. Davids). Two committees then met to revise the noted errors. At the sixth session, Gardiner of Winchester read out a list of one hundred Latin words which he wished to retain or anglicize. Half of these, as Mozley notes, had been fully incorporated into the English language, words such as contritus, baptizare, martyr and hospitalitas.[212] Cranmer broke off the revision by reporting the king's will to the ninth session of March 10. Henry VIII wanted the universities to examine both Testaments. Nothing further seems to have been done with an official episcopal version.[213]

In April of 1543, with the Great Bible in check by Convocation, Parliament passed an Act for the Advancement of True Religion which forbade all books of the Old and New Testament "of the crafty, false and untrue translation of Tyndale."[214] After October 1, all annotations or preambles must be cut or blotted out of other bibles and New Testaments. No unlicensed person should after that date read or expound the English bible to others in any church or public assembly. On April 8, 1543 Grafton and Whitchurch were sent to prison for printing unlawful books contrary to the November 16, 1538 proclamation.[215] Though the royal order which set up bibles in every parish church was never rescinded, another proclamation of July 8, 1546 ordered that after August 31, 1546 no person should have "the text of the New Testament of Tyndale's or Coverdale's translation in English."[216] The Great Bible which incorporated their best work was - miracle of miracles - exempt from this royal decree. In spite of that prohibition, common folk desired access to the English text. A Gloucestershire shepherd wrote a note to that effect in a history book.

> "I bout thys boke when the Testament was offerogated [abrogated], that shepeherdys myght not red hit. I prey God amend that blyndnes. Wryt by Robert Wyllyams keppynge shepe uppon Synbury Hill, 1546."217

Two accounts dramatise the attempts to restrict circulation of the English bible. One is an Admonition by Bishop Bonner of London in 1542 which insisted that "no exposition be made thereuppon otherwise than is declared in the book itself" and that no reading aloud be permitted during any divine service or sermon.[218] The other account by William Malden describes a young man persecuted by his father for reading the scripture as was the habit of poor men of Chelmsford who read the bible in the parish church on Sundays.

William, whose father took him to Latin Matins to take his mind off the English text, determined to pool his money so that he and Thomas Jeffary, his Father's apprentice, could buy an English New Testament.

> drueres poore men in the towne of chelmysford in the county of Essyx where my father dwellyd & I borne & with hym brovght vp, the sayd poore men bought the newe testament of Jesus chryst & on svndayes dyd syt redyng in lower ende of chvrche, & manye wolde floke abovte them to here theyr redyng thenI cam amonge the sayd reders to here them, redyng of that glade & swete tydynges of the gospell, then my father seyng this that I lestened vnto them euery svndaye, then cam he & sovght me amonge them, & brovght me awaye from the heryng of them, and wold have me to saye the lattyn mattyns with hym, the which greued me very myche & thvs did fete me awaye dyueres tymes, then I see I covlde not be in reste, then thovghte I I will learne to read engelyshe, & then will I haue the newe testament & read ther on myselfe...
>
> I plyed my boke, then shortly after I wold begyn to speke of the schryptores,...
>
> Then I went to bede, &, then my father awakyd, & my mother, tovlde hym of our commvyncatyon, then came he vp in to our chamber with a greate roode,... then he toke me by the heare of my heade with bothe his handes & pvllyd me out of the bed behynd Thomas Jeffary bake he syttyng vp in his bedde, then he bestowed his rodd on my bodye... I reioysyd that I was betten for chrystes sake, & wepte not one tarre out of myne eyes & I thynke I felte not the strypes my reioysynge was mvche...

The father let his son sleep, but as time went by, his anger increased to the boiling point.

> then sayed my mother, thomas Jeffary aryse, & make the reddy for I cannot tell what he will doo in his anger, & he sat vp in his bed pvttyng on of his clothis & my father cometh vp with ye havlter & my mother intretyd hym to lette me alone but in no wise he wolde be intretyd but pvtte the havlter aboute my neke I lyinge in my bedde & pvlled me with the havlter behynde the sayd Thomas Jeffarsyes bake almoste clene ovt of my bede then my mother cryed out & pullyd hym by the arme awaye, & my brother rycherd cryed out that laye on the other

syde of me, & then my father let goo his hovlde & let me alone & wente to bede. I thynke vj. dayes after my necke greved me with the pvlling of the havlter.219

END NOTES to SECTION II

[1]A. G. Dickens, The English Reformation (New York: Schocken Books, 1964), pp.28-29.

[2]Ibid., p.30.

[3]Richard Wunderli, London Church Courts and Society on the Eve of the Reformation (Cambridge, Mass: Medieval Academy of America, 1981), p.126.

[4]Carl S. Meyer, "Henry VIII Burns Luther's Books," Journal of Ecclesiastical History IX (1958), p.173

[5]Falconer Madan, Day-book of J. Dorne, bookseller in Oxford, A.D. 1520 (Oxford: Oxford Historical Society Publications, 1885), nos. 1281, 1429 and 1569.

[6]The Sermon of John the bysshop of Rochester made agayn ye pnicious doctryn of Martin Luther (London: Wynkyn de Worde, 1521?), sig. Aii[v] Cited by Meyer, p.186.

[7]John Skelton Poems, edited by Robert S. Kinsman (Oxford: Clarendon Press, 1969), p.111.

[8]S.T.C.2 22600.5-22603b [1531?-1558?]

[9]Christopher Haigh, "Anticlericalism and the English Reformation," History 68 (1983), p.391. See A. G. Dicken's response in the forthcoming Essays for G. R. Elton.

[10]Ibid., p.394.

[11]John Skelton Poems, p.98.

[12]Cited in A.R. Heiserman, Skelton and Satire (Chicago: Univ. of Chicago Press, 1961): 225.

[13]Paul E. McLane, "Prince Lucifer and the Fitful 'Lanternes of Lyght': Wolsey and the Bishops in Skelton's Colyn Cloute," Huntington Library Quarterly 43 (1980): 168.

[14]Robert S. Kinsman, "The Voices of Dissonance: Pattern in Skelton's Colyn Cloute," Huntington Library Quarterly xxvi (1963): 297.

[15]Susan Brigden, "Youth and the English Reformation," Past and Present 95 (May 1982): 43, 45-46.

[16]D.M. Palliser, The Age of Elizabeth: England Under the Later Tudors 1547-1603 (London: Longman, 1983): 34-37. See also

chapter 6: "Inflation of Population and Prices" in Joyce Youings, Sixteenth-Century England (London: Penguin Books, 1984): 130-153.

[17]Brigden, op.cit., p.59 and n.133.

[18]Mercers' Company, Acts of Court, fo. ccxxiiii, cited in D. Hoak, The King's Council in the Reign of Edward VI (Cambridge: Cambridge Univ. Press, 1976): 215.

[19]Philip Henderson, editor, The Complete Poems of John Skelton Laureate (London/Toronto: J.M. Dent and Sons Ltd., 1948): 420.

[20]Ibid., p.422.

[21]On the celebrated case of Richard Hunne who was murdered in 1514, see Richard Wunderli, "Pre-Reformation London Summoners and the Murder of Richard Hunne," Journal of Ecclesiastical History 33 (1982): 209-24. See also J. Fines, "The Post-mortem condemnation for heresy of Richard Hunne," English Historical Review LXXVIII (1963): 528-31, and S.C.F. Milsom, "Richard Hunne's 'Praemunire'," English Historical Review LXXVI (1961): 81-82. According to the documents printed in Fines, Hunne had a Wyclif Bible and defended both its translation and Wyclif's works. See also Stefan J. Smart, "John Foxe and The Story of Richard Hun, Martyr," Journal of Ecclesiastical History 37 (1986): 1-14.

[22]Cited in Susan Brigden, "Religion and Social Obligation in Early Sixteenth Century London," Past and Present 103 (May 1984), p.76.

[23]John F. Davis, "The Trials of Thomas Bilney and the English Reformation," Historical Journal 24 (1981), p.789.

[24]Margaret Bowker, The Henrician Reformation the Diocese of Lincoln under John Longland, 1521-1547 (Cambridge: Cambridge Univ. Press, 1981), p.4.

[25]Ibid., p. 58

[26]Ibid., pp.58-59.

[27]Ibid., p.61.

[28]Ibid., pp.61-62.

[29]William A. Clebsch, "The Earliest Translations of Luther into English," Harvard Theological Review LVI (1963), p.77.

[30]Ibid., p.76.

[31]S.T.C. 24454-24461.

[32]On Frith see William A. Clebsch, England's Earliest Protestants (New Haven: Yale Univ. Press, 1964): 78-136.

[33]J.B. Trapp and Hubertus Schulte Herbruggen, 'The King's Good Servant' Sir Thomas More 1477/9-1535 (London: National Portrait Gallery, 1977), p.79.

[34]Iohan Harryson [John Bale], Yet a course at the Romyshe fox/A DYSCLOSYNGE/or openynge of the Manne of synne, Co-/tayned in the late Declaration of the Po/pes olde faythe made by Edmonde Bo-/ner bysshopp of London/ (18 lines)/ (Zurich: Oliver Jacobson, 1543), sig. Fvii^{r}

[35]Ibid., sig. Hiiij^{v} See S.T.C.2 11381, 11387, 11386, 11390, 11385 and 24436.

[36]loc.cit. See Leslie P. Fairfield, John Bale Mythmaker for the English Reformation (West Lafayette: Purdue Univ. Press, 1976). Neither Clebsch nor Fairfield refer to this defence of Frith.

[37]John K. Yost, "German Protestant Humanism and the Early English Reformation: Richard Taverner and Official Translation," Bibliotheque d' Humanisme et Renaissance XXXII (1970), p.615. See James H. Pragman, "The Augsburg Confession in the English Reformation: Richard Taverner's Contribution," Sixteenth Century Journal XI (1980), pp.75-85.

[38]Cissie Rafferty Bonini, "Lutheran Influences in the Early English Reformation: Richard Morison Re-examined," Archiv für Reformationsgeschichte 64 (1973), p.223.

[39]Reset of text observed in comparing Pembroke College Cambridge copy (1538) and Emmanuel College Cambridge copy (1603).

[40]S.L. Greenslade, The Work of William Tindale (London/ Glascow: Blackie & Son Limited, 1938), p.9: "If this quarto edition, with its prologue and glosses, was completed at Worms, all copies have perished."

[41]Alfred W. Pollard, Records of the English Bible (Folkestone: Wm. Dawson & Sons Ltd., 1974), p.122.

[42]A.G. Dickens, op.cit., p.34. John Strype, Ecclesiastical Memorials (London: Samuel Bagster, 1816), V: 369.

[43]Greenslade, op.cit., p.78.

[44]Edited by R. Mercer Wilson (London: R.T.S.-Lutherworth Press, 1939), pp.224-25.

[45]J.F. Mozley, William Tyndale (London: Society For Promoting Christian Knowledge, 1937), pp.12-13.

[46]Ibid., pp.19 and 23.

[47]Ibid., pp.26-27.

[48]Ibid., p.28.

[49]John Archer Gee, "Tindale and the 1533 English Enchiridion of Erasmus, "Modern Language Association of America Publications 49 (1934), p.461

[50]Ibid., p.9. See also J.F. Mozley, "The English Enchiridion of Erasmus, 1533," Review of English Studies 20 (1944), pp.97-107.

[51]Mozley, op.cit., pp.33-34.

[52]William Tyndale's Five Books of Moses called The Pentateuch (Carbondale: Southern Illinois Univ. Press, 1967), p.3.

[53]S.T.C. 24438. Worms: P. Schoeffer, 1526.

[54]L.J. Trinterud, "A Reappraisal of William Tyndale's Debt to Martin Luther," Church History XXXI (1962), pp.28-31.

[55]Ibid., pp.31-33.

[56]The parable of the wycked mammon (Antwerp: J. Hoochstraten, 1528), fols. 6-7. Cited in Paul Alan Laughlin, "The Brightness Of Moses Face: Law And Gospel, Covenant and Hermeneutics in the Theology of William Tyndale," Emery Univ. Ph.D. thesis, 1975, p.166.

[57]Pentateuch, op.cit., pp.12-13.

[58]J.G. Møller, "The beginnings of Puritan covenant theology," Journal of Ecclesiastical History XIV (1963), pp.51-52.

[59]Cited in Michael McGiffert, "William Tyndale's Conception of Covenant," Journal of Ecclesiastical History XXXII (1981), p.170. See N.H. Wallis, The New Testament Translated by William Tyndale 1534 (Cambridge: At the Univ. Press, 1938), p.4.

[60]Trinterud, op.cit., p.33 and 39.

[61]Møller, *op.cit.*, p.51.

[62]Robert Williams, "Patterns of Reformation in the Theology of William Tyndale," *Christian Spirituality Essays In Honour of Gordon Rupp*, edited by Peter Brooks (London: SCM Press Ltd., 1975), p.133.

[63]*Ibid.*, p.138. Wallis edition (1938), pp.9-10.

[64]McGiffert, *op.cit.*, p.171.

[65]*loc.cit.* William A. Clebsch, *England's Earliest Protestants, 1520-1535* (New Haven: Yale Univ. Press, 1964), pp.191, 138, 146, 154.

[66]*Ibid.*, p.172.

[67]*Ibid.*, p.175. See note 36 where McGiffert faults Clebsch on two counts, i.e., 1) *The Mammon* (1528) which Clebsch finds occupied with faith actually focuses on works pace Tyndale's own summary of its contents in *Obedience of a Christian Man* (1528), and 2) Covenant teaching comes from Tyndale's preference for the New Testament Beatitudes rather than a discovery of the law in the *Pentateuch* (1530).

[68]A Compendious introduccion... vn to the pistle off Paul to the Ro=mayns (1526), fascimile reprint of unique Bodleian Library, Oxford copy (*S.T.C.* 24438) (New York: Walter J. Johnson Inc., 1975) sig. Cii^{r}.

[69]*loc.cit.* Reprinted in 1535 (*S.T.C.* 16818) and 1536 (*S.T.C.* 21789.5)

[70]*Ibid.*, sig. Cii^{v}

[71]The Workes of Sir Thomas More Knyght, sometyme Lord Chauncellour of England, wrytten by him in the Englysh tonge (London: J. Cawood, J. Waly, A. R. Tottell 1557), p.1037.

[72]Note by Gervase Duffield, editor, *The Work of William Tyndale* (Philadelphia: Fortress Press, 1965), p.368.

[73]P.S. Allen, *Opus Epistolarum Des. Erasmi* (Oxford: Oxford Univ. Press, 1913), III, p.239.

[74]John M. Headley "Thomas More and Luther's Revolt," *Archiv für Reformationsgeschichte* 60 (1969), p.146.

[75]*Ibid.*, p.148.

[76]*Ibid.*, pp.149-150.

[77]Ibid., p.151. See E.F. Rogers, "Sir Thomas More's Letter to Bugenhagen," The Modern Churchman 35 (1946), pp.350-60.

[78]Louis A Schuster, "Thomas More's Polemical Career, 1523-1533," The Confutation of Tyndales Answer, The Complete Works of St. Thomas More (New Haven: Yale Univ. Press, 1973), Volume 8, Part III, pp.1153-1154.

[79]E.F. Rogers, "Letter to Bugenhagen," p.452 from Richard S. Sylvester and Germain Marc hadour, Essential Articles for the Study of Thomas More (Handon: Archon Books, 1977).

[80]Scholar Press facsimile 1970 of Emmanuel College, Cambridge copy, sig. Cv^r.

[81]Ibid., sig. Rv^r.

[82]Ibid., fol. Cxl^v.

[83]Cited in Schuster, op.cit., p.1185 from sig. S^v.

[84]William Tyndale, An Answer to Sir Thomas More's Dialogue, edited by Henry Walter (Cambridge: The Univ. Press, MDCCCL), p.14.

[85]Ibid., p.11.

[86]loc.cit.

[87]Ibid., p.88.

[88]St. Thomas More: Selected Letters, edited by Elizabeth Frances Rogers (New Haven and London: Yale Univ. Press, 1961), p.176. More also responded to Robert Barnes, John Frith, George Joye, Simon Fish and Christopher St. German. The Letter against Frith is dated December 7, 1532 while the Apology against St. German appeared in Easter of 1533. See on Fish, The Supplication of Souls, edited by Sister Mary Thecla (Westminster, 1950) and Frederick le Van Baumer, "Christopher St. Germain: the political Philosophy of a Tudor Lawyer," American Historical Review XLII (1940), pp.631-51. More answered Barnes's Supplication (1531) in Book VIII of his Confutation of Tyndale.

[89]Ibid., p.177.

[90]E.F. Rogers, op.cit., p.454: Roper, Life of More, edited by Hitchcock, pp.34-35.

[91]Gordon Rupp, Thomas More The King's Good Servant (London: Collins, 1978), p.43.

[92]J. Payne Collier, editor, Illustrations of Old English Literature (New York: Benjamin Blom, 1966 reprint), Vol. I: 14.

[93]Ibid., p.23.

[94]Ibid., p.26.

[95]J.E. Devereaux, "John Rastell's Press in the English Reformation," Moreana XIII (1976), No. 49, p.39. See R.J. Roberts, "John Rastell's Inventory of 1538," The Library, Sixth Series (1979), p.41 which shows ten copies of Miles Coverdale's Ghostly Psalms!

[96]A Treatise concer-/nynge the diuisi-/on betwene/the spi=/ritu=/alitie and tem-/poralitie./ (device) [London: Thomas Berthelect, 1530 (?)], sig. A2^{v}.

[97]Ibid., sig. A3^{r}.

[98]Ibid., sig. A6^{r}.

[99]Ibid., sig. C1^{v}.

[100]A Dialogue Concerning Heresies, edited Thomas Lawler, German Marc'hadour and Richard Marius, The Collected Works of Thomas More Volume VI (New Haven: Yale Univ. Press, 1981), pp.314-15 and 409.

[101]S.L. Greenslade, "The Morean Renaissance," Journal of Ecclesiastical History XXIV (1973), p.398.

[102]Dialogue Concerning Heresies, pp.105-106. This point developed by Alistair Fox, Thomas More History and Providence (New Haven/London: Yale Univ. Press, 1982), p.155.

[103]Ibid., p.166.

[104]Dialogue, edited W.E. Campbell (London: 1927) cited in Brian Gogan, The Common Corps of Christendom. (Leiden: E.J. Brill, 1982), pp.141-142. Campbell is a facsimile edition of The Workes of Sir Thomas More Knyght (London: J. Cawood, J. Waly, and R. Tottell), pp.103-288 which is itself a reprint of W. Rastell's 1530 edition. The 1981 Yale edition was not available to Gogan.

[105]Complete Works 8.I., p.146.

[106]Ibid., p.149.

[107]Ibid., p.150.

[108]Ibid., p.158.

[109]Ibid., p.157.

[110]Ibid., pp.363-364.

[111]Louis L. Martz, "More as Author: The Virtues of Digression," Moreana XVI No. 62 (1979), p.107. See Norman Davis, William Tyndale's English of Controversy (London: 1971).

[112]Ibid., p.110.

[113]loc.cit. (Yale Edition: 48)

[114]E.G. Rupp, Studies In The Making Of The English Protestant Tradition (Cambridge: At the Univ. Press, 1947), p.48.

[115]Judith H. Anderson, "3. Roper: Deliberated Design and Designer," p.46 in Biographical Truth The Representation of Historical Persons in Tudor-Stuart Writing (New Haven: Yale Univ. Press, 1984).

[116]W.T. Vnto The Reader, The New Testament (1534) edited by N.H. Wallis, p.3.

[117]G.R. Elton, "The Real Thomas More?" Reformation Practice and Principle, edited by Peter Newman Brooks (London: Scholar Press, 1980), p.23.

[118]Ibid., p.27.

[119]Ibid., p.31.

[120]Luther's Works: 22-23. See "More, Politics and Heresy" in J.A. Guy, The Public Career of Sir Thomas More (New Haven: Yale Univ. Press, 1980), pp.141-174.

[121]Tyndale, New Testament (1534), edited by Wallis p.515.

[122]R. Mercer Wilson, editor, Tyndale Commemoration Volume (London: R.T.S.-Lutherworth Press, 1939), pp.143-144. Obedience (1970 fascimile), sig. Qv^{r}-^{v} Lines 7 and 10 above should read "mine," line 15 should read "doist to me" and line 16 should read "thine".

[123]John Strype, Ecclesiastical Memorials V: 364 and 366 (London: Samuel Bagster, MDCCCXVI).

[124]Ibid., p.369.

[125]loc.cit.

[126]The Acts and Monuments of John Foxe, edited by George Townsend and Stephen Cattley (London: R.B. Seeley and W. Burnside, MDCCCXXXIII) V: 40.

[127] Letters and Papers, Foreign and Domestic of the Reign of Henry VIII, edited by J.S.Crewer, J. Gardiner and R.H. Brodie (London: His Majesty's Stationary Office, 1862-1908), IV/I 884-886, no. 1962. Cf. M.E. Kronenberg, "A Printed Letter of the London House Merchants (2 March 1526)," Oxford Bibliographical Society Publications, n.s.l (1948), pp.25-32.

[128] Acts and Monuments V: 120.

[129] Ibid., p.415.

[130] See Appendix B in C. Carlyle Haaland, "A Chapter In International Protestantism: Miles Coverdale, Henrician Migrant" (Unpublished Yale Univ. Ph.D. thesis, 1967), pp.249-267.

[131] Celia Hughes, "Coverdale's Alter Ego," Bulletin of the John Rylands Library, Mancester 65 (1982), p.106.

[132] Remains of Myles Coverdale, Bishop of Exeter, edited by George Pearson for The Parker Society (Cambridge: At the Univ. Press, MDCCCXLVI), p.550. See Luther's Works (Philadelphia: Fortress Press, 1965), 53: 217-220 which prints a slightly revised translation by McDonald.

[133] English Historical Documents 1485-1558, edited by C.H. Williams (New York: Oxford Univ. Press, 1967), p.829.

[134] Ibid., p.830.

[135] Ibid., p.831.

[136] J.A. Guy, The Public Career of Sir Thomas More (New Haven: Yale Univ. Press, 1980), p.151. Public Record Office, State Papers, Henry VIII, Theological Tracts, 6/7, art. 14.

[137] Ibid., p.152.

[138] Frederick le Van Baumer, "Christopher St. German: the political Philosophy of a Tudor Lawyer," American Historical Review XLII (1940): 631-51. Doctor and Student edited by T.F.T. Plucknett and J.L. Barton, Selden Society XCI (1974).

[139] S.T.C. 21586, 21587, 2158.3, 21587.5, 21587.7.

[140] Guy, op.cit., p.156. On Cromwell see G.R. Elton, "Thomas Cromwell Redivivus," Archiv für Reformationsgeschichte 68 (1977), pp.192-208.

[141] The Coverdale Bible 1535, Holkham copy British Library Facsimile Edition (Folkestone: Wm. Dawson & Sons Ltd., 1974), colophon.

[142]Guppy, *op.cit.*, illustration 16.

[143]*Ibid.*, illustration 15.

[144]S.L. Greenslade, Introduction to 1974 Facsimile, p.11.

[145]*Ibid.*, p.11.

[146]Herbert, *op.cit.*, p.10. For letter to Cromwell see Mozley, *Coverdale and His Bibles*, p.111.

[147]Facsimile 1974, p.33.

[148]*Ibid.*, p.36.

[149]Herbert, *op.cit.*, p.25.

[150]Mozley, *Coverdale*, pp.79-80, 327.

[151]Herbert, *Historical Catalogue* (1968), p.17.

[152]*Ibid.*, p.17. The description comes from Herbert.

[153]William Fulke, *Defence of the Translations of the holy scriptures into the English tongue* (1583), cited in Mozley, *op.cit.*, p.113.

[154]James K. McConica, *English Humanists and Reformation Politics under Henry VIII and Edward VI* (Oxford: 1965), pp.117-18.

[155]John K. Yost, "German Protestant Humanism and the Early English Reformation: Richard Taverner and official translation," *Bibliotheque d'humanisme et Renaissance* XXXII (1970), pp.613-25.

[156]A.F. Pollard, "Thomas Cromwell," *Encyclopaedia Britannica*, 11th edition, cited by G.R. Elton, "Thomas Cromwell Redivivus," *Archiv für Reformationsgeschichte* 68 (1977), p.207.

[157]*loc.cit.*

[158]Yost, *op.cit.*, p.622.

[159]*Ibid.*, p.634.

[160]Mozley, *William Tyndale*, pp.184-85.

[161]*Ibid.*, p.355 where Mozley cites from Bale (1548), Foxe (1559) and three Marian documents of 1553/1555.

[162]*D.N.B.*, "Rogers, John (1500?-1555)," p.126.

[163]A.W.Pollard, *Records of the English Bible*, pp.214-215.

[164]*Ibid.*, pp.219-221.

[165]Mozley, *op.cit.*, pp.347-348.

[166]Harold H. Hutson and Harold R. Willoughby, "The Ignored Taverner Bible of 1539," *Crozer Quarterly* XVI (1939), p.164.

[167] *Ibid.*, p.169.

[168] *Ibid.*, pp.169-170.

[169] *Ibid.*, p.171.

[170] Cambridge Univ. Library copy.

[171] Noted by Hutson & Willoughby, *op.cit.*, p.174.

[172] A.W. Pollard, *Records*: 240-242.

[173] *Ibid.*, p.261, note 1. From Wilkins, *Concilia* III: 815.

[174] A.G. Dickens, *The English Reformation* (New York: Schocken Books, 1964), p.111. Now see A.J.Slavin, *The Precarious Balance: English Government and Society, 1450-1640* (New York: Knopf, 1973).

[175] *Ibid.*, pp.112-115.

[176] Elton, *op.cit.*, p.208.

[177] Arthur J. Slavin, *Thomas Cromwell On Church and Commonwealth Selected Letters, 1523-1540* (New York: Harper & Row Publishers, 1969), p.xvii.

[178] See Dickens, *op.cit.*, pp.109-113, 129-132 and 167-182.

[179] W. Gordon Zeeveld, "Thomas Starkey and the Cromwellian Polity," *Journal of Modern History* XV (1943), 177-191 and Cissie Rafferty Bonini, "Lutheran Influences in the Early English Reformation: Richard Morison Reexamined," *Archiv für Reformationsgeschichte* 64 (1973), pp.206-224.

[180] R.M. Fisher, "Thomas Cromwell, Humanism and Educational Reform, 1530-40," *Bulletin of the Institute of Historical Research* L (1977), pp.151-163.

[181] See J.E. Devereaux, "English Translators of Erasmus, 1522-1557" in Richard J. Schoeck, *Editing Sixteenth Century Texts* (Toronto: Univ. of Toronto Press, 1966), pp.42-58.

[182] A.G. Dickens, *op.cit.*, p.129.

[183] A.J. Slavin, *op.cit.*, pp.150-153.

[184] *Ibid.*, pp.168-169.

[185] A.G. Dickens, *Thomas Cromwell and the English Reformation* (London: Hutchinson, 1959), p.115.

[186] A.J. Slavin, "The Rochepot Affair," *Sixteenth Century Journal* X (1979), p.8 notes 24 and 25.

[187] Letters and Papers of Henry VIII XI, no. 1488. Coverdale and Grafton also wrote on his behalf to Cromwell. See L.P.XIII, part ii, no. 336.

[188] S.T.C. Between nos. 15820 and 16239.

[189] S.T.C. 16003, 16004, 16008.3 and 16008.5.

[190] C.L. Oastler, John Day, The Elizabethan Printer (Oxford: Oxford Bibliographical Society/Bodleian Library, 1975), p.28.

[191] See further Robert Kingdon, "The business activities of printers Henri and Francois Estienne," Aspects de la propagande religieuse (Geneve: Librairie E. Droz, 1957), pp.258-275.

[192] A.G. Dickens, Thomas Cromwell, pp.116-117.

[193] Ibid., p.117. For letters see Pollard, Records of the English Bible, pp.232-236.

[194] Pollard, op.cit., p.248.

[195] Ibid., pp.249-253.

[196] A.J.Slavin, "The Rochepot Affair," p.13.

[197] Foxe, Actes and Monuments V: 411.

[198] Slavin, op.cit., p.16.

[199] Ibid., pp.5-6.

[200] Ibid., p.14.

[201] Herbert, Historical Catalogue, p.25.

[202] Ibid., p.29.

[203] Ibid., p.30.

[204] "A prologue or preface" (1540), The Byble in/Englyshe (MDXL) Univ. Library Cambridge, fol. 10.

[205] Herdon Wagers' edition in Harold R. Willoughby, The First Authorized English Bible and the Cranmer Preface (Chicago: Univ. of Chicago Press, 1942), pp.38-49.

[206] Ibid., p.44.

[207] Herbert, op.cit., p.32.

[208] Ibid., pp.33-35.

[209] Francis Fry, A Description of the Great Bible, 1539 and the six editions of Cranmer's Bible, 1540 and 1541 (London. 1865).

[210] Mozley, Coverdale and His Bibles, pp.250-251.

[211] Ibid., p.252.

[212] *Ibid.*, p.274.

[213] *Ibid.*, pp.272-276. Wilkins, *Concilia* III: 860, Fuller III: 196, Parker, *De antiquitate* (1572), p.396, Pollard, *op.cit.*, pp.272-5.

[214] Cited in Mozley, p.283.

[215] Pollard, *op.cit.*, p.230 from Foxe's 1583 edition. Mozley, *op.cit.*, p.285 prints 1570 account based by Fox on the Acts of the Privy Council.

[216] Foxe V: 565.

[217] Dickens, *The English Reformation*, p.191.

[218] Pollard, *op.cit.*, pp.267-268.

[219] *Ibid.*, pp.270-71.

SECTION III. EXEGESIS IN EXILE

When Henry VIII authorised an English Primer on May 6, 1545, he set up the use of English on a par with Latin, "aswell of the eldre people, as also of the youth, for their common and ordinarye praiers, willyng commaundyng, and streightly chargyng, that for the better bringyng up of youth in the knowledge of their dutye towardes God, their prince, & all other in their degre, ..."[1] Grafton published this Primer on May 29, 1545.

During 1545/46 ten English, two English/Latin and one Latin editions appeared in print. The thirty-six Psalms compared to the fifty-eight in the Sarum Primers are drawn from the Rouen version as set forth in the Primer of 1536 and emended in the Redman Primer of 1537.[2] One Primer of 1529 had on its title-page a quaint prayer which was added to the 1536 Tyndale New Testament [Herbert #19].

God be in my hede
And in myn understandynge.
God be in myn eyen
And in my lokynge.
God be in my mouth
And in my spekynge.
God be in my herte
And in my thynkynge.
God be at myn ende
And at my departynge.[3]

The Rouen Primer (1536) shows extensive revision from Redman (1535) as well as dependance on George Joye's Psalter (1534) and the Marshall Goodly Primer (1535). Redman announced that his version of the Psalms were Englished according to the version of Felinus.[4] The point is that these primers were different translations than the existing English bible versions of Tyndale/Coverdale/Matthew/Taverner/Great Bible. This was also true in the primers of 1537 with epistles and gospels.[5] There is, as Butterworth remarks, a certain fresh quality about the Byddell Primer of May 1536/October 1537. The following section here and in the Redman Primer is based on Tyndale (1534):

> My brethren, be stronge in the lorde/... yt ye may stand stedfast against ye crafty awayte layinges of the deuyl/ for we wrastle not agaynste flessh & blode, but agaynst rulers/ against power/ & agaynst ye worldly lordes & rulers of the darknes of this worlde/ euen agaynst the spiritual craftynes aboue ye erth. For this cause take vnto you ye complete armure of god/ yt ye may resist in ye troublous tyme, & to stande vp after all the batayle be done.6

When Henry VIII died on January 28, 1547, his minor son Edward VI succeeded to the throne of England. Edward Seymour, Duke of Somerset, was protector and after his execution, the Duke of Northumberland replaced him as the power behind the crown. During the six years of Edward's Protestant sympathies, several editions of the English Bible effectively cancelled the Henrician prohibitions against use of Tyndale or Coverdale's Version.

In May of 1547 the Church of England proclaimed a General Visitation. The Royal Visitors' published their _Injunctions_ on July 31, a date which coincided with the first _Book of Homilies_ and the official translation of Erasmus' _Paraphrases of the Gospels_. The _Injunctions_ required each parish church to provide "one whole book of the Bible of the largest volume" in English and within a year a copy of the _Paraphrases_. The clergy were to have a copy of the New Testament in English as well.

A glance at Herbert's _Historical Catalogue_ shows several bible editions printed during Edward's reign. Five separate editions of the New Testament were printed in 1548, seven in 1549, five in 1550, three in 1551, and four in 1552 for a total of twenty-four. Fifteen complete Bibles were also printed according to Herbert's list, seven of which were Matthew's Bible, five the Great Bible, two of Coverdale and one mixed version of Taverner/Tyndale. In addition to these thirty-nine printings, four separate parts of Taverner's Old Testament add up to forty-three printings in whole or in part of the English bible during Edward's short reign.[7]

All of this printing of the English bible in turn collapsed with the early death of Edward, the accession of Mary Tudor to the English crown, the flight of Protestants known thereafter as the Marian Exiles and the execution of Bishops Latimer, Ridley and Archbishop Cranmer at Oxford in 1555/56. An English bible had been licensed for only a decade when its free circulation encountered severe opposition.

John Standish listed more than thirty proofs why the bible should not be available in the vernacular. His 1554 Discourse wherein it is debated whether it be expedient that the Scripture should be in English for all men to read that will, went into a second edition in 1555. John Strype summarised it in his Ecclesiastical Memorials.

> And some of his proofs were such as these: "That the reading of the scripture in English tended to the people's spiritual destruction. That by this damnable liberty (as he styled it) all holy mysteries had been despised, and the people had utterly condemned every thing that was not expressed in the letter of their English Bibles. That it was the occasion of many heresies; and that it ministered occasion to the common sort to fall into error, since the rude ignorant sort were ever prone perversly to wrest the scripture. That the universal church of Christ did never allow nor approve the scripture to be in the vulgar language, weighing the manifold inconveniencies that issued thereof; but ever, from time to time, among other errors, did tread that down, and suppress it. That like as God appointed the old law to be written in stone, tables, or books, so did he appoint (as Jeremie witnessed) the new to be written only in the heart of man. Why should the writing in books then be so highly regarded?8

Standish then added an anti-Semitic twist to his argument, which preferred the authority of the church to scripture written either in books or on the walls of churches.[9]

> Here also we read, "That as the people had the scripture in their own handlings these dozen years past, so it was to their utter spiritual destruction." He produced also that of our Saviour, "That which ye have heard in secret places, shall be preached on the tops of the houses." Which he made this use of: "He said not, it shall be written in your churches (as it was Jewishly used of late here in England) nor written in Bibles, to be read of every one in his mother tongue, and set up for that purpose in every church. He could not but mervail, that men, to their own confusion, were so desirous to have the scripture in their mother tongue. Therefore, away,

> said he, with the English damnable translation, and let them learn the mysteries of God reverently by heart, and learn to give as much credit to that which is not expressed in scripture; knowing, that in three points the authority of the church is above the authority of the scripture: one is, in fortyfing verities, not written, to be necessary to salvation, & c. And finally, as he concluded, seeing that by no means, so soon as by the scriptures in English, heresies did both spring daily, and were also maintained, wherein should good men be more diligent than in the extirpation thereof?"[10]

Chapter 6) John Knox: Pastor to the English

These events which would end the circulation of the vernacular scriptures led the English exile congregation in Geneva under John Knox to produce a fresh translation of the Old and New Testaments into the Anglo-Saxon accents of their homeland. Though they lived in Geneva and longed for London, God had prepared for them another city. This heavenly residence they described in their translation of 1560: "All these dyed in faith... and confessed that they were strangers and pilgremes on the earth... God... hathe prepared for them a citie."[11] English Catholics in turn were exiled under Elizabeth. Dr. William Allen, who was their leader, founded a seminary, proposed a Catholic edition of the English bible and incorporated these into a program of political resistance to Tudor Protestantism. Two communities in exile on the continent each then produced an English bible which sparked controversy. In the center of this ideological maelstrom stood John Knox of Scotland, who was pastor of the Genevan exiles, and Theodore Beza whose biblical scholarship became the focus of controversy from 1575.

The middle Rhine lands held several havens for Protestant refugees, protected by the Palatinate to the south and Hesse to the north. In the middle was the ancient free city of Frankfurt on the Main. Here Valerand Poullain, pastor of the French refugee church in Glastonbury, arrived from England with twenty-four families. They waited at Köln while Poullain negotiated for refuge with the city government. This was granted and the first worship service was held on April 19, 1554 at the Church of the White Ladies.[12]

The English soon arrived in Frankfurt, worshipping as early as July in the Weissfrauenkirche. As others arrived, so many services needed to be held that the church was busy on Sundays from six in the morning to eight at night. The English were unhappy with Poullain's order of worship, which did not permit the congregational responses of the English Prayer Book (1552).

The Frankfurt church now sought for two ministers to fill the pastoral office. They wrote to Haddon in Strasbourg, Lever in Zurich and Knox in Geneva to encourage them to consider the post. Meantime, William Whittingham and his colleagues urged their fellow English refugees to migrate to Frankfurt. Several at Emden accepted the invitation; Strasbourg offered Ponet, Bale or Cox; and Grindal actually invited Scory at Emden to go to Frankfort. Ponet, Bale and Scory were all bishops in England under Edward VI while Grindal would become both a bishop and an Archbishop under Elizabeth. Calvin urged Knox to accept the invitation to Frankfurt which he did. Since only Knox gave a favorable reply to the pastoral invitation, Whittingham and his colleagues invited Knox to be their pastor at Frankfurt.[13]

A. English Jeremiah

During the winter of 1550-51 all the St. Andrews prisoners in the French galleys were set free. Knox was released earlier than the others in February 1549 and came to England in April. The privy council gave him five pounds and sent him to preach at Berwick. After two years of preaching to a large congregation of illegal Scottish immigrants at Berwick, Knox spent a further three years in England, making a stay of five years in all south of Hadrian's Wall. By the summer of 1551 Knox preached regularly in Newcastle, devising his own order of worship which permitted the Berwick congregation to sit while receiving communion.[14]

Knox preached before Northumberland at Newcastle in June 1552, describing the punishment which would fall on England if her rulers continued their sin, vice and misconduct. Northumberland invited Knox to preach at court in a move which may be interpreted as a check of Archbishop Cranmer. Whatever the motive, Knox upset the careful timing behind Cranmer's second Prayer Book of 1552. Knox lashed out at its rubric which required the communicants to receive communion on their knees, holding that such an act implied adoration of the bread. This was sheer idolatry! Cranmer wrote to the Council on October 7 that neither Ridley nor Peter Martyr agreed with Knox. As late as October 27 the Council decided to retain the requirement for kneeling and to insert an additional passage that such was neither adoration of the elements in communion nor was Christ really present. The black rubric, as it was called, gave the printers real problems as well as the book binders. Three copies in the British Library each have the addition pasted in different places, one in the front of the Prayer Book, another in the end of the service and a third where it belonged.[15] Knox then instructed his congregation at Berwick to kneel at communion.[16]

Knox refused Northumberland's offer of October 28 made to William Cecil that Knox become bishop of Rochester. In February of 1553 the Privy Council ordered Cranmer to appoint Knox as vicar of All Hallows Church in Bread Street, London. Knox again refused. When Edward VI died on July 6, 1553, Knox was in Buckinghamshire. A week later he preached before a large congregation at Amersham, calling the Emperor Charles V no less an enemy of Christ than was Nero. This would haunt Knox two years later at Frankfurt. The sermon made an explicit reference to Jeremiah (42-44).[17]

Knox left England secretly and arrived in France in February 1554. In Dieppe he completed his _Exposition on the Sixth Psalm_ and went on to finish _A Godly Letter of Warning_ which again drew parallels between England and the Judea of Jeremiah. Knox indicates that he used Calvin's commentary to prepare this epistle.[18]

Knox arrived in Geneva in March of 1554, traveling to Zurich to enquire of Bullinger whether any of four special conditions permitted political resistance.[19] Bullinger was cautious in his reply.[20] In July of 1554 Knox promoted political resistance.

In July 1554, Knox published A Faithful Admonition to the Professors of God's Truth in England, which was the longest tract Knox thus far had written.[21] This tract indicates that the six weeks which intervened between his Comfortable Epistle and A Faithful Admonition brought a radical change in Knox's thinking about political resistance. Stanford Reid even suggests that the publication of A Faithful Admonition represented a turning point in his religio-political view.[22] Knox first denounced the Protestant nobles for their covetousness and insincerity during Edward's reign, and for now submitting to idolatry, but blamed himself for not having denounced Northumberland and the rest more vigorously.[23]

Knox then tried to rouse the sentiment of English nationalism.

> And who ever could have beleved that gloriouse Gardener, and trecherouse Tunstal (whome al Papistes praysed for the love they bare to theyr countrey), could have become so manifest traytoures, that not only agaynst theyr solemne othes, that they sould never consent nor agre unto, that a foren straunger shuld raygne over England, but also that they wold adjudge the Imperial Croune of the same to appertayn to a Spaniarde by inheritaunce and lyneal dissent? O traytours, traytours, how can yow for very shame shewe youre faces?[24]

In this tract, Knox also attacked Mary Tudor and shocked many of his Protestant colleagues as deeply as the Catholics. Knox hesitated to say directly that Mary should have been executed in the reign of Edward VI, but his reference to the posibility of her execution was sufficient for the Catholics and many Protestants to accuse him of treason.[25]

> And of Lady Marye, who hath not herde, that she was sober, mercyful, and one that loved the common wealthe of Englande? Had she, I saye, and suche as now be of her pestilent counsel, bene sent to hell before these dayes, then should not ther iniquitie and crueltie so manifestlye have appeared to the worlde. For who coulde

> have thought that suche crueltie coud have entered into the hert of a woman, and into the hert of her that is called a virgine, that she would thirst the bloud of innocentes, and of suche as by juste lawes and faythful wytnesses, can never be proved to have offended by them selves?26

As the result of Knox's indirect reference to Mary's execution, the stage was set for the development of his active resistance theory as well as his antagonism against woman rulers. In this sense, A Faithful Admonition constituted a stepping stone for his later arguments, especially in the Appellation and The First Blast Against the Monstrous Regiment of Women.

But soon after July 1554, Knox left Dieppe to return to Geneva for the study of Greek and Hebrew, which helped his deeper understanding of the Scripture. Then within a few weeks of his arrival at Geneva, Knox received an invitation from the English Protestants at Frankfurt asking him to be their minister. There Knox was deeply involved in the controversy over the style of worship. It was a dispute over the use of the second Book of Common Prayer. Knox's frontal attack upon the Book of Common Prayer represents a breach between Knox himself and the English Church.[27] It marks a proto-Puritan protest against popish dregs in the English Book of Common Prayer.

The First Blast of the Trumpet Against the Monstrous Regiment of Women was written as an attack on Queen Mary of England. This work gained for Knox a reputation as a revolutionary among his contemporaries. The First Blast argues that it is wrong for women to rule in the state, or even for a woman ruler to turn over the power of government to her husband, espcially if he is a foreign monarch. Knox insists:

> That it is a thing most repugnant to nature, to Goddes will and apointed ordinance,... that a Woman shuld be promoted to dominion or empire, to reigne over man, be it in the realme, nation, province, or citie.28

Criticism of Knox's view came from every quarter. Knox knew that Calvin would not approve, for Calvin believed that as government by women was a deviation from the original and proper order of nature, it must have been imposed as a punishment for the fall of man. In some countries women were entitled to succeed to the throne.[29] Even Francis Hotman expressed his opposition in 1559 to Knox's point of view.

However, the most significant point of the First Blast is not Knox's criterion that the ruler must be a man who has the fear of God before his eyes. One should instead note the fact that Knox had now openly repudiated the doctrine of Christian obedience and called on the nobility to revolt against the Sovereign.

> The same is the dutie of the Nobilitie and Estates, by whose blindnes a Woman is promoted... and, being admonished of their error and damnable fact, in signe and token of true repentance, with common consent, they oght to retreate that which unadvisedlie and by ignorance they have pronounced; and oght, without further delay, to remove from authority all such persones as by usurpation, violence, or tyrnannie, do possesse the same.30

B. From Reformer to Revolutionary

Knox began his presentation of the case for active resistance by assuring the Scots' nobility that they were powers ordained by God for the protection and defense of the people against the rage of tyrants.[31] Appealing directly to the nobles and the Scottish Parliament, Knox claims:

> God hath appointed you princes in that people, and, by reason therof, requireth of your handes the defence of innocentes troubled in your dominion, in the meane tyme, and till the controversies that this day be in Religion be laufully decided, ye receave me, and suche others as most unjustlie by those cruell beastes are persecuted, in your defence and protection.32

Both governing assumptions of the constitutional theory are already implicit in this. One is that the nobility no less than the monarch must be regarded as powers ordained of God.

> And the same, I say, is the duetie of every man in his vocation, but chefely of the Nobilitie, which is joyned with theyr Kinges, to bridel and represse theyr folie and blind rage.33

Knox's use of the constitutional argument does not seem to have been used by him until his writing of the Appellation. There was one more source upon which Knox seems to have based his active resistance theory, i.e., the concept of covenant. This concept appears in most clear-cut form in A Letter Addressed to the Commonalty of Scotland. The constitutional argument crystallized in the theory of inferior magistrates was by comparison a less radical form of the active resistance theory than that espoused by the English writer John Ponet. On the other hand, the argument from the concept of covenant was likely to support the popular revolution. In fact, this argument was made already at the end of his Appellation to the nobility, and was repeated in his Letter Addressed to the Commonalty of Scotland. As well, the concept of covenant provided the implicit foundation of the latter.[34]

For example, in the Appellation, Knox referred to the covenant that God made with Asa:

> And this is the fyrst, which I would your Honours should note, of the former wordes, to witt, That no person is exempted from punishment, if he can be manifestly convicted to have provoked or led the people to idolatrie. And this is most evidently declared in that solemned othe and covenante, which Asa made with the people to serve God,...35

Knox developed the concept of covenant and said:

> To this same law, I say, and covenante are the Gentiles no lesse bounde, then somtyme were the Jewes, whensoever God doth illuminate the eyes of anie multitude, province, people, or citie, and putteth the sworde in their own hand to remove such enormities from amongest them, as before God they know to be abominable... And moreover, I say, if any go about to erect and set up idolatrie, or to teach defection from God, after that the veritie hath bene receaved and approved, that then, not only the Magistrates, to whom the sword is committed, but also the People, are bound, by the othe which they have made to God, to revenge to the uttermost of their power the injurie done against his Majestie.36

Thus Knox maintained that the punishment of idolatry and tyranny is committed not only to the hands of the magistrates but also to the people.

Richard Greaves argued in 1973 that the sources of this covenant theory came alternately from Tyndale, Hooper or Calvin. Greaves prefers Tyndale's An Exposition uppon the V. VI. VII. Chapters of Matthew as the most likely direct source for Knox on the covenant. S.T.C.2 lists editions of 1533(?), 1536(?), 1537(?), 1548, and 1549. Finality in identifying these sources "can never be attained."[37] There is no direct citation of Tyndale's Exposition by Knox, Calvin's Sermons of 1549 on Jeremiah 42-44 have not survived, and contact with Hooper in England did not lead to any immediate use of the covenant as Hooper understood Bullinger.

More recently Greaves has argued that Deuteronomy 13 provided the Biblical sanction for Knox's call to revolution. Knox's extension of the principle of active disobedience to the people occured because of covenant responsibilities.[38] In this sense, Knox was a leading Deuteronomic dissenter. Knox probably received the concept of covenant from Anthony Gilby who was his colleague during the Frankfurt dispute, and then developed it to its extremity, while Gilby failed to push it to its natural conclusion. In spite of this difference, the fact that Gilby's Admonition to England and Scotland formed a portion of the volume containing Knox's Appellation will be one indication of Gilby's influence.[39]

In the Appellation Knox appealed to the nobility and the estates, which was composed of the three estates including the commonalty. But, according to Ridley, the commonalty was represented only by delegates from the burgh councils and the lairds were not represented in Parliament. If this is the case, Knox could have directed his Letter Addressed to the Commonalty of Scotland to the Protestant lairds who were the active force in the Scottish Reformation. Whoever was included by the term "Commonalty," Knox was not content to leave such matters in the hands of the nobles, whom Knox felt had once before let him down. Knox then proceeded to pen an exhortation to the commonalty of Scotland. The Appellation which was printed in Geneva in 1558 has a final leaf which the printer filled up with William Kethe's metrical version of Psalm (94):

O Lorde sith vengeance doth to thee,
And to none els belonge:
Now showe thy self (O Lord oure God)
With spede reuenge oure wronge.40

Knox maintained a similar view in his summary of the proposed Second Blast of the Trumpet. In this work, Knox set down four propositions:

1. It is not birth onely, nor propinquitie of blood, that maketh a Kinge lawfully to reign above a people professing Christe Jesus and his eternall veritie; but in his election must the ordenance, which God hath established in the election of inferiour judges, be observed.

2. No manifest idolater, nor notoriouse transgressor of God's holie preceptes, oght to be promoted to any publike regiment, honour, or dignitie, in any realme, province, or citie, that hath subjected the self to Christe Jesus and to his blessed Evangil.

3. Neither can othe nor promesse bynd any such people to obey and maintein Tyrantes against God and against his trueth knowen.

4. But if either rashely they have promoted any manifest wicked personne, or yet ignorantly have chosen such a one, as after declareth himself unworthie of regiment above the people of God (and suche be all idolaters and cruel persecuters), moste justely may the same men depose and punishe him, that unadvysedly before they did nominate, appoint, and electe.

In these propositions, Knox's fundamental format was again present. In the first proposition, Knox referred to the idea of inferior magistrates. He declared that the nobles had a right to remove a recalcitrant monarch. But in his third and fourth propositions, Knox stated that the people were not bound by any oath or promise to obey tyrants but might justly depose them. What had been proclaimed in the Appellation and the Letter Addressed to the Commonalty of Scotland was now outlined in this proposed Second Blast. The fourth proposition clearly suggested the concept of covenant, which was now applied to the relationship between the people and their rulers.[41]

Inferior magisterial and covenantal concepts of resistance thus form the background of the Appellation and Letter Addressed to the Commonalty of Scotland, which in their limited definition of commonalty completed the breakaway from Calvin's own doctrine of non-resistance. Two more sources of this resistance theory should be mentioned. Knox noted a passage from Sleidan in his An Answer to a Great Number of Blasphemous Cavillations written by an Anabaptist and Adversary of God's Eternal Predestination. This was written during 1558 and published in Geneva in 1560. In the same year the Geneva Bible appeared with its explicit notes on regicide attached to several Old Testament passages. Dan Danner suggests that Gilby wrote these notes.[42] Professor Owen Chadwick has noted the passage from Sleidan's 1558 Commentary on the State of Religion and the Republic of the Emperor Charles V. After a long extract on the Peasants War and the Münster revolution, Knox made a characteristic yet unexpected remark:

> What does this fearful tragedy show? First, what the innocent and godly may look for if these fanatics get power, and second, what doth the world and the rulers now on earth, for the most part, deserve. The world, I say, and the princes of the earth,... most justly deserve to be punished with such confusion as ye intend. For the one and the other (I mean the princes and the people) conspired to this day asgainst God, against his Son Jesus Christ, and against his eternal verity. They maintain impiety, superstition and idolatry, they cruelly murder the saints of God, and so do they rejoice in all kind of tyranny, that God's just judgments cannot long delay punishment.43

Knox by condemning these revolutionaries has in all honesty put himself half upon their side -- though we deny not the magistrate, though we abhor communism in property or in wives, though these revolutionaries were vile, the blood which they shed is no less than the world and its princes merit.[44]

In 1558, Knox's theory of active resistance was complete. Knox's sources could have been outside influences such as the theory of inferior magistrates exemplified in the resistance of Magdeburg or the Covenant concept of Gilby, or Knox might have developed it through his own search through the Scriptures.

Whatever the source, Knox by 1558 was armed with a complete theory of active resistance. With this theory in mind, Knox in 1559 sailed from Dieppe to Scotland. In 1560 the Geneva Bible with its revolutionary notes followed its English congregation's pastor across the channel to England. In Scotland it was Knox or nothing; in England it was Puritans and predestination. The Geneva Bible would play a central role in both kingdoms.

Chapter 7) Geneva Bible

After Richard Cox arrived in Frankfurt, a day or so later he and the English refugees of his party attended a service of the English congregation. When Lever said the prayer, Cox and the newcomers answered with the responses of the Book of Common Prayer. The elders tried to silence them to no avail as Knox who was in the audience remonstrated them.

Cox retorted that the Frankfurt congregation should have the face of an English Church. Knox responded with his hope that it would have the face of the Church of Christ. On Sunday March 17 Cox again led responses from his party. In the afternoon sermon Knox struck back with a sermon which attacked the Prayer book. Cox and Knox had a heated interchange which spilled over into the evening congregational meeting. At the postponed session of March 19 the rupture took place which would affect Puritan development in Scotland and England.[45]

The civic authority in the person of Glauburg accepted a compromise which would use Poullain's service on March 24. On Saturday news came from Isaac and Parry that two years before Knox had compared the Emperor Charles V to Nero and incorporated into his sermon seditious comments about Philip and Mary. Frankfurt was alarmed that Charles might use this published statement in the Admonition to England to rescind its free status as a city. On Monday, March 25, they expelled Knox from Frankfurt. William Whittingham, who was presently in Frankfurt, said that if the English Prayer Book were used, he and others might join themselves to some other church. When Cox did not wish this, Whittingham answered "that it would be to great crueltie to force men contrary to their consciences to obei all thier disorderly doinges," then offered to dispute the matter against the contrary part.[46]

Whittingham then sent a letter to England supporting Knox, only to leave Frankfurt himself in September for Geneva. On December 16, 1555 and again in December of 1556 he was elected an elder of the church at Geneva. On December 16, 1558 he became a deacon and in 1559 he succeeded Knox as minister.[47] Meantime in 1557 he produced a version of the English New Testament. When the Genevan English congregation prepared A Service Book, Whittingham wrote the introductory letter to _The forme of prayers and Ministration of the Sacraments, etc. used in the Englishe Congregation at Geneva_ (1556). It was printed by Jean Crespin.[48] The letter is a call to repentance over the plague which God has sent upon England, so that His favour and mercy might once again return to that fair land. Instrumental in that hope is this joint confession of faith in which youth can be brought up.[49]

> For the false prophets are sent forthe with lies in their mouthes to deceyve England; and the scarsitie of God's Worde is so great, that althogh they seke it from one sea coaste to an other, yet they can not finde yt, but as men affameshed devoure the pestiferous dounge of Papistrie, to the poisoninge of their owne sowles.50

William Whittingham (1524?-1579), dean of Durham, was born in the West country at Chester about 1524. He attended the Oxford colleges of Brasenose (B.A.) and All Souls where he became a fellow in 1545. Whittingham traveled in 1550 to several continental universities at Orleans, Lyons, Paris, Germany and Geneva. His return to England in May 1553 bode ill for such an extreme protestant. From 1554/55 in Frankfurt and 1555/60 at Geneva, Whittingham participated in several significant enterprises as a Marian exile. While in Geneva he prepared the 1557 version of the New Testament, revised several of Sternhold's Psalms and saw Knox's _Predestination_ through the Geneva Press.[51] It used to be thought that Whittingham wrote the Brieff Discourse but Professor Collinson quite convincingly assigns it to Thomas Wood.[52]

A. Translators

1. William Whittingham

A contemporary life states that Whittingham was associated with Miles Coverdale, Christopher Goodman, Anthony Gilby, Thomas Sampson and William Cole in the translation of the 1560 Geneva Bible.[53] Most of the work was done by the date of the February 10, 1559 dedicatory letter to Elizabeth in The Boke of Psalmes, and many returned to England after Elizabeth's accession on November 17, 1558. Whittingham seems to have supervised the New Testament and Anthony Gilby the Old Testament. Whittingham prepared the June 10, 1557 Badian New Testament and Gilby the 1557 Psalms of David.[54] Therefore, it seems prudent to look at these two translators as well as the text itself.

The 1557 New Testament added textual and explanatory notes to the translation which followed Stephanus' Greek New Testament (1551) and Beza's of 1556. It most likely followed Jugge's Tyndale revision of 1552. This "neat octavo" as Herbert describes it was the earliest English Testament to use verse division and the clearer roman type. Arguments to almost all the books are included as well as a list of dates from Adam to Christ and Calvin's Epistle declaring that "Christ is the end of the Lawe." The title-page has a symbolic engraving of Time leading Truth up out of a cavern, with the inscription: Go by Tyme restoreth Truth/and maketh her victorious.[55] The epistle to the reader is of value in ascertaining how this version formed the groundwork for the Geneva Bible of 1560.

> To these therfore which are of the flocke of Christ which knowe their Fathers wil, and are affectioned to the trueth, I rendre a reason of my doing in fewe lines. First, as touching the perusing of the text, it was diligently reuised by the moste approued Greke examples, and conference of translations in other tonges,... Forthermore that the Reader might be by all means proffited, I hbve deuided the text into verses and sections, according to the best editions in other langages,... And

> because the Hebrewe and Greke phrases, which are strange to rendre in other tongues, and also short, shulde not be to harde, I haue sometyme interpreted them without any whit diminishing the grace of the sense, as our langage doth vse them.

Whittingham(?) then concludes his remarks with gratitude that God has preserved his gifts to the church which are the vernacular scriptures of the Old and New Testament.

> So may we glorifie him (God) more and more rendring to him eternal thankes and praises for his heauenly and inestimable giftes bestowed vpon his churche, that all thogh Satan, Antichrist, and all his ennemies rage and burste, yet are they not able to suppresse them, nether wil he diminishe them: ... what shulde we doute of his bontiful liberalitie towards vs... which is God blessed foreuer?56

One of the interesting changes occurs at Matthew (1:19) where Tyndale wrote: "Joseph her husbande beynge a perfect man, and loth to make an ensample of her, was mynded to put her away secretly." Matthew and Taverner follow Tyndale while Coverdale changed "beynge" to "was" and the middle phrase to "and wold not bringe her to shame." Whittingham had "beying a just man, and loth to make her a publike exemple of infamie, was mynded to put her away secretly." The Geneva Bible adopted this reading by leaving off the words "of infamie."[57]

An analysis of the passages cited in our previous discussion of Tyndale seems to indicate that Whittingham's version was the working copy for the Geneva New Testament of 1560. The following table of borrowings reflects that process.

Matthew (6:24-33)

	Whittingham (1557)	Tyndale (1534)	Great Bible (1539)	Geneva (1560)
24	riches	mammon	Mammon	riches
29	royalty	royalte	royalty	glory
30	oven	fournace	fournasse	oven
33	heaven	heven	God	God

1557: The day present hath ever inough to do with its owne grief
1534: the daye present hath ever ynough of his owne trouble

1539:	sufficient unto the daye, is the trouayle therof
1560:	the day hathe ynough with his owne grief

In these eleven verses there are five vocabulary variations. In verses 24, 30, and 34 three of these are unique to Whittingham and Geneva, in verse 33 one is common to the Great Bible and Geneva and one in verse 29 is unique to Geneva. In this limited section, 60% of the vocabulary changes come to the Geneva Bible from Whittingham's version, 20% from the Great Bible and 20% are unique to the Geneva Version.

John (14:1-7)

	(1557)	(1534)	(1539)	(1560)
2	dwelling places	mansions	mansions	dwelling places
5	possible	possible	possible	can
7	sholde	had	had	shulde

Romans (8:31-39)

32	to death	----	----	to death
34	intercession	intercession	intercessyon	request
35	honger	honger	honger	famine
36	slayne	slayne	slayne	slaughter
37	more then conquerers	overcome strongly	overcome	more then conquerers
38	principalities	rule	rule	principalities
39	depth	loweth	loweth	depth

James (4:1-17)

1	contentions	fighttynge	fyghtyng	contentions
1	volupteousnes	volupteousnes	lustes	lustes
1	fyght	rayne	fight	fight
2	luste	lust	enuye	enuie
2	gayne	receave	receave	receive
3	voluptuousnes	volupteousnes	lustes	lustes
4	friendship	frenshippe	frend shyp	amitie
6	the scripture	----	----	the scripture
8	nye	nye	nye	nere
9	sorowe ye	sorowe ye	mourne	sorowe ye
10	Cast downe	Cast daune	Humble	Cast downe
10	shal	shall	shal	will
11	Backbyte not	Backbyte not	Backbyte not	Speak not evil
11	condemneth	iudgeth	iudgeth	condemneth
12	another man	a nother	another man	another man
13	get gayne	wynne	wynne	get gaine
14	----	----	----	afterward

15 we wil	let us	let us	we wil
17 to do wel	to do good	to do good	to do wel

The above passages from John (14), Romans (8) and James (4) show thirty-two vocabulary changes in twenty-three verses. Thirteen of these or 40.6% are unique to Whittingham and are taken over from his version into the Geneva New Testament. One of these at James (4:4) reflects a stylistic alteration in the 1560 Genevan text: "the amitie of the worlde is the enimitie of God?" From this limited sample of four passages the borrowings are statistically significant in that 43.24% are unique to Whittingham's text and the Geneva New Testament. The 1557 version is the prototype for the 1560 edition in verse divisions, roman type and vocabulary selection. More than 80% of the text common to all four New Testament versions is Tyndale (1534), reflecting the dominant position of the printed Erasmian text used alike by each translator. None the less, one is overwhelmed by the permanance of the Tyndale revision in its literary impact to 1560 and in the more than one hundred and fifty reprints of the Geneva New Testament to 1644.[58]

2. Anthony Gilby (1510-1585)

Anthony Gilby was a Cambridge man, educated at Christ's College in the 1520's and 1530's. He graduated B.A. (1531/32) and M.A. (1535), entered the ministry and early on became a Protestant. By 1547 his position was clear enough to those who read his *A Brief Treatise of Election and Reprobation* and *An answer to the Devillish Detection of Stephane Gardiner, Bishoppe of Wynchester, published to the intent that such as be desirous of the truth should not be seduced by hys errours, nor the blind & obstinate excused by ignorance*. Gilby's scholarship made its appearance in two Old Testament commentaries, one on Micah (1551) and another on Malachi.[59] That he held a living in Leceistershire is certain from the epistle prefixed to Knox's *Faithful Admonition* (1554). Gilby's rhetoric is best sampled from his 1558 *Admonition to England and Scotland to call them to Repentance* (Geneva: Jean Crespin).

> For your consent and assistance is the cause that strangers now oppresse and devoure the poore within your Realmes, who shortly, if God call you not to repentance, shall recompence you as ye have deserved. For the cupp which your brethren do now drink shall be put in your handes, and you shall drink the dreggs of yt to your destruction. And wonder it is if ye be becomme so foolishe and so blynd, that ye think yourselves able long to continue, and to be safe when your brethren rounde abut you shall perishe; that you can pack your matters well enough with the Princes; that ye can make you stronge with mariages, with flateries, and other fonde practises; or that with your multitude or strengthe ye can escape the daies of vengeance; or that you can hide yourselves in holes or corners. Nay, thoghe you should hyde you in the hels, God can drawe you thence: if you had the egles wynges to flie beyonde the east seas, you cannot avoid Goddes presence. Submitt yourselves therefore unto Hym, which holdeth your breath in your nostrels, who with one blast of his mouth can destroy all his ennemies.60

Contempt of God's Word and the idolatry of the Roman mass coupled with foreign marriages led Gilby to rail against Henry VIII and Mary Tudor.

> In the tyme of King Henrie the Eight, when by Tyndale, Frith, Bylnay, and other his faithfull servantes, God called England to dresse his vineyard, many promised full faire, whome I could name; but what frute followe? Nothing but bitter grapes, yea, breeres and brambles, the wormewood of avarice, the gall of crueltie, the poison of filthie fornication flowing from head to foote, the contempt of God and open defense of the Cake idol, by open proclamation to be read in the churches in the stead of Goddes Scriptures. Thus was there no ref-ormation, but a deformation, in the tyme of that tyrant and lecherous monster. The bore I grant was busie wrooting and digging in the earth, and all his pigges that folowed hym. But they soght only for the pleasant frutes that they winded with their longe snowtes; and for their own bellies sake, they wrooted up many weeds; but they turned the grounde so, mingling good and badd together, swete and sowre, medecine and poyson, they made, I say, such confusion of religion and lawes, that no good thing could grow, but by great miracle, under such Gardners.61

Gardiner came under special scrutiny as one might expect from Gilby's 1547 tirade. In all of this one detects Gilby's association with Knox.

> And one crafty Gardener, whose name was Stephen, having wolf-lik conditions, did maintain many a wolfe, did sow wicked seed in the garden, and cherished many weedes to deface the vineyard. And his maid Marie, who after was his mastres, now maried to Philip, wanting no wil to wickednes when she was at the weakest, nor stomake to do evill when she gatt the mastrie, did cherishe many weedes. Those two, I say, have so broken the hedges of the same vineyarde, (God so punishing the sinnes of those that oght to have made better provision for the same), that the husbandmen are hanged up, the diggars, dressours, and planters are banished, prisoned, and burned. Such havock is made that all wild beastes have power to pollute the sanctuarie of the Lorde. O heavens! beholde her crueltie; O earthe! cry for vengeance; O seas and deserte mountains! witnesses of her wickednes, break furthe against this monster of England.[62]

Knowledge of Hebrew improved in England during the 1540s with the arrival of scholars such as Paul Fagius and Tremellius, the one with Bucer at Cambridge and the other with Martyr at Oxford. This third scholarly language had gained impetus when John Fisher revised the statutes of St. John's College, Cambridge in 1524.[63] In 1547 Edward VI produced two coronation medals bearing Hebrew inscriptions.

Jones points out that Gilby showed independance of judgement on Hebrew matters in his commentary on Micah. There are several explicit references to the Hebrew text such as the comment on Micah (2:1): kî yesh l^{e}'ēl yādhām. Coverdale followed the Septuagint and Vulgate in translating the phrase as "for their power is against God." Gilby prefers instead to read it as "because power is in their hands." His note prefers 'el as "strength" rather than "God," the precise explanation offered by the Targum, David Kimchi and Ibn Ezra.[64]

Such use of Rabbinic exegesis had been observed first hand at Strasbourg where Peter Martyr was lecturing on Judges to the Marian exiles and in Zurich on Samuel.[65] The latter manuscript was used by Beza in his 1558 work against Castellio.[66] Lectures on Isaiah and Hosiah given by Zanchi at Strasbourg from 1553-1560 required Munster's Dictionary and Kimchi's commentary on the minor prophets.[67] Martyr lectured on Judges from the Hebrew text in his own house. William Cole and Thomas Sampson who aided Whittingham in the Geneva translation of 1560 had attended Martyr's lectures at Strasbourg (Sampson) and Zurich (Cole). Cole had been Master of Corpus Christi Oxford when Martyr was in residence during 1548-1553. Cole enjoyed Christopher Froschover's hospitality while in Zurich and no doubt profited from Martyr's lectures on Samuel as well as those of Rudolf Gualter.[68]

One must not neglect the polemical context within which such a translation was prepared at Geneva. Whittingham and Gilby are clear examples of translators/editors who viewed their biblical edition in such terms. Given the attitudes in England which would yet root out a vernacular bible, one needs to keep this tension in mind. The closing Prayer for the Faythefull appended to Gilby's Pleasaunt Dialogue (1581) describes this attitude very well. The prefatory letter speaks of the "wicked weedes of Poperie."[69]

> Lord God, & most mercifull father/We beseeche thee/for the honour of thy holy Name/to defende us from that Antichrist of Rome/and from al his detestable enormities/manners/lawes/garments/& ceremonies: Destroye the counsel of al Papistes and Atheistes/enemies of thy Gospell/& of this realme of England. Disclose their mischiefes and subtill practises: confounde their devices: let them be taken in their own wylinesses: and strengthen all those that maintayne the case and quarell of they Gospell/With inuincible force and power of thi holie Spirite: so that/though they bee destitute at anie tyme of worldlie ayde and comforte: that yet they fayle not to proceede and goe forward towardes that true godlinesse commaunded in thy holie worde/with all simplicitie and sinceritie: to thy honor and glorie/the comforte of thine electe/and the confusion of thine enemies/through Christ our Lorde and Sauiour. Amen. Amen. And say from the harte/AMEN.[70]

B. Publication and Propagation (1560-1570)

1. Old Testament Notes

Micah (2:1) in the Geneva Bible concludes with the phrase, "because their hand hathe power." This is the same reading found in Gilby's 1551 commentary on Micah. In fact, the text of Micah is a revised form of Gilby's earlier version. A check of Micah (1:2), (3:12) and (7:19) shows major agreement between the text of Coverdale (1535), Great Bible (1539), Gilby (1551) and Geneva (1560). There are six unique expressions in Geneva and eight common only to Gilby and Geneva in these three verses. The translators clearly used Gilby in their version of Micah.[71]

The bulk of the Old Testament notes are explanatory comments free of controversy. II Kings (2:9) is of interest since it provides the reader with three choices of meaning. The text says that Elijah told Elisha to ask what he could do for him before God took him away. Elisha responds, "I pray thee, Let thy Spirit be double upon me." The note reads:

> Ley thy Spirit have double force in me because of these dangerous times: or let me have twice so much as ye rest of the Prophetes: or thy spirit being devided into thre partes, let me have two.

The historical reflection in the notes to Daniel (7) catches the reader's eye. The leopard in verse six is Alexander the Great, while the four wings are his captains Seleucus, Antigonus, Cassander and Ptolemy. The fourth beast in verse seven is the Roman Empire whose tyranny and greed was legendary. Verse 14 speaks of Christ's kingdom as the everlasting one, in spite of verses 21-22 which say that the "horne made battel against the Sainctes, yea, and prevailed against them, vntil the Ancient of daies came, and judgement was given to the Sainctes of the moste high: and the time approched that the Sainctes possessed the kingdome." The note to verse 25 identifies the fresh adversary with the Roman Emperors Octavius, Tiberius, Caligula, Nero, Domitian, etc. Such comments are conservative in nature because they identify past rather than present political powers who trouble the elect people of God.

An example of theological interpretation is found in the arguments to Joshua and to Job. The Joshua summary concludes with a reference to Christ as the "valiant captaine." "This historie doeth represent Iesus Christ the true Ioshua, who leadeth vs into eternal felicitie, which is signified vnto vs by this land of Canaan." The Job argument opens up the hermeneutical framework of the Genevan translators. It is translated almost word for word from a 1559 French Octavo Bible printed at Geneva.[72]

IOB
THE ARGUMENT

> In this historie is set before our eyes the example of a singular pacience. For this holy man Iob was not onely extremely afflicted in outwarde things and in his body, but also in his minde, and conscience by the sharpe tentations of his wife, and chief friends: which by their vehement wordes, and subtel disputations broght him almoste to dispaire: for they set forthe God as a seuer judge, and mortal enemie vnto him, which had caste him of, therefore in vaine he shulde seke vnto him for succour. These friends came vnto him vunder pretence of consolation, and yet they tormented him more then did all his affliction. Not withstanding he did constantly resist them, and at length had good successe. In this storie we haue to marke that Iob mainteineth a good cause, but handeleth it euil: againe his aduersaries hauve an euil matter, but they defend it craftely. For Iob helde that God did not alway punish men according to their sinnes, but that he had secret iudgements, whereof man knewe not the cause, and therefore man colde not reason against God therein, but he shoulde be conuicted. Moreouer he was assured that God had not reiected him, yet through his great torments, & affliction he brasteth forthe into manie inconueniencies bothe of wordes and sentences, and sheweth him selfe as a desperate man in manie things, and as one that wolde resist God: and this is his good cause which he doeth not handel wel. Agayne the aduersaries mainteine with manie goodlie arguments, that God punisheth continually according to the trespas, grounding vpon Gods prouidence, his iustice, and mans sinnes, yet their intention is euil: for they labour to bring Iob into dispaire, and so they mainteine an euil cause. Ezekiel commendeth Iob as a iuste man, Ezek. 14,14, and Iames setteth out his pacience for an example, Iam. 5,11

The ultimate reflection for the Genevan translators was their escape across the sea from Queen Mary's "jolly captaines" like the ancient people of God who fled from Pharoah. The woodcut on the general title-page and the New Testament title is reproduced at Exodus (14:10) without the twin references of the outer margin to Psalm (34:19) and Exodus (14:14) about God's delivery of the righteous from all trouble and the one who shall fight for them. Four points are made about their English Exodus, best read in the patois of the Genevan translators.

> In this figure foure chief points are to be considered. First that the Church of God is euer subiect in this worlde to the Crosse & to be afflicted after one sort or other. The second, that the ministers of God following their vocation shalbe euil spoken of, and murmured against, euen of them that pretend the same cause and religion that thei do. The third, that God deliuereth not his Church incontinently out of dangers, but to exercise their faith and pacience continueth their troubles, yea and often tymes augmenteth them as the Israelites were now in lesse hope of their liues then when thei were in Egypt. The fourth point is, that when the dangers are moste great, then Gods helpe is moste redy to succour: for the Israelites had on ether side them, huge rockes & mountaines, before them the Sea, behinde them moste cruel ennemies, so that there was no way left to escape to mans iudgement.

2. Old Testament Text

To test the assumption that the Genevan translators utilized the Hebrew text for their Old Testament version, six passages will be examined.

The reader will recall that these were the same ones given in the previous chapter from Tyndale and Coverdale. The first of these is Genesis (3:1-17). The famous term "breeches" in verse seven has the note, "Ebr. things to girde about them to hide their priviries." The phrase patterns more often utilize the active voice of the verb with commas setting off individual phrases. The apurns (Tyndale) or breeches (Geneva) are both sown with leaves from the fig.

Exodus (15:1-8) shows interpretive comments inserted into the text. At verse two where Tyndale read the Hebrew as "The Lorde is my strength and my songe, and is become my salvation. He is my God and I will glorifie him...," Geneva after "God" reads, "and I wil prepare him a tabernacle." At verse four Pharoah's "iolye captaynes" are now "chosen." In Tyndale's Pentateuch (1530) and Gilby's Geneva, they sink to the bottome like a stone. Also in verse seven Geneva retains Tyndale's stubble, as it does Tyndale's "depe water congeled together in the myddest of the see" in verse eight with the slightly altered "the depths congeled together in the heart of the Sea." It seems obvious that Tyndale's wording was quite familiar. The Hebrew at this place in verse eight means to thicken.

Deuteronomy (32) reflects greater dependance on Tyndale than either Genesis (3) or Exodus (15). Tyndale translated verse ten as "He found him in a deserte lande, in a voyde ground and a rorynge wildernesse. he led him aboute and gave him understandynge, and kepte him as the aple of his eye." Geneva reads this as "he founde him in the land of the wildernes, in a waste, and roaring wilderness: he led him about, he taught him, and kept him as the apple of his eye." The structure, imagery and vocabulary is still Tyndale. At verse 33 the parallels are even closer.

Tyndale (1530)	Geneva (1560)
Their wyne is the poyson of dragons and the cruell gall of aspes	Their wine is the poyson of dragons, and the cruel gall of aspes.

At verse 35 the sliding foot, destruction at hand and make haste are taken over from Tyndale. In this case all three images are also in Coverdale's text.

Proverbs (9) reflects dependance on Coverdale's text, especially at verse ten where the first part is reversed and the second is identical.

Coverdale (1535)	Geneva (1560)
The feare of the LORDE is the begynnynge of wysdome, and the knowlege of holy thinges is understandinge	The beginning of wisdome is ye feare of the Lord, and the knowledge of holy things is understanding

When one reads through the above passages it becomes clear that in the Geneva Old Testament translation the Pentateuch follows Tyndale, that Coverdale was used for Proverbs and Isaiah, and that the bulk of the translation is not a fresh start but rather a careful revision of existing English versions compared with the Hebrew text. On the other hand, this version marks a break with the Vulgate tradition. A. C. Partridge compares Song of Solomon (2:1-4) with the Septuagint rather than Tyndale, giving an impression that there was no slavish reliance on previous English versions. At verse 14 he suggests that Geneva renders the Hebrew intelligently as well as poetically, for "'the secret places of the staires' suggests the Hebrew words 'seter' (covert) and 'madregah' (step or terrace)."[73] A glance at both Tyndale and Geneva, however, indicates borrowing from Tyndale.

Tyndale (1534)	Geneva (1560)
Vp hast my loue, my doue, in the holes of the rocke and secret places of the walles	My dooue, that art in the holes of the rocke, in ye secret places of ye staires

3. New Testament Text & Notes

It is already apparent that the 1557 Genevan New Testament in English was the prototype for the 1560 text. Analysis of Acts (12) and I Peter confirms that impression which has been derived from the 43.24% common vocabulary changes in Matthew (6:24-33), John (14:1-7), Romans (8:31-39) and James (4:1-17). Results of the Acts (12) comparison are as follows: At verse 19 Whittingham and Geneva have "punished." Verse 20 has "intended to make warre against them," while Tyndale and Great Bible have "was displeased with them." Acts (12) shows a high correlation between Tyndale (1534), Great Bible (1539), Whittingham (1557) and Geneva (1560). The text in all three versions is 95% set by Tyndale.

Selected passages from I Peter (1:1-25) show the following results: Verse seven indicates that the translators followed Whittingham rather than the Great Bible. Verses eight and nine are identical in Tyndale, Great Bible, Whittingham and Geneva except for the "even" at the end of verse nine. In verse eleven Geneva prefers the Great Bible to Whittingham. Then in verse thirteen Geneva adopts Whittingham word-for-word and phrase-for-phrase. Where Tyndale and Great Bible have "declaring," Whittingham has "reuelation" as does Geneva. In verse seventeen the "pilgremage" of Tyndale/Great Bible becomes "dwelling" in Whittingham/Geneva. Verse 22 reads as an active voice in Tyndale/ Great Bible (have purified your souls), but Whittingham/Geneva turns the voice to the passive (your souls are purified).

I Peter (2:2 and 9) and (5:1-3) are worth mention. (2:2) is "reasonable mylke" in Tyndale ('34), "milke" in Great Bible ('39) but "syncere mylke of the worde" in Whittingham ('57) and in Geneva ('60). (2:9) has "peculiar people" in Tyndale ('34), Whittingham ('57) and Geneva ('60) but not in the Great Bible ('39).

I Peter (5:1) is identical in all four versions with the exception of "reueiled" in Geneva ('60) for "open" in the other three. Verses two and three are taken directly from Whittingham rather than Tyndale or the Great Bible. The three versions are listed below.

Great Bible (1539)	Whittingham (1557)	Geneva (1560)
(2): Fede ye Christes flocke as moch as lyeth in you takynge the ouersyght of them not as compelled therto	Feed the flocke of God which dependeth vpon you caring for it not as though ye were compelled therto	Fede the flocke of God which dependeth vpon you caring for it not by constraint
but wyllyngly (after a godly sorte) not for the desyre of fylthy lucre but of a good mynde	but wyullingly not for the desire of filthy lucre lust of a good mynde	but willingly not not for filthie lucre lust of a readie minde
3): not as though ye were lordes ouer the parrishes but that ye be an ensample to the flocke (and that wyth good wyll)	Not as thogh ye wer lordes ouer Gods heritage but that ye be ensamples to the flocke	Not as thogh ye were lords ouer Gods heritage but that ye may be ensamples to the flocke

"Ouer the parisshes" came from Tyndale into the Great Bible version. Our limited random sample from six separate sections of the New Testament indicates that the translators used both the Great Bible and Whittingham in their revision. These samples suggest that the 1557 New Testament is the prototype for the 1560 version with the underlying literary core that of Tyndale.

The notes are exegetical for the most part with several cross references to other sections of the New Testament more prominent than even these. Some notes are explicitly Protestant in tone, such as the comment on John (20:30): "It is finished." The note adds: "Mans salvation is perfected by the onlie sacrifice of Christ: & all ye ceremonies of the Law are ended." For the most part these first set of notes are aids to the reader, as in Luke (15:8) that the pieces of silver are drachmae, "which is some what more in value then fyue pence of olde sterling money, & was equal with a Romaine penie."

Even the notes to Romans (9-11) are mild in tone, given the Genevan setting of this enterprise. The word election is mentioned only twice in this *locus classicus* for a doctrine of predestination. At Galatians (2:20) the expression "Thus I live yet" provokes the comment: "Not as I was once, but regenerat, and changed into a new creature, in qualitie, & not in substance."

The descriptive rather than dogmatic tone of this translation shines forth in the "arguments" to several of the New Testament letters. There is one summary for the four gospels and none for II or II John, making twenty-two arguments in all. I Peter is a good example of this modesty:

> He exhorteth the faithful to denie them selues, and to condemne the worlde, that being deliuered from all carnal affections and impediments, they may more spedely atteine to the heauenlie kingdome of Christ, whereunto we are called by the grace of God reueiled to vs in his Sonne, and haue already receued it by faith, possessed it by hope, and are therein confirmed by holines of life. And to the intent this faith shulde not faint, seing Christ contemned and rejected almost of the whole worlde, he declareth that this is nothing els but the accomplishing of the Scriptures which testifie that he shulde be the stombling stone to the reprobate and the sure fundation of saluation to the faithful: therefore he exhorteth them courageously to go forwarde, considering what they were, and to what dignitie God hathe called them. After, he entreateth particular points, teaching subiects how to obey their gouernours, and seruants their masters, and how maried fokes oght to behaue them selues. And because it is appointed for all that are godlie, to suffre persecutions, he sheweth them what good yssue their afflictions shal haue, and contrarie

> wise what punishment God reserueth for the wicked. Last of all he teacheth how the ministers oght to behaue them selues, forbidding them to vsurpe autoritie ouer the Church: also that yong men oght to be modest, and apt to learne, and so endeth with an exhortation.

This 1560 edition swiftly made its way to England. The costs of initial publication were borne by John Bodley, who was given a seven year licence to print the Geneva Bible in England.[74] Bodley failed to exercise his monopoly, however, and the first English printing was that by Thomas Vautroullier in 1575.[75] That the Bishops Bible appeared in 1568 and a clause in Bodley's licence reserves judgement to the authorities may mean that the notes posed a problem for the Crown. Therefore the several versions of this period were printed on the continent.

A separate octavo New Testament came from Geneva in 1560 and the first folio in 1562 was also printed at Geneva. A second quarto edition came from Crespin's press in 1570. This version is worth an extended comment for its format which shows that the Sternhold and Hopkins Metrical Psalter was intended as a part of this book. The twelve preliminary leaves contain an historical calendar as well as a count of the world's age from creation to 1569 by Martin Luther. The Kalendar has a small woodcut at the head of each month, signs of the zodiac and references to contemporary events. One page lists the "Faires in Fraunce and elsewhere."[76]

C. England (1575-1611)

Prior to its first printing in England, the Geneva New Testament text appeared in translations of Luther and Calvin. One of these is the committee translation of Luther's Galatians, printed in 1575 by Thomas Vautroullier. This London printer also published that same year the first Geneva Bible in England. Luther's Galatians went through reprints in 1577, 1580, 1588 (twice), 1602, 1616 and 1635. Not only is the text of Galatians in the Genevan mode, but other citations follow the text, though not always word for word. One example is the citation from Acts 15:8-10 in Luther's extended comment on Galatians (3:2).

Luther (1588)[77]	Geneva (1560)
God who knoweth their heartes,	God which knoweth the hearts,
bare them witnesse	barre them witnes,
in giuing vnto them	in giuing vnto them
the holy Ghost,	the holie Gost,
euen as he did vnto vs.	euen as he did vnto vs.
And he put no difference	And he put no difference
betweene vs and them,	betwene vs & them,
purifying their hearts	after that by faith
by faith	he had purified their hearts.
Nowe therefore,	Now therefore,
why tempt ye God,	why tempt ye God,
to lay a yoke on	to lay a yoke on
the disciples neckes,	ye disciples neckes
which neither our fathers	which neither our fathers,
nor we were able to beare?	nor we were able to beare?

The 1575 London octavo has the arms of Sir Francis Walsingham on the sides of the title-border. At the front is an Epistle by John Calvin. The two printings of 1576 were by Christopher Barker, folio in size, each with the tiger's head crest of Walsingham at the top of the title-page. In 1576 Barker published Tomson's English version and revision of Beza's New Testament text and notes. Two preliminary epistles are from Laurence Tomson (1539-1608), secretary to Walsingham, and that of Theodore Beza dated 1565 at Geneva. This final and popular form of the Geneva New Testament was based on Beza's 1565 Greek-Latin New Testament published by Robert Stephanus.

Beza's impact on the 1560 notes was considerable; that on the 1576 notes was dramatic. Irena Backus examines eleven notes in the 1560 edition which indicate a larger than expected impact.[78] Beza published major annotations in a separate 1557 folio which the Genevan translators used. The minor annotations were first printed in the 1565 Latin New Testament margin. In 1574 Pierre L'Oiseleur de Villers, a Huguenot refugee in London, produced an edition of Beza with both the shorter marginal notes and the harder passages explained from the major Annotations. Oiseleur added some notes from Carmerarius in the Gospels and Acts to fill out Beza's sparse comments, using Camerarius' 1570 _Commentarius_ and 1572 _Notatio_. This edition was translated into

English by Tomson, published in London by Barker in 1576 and in 1586 replaced the 1560 New Testament in some copies. The text on original sin at Romans (5:12) is changed from "insomuch that all men have sinned" to "in whom all men sinned." Beza read the text as the Vulgate rather than the Greek. This change from Tyndale, Whittingham and Geneva (1560) passed into the King James Version of 1611.[79]

If one counts the editions listed in Herbert, there were 150 printings of the Geneva Bible in whole or in part between 1560 and 1644. A table will summarize these by size and contents.

Type	Complete	New Testaments	Third Part (Job-Song of Solomon)
Folio	19		
4°	65		
8°	24	16	
12°	1	2	
16°	1	9	3 (1580,1583,1614)
24°		2	
32°		8	
	110	37	3

There are sixty-eight more editions in Eason's 1937 supplemental list. A glance at this list shows that none of these appear in Herbert's 1968 Historical Catalogue. Seventeen of these additional copies are given precise locations in Glascow, London, Oxford, Dublin and private libraries.

One can list ten features of the Geneva Bible taken from Herbert and Eason.

1) 1560: Complete Bible printed in Geneva.
2) 1560: Separate New Testament printed in Geneva.
3) 1575: Geneva Bible printed in England.
4) 1579: First Scottish Bible in a Genevan Version.
5) 1580: Third Part (Job-Song of Solomon) printed separately.
6) 1586: Tomson translation of Bezan text & notes issued.
7) 1590: First Cambridge Geneva Bible published.
8) 1599: Junius' notes on Revelation replace Tomson.[80]

9) 1640: First English Bible to omit Apocrypha.

10) 1642: King James Version with Genevan notes and Junius on Revelation.

Many more features of the Geneva Bible editions could be described than these tables summarize. From 1560 until the Great Ejection of 1662 the Geneva Bible with its variant notes played a parallel role with John Foxe's Actes and Monuments in shaping the view of England as an elect nation. One note from Revelation (14:6) reflects that image. The Apostle saw "Another Angel flie in the mids of heauen, hauing an euerlasting Gospel to preach..." The note from Junius reads:

> This Angel is a type or figure of ye good and faithfull seruants of God, whom God especially from that time of Boniface the 8. hath raised up to ye publishing of the Gospel of Christ, both by preaching and by writing. So god... used... Iohn Wicklife an Englishman, and so continually one or another vnto the restoring of the trueth, & enlarging of his Church.[81]

The means to accomplish the restoration of Gospel truth in the English church was well in hand. James (4:6) in the Genevan version summed it up in a phrase: "But the Scripture offereth more grace & therefore faith."[82]

Chapter 8) Beza in England

Before one explores the doctrinal impact of these notes, some attention should be given to Beza's background and subsequent influence in Elizabethan England. Theodore Beza became Professor of Theology at Geneva from 1559 to 1599, was Rector of the Academy for forty-four years until 1603 and a pastor at Geneva for forty-six years during which he was moderator of the Company of Pastors from 1564 to 1580.[83] While at Geneva, Beza undertook a number of diplomatic journeys in support of the French Protestants, from Poissy (1561) with the Catholics to Göppingen (1557) and Montbéliard (1586) with Lutherans.

A. Theological Tomes and Translations

Biblical scholars are familiar with Beza through his valuable gift of Codex Beza, a manuscript which contained significant variations from the Erasmian Byzantine text type. He presented this bilingual fifth or sixth century Latin/Greek copy of the Gospels and Acts to Cambridge University in 1581. One must move from this well known symbol of Beza's influence to a review of Beza's contacts with England through the dedications of his Latin books, his correspondance and his treatises. Ian McPhee has summarized these contacts in a unpublished essay. What follows is adopted from his survey.[84] It reveals sufficient material to support a claim that Beza was highly respected by Englishmen.

The collection of Beza's Latin theological works was published in three volumes in 1570, 1573 and 1582, each being dedicated to Walter Mildmay, founder of Emmanuel College, Cambridge in 1583/84. He sent Mildmay his dedicatory epistle in February, 1570 to which Mildmay replied in April 1572. In 1582 Beza dedicated his Christian Meditations on several Psalms to Ann Bacon. Anthony Bacon had stayed with Beza for several months and after reading the manuscript which Beza had buried amongst his papers, he encouraged Beza to publish it. Beza's high regard for Anthony's parents -- Ann and Nicolaus Bacon -- shines through in his dedicatory epistle. The Earl of Huntingdon, the famous patron of Puritans, received Beza's paraphrase of the Psalms in 1579. The Queen received his New Testament in 1565 and again in 1582. Much to Beza's chagrin she never acknowledged his gift. But her resentment of Geneva had perhaps been drained of its ardour, for Samuel Clark reports that Elizabeth solicited Beza's help to refute the Rheims New Testament in 1581.[85] Again in 1589 Beza, undaunted, dedicated his lectures on Job to Elizabeth and the year previous, after the defeat of the Armada, Beza wrote his Latin poem depicting Elizabeth as God's agent of providence.

Among Beza's early correspondents were Cecil, Huntingdon, Mildmay and the churchmen Grindal, Whitgift, and Cartwright. His letters to the strangers churches in London are also substantial.

Between 1568 and 1580 there are eleven extant letters between Beza and prominent members of the French, Dutch and Spanish churches in London.[86]

Statistically Beza occupies a prominent place among the foreign divines whose works were made to speak English. Between 1559 and 1603 forty-five editions of his works appeared in English, not to mention eleven of his Latin works printed in London [S.T.C. 2 1997-2054 in proof]. In the same period Calvin ranks first with one hundred thirty-four Latin and English editions [S.T.C.2, 4372-4468 in proof]. Bullinger and Luther together approximate Beza's output, with Viret (thirteen English editions) standing third in popularity among Reformed writers in England.[87]

These statistics for Beza do not include his Biblical translations with annotations, nor Tomson's revision of the New Testament in 1576 which incorporated many more of Beza's notes into the Geneva Bible. Beza's influence through this Bible unquestionably represents a major avenue for Beza's theology and, because of its wide reading public, an influence of major proportions.

The selection of Beza's works for translation tells us what Englishmen found most useful and edifying in his thought.[88] His chief work on Predestination was translated by two different men, in 1556 by Whittingham and in 1576 by John Stockwood. Whittingham's translation was published three times.[89] Stockwood's version is based on Beza's 1570 revision and was published twice in Elizabeth's reign and once in the seventeenth century.[90] Beza's original Latin treatise has been lost, but we have access to its contents through Whittingham's translation. A detailed comparison of the two texts shows that there were no significant alterations. What does emerge is that Whittingham was more free in his translation which flows more smoothly than Stockwood's crabbed sentences.

None of Beza's confessional theologies achieve the magnitude of Calvin's Institutes, but they range over the spectrum of Christian doctrine with considerable depth. Of these the most popular work was his earliest expression of theology, the Briefe and Pithie Summe of the Christian Faith with seven editions between 1563 and 1585. Also important was his Questiones and Answeres Part One in four editions and another part in one edition, which represents Beza's most comprehensive treatment of Christian doctrine. Between them, these two works account for twelve editions of the English translations, or 26.67% of the sixteenth century English translations of Beza.

The Brief and Pithie Summe is a translation of the 1559 Confession de la Foi Chretienne. It contains seven sections, i.e.:

I. Unity and Trinity of God
II. The Father
III. The Sonne
IV. Holy Ghost
V. Church
VI. Last Judgment
VII. Papal doctrine compared to that of the Holy Catholic Church 91

The 1563 edition is dedicated to Lord Hastings, Earl of Huntingdon. Section V states that Jesus Christ is the sole head of the Christian Church.

> He hath no need of anye successor, (for he is God lyuyng eternallye) nor anye Vicare or Lieutenaunt, for we haue all his wyll by writynge... and in deed the blindest man in the worlde maye see whether those men be tumbled and fallen headlonge, which would robbe and depriue Jesus Christe of this preeminence...92

Section V.7 gives the marks of the "trewe/false" Church.

> The marke of the trew Churche is the preachynge of the lyvely worde of the sonne of God, according as it was reuealed to the prophets and apostles, & by them declared to the worlde, therein comprehendinge consequently the sacramentes & the administration of the ecclesiasticall discipline, so as god hath ordeined it: for there is none other worde of god, nor other maner to preache it."93

A curious feature of the Questiones has been obscured by the improper identification of two editions in the Short Title Catalogue (1926). Both the 1578 and 1581 editions printed for J. Harrison prove to be spurious.[94] While they have the same title and style, the content is patently different. Harrison's editions run to only 20% of the original length and focus on several anti-Catholic questions. Harrison figures prominently, as we shall later see, in the printing of foreign Protestant treatises. The anti-Catholic temper of the tract no doubt suited his ideology, but unfortunately the real author is not Beza.

A third treatise which attempts to set forth a systematic theology was the work of students at the Academy closely supervised by Beza. We may safely assume that Beza endorsed the theology expressed in this work. It went through three editions in Edinburgh, printed by the exiled zealot Robert Waldegrave and translated by the equally zealous John Penry. The significance of this translation is accentuated both by its date and its ruthlessly logical style. Printed in Latin in 1586, the Theses Theologicae reflects the more mature and developed thought of Beza. The complexity and more academic tone of the work make it an excellent testing ground for any signs of scholasticism. Thus, Elizabethans had three comprehensive, systematic accounts of Christian doctrine from Beza's Geneva, all of which attained a relatively high degree of popularity.[95]

Besides these more sweeping surveys of doctrine many of Beza's treatises on specific doctrines were made available in English. His reply to Castellio in 1558 grinds out the vital themes surrounding Calvin's doctrine of double predestination. Significantly it was not until 1578 that Hopkinson translated this exhaustive polemic, at a time when Baro at Cambridge was beginning to arouse opposition to strict predestinarianism. Beza's many tracts on theology were sought and made available to Englishmen. From his succinct presentation at Poissy to his two lengthy sermons on the supper, Beza's eucharistic thought was well represented in English.[96] In addition, his ecclesiology would have been impressed upon Englishmen most vividly in the translations of his De Veris Et Visibilibus Ecclesiae Catholicae Notis (1579) (published by Waldegrave in 1582 (?) [S.T.C. 2014] and twice in the seventeenth century) and The Threefold Order of

Bishops, a boldly stated plea for Presbyterianism. Finally, besides his devotional work on the Psalms and his treatise on the Plague, Beza was well represented in England by his sermons, lectures and Biblical annotations.[97] Altogether an impressive list of books by Beza on a variety of subjects circulated in English during Elizabeth's reign.

B. Printers and Translators

The circle of men who translated and printed Beza's books appears to follow a similar pattern to that reflected in the wider circle who were involved with the production of all the foreign divines' works. Included in this pattern are thè patrons who are found in the dedications of this body of literature. It wold be impossible to separate Beza from this larger circle for purposes of establishing the uniqueness of his circle of translators and printers. Nevertheless, the men involved and the lines of patronage which emerge, all help to clarify the most consistent and zealous Protestant body in Elizabeth's reign.

Among the most influential printers of Beza's works were men of strong religious character and several who were firm "Calvinists." Men like George Bishop, Thomas Vautroullier, Henry Middleton, Abraham Beale, Lucas Harrison and the radical Robert Waldegrave were prominent in the printing of Beza's books. They all figure significantly in the printing of religious works and particularly the works of foreign divines in English.[98] Linder has described many of these men as "devout and reputable Calvinists" and several as "more radical Protestants, all with definite Puritan leanings."[99]

John Day can certainly be classified as a devout Protestant with Puritan leanings. He printed Zwingli, Calvin, Bullinger, Martyr, Viret, and Ochino in English.[100] More prolific in their output of foreign divines were men like George Bishop, Lucas Harrison and Vautroullier. Bishop and Harrison had formed a partnership at least by 1573. Bennett has pointed out their relationship with Arthur Golding's many translations.[101] They printed two of Beza's Latin texts, and, between them, five of his English translations. Their affinity for Calvin is clearly seen in their involvement in thirteen of Calvin's books, many of which Thomas Dawson and Henry Bynneman printed for them, as well as two of Bullinger's, and one each of Hemmingsen and Marlorat.[102] Vautroullier, a prominent Huguenot refugee printer, had a monopoly on Beza's Latin translation of the New Testament which went through nine editions by 1587. He also printed four other Latin texts by Beza, one English translation, five of Luther's works in English, and those of numerous other divines.[103]

Thomas Dawson and Robert Waldegrave rank among the most radical printers in connection with Beza. Dawson printed Beza's treatise on the Plague, several works by Bullinger, Melanchthon, Viret and over ten of Calvin's books. Waldegrave was notorious for his involvement in the printing of the Marprelate Tracts which forced him into exile in Scotland where he continued to print. He published six editions of Beza's works, among which were three of Beza's most anti-Catholic treatises.[104]

Waldegrave's first published work is a book of prayers and meditations printed by Thomas Dawson in 1578 known as, The Castle for the Soule (S.T.C. 24911). During his ten years as a London printer Waldegrave made a name as a printer of Puritan works, including in his publishing list two books by John Field, at least one by Oliver Pigge and another by Laurence Chaderton that went through several editions.[105] In 1584 Waldegrave printed two sermons of John Udall on Peter's fall which he reprinted in 1587 (S.T.C.2 24503.7 and 24504). In 1588 he reprinted three sermons of Udall on Acts (2:37-38) as well as four sermons on the combat between Christ and the devil (S.T.C.2 24490 and 24492). These were followed by a Udall Dialogue between a bishop and a papist printed three times in 1588 (S.T.C.2 24505, 24506 and 24506[a)], five sermons on Joel (1) (S.T.C.2 24507) also in 1588 and A demonstration of the trueth of that discipline which Christe hath prescribed for the gouernement of his church (1588: S.T.C.2 24999).

Waldegrave's press and type were seized on April 16, 1588 and destroyed on May 13. Waldegrave escaped with one box of type and his wife may have rescued another. John Penry and Waldegrave then retired from London to East Molesey near Kingston on Thames where John Udall was minister. That summer he issued two of Penry's Puritan tracts. The second of these was An exhortation vnto the gouernors and people of Wales, which was reprinted with several pages of new material which in turn were cancelled and replaced by a single leaf (S.T.C.2 19605, 19605.5, 19606). Then in October 1588 he printed the first Marprelate tract, O read ouer D. John Bridges (The Epistle).[106] When he arrived in Scotland (1590) Waldegrave printed several works at Edinburgh which include editions by William Perkins, whose A golden chaine Waldegrave reprinted in 1592 (S.T.C.2 19661). When Penry translated the Genevan Propositions and Principles of Diunitie, Waldegrave printed it in 1591 and again in 1595 (S.T.C.2 2053 and 2054). He became the royal printer to James VI and only a premature death in 1604 kept Waldegrave from a prosperous publishing career in London when James assumed the English crown.[107]

Richard Schilders, although not a printer of Beza's works, must also be classified as one connected with the radical fringe of Puritanism. After 1580 he was the chief printer for such Puritans as Dudley Fenner and Cartwright and printed Browne's A Treatise of Reformation without Tarrying for anie in 1582.[108]

The Queen's printer, Christopher Barker, published Tomson's revision of the New Testament and Beza's Christian Meditations, and William How printed five editions of Beza.[109] How printed Beza's Briefe and Pithie Summe, three editions of Questiones and Answeres for A. Veale and a work each of Bullinger, Calvin and Erasmus. Apart from these he printed almost entirely non-religious works. Linder identifies A. Veale as a Puritan; he may have been. But this is difficult to determine from his publications. He did have How publish the three editions of Beza's Questiones and Answeres, a work of Viret and of Bullinger. Men like Thomas Woodcocke, Henry Denham, Hugh Singleton, Henry Bynneman, Thomas East, Thomas Purfoot, Ralph Newbery, Thomas Man, Arthur Maunsell, Hugh Middleton, John Perrin[110], John Lefatt of Cambridge, Joseph Barnes of Oxford and others were active in the dissemination of foreign divines' books in English translation. More detailed studies on their publications and patrons may clarify this circle which played such a vital role in English Protestantism.

The translators of Beza's treatises also tend to come from the more Puritan wing of the English Church. Most prolific among them was Arthur Golding who translated two of Beza's works and six of Calvin. Golding was widely recognized as a Puritan sympathizer and had many patrons of influential standing. He had intimate friendships with men like Cecil, Leicester, Huntingdon, Mildmay, Hatton and others. Golding was probably one of the most skilled translators in this period.[111]

Several of the more radical Puritans helped their cause by translating Continental books. Beza obviously had appeal to members on the left, for several of the more zealous of their circle translated his works. Mention has already been made of Whittingham and John Stockwood. Even the leader of the radicals, John Field, translated two of Beza's tracts. Anthony Gilby and Thomas Wilcox also Englished Beza; both were fervent Puritans. John Penry, the radical associated with the <u>Marprelate Tracts</u>, also translated Beza when exiled in Scotland.[112] John Stubbs, who had his right hand removed for a treasonable tract against the Queen, translated two of Beza's works. William Hopkinson, a graduate of St. John's college in Cambridge in 1567, also had Puritan sympathies, as is evident from his book.[113] Henry Aires,[114] Robert Fyll, John Harmer, Lawrence Tomson and John Baron complete the number of those who thought it profitable for their countrymen to read some aspects of Beza's thought.

Several dedications of Beza's works, however, show definite alignment with vital Protestants. Sir John Pelham, a Marian exile, had only two books dedicated to him, one being Beza's treatise on Predestination. John Field chose to dedicate Beza's work on the sacraments to the Protestant zealot Catherine, Duchess of Suffolk. She had been a distinguished Protestant in Edwards' reign, had gone to the Continent in Mary's reign and became the recipient of many dedications of religious works by Calvin, Tyndale and Latimer. Indeed the latter was supported by Catherine and figures prominently in her dedications.[115] Another lady of a similar persuasion was Ann Bacon, Sir Nicolas Bacon's wife, and mother of Anthony and the famous Francis Bacon. She was a distinguished classical scholar and was widely known both for her translation of Jewel's Apology and for her Puritan piety and zeal. Prompted by Anthony, who was staying as a guest in Beza's house, Beza published his meditations on the Psalm and dedicated them to Ann.

Two of the most powerful houses in England were those of the Earl of Leicester and the Earl of Huntingdon. Both were zealous Protestants. The former was a somewhat enigmatic character whose real intent is often difficult to judge. He had one of Beza's books dedicated to him by John Harmer of Oxford. Harmer, who had studied with Beza in Geneva, was helped by Leicester to a fellowship at New College. The Hastings family was, however, the most influential among zealous Protestants. Claire Cross has already demonstrated that Henry and his nephew Francis patronized Protestants of a Puritan leaning.[116] In fact Henry is an example of how the theological and popular movements for reform united. Ministers such as Anthony Gilby, Thomas Sampson, and Richard Hildersham were all patronized by Henry. Many of the more radical members of the Puritans like John Udall dedicated works to him.[117] Thus the ideas of Continental theologians like Calvin and Beza took on living flesh in these Puritan households which become virtually nonconformist centres.[118] Hastings' placement of Puritan clergy in his own livings and in others where his influence opened doors to them, helped to give impetus to the spread of a more rigorous Protestantism.

One other way in which Beza appears in English works was through translations of his 1569 Poemata. Timothy Kendall in his anthology Flowers of Epigrams (1577) chose fifteen poems from the 1569 Poemata. One of these celebrates Calvin and another, Luther.[119] Anne Prescott has noted that when Thomas Rogers translated Geveren's Of the end of this world, and second comming of Christ (1577), he placed a translation of Beza's poem on the reverse of the title page, a poem which interpreted the nova of 1572 as a star which presaged the demise of Charles IX.[120] Anti-Catholic epigrams also circulated in English from Beza's collection, such as the one on Julius III at the table, which detailed the behaviour of the Pope's bladder and lower colon.[121]

The most popular epigram of all was printed in 1588 with translations into seven languages. This was a celebration of England's victory over the Spanish Armada. It was reprinted with a new translation after the preface to Beza's Job expounded (1589?) and was included in Hakluyt's Voyages as well as Speed's Historie of Great Britaine (1611). It tells about Philip aflame with "Pride, and never quencht desire,/To spoile that Islands wealth, by Peace made great..." How "well have winds his proud blasts overblowen."[122]

A recent study of Oxford Protestant reformers finds Beza in vogue at that other university during Elizabethan times. Wills and inventories of book bequests show more Zurich and Heidelberg imprints than Geneva until the 1580's. Thomas Morrey of Christ Church owned a fine selection of Beza.[123] Edward Higgins, fellow of Brasenose, owned Beza's annotations along with other Beza volumes. New College received Beza's tracts in 1593 and there is a substantial list in the 1617 bequest of Arthur Lake, Bishop of Bath and Wells. William Mitchell of Queens had many volumes by Beza at his death in 1599.

At the local level, John Brinsley who was a 1588 M.A. of Christ's College, Cambridge, included Beza in his puritan school at Ashby. His popular system of education based itself on Sturm of Strasbourg, Erasmus and Melanchthon. Brinsley asked his students to spend fifteen minutes each evening on Eusebius Paget's history of the Bible.

> Brinsley recommended the Biblical translations of both Erasmus and (especially) Theodore Beza, who was both more 'religiously' correct and who 'more fully [expressed] the sense and drift of the Holy Ghost.'124

C. Beza/Tomson Notes

Not only did Tomson serve as secretary to Francis Walsingham, but he dedicated his 1576 translation of Beza's notes and summaries to Francis Hastings as well as Walsingham.[125] The notes are theological at several points. It will suffice to explore those at John (14), Romans (8), Romans (9), I Corinthians (11), Ephesians (3) and Revelation (13).

The focus of John (14:6-7) that Christ is the true and living way to God finds support in the note:

> This saying showeth vnto us both the nature, the will and office of Christ.
>
> It is plaine by this place, that to know God and to see God, is all one: Now whereas he sayd before, that no man sawe God at any time, that is to be understood thus, without Christ, or merit not through Christ, no man could ever see nor God at any time: For as Chrysostom said the Sonne is a very short and easie setting forth of the fathers nature to us.126

Romans (8) adds to this focus on Christ the benefits which accrue to the believer known as sanctification. Here Beza strikes the same cord as in his letter of March 8, 1555 to Peter Martyr Vermigli on union with Christ. The Spirit of Christ provides life even though one's body is mortal.

> You have the selfe same Spirit which Christ hath: Therefore at length it shall doe the same in you, that it did in Christ, to wit, when all infirmities being vtterly laide aside, and death ouercome, it shall cloth you with heavenly glory.

Beza closes chapter eight of Romans with a confession of hope in the living Christ. "What can there be so waightie in this life," he asks, "or of so great force and power, that might feare us...?" Beza concludes that nothing can do this since God's love in Christ is confirmed in us "by steadfast faith."

Notes to Romans (9-11) introduce the reader to Beza's views on predestination. Recent studies have shown that Beza is faithful to Calvin's theological concern, that the scholasticism which the later Reformed tradition incorporates in its theological statements is not Bezan in origin and that the standard biography fails to chart the intellectual currents in Beza's career. In addition to all of these, Kickel's study misrepresents Beza's mental horizons.[127]

Beza treated predestination in his _Tabula Praedestinationis_ (1555), _Confessio Christianae fidei_ (1556), _Questionum & responsionum christianarum libellus_ (1570), _Catechismus compendarius_ (1572), _Latera brevis fidei Confessio_ and the _De Praedestinationis doctrina_ with its exegesis of Romans (9).[128] The Catechism introduces the _syllogismus practicus_ as the primary ground of assurance. Though here Beza departs from Calvin's devotional doctrine of assurance, he does not indulge in either metaphysical speculation or rationalization based on a doctrine of the decrees. Even this departure is absent from the _Tabula_. Beza has this moral theory of experience which the English Puritans pick up, and it is to be distinguished from seventeenth century metaphysical speculation.[129] Beza cautioned his readers that though God's glory is necessarily achieved, it is so freely and spontaneously. No one is coerced into sin. "You must remember," Beza wrote in the _Quaestionum et Responsionum_, "that Coercion differs from Necessity since many things are simultaneously necessary and voluntary, as you must agree, was the death of Christ. But nothing can be both coerced and voluntary..."[130]

All of the above nuances about Beza as a scholastic Protestant are helpful when one approaches his notes on Romans (9) in the Tomson translation. Beza commences with a comment on Romans (9:6): All are not Israel which are of Israel. God's word is true even though Israel be cast off. God's election of Israel is so common and general that its efficacy pertaineth only to the elect whom he chooses by his "secret councel." At verse eleven, on the Pauline assertion that God's purpose is according to election that he loved Jacob and hated Esau, Beza concludes that "they are deceued which make foreseen faith the cause of election, and foreknowen infirmitie the cause of reprobation."

Beza moves on to the benefits of election in his comments on verse twenty-four: "Euen vs whom he hath called, not of the Iewes onely, but also of the Gentiles." The use of eternal predestination is for the reprobate, which is lenient in permitting them "to enjoy many and singular benefits untill at length he iustly coondemne them," and for the elect, to whom is demonstrated his great mercy by degrees of calling, faith, justification, sanctification and glorification. "We aught not to seeke, the testimonie of it in the secret counsel of God," Beza writes," but by the vocation which is made manifest and set foorth in the Church, propounding vnto vs, the example of the Iewes and Gentiles, that the doctrine may be better perceived." So then Beza concludes that the declaration of our election is our calling apprehended by faith, while the pride of men is the cause of their damnation which "needs not to be sought for any other where but in themselues."[131]

Beza puts the matter of election another way in his comments on Ephesians (2:4): "But God which is rich in mercy, through his great loue wherewith he loued vs..." Here he uses Aristotelian categories of causation to explain the function of God's mercy in Christ, to wit, "that the efficient cause of this benefit is the free mercie of God: and Christ himselfe is the materiall cause: and faith is the instrument, which also is the free gift of God: and the end is Gods glory." Beza omits the first cause, deliberately one thinks, thereby stressing the benefits of mercy as the assurance of the believer. The categories may be Aristotelian, but the assumptions are not pagan but are Christian. The concern is pastoral and not purely philosophical at this point in the notes on the text of Ephesians (2).

Richard Hooker noted Beza's significance for his Puritan opponents when they challenged Book V of Hooker's Laws of Ecclesiastical Polity. In 1599 A Christian Letter of Certaine English

Protestants protested that Hooker set up reason over against scripture and reading against preaching.[132] "Will you bring us to Atheisme, or to Poperie" they asked, "or to prepare a plott for an Interim, that our streets may runne with blood, when all religions shal bee tollerated?"[133] Hooker's response was only sketched out in marginal comments of his copy of A Christian Letter now in the Bodleian and in Trinity College Dublin MS. 364. There Hooker draws a comparison between the "Stiffe nature" of Calvin and Beza whom he thought more pliable. Hooker underscores Beza's influence on the English Church when he writes this note, "Remember to make a comparison betweene Calvin and Beza."[134]

Almasy sees Hooker's appeal to rationality as more polemical than his modern editor W. Speed Hill allows.[135] The response to Thomas Cartwright on this score makes up for the deficiency in Archbishop Whitgift's appeal to learned continental interpreters which resulted in one set of exegetical citations from these authorities matched against another.[136]

D. Junius on Revelation (1592)

Franciscus Junius (1545-1602) studied oriental languages and theology at the Genevan academy (1562-65). Serving for a short time as a reformed minister in Antwerp (1565-7) he fled from the Netherlands to the Palatinate where he pastored the French speaking congregation of Schonau (1567-73). Junius then joined Immanuel Tremellius at Heidelberg to assist in the Latin translation of the Old Testament (1575-79). From 1578 to 1584 he held a chair of Theology at Neustadt where he taught Hebrew and Old Testament exegesis, interrupted by a stint back in the parish ministry. In 1584 Junius became a professor at Heideberg, which post he exchanged for the principal chair of theology at Leiden until he died of the plague in 1602.[137]

The 1560 notes to Revelation derive from Bale and Bullinger, while after 1599 some editions take their notes from Junius. John Bale's The Image of bothe churches went through several editions and its framework was incorporated into the 1560 Geneva Bible as well as John Foxe's Actes and Monuments.[138]

Junius' A brief commentary upon the Revelation of St. John appeared in 1592 and was reprinted in 1594, 1596 and 1600.[139] The 1592 edition was eighty-eight pages in octavo which replaced Tomson's text in some versions from 1599.[140] The 1599 date is probably untrue in most cases because it was a date used by Barker for editions published at different times in Amsterdam and Dort. Some copies bear both the 1599 imprint and 1633 by Stam of Amsterdam.[141]

One 1607 edition has a sheet with the title The Order of Time which comes before Revelation. It seems to be unnoticed by modern scholars.

THE ORDER OF TIME

WHERVNTO THE CON-tents of this booke are to be referred.

1, etc. The dragon watcheth the Church of the Iewes, which was ready to trauaile: Shee bringeth foorth, fleeth, and hideth her selfe, whilest Christ was yet vpon the earth.34. The dragon persecuteth Christ ascending into heauen, hee fighteth and is throwen downe: an after persecuteth the Church of Iewes.67. The Church of the Iewes is receiued into the wildernesse, for three yeeres and an halfe.70. When the Church of the Iewes was ouerthrowen, the dragon inuaded the Catholike Church: all this is in the 12 chap.

The dragon is bound for a thousand yeeres, chap. 20.

The dragon raiseth vp the beast with seuen heads, and the beast with two heads, which make hauocke of the Church Catholike and her Prophets for 1260. yeeres after the passion of Christ, chap. 13 and 11.97. The seuen Churches are admonished of things present, somewhat before the end of Domitian his reigne, and are forewarned of the persecution to come under Traiane for tenne yeeres, chap. 2 and 3.

God by word and signes prouoketh the world, and sealeth the godly, chap. 6 and 7.

He sheweth foorth exemplars of his wrath vpon all creatures, mankinde excepted, chap. 8.1073. The dragon is let loose after a thousand yeeres, and Gregory the seuenth, being Pope, rageth against Henry the third, then Emperour, chap. 20.1217. The dragon vexeth the world 150. yeeres vnto Gregory the ninth, who writ the Decretals, and most cruelly persecuted the Emperour Fredericke the second.

> The dragon by both the beasts persecuteth the Church, and putteth the godly to death, chap. 9.1295. The dragon killeth the Prophets after 1260. yeeres, when Boniface the 8. was Pope, who was the author of the sixt booke of the Decretals: hee excommunicated Philip the French King.1300. Boniface celebrateth the Iubile.1301. About this time was a great earthquake, which ouerthrew many houses in Rome.1305. Prophecie ceaseth for three yeeres and a halfe, vntill Benedict the second succeeded after Boniface the 8. Prophecie is reuiued, chap. 11.
>
> The dragon and the two beasts oppvgne Prophecie, chap. 13.
>
> Christ defendeth his Church in word and deede, chap. 14. With threats and armes, chap. 16.
>
> Christ giueth his Church victory ouer the harlot, chap. 17 and 18. Ouer the two beasts, chap. 19. Ouer the dragon, and death, chap. 20.
>
> The Church is fully glorified in heauen with eternall glory, in Christ Iesus, chap. 21 and 22.

At Revelation (12:14) the "time, and times, and halfe a time" for the woman with the wings of a great eagle is calculated from Nero's reign in the first century. The time is three and a half years as in Daniel (7:25).

The note cites Josephus and Hegesippus. In chapter thirteen the ideology is more complex with two parts to describe the meaning of the beast risen from the abyss, the one being Imperial Rome and the other, ecclesiastical Rome or the Papacy. The latter comes under attack in these notes by Francis Junius.The notes claim that the _Decretals_, _Clementines_ and _Extravagants_ are full of papal pretension. Pope Sixtus IV is singled out for having posted a verse on the gates of Rome to celebrate his pageant of entry to his seat of rule. The blasphemous verse reads as follows:

> By oracle of thine owne voyce,the world thou gouernest all, And worthily a God on earth, men thinke and doe thee call.

The infamous number of the beast in Revelation (13:18) calls forth a papal application of the "sixe hundreth three score and sixe." The series of sixes, which are in unities, tens and hundreds, speak of the hierarchical pattern of the papacy. When Boniface VIII commended six books of decretals he marked himself with the number of that beast. Junius does not agree with the common interpretation of this number, prefering his own pattern as described above.

> It seemeth vnto mee neither profitable, nor like to be true, that the number of the beast, or the name of the beast shold be taken as the common sort of interpreters doe take it.

The common interpreters are reflected in the original note to Revelation (13:8) which used the Greek letters of the small number which makes up 666 and signifies lateinas or Latin, i.e., the language of the papal antichrist. This came from Heinrich Bullinger's Latin commentary of 1557 in which the Zurich reformer added 666 years to the reign of Domitian who was Emperor of Rome when the Book of Revelation was written. This placed the reader at the reign of Pepin the Short, King of the Franks, who was annointed in 754 by Pope Stephen II with the title of Roman Patrician. Pepin used the Donation of Constantine to grant lands to the papacy known as the Pentapolis and the Exarchate of Ravenna. Bullinger's commentary was translated into English in 1561, making such an historical application more prominent among the readers of the Geneva Bible.

John Foxe worked out a whole scheme in his Actes and Monuments (1563), using the Lateinas to argue against Nicholas of Lyra that the 666 was not the Turk who established supremacy about A.D. 666, but was the Papacy instead. In Foxe's commentary on the Apocalypse of 1587 he preferred Romanus ("a man of Rome") which would produce the number 666 whether written in Greek or Hebrew.[142] Political (Pepin III), pestilential (Turk) and papal (Boniface VIII) interpretations of Romans (13) circulate among the readers of the two Genevan versions of the Apocalypse in the late 1590s and beyond.

Chapter 9) Catholics and Controversy

A. Rheims New Testament

Religious controversies of the Elizabethan age raged from the first return of the Marian exiles in 1559 to the Hampton Court scene of 1604 where King James vowed to harry the Puritans out of the realm. Whether in the middle of the Tudor period or a year after Astreia's death, polemical exchange was endemic to England. The English Catholic community occupies a central role in such controversy, fueled by another group of exiles who also produced a bible -- this time at Rheims rather than Geneva. The leader of these exiles was William, Cardinal Allen, whose "articles of the catholicke faith"(1567) escalated the rhetorical interchange with the English Protestant community. The English Catholic New Testament symbolises the continuing quarrel over a vernacular bible which since 1408 had been the vehicle of heretical opinion. When the Old Testament came from Douai in 1610, after two centuries the English Bible was available for Catholics as well as Protestants. Lest anyone think that 1610 for the Catholics and 1611 for the Protestants with the new King James Version settled the matter of biblical versions, one needs to be reminded of the heat which the Rheims New Testament created in its four editions from 1582 to 1633.[143]

1. William Allen (1532-1594): Exile and Cardinal

William Allen entered Oriel College, Oxford in his fifteenth year. 1547 was a transition year as Edward VI succeeded his Cathlic father Henry VIII and the Italian Protestant exile Peter Martyr Vermigli entered England in November to be ensconced the following spring at Christ Church, Oxford. Allen took his B.A. in 1550, M.A. in 1554 and became principal of St. Mary's Hall, Oxford in 1556. He was able to reside at Oxford in Elizabeth's reign until his zeal for the catholic faith obliged him to leave England for Louvain in 1561.

Allen paid a secret visit to Lancashire in 1562 with frequent visits to Oxford to make several converts. He eluded the authorities in Lancashire by retiring to Oxford where he composed treatises, found shelter with the Duke of Norfolk when Oxford was unsafe and wrote Certain Brief Reasons concerning Catholic Faith. After a return to Oxford, Allen escaped to the Low Countries in 1565, never to return again to his native England.[144]

When Allen reached the continent, he was ordained a priest and read theology lectures at the Benedictine College at Mechlin. A pilgrimage to Rome in 1567 followed these lectures, after which Allen seized the opportunity to found a college for training English Catholic priests at Douai in 1568. The Seminary lasted ten years until political changes in the Low Countries led to expulsion of the English in March 1578. The college was relocated in Rheims with an annual gift from Philip II of Spain and a papal donation of 500 crowns! Allen became a Cardinal in 1587 as a papal response to his political career in which Allen and Robert Parsons supported Philip's claim to the English crown over against the succession of James VI of Scotland, son of Mary Queen of Scots. Sixtus V created Allen a cardinal to please Philip.[145]

Allen's impact on England began to intensify when Richard Bristow prepared forty-eight items at Douai known as Allen's Articles. These were published in 1574 and restated in 1576.[146] Since William Fulke responded to these as early as 1568, manuscript versions of Allen's Articles seem to be circulating in advance of their publication. Allen was the 'dark beast' for his Protestant respondants,[147] as a 1592 pamphlet demonstrates which calls the Seminary Priests of Rheims "Angelles of darknes."[148]

The English recusants, as these catholic exiles are called, had their own mission to develop as time passed. They had their own martyrs as well, among whom Edmund Campion was legendary. Campion was a brilliant scholar among the more than one hundred senior members of Oxford who became academic emigrees in the first decade of Elizabeth's reign. Gregory Martin and Robert Parsons along with Campion were the most distinguished of this group. Campion left Oxford in 1569, went to Douai in 1571 and became a Jesuit at Rome in 1573. Campion was chosen for the English Mission, arriving in England in June of 1580. He was caught in July, 1581, examined before the Queen, tortured and executed in December of 1581. The Catholic community regarded Campion as a martyr while the Elizabethan government viewed him as a traitor. One of Campion's writings published in 1581 began with a discussion of the Bible in its presentation of ten topics (Rationes Decem).[149]

William Allen entered the fray which the Queen's chief minister, William Cecil, Lord Burleigh created with his 1583 tract, The Execution of Justice in England. Cecil defended the government's action against "certain stirreres of sedition." This 1584 True Sincere and Modest Defence of English Catholiques is a classic defense of justice, which Allen defined as a prince and prelate moving against heretics. Persecution, he adds, is when prince or people rebel against their bishops. This struggle over the obedience of the faithful lies behind the Rheims New Testament and its printed apparatus.[150] Protestant apologists now enter the fray with several tracts on the marks of a true church. Among the French Protestant material which they found useful was a speech which Theodore Beza made at Poissy. This 1581 Briefe collection of the Church is a translation and adaptation which Thomas Sampson made of Beza's 1561 address to the Catholics.[151]

Cecil's Execution of Justice was published on December 17, 1583 and a revised edition appeared in January 1584. Cecil begins with a reference to the Rising in the North in 1569 and the Irish invasion of a decade later. The Northern Earls of Westmorland and Northumberland consulted with a secret papal agent even as a papal bull declared Elizabeth to be excommunicate and absolved all English subjects from their allegiance to her. Cecil draws a connection between these bloody revolts and the Mission to England. Dr. Allen quickly countered this charge of treason in his True, Sincere, and Modest Defense of English

Catholics, one of whose first copies was smuggled into England and went to Mary, Queen of Scots, then under house arrest.[152]

Allen argues for the right to depose Elizabeth, supporting his contention from Scripture, canon law, ecclesiastical history, St. Thomas Aquinas and, wonder of wonders, from Protestant theologians including Calvin, John Knox and Beza. The latter argument had a double-edge to its point that every Christian society has a right to resist secular authority, and that English Protestants were not always loyal and obedient subjects.[153] Allen presented a 1585 memorial to Pope Sixtus V which reported that almost three hundred priests were ready in England amongst the nobility "who will direct consciences and actions of the Catholics in this affair when the time comes."[154] The Douai seminary, Campion and Parsons' mission to England, the Papal bull Regnans in excelsis and the True Defense create the setting for the controversial Rheims New Testament of 1582. That volume contained a history of the early church in which Peter and John face down the magistrates. The marginal comment applied Acts (4:19) to the lives of English Catholic readers: "Whether it be right in the sight of God, to obey you rather than God, iudge ye."[155]

> Marke their countenance and courage after their confirmation, being so weake before. And if any magistrate command against God, that is to say, forbid Catholike Christian men to preach or serve God this same must be their answer; though they be whipped and killed for their labour.156

Peter Holmes points to Robert Parsons' A Conference about the next succession to the crown of England (1594) as a significant English Catholic tract on political resistance. The coronation oath becomes a political contract which when broken by not ruling justly "according to law, conscience, equity and religion" gave people the right to withdraw the power they had bestwed on the king. Parsons writes:

> "which oath and promise being not observed, they [kings] break with God and their people; and their people may and, by order of Christ's supreme minister, their chief pastor in earth, must needs break with them.157

In all fairness to the context of Allen and Parsons' pro-Spanish policy, a group of English Catholic Appellants attacked these Catholic resistance arguments from 1595. William Watson in particular at Rome quoted as an inducement to non-resistance the words of Pierre Grégoire, that these are "new smattering divines... who in their pulpits and lectures cast out not words of modesty or of the word of God, but lightnings and thunderings-..."[158] Watson objected to political resistance by English Catholic clergy. One can agree with Holmes that the Catholic period of resistance ended with Parsons' Memorial of the Reformation of England (1596), yet the ideological slant of the Rheims New Testament intensified between the first edition of 1582 and the second of 1600, pouring more oil than water on the flames of Catholic resistance to Bezan exegesis.

2. New Testament (1582)

Thomas Harding and Nicolas Sander wrote to Cardinal Morone on June 11, 1568 to suggest a Catholic translation from the Vulgate to counter various Protestant versions in English.[159] Dr. William Allen set Gregory Martin to the task some ten years later. In a letter of 16 September 1568 Allen writes:

> We (i.e. the students of Douay College) preach in English, in order to acquire greater power and grace in the use of the vulgar tongue, a thing on which the heretics plume themselves exceedingly, and by which they do great injury to the simple folk. In this respect the heretics, however ignorant they may be in othyer points, have the advantage over many of the more learned catholics, who having been educated in the universities and the schools do not commonly have at command the text of scripture or quote it except in Latin. Hence when they are preaching to the unlearned, and are obliged on the spur of the moment to translate some passage which they have quoted into the vulgar tongue, they often do it inaccurately and with unpleasant hesitation, because either there is no English version of the words or it does not then and there occur to them. Our adversaries on the other hand have at their fingers' ends all those passages of Scripture which seem to make for them, and by a certain deceptive adaptation and alteration of the sacred words produce the effect of appearing to say nothing but what comes from the bible. This evil might be remedied if we too had some catholic version of the

bible, for all the English versions are most corrupt.160

In the storm which followed the release of Martin's translation in 1582 with Bristow's notes, more often than not it was Beza's version which was in view. John Keltridge preached sermons in the Tower which makes this explicit. The sermons were preached on May 7 and 21, 1581. The "Bezites" teach that white shall be black and chalk shall be cheese: "and al this their euident false translation, must be to our miserable deceiued poore soules, the holy Scripture and Gods word."[161] William Rainolds reinforced the Bezan complaint in his refutation of Whitaker published at Paris in 1583.

> ... must therefore Christ be sett to schole to learne his lesson of that firebrande of sedition, that sinke & gulfe of iniquitie Theodore Beza? and what is the absurditie you find in these words? mary that that which was in the chalice was shedde for our sinnes, and therefore consequently, it was the real bloud of our Sauiour, which is plaine Papistrye and against our commuinion booke. Is it so? Then to hell with your Communion booke, and you to, if that be so opposite to the Gospel of Christ, & you dare mainteyne it by open checking and controling Christ the eternall wisdome of God.162

Gregory Martin (d. 1582), was admitted to St. John's College, Oxford in 1557 where he took the B.A. in 1561 and The M.A. on February 19, 1565 with Edmund Campion. Afterwards he entered the household of Thomas Howard, fourth duke of Norfolk as tutor to the future Earl of Arundel and his brothers. After the duke was committed to the Tower, Martin escaped to the English College at Douai where Dr. Allen welcomed him. Martin became a priest in 1573, took a divinity title in 1575 and taught Hebrew. In 1578, after a brief stay at Rome, Martin transferred with the others to Rheims. He devoted his remaining years to the translation of the English Catholic Bible.[163]

Richard Bristow (1538-1581) was born at Worcester and matriculated at Oxford (Exeter College?) where he took the B.A. on April 17, 1559 and M.A. at Christ Church on June 25, 1562. He and Campion entertained the Queen with a public disputation at Oxford on September 3, 1566. Bristow was admitted to a fellowship at Exeter college on July 2, 1567. In 1569 the brilliant Bristow left Oxford for Louvain as a recognition that he had erred in his religious adherence while in attendance at Elizabethan Oxford. Dr. Allen at once appointed Bristow to be the first director of studies at Douai, placing the Rheims exodus under his care in the new location after 1578. Bristow and Allen revised Martin's English New Testament for which Bristow prepared the notes.[164]

John Fogny published the Rheims New Testament in 1582 which Martin had translated from October 1578 to March of 1582. It is a handsome quarto of 400 sheets with fifteen used for preliminaries. The Annotations are placed at the end of each chapter with shorter notes in the outside margin and references on the inside margin. Contents precede each chapter with arguments before most of the twenty-seven books. The Explication at the end lists many words now familiar to modern readers, terms such as advent, evangelize and resuscitate.[165] Dr. Allen seems to have had copy in hand when he wrote to George Gilbert from Rheims on January 15, 1582 that the Testament which they thought might not exceed 1000 scudi will cost 500 scudi. However, Allen suggests, it will be necessary to print Martin's book "on the corruptions and falsifications of the heretics on the Bible..."[166]

The Preface makes several pointed remarks about Protestant translations, singling out for example Theodore Beza's addition to the Greek text of Acts (1:14). The text should read "with the women" but Beza puts it "with their wives."[167] The Preface complains about the invention of printing, which after thirteen decades was the ultimate exercise in futility.

> yet we must not imagin... that the translated Bibles into the vulgar tonges, were in the handes of euery husband man, artificer, prentice, boies, girles, mistresse, maide, man: that they were for table talke, for alebenches, for boates and barges, and for euery prophane person and companie. No, in those better times men were neither so ill, nor so curious of them selues, so to abuse the blessed booke of Christ: neither was there any such easy meanes before printing was invented, to disperse the copies into the handes of euery man as now there is...

> Then the scholar taught not his maister, the sheepe controuled not the Pastor, the yong student set not the Doctor to schoole...168

Four selected chapter annotations demonstrate the polemical purpose of the translation which would be unnecessary in more obedient times when printed bibles were not in general circulation. The first annotation comments on the phrase "Life euerlasting" in John (17:3).

> Both the life of glorie in heauen, and of grace here in the Church, consisteth in the knowledge of God: that, in perfect vision: this, in faith Working by charitie. For, knowledge of God without keeping his commaundments, is not true knowledge, that is to say, it is an unprofitable knowledge.169

The second note is a complaint about the Protestant view of "only faith" at Romans (3:28): "By faith, without workes."

> This is the place where vpon the Protestants gather falsely their only faith, and which they commonly auouch, as though the Apostle said, that only faith doth iustifie. Where he both in wordes and meaning exepteth only the works of the Law done without Christ before our conuersion.170

The third example is taken from I Corinthians (4:4) where St. Paul speaks about the certainty of salvation which comes not from a clear conscience but from God's judgement. Bristow could not restrain himself at this point in the Pauline discourse. The phrase reads, "But not iustified."

> The Heretikes are certaine that they be in Gods grace, but S. Paul though guiltie of no crime in his conscience, durst not assure him self that he was iustified, neither could take vpon him to be iudge of his owne hart and cogitations, whether they were pure or no: but the trial therof he left onely to Gods iudging day.171

The fourth annotation is the final comment on the text at Revelation (22:20): "Come Lord Iesus."

> And now O Lord Christ, most iust and merciful we thy poore creatures that are so afflicted for confession and defense of the holy, Catholike, and Apostolike truth, conteined in this thy sacred booke, and in the infallible doctrine of thy deere spouse our mother the Church, we crie also vnto thy Maiestie with tendernesse

> of our hartes vnspeakable, COME LORD IESUS QUICKLY, and iudge betwixt vs and our Aduersaries, and in the meane time giue patience, comfort, and constancie to al that suffer for thy name, and trust in thee. O Lord God our onely helper and protector, tarie not long. Amen.[172]

B. Circulation and Controversy

A second edition of the Rheims New Testament came from the Antwerp press of Daniel Vervliet in 1600. A notable addition is a Table of Heretical Corruptions summarized from Martin's Discouerie (1582). The longer title reveals the polemical intent of this insertion made by Richard Gibbons a Jesuit.[173] It reads, "A table of certaine places of the New Testament corruptly translated in favour of heresies of these dayes in the English Editions: especially of the yeares 1562, 77, 79 and 80..."[174]

The charge is that the Protestants under the pretense of translation directly from the Greek text have instead corrupted it. I Peter (1:25) becomes an example where they add to the word "evangelized" the qualification "by the Gospel is preached." That addition introduces the heresy "that there is no other word of God, but the written word only."[175] The fresh notes to II Thessalonians (2:3) call Protestants and Calvinists "near forerunners of Antichrist" and inserts a six page discussion of the term Antichrist. The note charges Protestants with confusion, since Calvin

> And his fellowes and followers Illyricus and Beza, and the rest are... so contrarie to him, that it is horrible to see their confusion, and a pitieful case that any reasonable man will follow such companians to evident perdition.[176]

That would remind the reader that William Fulke responded to Martin in his own Defense of the Sincere and true translations of the holie scriptures into the English tong (1583), which was reprinted twice in 1611, in 1617 and again in 1633. In 1589 Fulke edited the Rheims New Testament in parallel columns with the Bishops Bible (1568). He then appended the notes interspersed with his own objections.

One interesting exchange occurred at Matthew (3:2), where Erasmus had earlier altered the Vulgate text away from "do penance." Martin had preserved the literal Vulgate, rendering verse two, "And saying, Doe penance: for the kingdom of heaven is at heand." Fulke opposed this with the Bishops' Bible text, "And saying Repent ye: for the kingdom of heaven is at hand."[177] Martin, in the Rheims' note on Matthew (3:2) stated in part,

> So is the Latine, word for word so readeth all antiquitie, namely S. Cyprian ep.52. often, and S. Augustine li 13. Confes.C.12. and it is a uery vsuall speach in the New Testament, specially in the preaching of S. Iohn Baptist,* Christ him selfe, and * the Apostles: to signifie perfect repentance, which hath not onely confession and amendment, but contrition or sorow for the offence, and painefull satisfaction:...178

Since the 1582 text was reprinted in 1600, 1621, and 1633 as well as reproduced in Fulke's Confutation of 1589, 1617 and 1633, one can see the wide dissemination of these notes. Fulke answered the above charge that 'penance' was to be preferred over 'repent' in the English text of Matthew (3:2).

> And Beza doth iustly mislike your translation because in shewe of wordes... it fauoreth that blasphemous doctrine of satisfaction for sinne vnto the righteousnes of God, which was throughly performed by the sacrifice of Christes death.179

The mention of Beza seemed to animate Fulke's response as in his retort to Martin's charge that the heretics correct themselves in their translations. Martin said:

> the Puritans controll the grosser Caluinists of our Country... of wilfull falsification, as it is notorious in the latter editions of Luther and Beza, and in our English Bibles, set forth... from Tindall their first Translator vntill this day: yea (which is more) the English Translators of Bezaes new Testament, controll him and his translation which they protest to follow, being afraid sometime and ashamed to express in English his false translations in the Latine.180

Fulke answered that the beasts to whom Ambrose ascribed the art of making syllogisms would not reach such a brutish conclusion that the differences in translation are a willful and deliberate distortion of biblical doctrine. He then cites Augustine to the effect that the multitude of translations in all their diversity is for the benefit of the ignorant and learned alike.[181] More extended controversy came from the pens of Thomas Cartwright, John Reynolds, William Whitaker, Thomas Bilson, George Wither and Edward Bulkeley.[182]

John Howson's reaction to the Geneva notes in 1612 provides a case study in controversy. As a canon of Christ Church, Oxford he objected to their misinterpretation of the divinity of Christ. For this Howson was suspended by the pro-vice chancellor, Dr. Robert Abbot, later bishop of Salisbury (1615) and elder brother of George Abbot, Archbishop of Canterbury. Howson had himself suspended Henry Airy from preaching for a term in January of 1603.[183]

In June 1615 Howson appeared before James I at Greenwich charged by Archbishop Abbot with creating factions. Howson's account survives in the State Papers.

> In the meane tyme I said I would tell him what I could remember, & beginning wth a reproofe of his for a sermo preached XXty yeares before att an Act in Oxon, wherein I taxed the Geneva Noats for calling Archb, Bps Drs & C the Locust of the Bottomless Pitt & C. He asked the Kinge if hee thought not that I was madd. I answeared, that I confessed indeed that I did lacke sleepe; for hearing of his violent threatenings ... upon whose favour or displeasure depended my very life or death.184

The Westminster Annotations of 1645 recall Howson's sermon of 1612 in which he charged that the Genevan notes were unsound. Sir Thomas Bodley, famous founder of the public library, defended Howson and Laud against such slanders.

Even though Bodley's sermon/tract has not survived, a letter to Thomas James is extant which confirms the account in the Annotations. Bodley wrote as follows:

> You shall do me a special pleasure to let me know from you the particularities... with Dr. Howson: when he is appointed to answer, and before whom, and who they are that have censured his sermon... For I repute it a mater much importing the honour and credit of the University: and to say the truth, the whole church of this realm that he should be censured severely...185

James I in 1604 attacked the politics of those Genevan notes where they urged execution of the Queen in Asa's day (II Chronicles 15:16) for after all Elizabeth had seen to the demise of his own mother Mary, Queen of Scots. The Genevan note to II Chronicles 15:16 reads as follows:

> & herein he shewed yt he lacked zeale: for she oght to have dyed bothe by the covenant, and by the Lawe of God: but he gave place to foolish pitie, & wolde also seme after a sorte to satidfie the Lawe.186

It is clear that controversy marked the circulation of the translations prepared by the two English exiled communities, the Marian Exiles who produced the Geneva Bible and the English Recusants who responded with the Rheims New Testament some two decades later.[187] One must comment on the significance of that interchange which found both translations encumbered with theological notes. One conclusion is surely that neither party trusted the bare text to circulate among those for whom it was intended -- English readers who saw either Papist or Puritan as the Antichrist of Revelation (13) or for whom Beza or Bristow were the beast slipping out of the abyss. Both parties were decades away from understanding St. Paul's concern as expressed in Ephesians (4:15): "Let us follow the truth in love." It was not yet time to listen to Tyndale's lyric of enemy love, that "Christ is the reason why I love thee."

END NOTES to SECTION III

[1]Charles C. Butterworth, The English Primers (1529-1545) (Philadelphia: Univ. of Pennsylvania Press, 1953), p.257.

[2]Ibid., p.261.

[3]Charles C. Butterworth, The Literary Lineage of the King James Bible, 1340-1611 (Philadelphia: Univ. of Pennsylvania Press, 1941), p.103.

[4]Butterworth, English Primers, p.133., i.e. Martin Bucer.

[5]Ibid., pp.140-161.

[6]Ibid., p.161.

[7]Herbert, Historical Catalogue, pp.36-60, nos.66-105.

[8]John Strype, Ecclesiastical Memorials (London: Samuel Bagster, MDCCCXVI) IV: 279.

[9]On this practice in Edwardian days see James E. Oxley, The Reformation in Essex to the Death of Mary (Manchester: Manchester Univ. Press, 1965).

[10]Strype, op.cit., IV: 280. See S.T.C.2 23207-23208.

[11]Geneva Bible (1560): Hebrews (11:13-16).

[12]Frederick A. Norwood, Strangers and Exiles (Nashville: Abingdon Press, 1969), I: 318.

[13]A Brieff discours/off the troubles begonne at Franckfort in Germany Anno Domini 1554 (MDLXXIIII), pp.XIII-XXVII.

[14]W. Stanford Reid, Trumpeter of God (New York: Charles Scribner's Sons, 1974), pp.76-77.

[15]Peter Lorimer, John Knox and the Church of England (London: Henry S. King & Company, 1875), p.102. Ridley, John Knox, pp.108-109.

[16]Lorimer, op.cit., p.259. Not in Laing, Works.

[17]John Knox, A Faithful Admonition to the Professors of God's Truth in England, Works III: 308-309.

[18]Works III: 201.

[19]Works III: 221-226.

[20]Calvin Opera XV: 90-91.

[21]Hereafter called A Faithful Admonition

[22]Reid, Trumpeter of God, pp.113-114.

[23]Jasper Ridley, John Knox (New York: Oxford Univ. Press, 1968), p.184. See Richard Kyle, "John Knox and the Purification of Religion: the Intellectual Aspects of his Crusade against Idolatry," Archiv für Reformationsgeschichte 77 (1986): 265-80.

[24]Works III: 296-7.

[25]Ridley, John Knox, pp.185-6.

[26]Works III: 294.

[27]Reid, Trumpeter of God, pp.125-127.

[28]Works IV: 389.

[29]Ridley, John Knox, p.268.

[30]Works IV: 415-6.

[31]Quentin Skinner, The Foundations of Modern Political Thought (Cambridge: Cambridge Univ. Press, 1978) I: 211. See critique of Skinner's secularization of this ideology in Carlos M. N. Eire, War Against the Idols (Cambridge: Cambridge Univ. Press, 1986), pp. 304-310.

[32]Works IV: 469.

[33]Ibid., p.497.

[34]Greaves, "John Knox, and the Development of Resistance Theory," offprint from Journal of Modern History 48 (September 1976): 17.

[35]Works IV: 500.

[36]Ibid., p.506.

[37]Greaves, "John Knox and the Covenant Tradition," Journal of Ecclesiastical History 24 (1973): 31.

[38]Greaves, "John Knox, and the Development of Resistance Theory," p.22. (See also Works IV: 500-1).

[39]See Richard L. Greaves, Theology and Revolution in the Scottish Reformation (Grand Rapids: Wm. B. Eerdmans, 1980), pp. 134-156 and Richard Kyle, "John Knox's Interpretation of the Bible: An Important Source of His Intellectual Radicalness," Journal of Religious Studies, forthcoming.

[40]John Knox, The Ap-/pellation of/John Knoxe From/the cruell and most iniust sentence/pronounced against him by the/false

bishoppes and clergie of Scot/land, with his supplication and ex-/hortation to the nobilitie, e-/states, and comunaltie/of the same re-/alme. Printed at GENEVA, MDLVIII. Balliol College, Oxford copy used by permission. Hopkins version replaced Kethe in the metrical psalter.

[41] Works IV: 539-40.

[42] Dan Danner, "Anthony Gilby: Puritan in Exile - A Biographical Approach," Church History 40 (1971), p.418.

[43] Knox, Works V: 461-2.

[44] W. Owen Chadwick, "John Knox and Revolution," Andover Newton Quarterly 15 (1975), p.262. See critique of Sleidan's secularizing of the Reformation in A. G. Dickens, "Johannes Sleidan and Reformation History," Reformation Conformity and Dissent, edited by R. Buick Knox (London: Epworth Press, 1977): 27-43.

[45] A Brieff discours off the troubles begonne at Franckford, pp.XXVIII-XLV.

[46] Ibid., p.XLVI.

[47] "Whittingham, William," Dictionary of National Biography, p.151.

[48] Knox, Works IV: 157-214. William D. Maxwell, The Liturgical Portions of the Genevan Service Book (London: The Faith Press, 1965), pp.85-168.

[49] Works IV: 157-168.

[50] Ibid., p.158.

[51] D.N.B., art.cit., pp.151-152. See further appendix of Peter Lorimer, John Knox in England, for a 1603 life of Whittingham.

[52] Patrick Collinson, "The Authorship of A Brieff Discours off the Troubles Begonne at Franckford," Journal of Ecclesiastical History IX (1958), pp.201-206.

[53] Lorimer, op.cit., appendix.

[54] Lloyd E. Berry, "Introduction to the Facsimile Edition," The Geneva Bible (Madison: Univ. of Wisconsin Press, 1969), pp. 9-10.

[55] Herbert, op.cit., p.61.

[56] The English Hexapla (London: Samuel Bagster and Sons, MDCCCXLI), pp.132-133.

[57] Geddes MacGregor, A Literary History of the Bible (Nashville: Abingdon Press, 1968), p.143.

[58] Examples taken from The English Hexapla (London: Samuel Bagster and Sons, MDCCCXLI).

[59] Dated to 1553 from Gilby's Treatise on Election.

[60] John Knox, Works IV: 555.

[61] Ibid., p.563.

[62] Ibid., p.562.

[63] G. Lloyd Jones, The discovery of Hebrew in Tudor England: A third language (Manchester: Manchester Univ. Press, 1983), p.98.

[64] Ibid., pp.129-130.

[65] Marvin Anderson, Peter Martyr A Reformer In Exile (1542-1562) (Nieuwkoop: B. DeGraaf, 1975), pp.369-70 and 383-394.

[66] Ian McPhee, "Conserver or Transformer of Calvin's Theology? A Study of the Origins and Development of Theodore Beza's Thought, 1550-1570," Cambridge Ph.D. thesis, 1979.

[67] G. J. Burchill, "Gerolamo Zanchi in Strasbourg 1553-1563," Cambridge Ph.D. thesis, 1979.

[68] R. Faerber, "La Communaute anglaise a Strasbourg pendant le regne de Marie (1553-1558)," pp.432ff in Livet and Rapp, Strasbourg au coeur religieux du XVI[e] siecle (1977). Article "Cole, William," Dictionary of National Biography. See Anderson, Reformer in Exile, pp.175-185 and 211-214.

[69] Anthony Gilby, A Pleasant/Dialogue,/betweene A Souldior of Barwicke,/and an Englishe Chaplaine... (1581), sig. A8[v].

[70] Ibid., sigs. N3[r]-N4[r].

[71] A Commen=/tarye upon the/Prophet Mycha. Wrytten by Anto=/ny Gilby. Anno Domi. MDLI. (London: Jhon Daye).

[72] Herbert, op.cit., p.61, no.107.

[73] A. C. Partridge, English Bible Translation (London: Andre Deutsch Limited, 1973), p.86.

[74]A. W. Pollard, Records of the English Bible, pp.284-285.

[75]Herbert, op.cit., p.81 no.141.

[76]Ibid., p.71 no.130.

[77]Martin Luther, A Commen-/tarie of M.Doctor/Martin, Lvther vpon the Epistle/ of S. Paule to the Galatians... (eleven lines) (London: Thomas Vautroullier, 1588), sig. DV[r].

[78]Irena D. Backus, The Reformed Roots of the English New Testament (Pittsburg: Pickwick Press, 1980), pp.14-18.

[79]Ibid., p.24.

[80]A.F. Johnson, "J.F. Stam, Amsterdam, and English Bibles," The Library, Fifth Series 9 (1954), 185-193. Stam printed all six of the Christopher Barker imprints of 1599 (see Herbert, Historical Catalogue nos. 188-94 and 364).

[81]Geneva-Tomson-Junius (1607), ad.loc.

[82]Greek text says, "he (God) giues more grace."

[83]Robert M. Kingdon, "Theodore Beza," New Catholic Encyclopedia (Washington: Catholic Univ. of America, 1967), vol. 2, p.379.

[84]Written for Professor Elton's doctoral seminar at Cambridge Univ. in 1975. Used by permission and updated.

[85]S. Clark, A General Martyrology (London 1677-original 1651) p.19.

[86]P. Collinson, "The Elizabethan Puritans and the Foreign Reformed Churches in London," Proceedings of the Huguenot Society of London, 20 (1958-64) pp.528-555.

[87]Robert Linder, "Pierre Viret and the Sixteenth Century English Protestants," Archiv für Reformationsgeschichte LVIII (1967), pp.151, 152. However, only in terms of the number of books is this data meaningful.

[88]Linder, op.cit., 157ff. He has shown that a similar selection of Viret's works appealed to radicals for their specific content on controversial matters.

[89]The first edition, published in Geneva, does not appear to have survived; no doubt only a limited number of copies were made. It was published in England in (1575) and appeared in "A

Discourse of the most Substancial Points of Divinity..." by S.I. and dedicated to Sir Henry Bromley in 1595.

[90]Stockwood claims that Beza revised the 1555 edition, but in reality Beza only restructured it.

[91]A briefe and pith-/thie summe of the christian faith/made in forme of a confession, with a con=/futation of all suche superstitious/errours, as are contrary/thereunto. Made by/ Theodore de Beza./ (two lines plus device)/ (London: Roland Hall, 1563) [S.T.C.2 2006.7].

[92]Ibid., sig. Mvi^{v}.

[93]Ibid., sig. Mviii^{r-v}. See S.T.C.2 2014: A/DISCOURSE, OF/ the true and visible Markes/of the Catholique/Churche/written by M. Theod. Beza. Vezelius./ (London: Robert Walde-grave: 1582?). Reprinted in 1622 and 1623.

[94]S.T.C., 2041 and 2042. J. Harrison financed the printing of these editions. W. Greg, Some Aspects and Problems of London Publishing Between 1550-1650 (Oxford: Clarendon Press, 1956), p.85.

[95]If we take Bennett's figures of 1250 as the average number of copies (pp.297, 298) per edition then Beza's systematic theologies reached the respectable number of 17,500 copies. Even if they were not all sold, the figure remains high enough to demonstrate his significance.

[96]"An Oration Made by Master Theodore de Beze." Beza's speech on September 9th was published twice, by R. Jugge in London and by R. Lekprewik in Edinburgh. The September 24th and 26th speeches were each published once. Also "Two Very Learned Sermons of M. Beza..." (London: R. Waldegrave for T. Man & T. Gubbins, 1588).

[97]Christian Meditations upon Eight Psalms (London: C. Barker, 1582) A Short Learned and Pithie Treatise of the Plague (London: T. Dawson, 1580) Master Beza's Sermons upon the Three First Chapters of the Canticle of Canticles (Oxford: J. Barnes, 1587) Job Expounded by T. Beza... (London: J. Legatt, 1590) Another translation of "Christian Meditations" was done in 1582

but not published. British Library, Additional Manuscripts, 38170. Also a translation of Beza's French Sermons, Sermons upon the Holy Historie of The Passion and Burial of our Lord Jesus Christ...was prepared for publication in 1597 but for an unknown reason remained in manuscript. British Library, Lansdowne Manuscripts, 395.

[98]All references to the wider circle of foreign divines translated into English have been gathered from a detailed check of all the S.T.C. numbers listed in Julia G. Ebel's "A Numerical Survey of Elizabethan Translations," The Library, 5th Series, 22 (1967) pp.104-127.

[99]Linder, op.cit., pp.163-164.

[100]In 1560 he printed Zwingli (S.T.C. 26135) and Calvin's sermons (S.T.C. 5560) and in 1561 Bullinger's sermons on the Apocalypse (S.T.C. 4061). In 1564 and 1568 he printed Martyr's Commentaries (S.T.C. 24670 and 24672). Altogether he printed three of Calvin's, two of Bullinger's and two of Viret's works. He also published the first edition of Foxe's Book of Martyrs in 1563 as well as Parker's translation of the Psalms in 1560. He received a monopoly from Leicester to print the A.B.C. and Catechisms. See D.N.B. Vol. V. pp.683-685.

[101]Bennett, op.cit., pp.26, 111. They printed eight of Golding's translations.

[102]It was Harrison and Bishop who sought out Arthur Golding to translate Nicholas Hemingsen's exposition of the Gospels: Bennett op.cit., p.26. Twelve editions of Hemingsen's works appear in the S.T.C., all of which reveal contacts with zealous Protestants. Marlorat's eight editions also reflect similar contacts. Now see C.L. Oastler, John Day, the Elizabethan Printer (Oxford: Bodleian Library, 1975), pp.1-28.

[103]A detailed check of Paul G. Morrison's Index of Printers and Booksellers... (Virginia, 1950) for only five years revealed the heavy religous orientation of his publications. Calvin, Viret, Marlorat, Fulke, Jewel, Thomas Sampson and P. De Mornay were all included.

[104] S.T.C. 2014, 2051 and 2053. Apart from his printing of Viret, however, he does not seem to have done much on other foreign divines. A check of Morrison's Index, op.cit. for the years 1578-1581 showed a definite inclination to print religious tracts in the "Calvinist" school.

[105] Katherine S. Van Eerde, "Robert Waldegrave: The Printer as Agent and Link between Sixteenth-Century England and Scotland," Renaissance Quarterly XXXIV (1981), p.44.

[106] Ibid., pp.50-51. See William A. Jackson, "Robert Waldegrave and the Books he Printed or Published in 1603," The Library, Fifth Series, XIII (1983), 225-233. There were fifteen books and broadsides of that year.

[107] Ibid., pp.76-77.

[108] J.D. Wilson, "Richard Schilders and the English Puritans" Transactions of the Bibliographic Society, Vol. XI (1909-11) pp.65-134.

[109] More research would be required to clarify the possible commitments of men like Barker. In 1578 Barker registered a sacramental work by Erastus and Beza, translated by John Shutt. See Arbor, The Registers of the Company of Stationers, Vol. II, p.151. It is listed by the Puritan, Andrew Maunsell, The First Part of the Catalogue of English Printed Bookes (London: 1595) p.94. This book evidently was never printed or it has not survived.

[110] John Perrin, the Protestant refugee from Switzerland, was also prominent. He printed the three editions of The Popes Canons, a work often associated with Beza. It was translated by Thomas Stocker who also translated the very similar work by Viret. The confusion may have resulted from their similar titles and their association with Stocker.

[111] See Louis Thorn Golding, An Elizabethan Puritan (New York: Richard R. Smith, 1937).

[112] The Folger and British Museum Catalogues associate Penry with Beza's Propositions and Principles of Divinity, published in 1591 by Waldegrave in Edinburgh. There was certainly every pos-

sibility for him to have done so since he was in exile during this time. See DNB, Vol. XV, pp.791-795.

[113]See his book, S.T.C. 13774. His translation of Beza's rebuttal of Castellio, published by Newbery and Bynneman in 1578, must have sold quite well. On Bynneman's death in 1583 his will included 61 copies of Beza's treatise. However, this does not include books in his Thames Street printing house, nor indeed any possible transfers of books to other booksellers. See Mark Eccles, "Bynneman's books," The Library, 5th Series, 12 (1957) pp.81-92.

[114]Aires' translation was registered but either was never printed or hasn't survived. See Arbor, Vol. II, p.294.

[115]F.B. Williams, Index of Dedications and Commendatory Verses in English Books (London: Bibliographic Society, 1962), p.23.

[116]M. Claire Cross, The Career of Henry Hastings... Unpublished Ph.D. Thesis, Cambridge Univ. (1959) pp.168ff. Much of this thesis was later published, but this particular chapter is most clearly stated in the thesis.

[117]*Ibid.*, pp.368ff. She lists all the books dedicated to him and his family -- nineteen out of twenty were religious. Rober Fyll (whom she says could have been the Robert Fielde who was a member of Knox's congregation in 1557), Golding, Villerius, Beza himself, Gilby, all dedicated Beza's works to him. Tomson dedicated his revision of the New Testament to Francis Hastings.

[118]Gilby's dedication of Beza's Psalms indicates that they were ideal for the nurture of religion in Huntingdon's household. Henry always had chaplains who without exception were zealous Protestants. Cross, *op.cit.*, p.197.

[119]cf. pp.156-166.

[120]Anne Lake Prescott, "English Writers and Beza's Latin Epigrams: The Uses and Abuses of Poetry," Studies in the Renaissance 21 (1974), p.92.

[121]John Bale, Pageant of Popes (1574), sig. Aa7.

[122]Prescott, *op.cit.*, p.93.

[123]C.M. Dent, Protestant Reformers in Elizabethan Oxford (Oxford: Oxford Univ. Press, 1983), p.97.

[124]Ibid., pp.98-99. John Morgan, Godly Learning (Cambridge: Cambridge Univ. Press, 1986), pp.197-198.

[125]See Claire Cross, The Puritan Earl. The Life of Henry Hastings, Third Earl of Huntingdon 1536-1595 (London: MacMillan, 1966).

[126]Geneva-Tomson-Junius (London: Christopher Barker, 1607), ad.loc. All references which follow are taken from this edition.

[127]Geisendorf, op.cit., omits the intellectual elements while Walter Kickel misinterprets them in his Vernunft und Offenbarung bei Theodore Beza (Neukirchen: Neukirchener Verlag, 1967). More recent narratives which tip the scales another direction are those of Ian McPhee, op.cit., and Tadataka Maruyama, The Ecclesiology of Theodore Beza The Reform of the True Church (Geneve: Librairie Droz, 1978). Quite helpful is the essay by Jill Raitt, "The Person of the Mediator: Calvin's Christology and Beza's Fidelity," Occasional Papers of The American Society for Reformation Research I (1977), 53-80; and her "Beza, Guide for the Faithful Life," Scottish Journal of Theology 39 (1986): 83-107. See Marvin Anderson, "Theodore Beza: Savant or Scholastic?", Theologische Zeitschrift 43 (1987), forthcoming.

[128]Tractationes theologicae (Geneva: 1582) III: 402ff.

[129]Muller, op.cit., pp.197-198.

[130]Q.R. I, 665 translated in Jill Raitt, "Theodore Beza 1519-1605," Shapers of Religious Traditions in Germany, Switzerland, and Poland, 1560-1600, edited by Jill Raitt (New Haven: Yale Univ. Press, 1981), p.95.

[131]Notes 27 and 28 to verses 30-31.

[132]Printed at Middelbourg by R. Schilders, sig. F2^{r}.

[133]John E. Booty, editor, Works of Richard Hooker IV: Lawes Attack and Response (Cambridge: Belknap Press, 1982), p.XLii.

[134]Ibid., p.xxxiii (see also p.55).

[135]R. Almasy, "The purpose of Richard Hooker's polemic," Journal of the History of Ideas XXXIX (1978), p.251.

[136] Ibid., pp.264-265. See also M.R. Sommerville, "Richard Hooker and his Contemporaries on Episcopacy: an Elizabethan Consensus," Journal of Ecclesiastical History 35 (1984), 177-187 and J.K. Luoma, "Restitution or Reformation? Cartwright and Hooker on the Elizabethan Church," Historical Magazine of the Protestant Episcopal Church XLVI (1977), 85-106.

[137] C. De Jonge, "Franciscus Junius (1545-1602) and the English Separatists at Amsterdam," in Derek Baker, editor, Reform and Reformation: England and the Continent C.1500-C.1750 (Oxford: Basil Blackwell, 1979), pp.165-166. See note 1 of Jonge.

[138] Paul Christianson, Reformers and Babylon (Toronto: Univ. of Toronto Press, 1978), pp.40-46.

[139] S.T.C.2 2988-91, 7296-97.

[140] Herbert, Historical Catalogue, p.107 (no.214), p.110 (no.224) and p.115 (no.247). But see his contradictory statement about the 1602 edition on p.121 (no.272).

[141] Ibid., pp.116-117 (no.252).

[142] David Brady, The Contribution of British Writers between 1560 and 1830 to the Interpretation of Revelation 13:16-18 (Tübingen: J.C.B. Mohr, 1983), p.40. See also Peter Lake, "The significance of the Elizabethan identification of the Pope as Antichrist," Journal of Ecclesiastical History 31 (1980):161-178.

[143] Herbert, op.cit., pp.95, 118, 151 and 169 (nos. 117, 258, 382 and 479).

[144] "Allen, William," Dictionary of National Biography I: 314-316. See M. Haile, An Elizabethan Cardinal: William Allen (London: 1914).

[145] Ibid., p.319. See Letters and Memorials of William Cardinal Allen, ed. T. F. Knox (London, 1882).

[146] A.F. Allison and D.M. Rogers, A Catalogue of Catholic Books In English Printed Abroad Or Secretly In England 1558-1640 (London: Wm. Dawson & Sons Ltd., 1968 reprint), p.26 (nos. 146 and 148).

[147] Peter Milward, Religious Controversies of the Elizabethan Age (Lincoln: Univ. of Nebraska Press, 1977), p.41.

[148] S.T.C.2 22185. Prose 1559-1582 (London: Sands & Co., 1950), pp. 519-523.

[149] Allison and Rogers, #192. See #193 for 1632 translation.

[150] Craig R. Thompson, The English Church in the Sixteenth Century (Ithaca: Cornell Univ. press, 1963), p.46.

[151] S.T.C.2 21587.3 (no. 3 of series) and, after .3 & .5.

[152] The Execution of Justice in England By William Cecil and A True, Sincere, and Modest Defense of English Catholics, edited by Robert M. Kingdon (Ithaca: Cornell Univ. Press, 1965), p. xxiii.

[153] Robert M. Kingdon, "William Allen's Use of Protestant Political Argument," From The Renaissance to the Counter Reformation: Essays in Honor of Garrett Mattingley, edited by Charles H. Carter (New York: 1965), pp.164-178. Peter Holmes, Resistance and Compromise (Cambridge: Cambridge Univ. Press, 1982), does not accept Kingdon's contention that Allen used Protestant resistance theory to buttress his own polemic (pp.157-158).

[154] Garret Mattingly, "William Allen and Catholic Propaganda in England," Aspects de la propagande religieuse, edited by E. Droz (Geneve: Librairie Droz, 1957), p.337.

[155] The English Hexapla, ad.loc.

[156] Cited by Thomas H. Clancy, Papist Pamphleteers (Chicago: Loyola Univ. press, 1964), p.141.

[157] Peter Holmes, Resistance and Compromise, p.150.

[158] Ibid., p.197. See now Christopher Haigh, "From Monopoly to Minority: Catholicism in Tudor England," Transactions of the Royal Historical Society, Fifth series 31 (1981).

[159] A.C. Southern, Elizabethan Recusant Prose 1559-1582 (London: Sands & Co. (Publishers) Limited, 1950), p.232.

[160] loc.cit.

[161] John Keltridge, Two Godlie and Learned Sermons (London: (J. Charlewood and) R. Jhones, 1581), sig. G4.

[162] William Rainolds, A Refutation of sundry reprehensions, cauils, and false sleightes..to deface the late English transla-

tion, and Catholike annotations of the New Testament (Paris: for Richard Verstegan?, 1583), sig. P8^{v}.

[163]"Martin, Gregory," *Dictionary of National Biography* XII: 1162.

[164]"Bristow, Richard," *Dictionary of National Biography* II: 1264-1265.

[165]Herbert, *Historical Catalogue*, p.96 (no.177).

[166]Thomas Francis Knox, *Letters and Memorials of William Cardinal Allen* (1532-1594) (London: David Nutt, MDCCCLXXXII), pp.109-110.

[167]The/New Testament/of Iesvs Christ (Rhemes: Iohn Fogny, 1582), sig. fiij^{v}.

[168]*Ibid.*, sigs. Aiij^{r-v}.

[169]*Ibid.*, sig. Llii^{r} (267).

[170]*Ibid.*, sig. Ccciij^{v} (390).

[171]*Ibid.*, sig. Ii^{r} (433).

[172]*Ibid.*, sig. Bbbbbb^{r} (745).

[173]Harry R. Hoppe, "The Copyright-Holder of the Second Edition of the Rheims New Testament (Antwerp, 1600), Richard Gibbons, S.J.," *The Library* Fifth Series 6 (1951), 116-120.

[174]THE/NEW TESTAMENT (Antwerp: Daniel Vervliet, 1600), sig. di^{r}.

[175]*Ibid.*, sig. d.iij^{r}.

[176]*Ibid.*, sig. Aaaiij^{v}.

[177]William Fulke, The/Text of the New/Testament of Jesvs/ Christ, Translated ovt of/the vulgar latine by the Papistes of the traite-/rous Seminarie at Rhemes... (London: Deputies of Christopher Barker, 1589), sig. D5^{r}o.

[178]*Ibid.*, sig. D6^{r}o.

[179]*Ibid.*, sig. D6^{r}o.

[180]Fulke, *Defense* (London: Iohn Bill, 1617), p.156.

[181]*Ad.loc*.

[182]Milward, *op.cit.*, pp.47-50.

[183]Ms. Oxford Univ. Archives, Congregation Book M.f 149^{v}-150^{r}.

[184]Public Record Office, SP 14/80/116. See also the altercation between Hawson and George Abbot going back to the 1590s reported from the same document in Kenneth Fincham and Peter Lake, "The Ecclesiastical Policy of King James I," Journal of British Studies 24 (1985): 194-97.

[185]T. Hearne (ed.), Reliquiae Bodleianae (1707): 297-8, 353-4. Letter of September 12, 1612. Above references provided by Mr. Nicholas W.S. Cranfield, Merton College, Oxford.

[186]Geneva Bible (1560), fol. 197^r.

[187]Thomas Clancy, "Papist-Protestant-Puritan: English Religious Taxonomy 1565-1665," Recusant History 13 (1976): 227-53.

SECTION IV. PURITANS AND PASTORS

In his 1562 Apologie of the Church of England John Jewel used the adverbial form of the term "puritan." This work which was published in nine Latin, four English, two Greek and one Welsh editions by 1639, circulated in some editions with Peter Martyr Vermigli's prefatory letter. Thomas Stapleton attacked the protestant heresy as ancient Donatism, calling the modern form "puritan" in his 1565 A fortresse of the faith: "... to be apparailled priestlike semeth so absurde to the Puritans off our countre, to the zelous gospellers of Geneva that ... they withstand ... their Soverain and Liege princesse ...."[1] In 1574 Thomas Cartwright asserted that English bishops had borrowed the term "puritan" from Catholic writers like Stapleton to discredit the pure pattern of the church defended by others such as John Jewel, bishop of Salisbury.[2] The term "puritan" emerges then from polemical religious writings early in the reign of Elizabeth I with more than one reference to continental reformed theologians such as Bucer, Bullinger and Beza. Neither the presence of the term "puritan" nor its polemical connotation should be ignored in attempts to define its use in the century from Jewel's Apologie to the Great Ejection of 1662.

The first puritans were those English who saw continental models of protestantism during the Marian exile of the 1550s and returned on the accession of Elizabeth. According to one preface of the Geneva Bible (1560), their hopes were placed in her support of two necessary purposes:

> First, that we have a lively and steadfast faith in Christ Jesus, who must dwell in our hearts... as the only means and assurance of our salvation... The next is, that our faith bring forth good fruits, so that our godly conversation may serve us as a witness to confirm our election and be an example to all others...3

If for a time the church lay dormant, covered with ashes, yet again could it be swiftly kindled by the wind of God's Spirit.

Though it seemed "parched and pined in the wilderness, yet God giveth ever good success."[4]

As the decades passed this agenda of faith and godly living animated puritanism in its accommodation with the parish structure of the English Church. Though preachers exchanged one parish for another with augmented stipends and on occasion their auditors conformed to reading of sermons which was not feeding, even so the modus operandi for reform of the church was an increased biblical literacy amongst the English people. The model that molded the puritan society was a continental one negotiated within the Tudor and Stuart structures of society.

A certain ambivalence about use of the term "puritan" pervades recent historical writing. C. M. Dent sees limitations in using the term at all, preferring protestant to puritan to describe Elizabethan men at Oxford and in its several colleges. Dent furnishes a billiant account of these "nurseries" such as Brasenose, Queen's and Exeter colleges who produced "a steady stream of ministers for the remoter parts of the realm."[5]

Peter Lake on the other hand prefers the term "moderate puritan" to describe those whose presence served to attach to that English church those evangelical loyalties which "prompted the whole affair in the first place."[6] By moderate Lake means the negotiated choice between principles animated by a vision of true religion and continuance in the English church of what puritans took to be corrupt elements. Men like Laurence Chaderton, Master of Emmanuel College, raise questions for Lake about a career which combined presbyterian radicalism with university administration. Does the style shift after 1590 over the central issues of conformity and polity? Lake's questions about the style of evangelical protestantism are compelling. Part of the answer lies in Christopher Hill's observation that if the millenium were around the next corner, temporary accommodation could be sustained to a less than perfect parish experience.[7] As the decades unfurled past 1588 and down to 1639, radical exegesis of the Apocalypse by a commentator like John Napier switched attention to the final stages of a cosmic struggle which was a revolution against Babylon.[8]

William Hunt prefers the term "professor" rather than "puritan" or "moderate" to describe those "advanced protestants" who sought commitment to a godly life. Hunt opts for godly preachers who used the sermon as a "code of redemption" to lead future saints from the agony of conscious sin to final assurance of salvation. In so doing, puritan ministers were painful preachers who cut away non-essentials with the Sword of the spirit.

> This exaltation of preaching constituted an audacious bid for social prestige, and implicitly for power, by the preachers themselves... If preaching was essential to salvation, then the "dumb dog" was not merely a parasite. He was, in the words of George Gifford, a "murderer of souls."[9]

This transfer of authority from altar to pulpit is more satisfactory an explanation of the different concerns of evangelicals and parish conservatives than the supposed distinction between moral commandments and ceremonial ones. The central "puritan" document on these matters in its nineteen editions, refuses to express a preference for the first four commandments of the Mosaic law as moral over against the final six as the ceremonial or second table of the law. The godly person in Stuart England would read for example in Dod and Cleaver's <u>Ten Commandements</u> (1614 edition) these cautionary words:

> God spake not the first commandement onely, nor the second or third, and left there: but hee spake them all; and gave as strict a charge to keepe every one, as any one; and no one was vttered by Gods voice, or written with his owne finger more then the other ... whosoever will have any true comfort by his obedience to Gods law, must not content himselfe to look to one, or two: but must make conscience, and have a care to keepe them all and every one. -- sig. $A8^{n-v}$

The power of the pulpit was that over the keys of the kingdom, i.e., the power on earth to forgive and retain sins in heaven.

Patrick Collinson finds in the end that this preaching task, which Hunt labels the 'syntax of redemption,' "exposed the imagination to the invisible word." Material remains of the post-

Reformation church in England are a poor means to measure the vitality of its religion. Collinson contrasts the material with his observation about the invisible means of grace which created a true and lively faith. The godly were chosen to walk in the Way which meant that "the godless behaviour of others was near conclusive evidence of their exclusion from God's mercy."[10] The protestant martyr John Bradford described that style of faith in which lively stones were built on the foundation of the apostles and prophets. Puritans then were not those who tore down but sought rather to rebuild the Elizabethan church on Christ the chief cornerstone. This was accomplished, said Bradford, "by the mason-work of God, hacking and hewing from you by the cross the knobs and crooked corners."[11]

Not all appreciated these godly architects called puritans who would trim their rough edges for them. John Manningham complained about such builders of the kingdom of God that though they loved God they despised their neighbors. His Diary describes the animosity which these godly created with their sermonic code of redemption. "A puritan is such a one as loves God with all his soul, but hates his neighbor with all his heart."[12] Such a parody of Protestant intensity indicates in itself the tensions which the Tudor Church passed on into the seventeenth century.

Social tensions were not always the result of theological opinion as is clear from the concern over use of tobacco. The London port books show that tobacco imports rose from £55,143 in 1620 to £230,840 by 1640, making it the most valuable import on the eve of the Civil War. Earle complained that unlicensed shops were "the rendezvous of spitting, where men dialogue with their noses, and their communication is smoke." Behind that smoke there may have been some fire, for in fact "brothel-keepers displayed tobacco pipes for their signs." A satire of 1614 which went through five editions in two years told that many "for Want of Wit, shall sell their Freehold for Tobaccopipes and red Petticoats."[13]

When one reads puritan literature one sees not only an intensity but also introspection and preoccupation with sin. It is as though the key scriptural text for a Puritan were "What ever is not of faith is of sin" (Romans 14:23) and hence a daily concern about the level of faith. Two writers comment on the specifics of that daily living under the shadow of the Almighty. The first is the Puritan Philip Stubbs who was active from 1581 to 1593. Stubbs wrote a dialogue which excoriated social abuses such as dancing when held on a Sunday, "leapings, skippings, & other unchaste gestures, not a few."[14] The Anatomie of Abuses abhors feminine pride in apparel, the "cousin of pride." Then Stubbs came to interpret cosmetic concerns.

> The Women of Ailgna [Anglia] use to colour their face ... whereby they think their beautie is greatly decored: but who seethe not that their soules are thereby deformed, and they brought deeper into the displeasure and indignation of the Almighty... Thinkest thou that thou canst make thyself fairer than God who made us all?... Therefore this their colouring of their faces importeth ... that they think them selues not faire enough, and then must GOD needs be untrue in his word.15

Not only must a Puritan scrub the soul, but also the face!

On the negative side, Oliver Ormerod sought to prove that the Puritans resembled the Anabaptists in more than four score ways. This 1605 dialogue between an Englishman and a German attacks Thomas Cartwright, Hay any worke, Martin Marprelate and the Admonition to Parliament of 1572.[16] Ormerod discounts Puritan motives as attempts to stir up the people to sedition rather than to reform. His tirade against the Puritan attack on the pulpit is quoted elsewhere in our narrative, but is cited here to underscore the intensity which Collinson reflects in his reference to John Manningham's Diary.

> So do our Sectaries likewise beate the Pulpit, and cry out against Non-residents, & double beneficed men,... that they are Idoll Sheyheards, dumbe Dogges, no ministers, and that they doe fleece, but not feede their flockes.17

Cliffe's impressive study documents the support which the Gentry gave to the Puritan cause in the Stuart period from 133 separate manuscript collections. Brampton Bryan is one such parish which Sir Robert Harley transformed into a godly Puritan living in the remote border county of Herefordshire. Thomas Pierson, close friend of William Perkins at Cambridge, was installed in 1612. Pierson was famous for his "labours in the Ministry of the Gospel."[18] So wide spread was support of the Puritan cause that one wonders who indeed was Anglican before 1630!

As Professor Collinson has well said in his recent comment on puritanism, Frere's 1904 study presented puritanism as a minority mouvement within the mainstream of an Anglican majority, while in the 1980s the taxonomy in vogue establishes a Puritan majority in religious society if not society at large throughout the Elizabethan and Stuart period.[19] Collinson calls this a moral majority view which should have the courage to discard "Anglican" as the greatest anachronism of them all. The "Ecclesia Anglicana was conscious of a solidarity with the whole body of the Reformed Church in Europe which was not compromised by a sense of national identity."

Thomas Cartwright in 1583 advised the young Arthur Hildersham to study the Bible daily. So far as commentaries went, he should concentrate on Calvin, Oecolampadius and Peter Martyr, read Calvin's _Institutes_ and Beza's _Confession_. Cartwright ended a list of Latin and Greek doctors such as Tertullian and Gregory Nazianzus with Luther, Bucer and Calvin. Collinson comments apropos of such lists that the continental stream had many rivulets, whether it be Zurich, Strasbourg, Basle or Geneva.

> But at the same time, the student who has only heard of 'Calvinism' must learn that English theologians were as likely to lean on Bullinger of Zürich, Musculus of Berne, or Peter Martyr as on Calvin or Beza, while they accorded a higher measure of authority to Ambrose, Athanasius, Augustine, Chrysostom, and Cyprian, for the apologetics of the Church of England (and not only the English Church) always rested on a patristic foundation. Such names were the missile weaponry of Elizabethan

> divinity, so much of which was polemical. But if we were to identify one author and one book which represented the centre of theological gravity of the Elizabethan Church it would not be Calvin's Institutes but the Common Places of Peter Martyr, described by his translator, Anthony Marten, as 'a verie Apostle'.20

Popular puritan mentality lies somewhere beneath the sea of sermonic literature and beyond the mountain ranges of theological tomes, whether biblical commentary or codes of conduct in scholastic format.[21] Nicholas Tyacke penetrates that mentality by using puritan baptismal names. The county of Sussex in particular used 'scriptural phrases, pious ejaculations, or godly admonitions' in the 1580s and 1590s. Eighteen east Sussex parishes in particular introduce these puritan baptismal names, the greatest concentration being in the parish at Warbleton.[22]

Dudley Fenner, curate at Cranbrook in Kent, seems to have been the chief national begatter of this practice which commenced in the 1580s. In December 1583 he named his daughter More-fruit and named the son of Thomas Hendley, esquire, From-above Hendley.[23] Fenner argued that "the father's duty is... to present the child for the first sacrament, and there to give a name in the mother tongue, which may have some godly signification..."[24] Tyacke sees the significance of this practice as akin to monastic entrants taking a saint's name as a sign of their new vocation. Hence a puritan separates and dedicates the new born child as the spouse of God. In east Sussex such names emerge as Comfort, Safety, Sure-hope, Hope-still, Fear-not, Good-gift, Deliverance, and Fear-God. Comfort would come from the Elizabethan Prayer Book which defines the third cause for which marriage was ordained as "the mutual society, help and comfort that the one ought to have for the other."[25] These names accentuate the ethos of the puritan movement which divided both family and community. As a symbol of their discovery of the Bible and as a code of public and private behaviour, such a baptismal practice helps one to understand the bravado if not braggadocio implicit among those who spoke God's will for the entire English Commonwealth. These names assist one to enter the world of a puritan counter-culture in late Elizabethan and Stuart England.[26]

Puritanism emerges as a description of that protestant intensity as early as 1562. Its doctrinal basis is taken from the Bibles of Tyndale, Coverdale and Geneva, whose scope of interpretation lead to a fresh obedience of faith. As Professor Collinson has noted, these "hotter sort of Protestants"[27] are those whom John Foxe depicts on the engraved title-page of his Actes and Monuments, sitting under the preacher with Bibles open on their laps.[28] Their ecclesiology, whether episcopal, presbyterian or congregational is derived from their voluminous commentaries and common-place books and finds its characteristic expression in their desire to hear and preach biblical sermons in the plain style. To be a Puritan meant among other considerations the desire to hear biblical preaching at the parish level. As Bindoff has well said, "there could not be an English Geneva, there could only be a Genevan England."[29]

Chapter 10) Mitres and Ministry

William Bradshaw (1571-1618), who entered Emmanuel College, Cambridge in 1589, confirms the puritan priority of preaching in his English Puritanisme. Chapter three of this work defines true ministers of the Word.

> And they cannot be persuaded that the faculty of reading in ons Mother tongue the scriptures etc. which any ordinary Turke or Infidell hath, can be called in any congruity of speech a ministeriall gift of Christ.30

Two recent studies underline that support which lay puritans gave to this conviction that preaching is a necessary mark of the ministry. Rosemary O'Day finds that though patronage was often blocked by the system, that fraction of livings in the hands of active puritans was vital to the movement.[31] The more recent account by J.T. Cliffe underlines the sermonic function expected by the Puritan gentry. Women were often most zealous in recording sermons and reviewing their contents, as Cliffe finds true about Lady Anne Waller, who was a "constant Writer of Sermons and wrote them in her Heart as well as in her book." Her life was thus an "exact commentary on the sermons which she heard."[32] Thomas Tymme wrote his Silver Watch-bell on just that theme, a work which went through eighteen editions between 1605 and 1640. "Many deal with God's word," wrote Tymme, "like the butterfly with the sweet flowers, who dyes its wings with them that they may seem to be of a fair painted cullor. Thes thinke yt holines consisteth in often, & much hearing, how little soeuer they practice."[33]

After a survey of puritan pastoral activity in this chapter, our next task will be to penetrate the theological thickets of puritan scriptural commentaries, which few have hazarded to explore, and to examine sermons on the plague which demonstrate a commonality of exhortation by the clergy at several levels in time of regional catastrophe. The reader will find that those commentaries and plague sermons document concerns held at several levels of a common religious culture between 1560 and 1640.

A. Episcopal Appointees

When the Genevan exiles dedicated their 1560 translation to Queen Elizabeth, they had high hopes that she would be a holy Deborah who would drive Catholicism from England's verdant land. Their rhetoric was not misplaced in its hope that light and liberty would restore the church. What shape was the English Church to take in those halcyon days of Elizabethan expectations? The Frankfurt dispute between Cox and Knox would soon enough revive itself in England as persons debated whether worship would have an English face or that of a Church of Christ. The initial arguments took place as several exiles assumed appointments to the episcopal bench. Subsequent attempts to introduce a presbyterian form of discipline in the decade from 1570 to 1580 and a congregational structure after 1582 failed to achieve permanence in the English parish structure. Among the several whom Elizabeth appointed to the episcopal bench, Thomas Bentham, John Jewel, Edmund Grindal, and Matthew Hutton were bishops with puritan sympathies. These four must suffice to describe the episcopal form of the continental reformed consensus in the Elizabethan Church.

The problems facing Tudor bishops can be seen in the visitations undertaken by John Hooper of Gloucester in 1551 and John White of Lincoln in 1556. Henrician conservatives were replaced by reformers whose compliance with the new religious policies was certain. The most vigorous of the Edwardian appointees was John Hooper. During his short stint at Gloucester, Hooper carried out a vigorous visitation in 1552, "launched a programme of supervised scriptural study by the clergy, who were to attend regular meetings in each deanery...," brought the consistory court under personal supervision and bypassed his rural deans to exercise direct contact within his diocese.[34] In his first visitation Hooper examined 311 priests, missing sixty-two incumbants who did not reside in the diocese. Of the 311 resident clergy, 171 could not repeat the Ten Commandments, ten could not repeat the Lord's Prayer, and twenty-seven could not identify its author.[35] John White of Lincoln was a Marian appointee whose discoveries in Lincoln were as telling as those by Hooper five years before. White visited 235 parishes where he found 133 churches whose fabric was in ruinous condition. Twenty-seven parishes were without vicar or curate; three priests were accused of simony and eight were married.[36] White did little to alter the situation.

Thomas Bentham was one of the three royal commissioners who visited Lincoln Cathedral in September of 1559 and deprived many of the higher clergy of their livings, including five of the six archdeacons. Even so, all of the cathedral dignitaries and resident canons were retained. One of these was the dean, Francis Mollet, faithful chaplain of Queen Mary who missed elevation as bishop of Salisbury on the double death of the Queen and Archbishop Pole.[37] The dean's conservatism must be flanked with the sympathies of the chancellor, one John Salisbury, who was a moderate protestant even though Foxe tells us that he accepted heretical books from Thomas Garret.[38] As late as 1562 choral vicars were paid to celebrate the Mass of the Virgin Mary at Lincoln Cathedral.

Not until 1564 did the new phase begin for the cathedral with the residence of the archdeacon Aylmer and the installation in 1566 of his fellow Marian exile Michael Reniger as new chancellor.[39] That hiatus of some seven years' duration is symptomatic of economic realities for which the Elizabethan episcopal appointees were ill prepared.

1. Thomas Bentham

One can sympathize with Thomas Bentham whom Elizabeth appointed to the see of Lichfield and Coventry in late 1559. Bentham was one of the seventy-six appointments to the episcopal bench which Elizabeth made between 1558 and 1603.[40] At least seven bishops besides Bentham were progressive in their resolve to rebuild the Tudor church through a revitalization of the more than eight thousand parishes in England and Wales. If one adds the committed protestants to that list of bishops, ten emerge from the first round of appointments who had every hope that Elizabeth would assist them in their diocesan desire to bring about a metamorphosis of the ministry. Not only was absenteeism a problem and the clerical arrangements for concubines a sordid affair, but some one must speak to that vicar who kept fish in the fount! The ten who make up the first phalanx of reformed prelates are as follows:

Thomas Bentham:	Coventry and Lichfield
Nicolas Bullingham:	Lincoln
Richard Cox:	Ely
Edmund Grindal:	London
Robert Horne:	Winchester
John Jewel:	Salisbury
John Parkhurst:	Norwich
James Pilkington:	Durham
Edwin Sandys:	Worcester
Edmund Scambler:	Peterborough

Pilkington set the tone which animated these bishops.

> In Durham I grant the Bishop that now is [i.e., himself] and his predecessor [Cuthbert Tunstall] were not... made Bishops after one fashion... This [Pilkington] has nether cruche [crozier] nor mitre, never sware against his Prince his allegiance to the Pope; this has neither power to christen bells, nor hallow chalices... and with gladness praises God that keeps him from such filthiness,... God defend all good people from such religion and bishops.41

Bentham's see sprawled across the Midlands with a mediocre income to match its moderate population. The four archdeaconries of Coventry, Derby, Stafford and Shrewsbury each posed a different problem. Staffordshire and Shropshire were said to contain troublesome Romanists, while Coventry had a sizeable radical Protestant congregation. The Diocese of Coventry and Lichfield had over 500 parochial units and by 1563 a population of 125,144.[42] Bentham's Letter Book has two hundred and forty-seven entries, one hundred fourteen of which touched on money or land in the see which supplied the bishop's living. This forty-six per cent of the entries was matched by another fifteen per cent or thirty-seven more entries which centered on fiscal woes in the collection of fees from leases, tenures and fees.[43]

The financial crisis had several components, among which were the practices of paying a year's diocesan income on assuming episcopal office, the awareness by Marian bishops of their deprivation so that they let out long leases at improper rents to friends and relatives,[44] and the Act 1. Elizabeth 19 which provided for the exchange of impropriated tithes from the crown for unencumbered episcopal possessions. The latter was the particular vehicle whereby the crown exploited episcopal lands as it earlier had monastic properties. Archbishop Parker in 1559 shared his apprehension when with several others he offered to give an annual pension of one thousand marks in exchange for the original scheme. The Queen refused for she could unload unproductive rectories and scattered livings with their pension obligations for the best and richest episcopal lands.[45]

Hanbury was a case in point for Bishop Bentham. Bentham could not take possession of this rich living because of a pretended title to it by Christopher Grene and Christopher Bayne. The previous bishop made over the parsonage of Hanbury in Staffordshire to two of his servants. Baynes declared that Bishop Baynes was his natural uncle.[46] As a result of legal action which consumed both the Bishop's time and his money, Bentham could not repay his debts incurred for entry into episcopal office nor even his daily expenses. In October 1560 he complained that not above five pounds remained in his house. In August he wrote Thomas Lever at Coventry to borrow £40. Seven days later he borrowed another £40 from an alderman of Coventry.[47] Overton stated that Bentham died £1000 in debt to the crown and £200 to the see.[48]

In spite of his fiscal problems, Bentham cared about the improvement of ministry in his diocese. Preaching would be the _modus operandi_ of diocesan renewal under the gospel. As early as 1560 Bentham noted the lack of livings to undergird qualified ministers. "I am far from good counsell and destitute of lerned men," he wrote to Grindal at London, "for lack of lyvynge to give theym and I can get no helpe of any Iustice."[49] His 1565 _Injunctions_ tried to enforce private study among his clergy:

> Item, that you leave haunting of alehouses, at all times spending your time in godly exercises, in prayer, study and reading of Holy Scriptures, bringing the youth in good literature, civil manners and good nurture, teaching them daily to increase in knowledge fear and love of God...50

Unfortunately Elizabeth mortgaged the hierarchy's future. "The harvest of her sowing was reaped in a puritan opposition which found an easy target in the too worldly... episcopate of her Stuart successors."[51] Felicity Heal calculates that Secretary Cecil listed the episcopal income in 1560 at £23,000 compared to £28,000 for gross revenues at the time of Mary's death.

Such a drop in income of 17.86% held disastrous consequences for the renewal of parish ministry, for surely poverty of body led to poverty of mind.[52] Heal concludes that the "Tudor bishops struggled as best they could to offer spiritual leadership in a cold climate. Their efforts should perhaps compel our sympathy, if not our unstinted praise."[53]

2. John Jewel (1525-1571)

Jewel entered Merton College, Oxford in July of 1535 where John Parkhurst educated him in biblical study. This he did by making Jewel compare the New Testament translations of Tyndale with Coverdale.[54] Jewel left Merton for Corpus Christi College as a scholar in 1539, taking a B.A. in 1540 and an M.A. in 1545. He had been elected fellow in 1542 and was a prelector in humanity and rhetoric when Peter Martyr Vermigli took up residence in early 1548. Martyr's influence on Jewel lasted until he left England in 1553 and while on the continent during Queen Mary's Catholic reign. Jewel served as notary in April of 1554 during Cranmer and Ridley's disputation. Jewel fled England to make his way to Frankfurt by March 13, 1555. He joined Cox in the opposition to Knox before answering Martyr's invitation to be his guest at Strasbourg. There Jewel listened to Martyr's lectures on Judges and followed him to Zurich in 1556 to assist in the lectures on Samuel. Late in 1558 Jewel left Zurich for England, a trip of fifty-seven days.

His letters to Martyr and others give valuable information on religious affairs. On June 15, 1559 Jewel preached at St. Paul's Cross. Jewel was consecrated Bishop of Salisbury at Lambeth on January 21, 1560. Martyr praises Jewel in the preface to his 1561 <u>Dialogus de utraque in Christo Natura</u> written against the Lutheran theologian John Brenz. Martyr comments on their glad days at Oxford and subsequent stay at Zurich.

> I write these things to show you, O Praetor, that I have not fulfilled my office in writing this Dialogue until the church is purged of disfiguring flaws and rendered more attractive. And you will be fulfilling your duty as Bishop if you see to it with all your energies that strange and false opinions of this sort be ejected from the sheep-fold of Christ... I have already set forth in a few words what I would like you to do, my reverend and

> most learned friend. All that is left now (as is the custom in literary dedications) is to praise your sterling qualities to the entire Christian world. If I were to summon up enough courage to do this, I would find myself running out of words before I exhausted the subject. And no one can be found better able to speak of your character and admirable life than I, for I speak not from second hand evidence but what I actually heard and saw and experienced. I speak of the quality of your genius, your eloquence and devotion, your capacity for hard work and the struggle for true religion, and above all, your modesty and moderation. When you and I were together at Oxford, I realized you had these qualities to an eminent degree. But since we were together there for only a short time, many began to think me a liar or dupe. For sly men usually give the impression of possessing many fine qualities when in reality they were filled with corruption. But later on, after you had moved to Germany from England, and lived for many years in the same house with me, there (at the same table with snakes!) we studied and conversed together every day. I believe that of all men I alone can accurately testify to your sincere faith, high moral standards, single-minded devotion and unwavering courage, not to mention the native ability, self-discipline, and sound judgment ...Your good example, upright life, and thorough commitment to your duties contribute more to your exalted reputation than anything a man could write... Finally, I shall appeal to you, my dear friend, a pillar of Christ's church and its most splendid ornament, to consider my little gift to you as a compliment and accept it with a grateful heart.55

John Jewel now took up a literary career as an English bishop in defense of religion derived from the primitive church. The Apology of the Church of England (1562) claims that wasps make honeycombs like bees do, yet there is no honey within.[56] Jewel goes on to argue for the "purity" of the ancient church whose pattern is preferred to that of Rome in his day.

> As for vs, we runne not for succour to the fire, as these mens guise is, but wee run to the Scriptures: neither do we reason with the Sword, but with the Word of God: and therewith, as saith Tertullian, doe feed our Faith: by it doe we stirre vp our hope, and strengthen our confidence.57

> These men have broken in pieces all the pipes and conduites: they have stopped vp all the Springs, and choked vp the Fountaine of liuing water with dirt and mire... these men, by damming vp all the Fountaines of GODS Word, haue brought the people into a pittifull thirst.58

Jewel then argues that his kind have ended the famine of the Word of God as Amos the prophet foretold, have renounced the Roman Church wherein no one could consider himself safe, and have rejected their curse "with booke, bell and candle."[59]

> And wee are come to that Church, wherein they themselves cannot deny... but all things be gouerned purely, and reuerently, and as much as we possibly could, very neere to the order vsed in old times.60

Thomas Stapleton attacked the protestant heresy as ancient Donatism revived in his day, calling the modern form "Puritan."[61]

Thomas Cartwright in 1574 asserted that the name "Puritan" had been invented by such Catholic writers and used by English bishops to discredit the Presbyterian party.[62] Jewel defended the pure pattern of the ancient church in 1562 which Catholic opponents like Stapleton labeled "Puritan" and Presbyterians such as Cartwright lamented as a term borrowed from Romanists to quash presbyterian aspirations. The episcopal Puritans such as Jewel attempted to restructure the _Ecclesia Anglicana_ along continental lines in 1563.

Jewel supported the Elizabethan Settlement of 1559 with its parliamentary faith by statute. Professor Jones has demolished the hypothesis set forth by Sir John Neale's _Elizabeth the I and her Parliaments_ that at first the Queen only intended an act of supremacy restoring the _status quo ante_ of 1547, which would be no Protestant Church, but rather a return to Catholicism without a Pope, leaving liturgical changes for a later session. A determined and radical core of Protestants revolted in the Commons to include restoration of the 1552 liturgy. Neal argued that a Puritan party in the Commons led by the Marian exiles forced a compromise between her ideal and their perception of Swiss Protestant models. Jones seeks to show that there was no radical core in 1559 which clearly sat in the Commons of 1566.[63] Jewel in particular looked with hope on the Queen's programme as did his mentor Peter Martyr who sent a December 1558 letter urging Elizabeth to follow David's Old Testament example "to restore again into his place the holy Gospel of Christ." In August of

1559 Martyr wrote to Richard Cox that Elizabeth "calls religion to evangelical purity."[64] Between 1559 and the parliamentary trauma of 1566 lie the convocation of 1563 and Jewel's challenge to men like Henry Cole, Thomas Harding and Thomas Dorman.

Elizabeth took advice from a number of quarters which included Richard Goodrich's "Divers Points of Religious Contrary to the Church of Rome" and the anonymous "Device for Alteration to Religion." Goodrich urged that the leaders of the Marian regime be imprisoned preparatory to religious alterations. The "Device" raised a series of questions and answers to dangers attending such an alteration, whether it be a French invasion through Scotland or papist trouble in the Shires. Its most famous suggestion urged an assembly of learned men to "review the Book of Common Prayer, and order of ceremonies, and service in the Church." Such a plan to disarm the religious extremists transpired in the months to follow. Its effects were felt in the Oxford Colleges soon enough.

Winthrop Hudson has recently suggested that there was a Cambridge connection which held together these episcopal, parliamentary, administrative and theological aspirations for an English church with a reformed or continental face. Chapters 4-5 of this 1980 study explore the role of Cheke, Bucer and Martyr as well as Cecil's contacts in London.[65] My own feeling is that Sir Anthony Cooke played a larger role than Hudson allows. Martyr dedicated his Romans commentary of 1558 to Cooke which links up the 1550 Oxford lectures at Christ Church with the London leanings toward a reformed English Church. That Latin commentary passed through printings of 1558, 1559, 1560, 1568 (Latin and English), 1612 and 1613. The prefatory letter to Cooke appears in all fourteen editions of the _Loci Communes_ from 1576 to 1656.[66] Martyr also corresponded with Cooke on October 15,1558,[67] February 12, 1559 and June 26, 1562.[68] In the case of Peter Martyr Vermigli one must talk of an Oxford connection.[69]

That Peter Martyr contributed a letter which circulated in Latin and some English copies of Jewel's _Apology_ is one more link in the continental chain of circumstances which impinges on Elizabethan Reform. In his letter Martyr praises the Apology which he says Bullinger, Gualter and Wolph likewise lauded as "neuer any Booke of this time was euer more accurately and perfectly penned."[70] If Martyr and the Zurich party praised Jewel's "famous renowned child,"[71] small wonder his catholic opponents poured venom on such a defense. Chief among these reactionaries were Dr. Henry Cole, deposed Dean of St. Paul's and Thomas Harding, formerly Regius Professor of Hebrew at Oxford. Both Jewel and Harding were from Devon and followed the hot gospellers at Oxford. Harding retracted his Protestant convictions under Mary, took a benefice in Salisbury but was ejected by the new Elizabethan bishop, John Jewel. Harding protested in 1567 that such invalidated their case by incestuous contacts between men and women, as did Jewel's "great frend and Maister, Peter Martyr."[72]

Jewel challenged the Catholics in a sermon which he preached at St. Paul's Cross on 26 November 1559 and repeated at Court on March 17, 1560. Jewel challenged the Catholics to respond to 27 articles taken from scripture and the Church Fathers of the first six centuries. Henry Cole responded first in 1560 with his Copie of a Sermon (S.T.C. 14599a) and The True Copies of the Letters betwene the reverend father in God Iohn Bisshop of Sarum and D. Cole (S.T.C. 14612). An anonymous Catholic answer in manuscript circulated widely, retorting to Jewel's first article on the subject of private Mass. It was thrice published in 1562 with a rejoinder by Thomas Cooper, later Bishop of Lincoln and Winchester (S.T.C. 14615, 14616, 14617).

The main challenge came from Doctor Harding. Thomas Harding (1516-1572) came from Devon and was educated at Winchester (1528). From Winchester he passed to New College, Oxford where after two years he became a fellow in 1536. Henry VIII selected Harding as Regius Professor of Hebrew for his skill in languages. During the reign of Edward VI Harding supported the protestant zealots, becoming Warden-elect of New College on Edward's direction. He also attended the private sessions which Peter Martyr held in his lodgings at Corpus Christi. Later as a convert to Romanism he attacked both Martyr and Jewel from personal memories of their Oxford connections.[73]

The sermon itself and Harding's challenge introduce one to a "puritan" bishop whose forte was patristic defense of the Protestant cause. Jewel marvels that catholics can challenge Theodoret who spoke of bread and wine joining God's grace to their nature which remains all the while bread and wine.[74] The reply to Harding's Answere (1564: S.T.C. 12758-9) takes up the issue of divine worship in the vernacular, for Harding's 35th division argued that if the Latin service were condemned because of its unintelligible language, so must the "new masters" condemn David's Psalms which they misconstrue. He quotes from St. Augustine whose North African people sang the Psalms "which they understood not," to the effect that the people needed to listen to his preaching lest they sang with voice only like the birds and not with human reason.[75] Jewel retorts that though the Psalms be hard, the key is better used and rightly so when it opens than when it shuts up. Chrysostom took the key of Matthew XXII to be "the word of knowledge of the scriptures"[76] and then Jewel quotes Gregory that the scriptures are a stream in which "the elephant may swim, and the lamb may wade afoot."[77]

Harding thought that the people were too simple to understand scripture in English, while Jewel defended the right of the simple to hear their shepherd's voice in scripture. Harding's argument about the complexity of scripture has had its exponents among preachers as well as scholars in every age, among those who seem unable to trust the Spirit to make scripture plain without pulpit pyrotechnics or an interpretive grid placed over the plain surface of the text. It is no act of charity, Jewel argues in effect, to drown the sheep in the waters stirred up by a hurricane of ecclesiastical or psychological insecurity, created by congregational shepherds unwilling to trust their sheep with knowledge or love of the glory of God derived from a vernacular biblical text free of commentary. Such clerical arrogance has as its effect to keep the people ignorant that Christ alone is the chief shepherd or bishop of their souls (I Peter 2:25).

Harding attacked the vernacular scriptures as the source of heresy, citing Cardinal Bessarion of the fifteenth century that either the Greek or Latin church is that against which Hades shall not prevail and there is no third option.[78] Jewel will not admit that such a general argument accounts for the heresies or the schisms of Muscovy, Armenia or Ethiopia where vernacular services and scripture nourish these national christians.[79] Then Harding specified why the English need nothing beyond the Latin which had served them well for most of a millenium. The English service devised in King Edward's time has much "repugnant to the faith and custom of the catholic church."[80] Jewel is at his best here when he defends the "puritan" understanding based on I Corinthians (14), that everywhere in the primitive church priest and people prayed together in a common tongue.[81]

Jewel's response to Harding's Conclusion is that he racks, alters and changes the plain meaning of the patristic witness to damn the protestant cause. "Your greatest grounds be surmises, guesses, conjectures, and likelihoods."[82]

> Surely, M. Harding, if you could behold the wonderful works that God hath wrought in the kingdoms of England, France, Denmark, Polonia, Suecia, Bohemia, and Scotland, and in the noble states and commonweals of Germany, Helvetia, Prussia, Russia, Lituania, Pomerania, Austria, Rhetia, Vallis Tellina, & c., ye would not greatly find fault with the number, nor think that they, whom it hath pleased God in all these kingdoms and countries to call to the knowledge and feeling of his holy gospel, are so few. And if ye could also consider the extremity and cruelty of your side, and the abundance of innocent blood that so constantly hath been yielded for the testimony of the truth, ye would not so lightly call them either unstable or light persons. Certainly they whom you seem so lightly to esteem are kings, princes, magistrates, councillors, and the gravest and greatest learned fathers of Christendom. If it please God of his mercy to bless and increase that he hath begun, within few years ye shall find but few that will so lightly be deceived and follow you. In all countries they flee from you and forsake you. Ye can no longer hold them,

> but either by ignorance or by force and tyranny. The people, whom it liketh you to call dogs and swine, are neither so beastly nor so unsensible and void of reason, but that they are able now to espy them by whom they so often have been deceived. They are able now to discern the truth from falsehood, and the true Shepherd from a stranger, and lament your pitiful case, that are so suddenly fallen back, and welter so miserably in your error.83

3. Convocation of 1563

The origins of Puritanism are to be seen therefore in the continental impact on England during the reign of Edward VI and the experiences of the Marian exiles in several reformed centers during Mary Tudor's catholic restoration. When Elizabeth appointed several of these persons to the episcopal bench, their programmatic approach to diocesan reform as well as their theological challenge are components which the convocation of 1563 sought to extend to the national church. Preaching was to be the *modus vivendi* as in Grindal's support of the Prophesyings. The doctrinal core is widely shared even if the external debates over vestments and liturgy seem to reflect widespread disagreement over essentials and non-essentials.

A.J. Carlson concludes that Convocation of 1563 introduced reforms at the same time that government bills were being undermined in the lower house of Convocation. These sessions from January 11 to April 14, 1563 are the source of Puritan demands for a "religion of individual conscience reacting within the circumstances of Tudor conformity."[84] Carlson views the Edwardians at Cambridge and Oxford as the first of "the godly who were hated for religion's sake." The second set of Puritan experiences comes during Mary's reign among the eight hundred some English exiled on the continent. So John Parkhurst among his first acts at Norwich as bishop imitates that reformed model and set up every Tuesday a conference among the diocesan clergy to produce literate preachers.[85] The third experience as Carlson would have it was the fear of existing popery. These three are common to any description of Puritanism, i.e., the cohesiveness of persecution, a common intellectual experience, and the perceived threat of popish tradition.[86] The Convocation of 1563 sorted out the implications of this common thread.

Alexander Nowell was the _agent provocateur_ of these early sessions in 1563. Nowell and a delegation of six others appeared before the bishops to present a "Petition for Discipline" on January 16. This turns out to be twenty-one articles signed by sixty-three members of the parochial clergy.[87] This was the first step of puritan petition, a hint of more radical demands ahead. The eighteenth article gives the impression of a protestant inquisition, for it would allow the bishop's ordinary to summon both lay and ecclesiastical persons whom he suspected in religious matters to examine them on these articles. Private baptism, idolatrous mass and superstitious images in the churches were to be abolished. All fellows in college must preach at least twice a year or leave the universities![88]

The _Thirty-nine Articles_ were under vigorous analysis in these clerical discussions of 1563. By February 13 the Commons were debating the new Supremacy Bill, i.e. "the Bill for Punishment of those who shall extol the Bishop of Rome or refuse to take the Oath." Those who refused the oath lost their property (praemunire) on the first offense and their lives (high treason) on the second. The Convocation debates heated up over seven articles presented on February 13 to the clergy by thirty-four members with Nowell as their leader. Twenty-one of these were Marian exiles though only five were from Geneva. These pressed home the crucial removal of papal dregs, such as organs which were to be replaced by psalm-singing, restriction of baptism to ministers without the sign of the cross and removal of cope and surplice in clerical dress.[89]

As Carlson puts the matter, the Puritans had a triple agenda. First of all, the Queen had ignored a lower house of 1559 dominated by Marian catholic clergy to publically proclaim that she was protestant. Now that the Council of Trent was in session she would allow no breach in the protestant facade.

Secondly, in 1563 the House of Commons held men of like religious conscience similar to the Puritans in Convocation. In the third place, the Puritans thought they could win. So a vote on the articles now reduced to six in number brought forty-five in favour and thirty-five against. But Convocation represented all of the Canterbury clergy with a total of 144 votes. Proxy votes determined the outcome as the Puritans mustered fifteen to match their forty-three and the resistance cast twenty-four votes by proxy to oppose the Puritan 58 votes with 59 of their own. Thus by one proxy vote the Puritan agenda was defeated in the lower house of Convocation.[90] Carlson explains how the Dean of Exeter who controlled three proxy votes chose to be absent as well as some others. Gregory Dodd would have swung the odds to the Puritan agenda. Bishop Alley of Exeter may have pressured him to be absent.[91]

The hopes were pinned on the bishops after the single vote defeat in Convocation. On two occasions Edwin Sandys, Bishop of Worcester, presented proposals for further reform in the Elizabethan Church. His first reform would eliminate private baptism and the crossing of an infant's head as superstitious -- both major points of the lower house proposal since they appear in both the seven article petition and its six article reduction of January 13. Sandys' second proposal listed seven reforms of episcopal administration. All clergy, for example, would catechize "every Sunday according to the injunction on that behalf."[92] That William Alley, Bishop of Exeter, responded to Sandys indicates tensions over the Puritan agenda in the upper house as well as the lower. A look ahead to the future 1566 argument against vestments is seen here as Alley inveighs against those preachers who "murmur, spurn, kick" against required vestments.[93]

Alexander Nowell, Dean of St. Paul's, was one architect of this 1563 reform. His long tenure in that post from 1560 to 1602 spans almost the entire reign of Elizabeth. Nowell was on Cecil's 1559 list of episcopal appointees and had been a vigorous member of the Frankfurt exile congregation. Nowell prepared a catechism for the 1563 Convocation which he adapted from John Calvin's Genevan Catechism.[94] The lower house subscribed to the Catechism while the bishops "allowed" it. Cecil sent it on to Elizabeth who did not approve its publication, returning it via Cecil with critical notes from learned persons attached. Nowell used these notes for further alterations before publishing the Catechism in 1570. Archbishops Parker and Grindal approved the publication which by 1571 circulated in Latin and English as mandatory for schoolmasters. Thomas Norton, who translated Calvin's Institutes into English, prepared the English version while a leader of the puritan cause in the House of Commons. This rather than the vestment controversy of 1566 gives one a glimpse at the continental accents of Calvin in England during the sixteenth and seventeenth centuries. King James I in 1604 ordered its use in either the larger or abridged form.[95] Nowell utilized 28% of Calvin and 13% of Poynet's Catechism where he also borrowed material. John Calvin was his mentor, especially in the section on sacramental observance of the Lord's Supper, with its language of communication with Christ's body in his supper "by the words and mysteries of God."[96]

4. Edmund Grindal (1559-1583)

Edmund Grindal was a third Elizabethan Puritan bishop whose career meshes with the concerns of a Bentham as well as a Jewel. Grindal likewise struggled to create a reformed church in England as Professor Collinson has so ably described in his recent 1980 biography. If Jewel was a protege of Martyr from Oxford and Zurich days, Grindal was a disciple of Bucer. Professor Collinson points this out in contrast to Beza, all in the context of their respective responses to the Strangers Churches in London and their crises of the 1560s. Grindal as Bishop of London had to intervene in the Dutch congregation over Adriaan van Haemstede, and in the Spanish church about Casiodoro de Reina and Antonio del Corro.

> There was a difference of mentality between those who lived and breathed in an atmosphere of continuing doc-

> trinal refinement, and whose theological organ was hypersensitive, and a bishop who while not ignorant of doctrine was content to rest on what he had learned and to apply it practically, in life and in pastoral administration. There was also a temperamental difference. Grindal's inclination was always to hope for the best of mankind, not to suspect the worst. He had no taste for witch-hunts, no capacity for dirty tricks. And in relation to Beza there was a kind of generation gap. Not a difference in age: although Beza would outlive Grindal by a quarter of a century they were born in the same year and had met in Strasbourg as contemporaries, each on the verge of seniority in their respective churches. But Grindal's charitable and even pragmatic spirit perpetuated the influence of Bucer and contrasts with the marked intolerance which Beza brought to bear on the affairs of the churches, together with a neo-scholastic theological method. It is fair to add that Grindal as a leader of a church established and peacefully enjoying the gospel was not engaged, as Beza was and the French in general were, in continual definition and defence of the truth, in circumstances where the support of the christian magistrate was not available, and often with respect to particular cases.[97]

Grindal was revered by his protestant contemporaries as a good man who "ground himself even to his grave by mortification."[98] Grindal went up to Cambridge with Edwin Sandys in the 1530s to study at Pembroke College. There as a fellow of the college in 1538 he listened first to Ridley and than in the 1550s to Bucer.[99] In 1550 Ridley used Grindal as an evangelist in his London diocese, giving the young Grindal invaluable experience. Grindal was named by Edward VI to be bishop of London until Mary's reign ended all talk of such a rapid promotion for one only thirty-four years of age. Grindal took refuge in Strasbourg where he assisted Foxe in collecting materials for the Acts and Monuments.[100]

Grindal was consecrated bishop of London in December 1559, translated to York as Archbishop in 1570 and transfered to Lambeth as Archbishop of Canterbury in 1575. Each segment of his career in high office faced Grindal with different challenges, from the trouble with the Stranger's Churches of which he was superintendant in London and the Vestments controversy to a partnership with the Earl of Huntingdon while at York and the conflict over preaching with Elizabeth as Archbishop of Canterbury.

The affair involving the two learned Spainards de Reina and del Corro illustrates as sharply as any other event the clash between free thought and discipline. These two had worked with Cipriano de Valera to translate the entire bible into Castilian, the so called Bear Bible printed at Basle in 1569. Casiodoro de Reina fled from England on 21 September 1563, convinced that the charge of sodomy (called buggery) was a hanging matter.[101] The joint charge of heresy involved suspicion of Servetism, that he had kissed a book by Servetus and supported his Tri-theistic views.[102] Beza ultimately condemned de Reina in Letter 59 of his _Epistolae_, whatever help Grindal did to clear him of a false charge. Grindal saved the manuscripts of the 'Bear Bible' which when published in 1569 praised Grindal for rescuing the work "from hostile hands." The real tragedy was Reina's cowardice seen in his sudden flight to the continent before any formal hearing could exonerate him.[103]

Corro was another matter indeed, for in his letter to Reina on Christmas Eve 1563 not only did he discuss the plans for the Spanish Bible but also Corro set forth some leading theological questions. Corro got a testimonial from Grindal on arrival in London, running to the bishop to qualify his theological view. The French National Synod barred him from ministry while Beza rejected Corro's _Apology_. Corro's ambition, slander, lies and jests led to his undoing by late 1568 and into the trial of 1569.[104] Then Corro digressed from the Calvinist orthodoxy with a broadside which was silent on the Trinity and casual on predestination. This case dragged on into the late 1570s.

Corro's _Dialogus Theologicus_ appeared in a second edition of 1587. There one can trace the predestinarian latitude at first hand.[105] The 1574 edition had been reprinted in England during 1575. Archbishop Parker said that Corro's _Dialogus_ showed his "purity of doctrine," including an orthodox statement on the Trinity.[106]

During his tenure as Archbishop of Canterbury, Grindal supported preaching after the Zurich pattern of prophesyings which catapulted him into conflict with the Queen and into national prominence. These were not paroxysms of puritan bibliolatry nor were they necessarily a threat to episcopal order, even though Beza's attack on bishops got printed by Field and Wilcox as part of their 1572 Admonition to Parliament.

Such sermons were delivered before a lay audience, perhaps on market days and in a central church. Two or three sermons would be preached on the same passage of scripture to clergy gathered for mutual encouragement. By 1576 such an institution was wide-spread. Because Archbishop Parker had supressed these "vain exercises" at the Queen's command in 1574, Parkhurst of Norwich seized on the word "vain" to permit the Norfolk gentry, patrons of the puritan preachers, to indulge in these exercises.[107]

Grindal refused to suspend the exercises, even though the Queen confronted her Archbishop on June 12 to enquire into them and if they were as reported, she would disband them. Grindal wrote to the bishops for their reports. Only four of the fifteen extant replies were hostile, such as Cox of Ely who wrote "the world is full of new fangles and fancies."[108] Bishop Edmund Gheast of Salisbury heard of three kinds of preaching. In one diocese a text was appointed for three sermons, in another a common place was assigned for one person to elucidate, and in the third every minister must comment on a set place from Calvin or Musculus.[109] David Kemp who was Archdeacon of St. Albins reported his reminder to the clergy about the authority of the scriptures, church, keys, law and gospel, and the sacraments of Christ's body and blood "accordynge to Mr. Cranmers and Peter Martyrs books." These they passed over three times in twelve years.[110] The exercise at St. Albins began in April 1572 with Mr. Nowell's Catechism, then the Epistle to the Galatians. At dinner the masters of the town and gentlemen of the contry send wine. "Wure horsmeate cost us nothynge, our dyner, farynge honestly, vi d. a peece."[111]

Grindal's letter reproved the Queen.

> But surely I cannot marvel enough, how this strange opinion should once enter into your mind, that it should be good for the Church to have few preachers. Alas, Madam! is the Scripture more plain in any one thing, than that the gospel of Christ should be plentifully preached; and that plenty of labourers should be sent into the Lord's harvest; which, being great and large, standeth in need, not of a few, but many workmen?[112]

When the Archbishop told Elizabeth: "Remember, Madam, that you are a mortal creature," she shot back with a reminder that she was Queen![113] Elizabeth suspended Grindal from his office as Primate of England for not suspending these scriptural exercises practiced in at least eighty-five locations.[114]

5. Matthew Hutton (1589-1606)

Matthew Hutton was born in the parish of Warton, North Lancashire in 1529. He became sizar in Cambridge University in 1546 where as a fellow of Trinity College he took the B.A. (1551/52), M.A. (1555) and B.D. (1562). In 1561 Hutton became Lady Margaret professor of divinity and in 1562 master of Pembroke Hall and regius professor of divinity. By 1565 Hutton distinguished himself in the theological disputations before Queen Elizabeth at Cambridge.[115]

Archbishop Parker opposed Hutton's nomination in 1570 to succeed Grindal as bishop of London, perhaps because of his suspected Puritan leanings.

In 1586 Archbishop Sandys brought thirteen charges against Hutton who defended himself with elan before submitting to nothing more than the use of violent and indiscreet language. Whitgift describes one of those indiscretions in a letter to Hutton of May 2, 1597. "In one of the letters there was put Christ's-tide for Christmas, which because of the novelty thereof... was by some of your friends misliked, and I marvel how it escaped you..."[116] The ending -mas(s) in Christ-mas was too catholic!

On 9 June 1589 through Burleigh's influence Hutton was elected to the bishopric of Durham. On 14 February 1595/96 he was elected Archbishop of York. One of his last public acts before his death on January 16, 1606 was to write a letter in which he urged relaxation in the prosecution of the puritans.[117]

To entertain the probability that Matthew Hutton was a puritan bishop as does Peter Lake is to widen the meaning of puritan to include episcopal variants as well as presbyterial and congregational. If our first bishop suffered economic constraints as did Bentham and the second introduced a patristic component into the polemical argument with the Romanists, as did Jewel, then Grindal as the third example and Hutton as the fourth can be seen as Archbishops of Canterbury and York who promote the doctrinal consensus which lay behind the puritan mentality. Those who would change Christ-mass to Christ-tide, or who would name children Fear-God and Hope-still, or again provide for prophesyings exibit a certain style of divinity which can also be identified in Matthew Hutton.

When Hutton went north to become Dean of York, he advocated Grindal as the archepiscopal appointee in 1568. He wrote to Lord Burleigh that the new archbishop should be:

> a teacher because the country is ignorant; a virtuous and godly man because the country is given to sift a man's life; a stout and courageous man in God's cause because the country otherwise will abuse him; and yet a sober and discreet man lest too much vigorousness harden the hearts of some that by fair means might be mollified.118

Grindal's former chaplain was loyal to his old patron. In 1573 Hutton could respond to the presbyterian challenge in a lengthy communique to Burghley. If one argued that conformity might offend those weak in the faith, Hutton countered that by disobedience one not only offended the Queen herself but "all those that like well of the law."[119]

In the 1590s Hutton commented on the ecclesiastical situation in an important sermon delivered at Whitehall and in letters to the great Lords such as Essex and Robert Cecil. When in his sermon Hutton urged the Queen to name an heir, Elizabeth rebuked him for his temerity.[120] The Roman threat animated his correspondance to the Earl of Essex who had a Mr. Wright in his household, a popish priest turned anti-Spanish informer. Hutton protested that Essex ought not to have sent Wright north to visit his father in York. Such a man was, in Hutton's words,

> without pardon, without keeper, with credit to be sent to his father an obstinant Recusant, to a country full of recusants, hath bred divers effects of sundry opinions in divers men.121

When the aged Archbishop entered the Stuart context, he attacked both superstitious papists and giddy-headed puritans alike, so that "neither the papists may obtain their hoped for reformation, nor the puritans their fantastical platform of reformation."[122] Here Hutton restricts the term puritan to the precisions whom James denounced in his Basilicon Doron (1603), i.e., the Brownists and sectaries who emerged in the 1580s. Dr. Lake views this as a cover for protecting the mass of puritan ministers. Again the difference between papist and puritan was crucial. There may well be many stripes of cat but all dogs are curs. During his visitations of 1600 and 1604/05 Hutton presented only four ministers for non-conformity though several well known dissenters retained their livings throughout Hutton's primacy.[123]

> "More generally Hutton's style of divinity was very much in accord with that of the puritans -- hence his protection of them from the hostile attentions of the central government. Hutton was sustained in his evangelical protestant vision of the English church by his close cooperation with a whole series of godly and well affected magistrates at both the local and national levels. In 1573 and again in 1589 Hutton had cited the protestant zeal and godly learning of such men as one of the major assets of the English church."124

The irenic spirit of Martin Bucer was alive and well in the English Church before the intensity of Beza precluded episcopal obedience. Men such as Bentham, Jewel, Grindal and Hutton belong to an English Church with a calvinist face, even if internal debate continued over whether that visage was more human than divine.

Chapter 11) Presbyterian Protest

By the 1570s events were crashing in on the moderate puritans and their supporters causing them to agitate for a religious consensus. Protestant enthusiasm reached into the family of Nicholas Bacon, Elizabeth's Lord Keeper who presided in the House of Lords and at theological disputations, such as the one in 1573 where he cooly informed Archbishop Parker that he and Bishop Sandys must hear what the puritans had to say. "We may not deal with them as in papish time."[125] Nathaniel Bacon and his brother Edward, contracted their protestant enthusiasm at Gray's Inn, one of the legal societies in London. Nathaniel resided in East Anglia where he cooperated as a magistrate with godly preaching, whereas Edward resided in London first and visited Beza, Danaeus and others abroad before relocating outside Ipswich. Such a familial intensification of religion mirrors the similar changes among the clergy for whom the Bezan option of ministry held chief attraction.[126] To assess the latter one must return to the Cambridge of Cartwright.

A. Cartwright and Cambridge

Thomas Cartwright was born the son of a yeoman farmer in 1535 in the small town of Royston which is situated ten to fifteen miles southwest of Cambridge. Little is known of his very early life but the record begins to speak when at the age of twelve he matriculates at Clare Hall, Cambridge in 1547 (this being the same year young Edward VI assumes the throne). His early schooling was marked by the arrival of two distinguished alumni from Heidelberg, Paul Fagius and Martin Bucer. Soon after their appointment at Cambridge, Fagius died, but the reformer Bucer lectured in Divinity until 1551. It is assumed by Cartwright's foremost biographer, A.F. Scott-Pearson, that the residence of Bucer did "much to kindle the interest of many members of the University in the Continental Reformation."[127]

Pearson wants to include Cartwright as one who was directly influenced by Bucer. This may indeed have been the case but one can not ascertain in Cartwright's writings any direct allusion to Bucer as a catalyst for his later thought. The same is true when trying to ascertain the influence left on Cartwright by Thomas Lever the Protestant reformer and Puritan divine who as Master of the School preached daily at St. John's. Though Cartwright must have heard many of Lever's sermons after becoming a scholar at St. John's in 1550, he is silent on the subject of Lever's particular persuasiveness on his own protestant views. It is safe to say, however, that the student life at Cambridge was rife with protestant ideologies. It was also a life of demanding discipline. Lever in a sermon preached at Paul's Cross to the citizens of London in December, 1550, throws light on this difficult life:

> There be dyvers ther whych ryse dayly betwixte foure and fyve of the clocke in the mornynge, and from fyve untyll syxe of the clocke use common prayer wyth an exhortacion of gods worde in a common chappell, and from sixe unto ten of the clocke use ever eyther pryvate study or commune lectures. At ten of the clocke they go to dynner, wereas they be contente wyth a penye pyece of byefe amongest foure havying a fewe porage made of the brothe of the same byefe, wyth salte and otemell, and nothynge els. After thys slender dinner they be eyther teachynge or learnynge untyll fyve of the clocke in the evenynge, whenas they have a supper not much better then theyr dyner. Immedyatelye after the whyche, they go eyther to reasonying in problemes or unto some other studye, untyll it be nyne or tenne of the clocke, and there beying wythout fyre are fayne to walk or runne up and downe halfe an houre, to gette a heate on their feete whan they go to bed.128

Needless to say, this was a rigorous life for any fifteen year-old and one which laid the groundwork for his later scholarly achievements.

On July 6, 1553 King Edward VI died and Mary became the Catholic Queen. A large number of Protestants were driven overseas by these events, leaving behind a relatively small group of dissenters. Cartwright was not a Marian Exile and remained at

Cambridge until he received his B.A. degree in 1554. Among his fellow graduates was his future antagonist John Whitgift. From 1556-1559 Cartwright was employed as a law clerk who returned to the University only after Elizabeth was installed as the head of state. On April 6, 1560 at the age of twenty-five Cartwright was admitted as a Lady Margaret Fellow.

Cartwright was already known in the university as an eloquent preacher, a rising theological scholar, and an able disputant. Owing to his skill as a theologian and rhetorician, he was elected to take part in a theological disputation held in the presence of Queen Elizabeth on the occasion of her visit to Cambridge in 1564. The DNB and John Whitgift's chief biographer, G. Paule, relate that Elizabeth showed a marked preference for Cartwright's antagonist in the disputation (John Preston) and that the former "from that time cherished resentful feelings, which ultimately led him to kick against her ecclesiastical government."[129] Paule sees this inattention on the Queen's part during the philosophical disputation as the catalytic agent in Cartwright's later puritanism. Paule goes so far as to attribute to Cartwright's character "pride and jealousy" as the "real reasons" for his flight to Geneva, that he might "feed on Presbyterian doctrine to return and get revenge."[130]

Pearson is quick to counter this character assassination by citing three documents (Nichol's eye-witness account of the debate, Stokys' narrative, and Hartwell's poem on the contest) to set the matter straight.[131] His contention is that Cartwright was not overly upset by the Queen's recognition of Preston and attributes Preston's victory to his many talents that made him highly visible before the Queen.[132] It is interesting to note, however, that even in the face of Pearson's argument Patrick Collinson still holds to the idea that Cartwright's response to the Queen and later his trips to Ireland and the Continent were a direct result of some personality deficiency. "A somewhat unheroic tendency to withdraw from the scene of conflict would always be characteristic of Cartwright, and it hampered his capacity for decisive leadership."[133] Cartwright's oration before the Queen seems more an academical disputation not all that determinative of his "motivation" for later opposition to Elizabeth's ecclesiastical policies.

A growing awareness on Elizabeth's part of the considerable diversity and "disunity" in the Church of England prompted her to reprimand Archbishop Parker for his inability to secure conformity in the Church. This reprimand was the result of Parker's providing the Queen with certificates describing the "varieties and disorders" existing in the ceremonies of the Church. Horton Davies comments on these varieties "that some ministers said the service in the chancel, others in the nave; some led worship from the pulpit, others from the chancel seat. Communion was administered by some clergy with a surplice and cope, by some with only a surplice, and by others wearing neither vestment, etc..."[134] Clearly some order was desirable. Parker drew up his "Advertisements" (1566) which set out the proper procedures for establishing ecclesiastical unity (conformity). The edict which precipitated the Vestiarian Controversy concerned the surplice.

The principal minister in cathedral and/or collegiate celebrations of Holy Communion was to use a cope, while the celebrant in a parish church "shall wear a comely surplice with sleeves."[135] The Universities soon became centers of opposition to Parker's "Advertisements." Although dissent was voiced by many students and faculty, the Bishops pursued their policy with vigor. In March of 1566 those of the London clergy who refused to obey the edict were summarily suspended which had the reverse effect of consolidating dissent. This opposition consolidated puritanism whose chief outcry was that Elizabeth's so-called reformation of the Church of England had become little more than a "leadened mediocrity." And Elizabeth, in the words of John Knox, was "neather gude Protestant nor yit resolute Papist."[136] This lack of clear-cut separation from the Roman Church was unsatisfactory to the Calvinist/Puritans who saw the vestments as mere "papal rags" which they denounced as "Romanish dregs" imposed on the English Church.[137]

At this point English dissent was cooled by correspondence from the Continental Reformers who urged them to tolerate the vestments because of their peripheral importance. Pearson sees the English Separatist Church (Plumber's Hall group, etc...) growing out of an unwillingness to relent in this matter by submitting to either the Continental Reformer's advice or English Church demands and choosing instead an alternative worship experience regardless of the consequences.[138] There seems to be a wide variance of opinion as to Cartwright's involvement in the controversy. DNB relies on Paule's view that Cartwright had preached three sermons encouraging the renouncement of the suplice which prompted some three hundred fellows and scholars to appear in chapel without them.[139] Pearson, on the other hand, thinks that Cartwright was a supporter rather than an instigator of the dissenting position.[140]

It is probable that Cartwright was merely a supporter of these early Puritans because it is clear that for the greater part of the controversy he was not even in England. For in 1565 he had become domestic chaplain to Adam Loftus, Archbishop of Armagh, and "in Ireland Puritans were not troubled for their nonconformity."[141] An inference might be made that Cartwright was influential in Loftus' later (1577) alleged conversion to puritanism. When Loftus is questioned on the origins of his puritanism, he denies being a puritan but is familiar with and holds complimentary ideas to those of Cartwright. This could suggest that by 1567 Cartwright's puritan/presbyterian doctrine was starting to emerge. Loftus returned to England because of ill health and Cartwright returned to Cambridge to complete and receive his B.D. degree in 1567.

A 1568 event propelled Cartwright into prominence as a spokesman for puritanism. He was elected as one of the twelve academic preachers at Cambridge. Apparently Cartwright was not only an eminent scholar but also a very popular preacher. During his week-day preaching at Great St. Mary's a contemporary, Clarke, states that "there was a great confluence af all sorts to heare him; grave men ran like boys in the streets to get places in the Church." adding that "the sexton was fain to take down the window, by reason of the multitudes that come to hear him."[142]

1569-1570 became landmark years for the growth of puritanism, for in those two years many puritans turned to presbyterianism, in part because they now saw the bishops as their opponents for reform. The occasion for this shift to presbyterianism was the promotion of Cartwright as Lady Margaret Professor of Divinity at Cambridge and his subsequent lectures on the first two chapters of the Acts of the Apostles. The consequences of this appointment and these lectures were of great moment, and need to be discussed in detail. The lectures aroused an enthusiastic response from the younger element in the University and a marked reaction from the University authorities.

Throughout the spring term of 1570 at Cambridge Cartwright delivered a series of powerful sermons on the first two chapters of the Acts of the Apostles. In these he dealt with ecclesiastical policy and its relationship to the current practices in the Church of England as well as his understanding of the authority of scripture and its proper exegesis. Cartwright compared the primitive church with the existing English system. His exegetical study led him to the conclusion that the Apostolic Church was the forerunner of what had become known in his era as presbyterianism. In proclaiming that the Apostolic Church was the "model for all time" he became both "interpreter and advocate of Presbyterianism."[143] The force of his hermeneutical method demanded that he become a critic of the established episcopal system.

Cartwright's lectures soon produced a sensation at the University and in gathering a party of sympathizers Cambridge was threatened with division and chaos. At this time Whitgift, who had earlier renounced puritanism, replied to Cartwright from the pulpit, but it is generally acknowledged that Cartwright was his oratorical superior and his popularity went unabated.[144] However, the University authorities soon took some action of their own. On June 11, 1570, William Chaderton (formerly Lady Margaret professor) officially complained to Cecil, the chancellor of the University. His complaint reads:

> one Mr Cartewrighte latelie chosen Into my place, reader of ye divinitie lector founded by Ladie Margaret, who hathe alwaies stubbernelie refused ye cappe, and such like ornaments agreable to gods law, and ye Queenes Majesties Injunctions, dothe now In his daylie lectors teache suche doctrine as Is pernitious, and not tollerable in christian commonwealthe: That is that in ye churche of Englande there is no lawfull and ordynarie callinge and chosinge or admittinge of ministers, nether anie ministrie: and that ye electyon of ministers and bishoppes at this daye is tyrannous.[145]

The force of his complaint is that Cartwright is attempting to overthrow both the ecclesiastical and civil authorities in England. This perceptive analysis saw the clear implications of Cartwright's theological tendencies.

John May, vice-Chancellor of the University, tried in vain to convince Cartwright to cease his teachings. Cartwright responded by sending May a letter containing six articles pertaining to church government which were a condensation of his lectures. A list of these "obnoxious doctrines" should clarify the specific reforms advocated by Cartwright:[146]

1) The names and offices of Archbishops and Bishops should be abolished and in their place the New Testament offices of Deacons and Presbyters (Elders) should be established.

2) The Presbyter should have a purely spiritual function and the Deacons should care for the poor.

3) Church government should not be entrusted to Chancellors of Bishops or Officials of Archdeacons, etc..., but to the minister and presbyter of the church.

4) Each minister should be attached to a definite congregation.

5) No one should "candidate" for the office of minister or be appointed by Bishops, but elected by the church.

6) All should promote this reformation according to their vocation.

Not only was the University in an uproar but the authorities began to move quickly to censure Cartwright. Cecil co-operated to the extent of allowing the ruling academic authorities to deny Cartwright his D.D. degree and order him to refrain from discussing what they saw as dangerous topics. In response counterpetitions were rained on the Chancellor by Cartwright's supporters. However, not only were these unsuccessful but Cecil allowed the authorities to restructure the University statutes which gave them the power to deprive professors of their Chairs. As soon as Whitgift became the new vice-Chancellor in December of 1570 one of his first acts was to deprive Cartwright of his position.[147] Cartwright tried to engage Whitgift in a public debate, but because neither could agree on the other's terms it never took place.

It would seem that the principal issue at stake between Cartwright and Whitgift (and other University/civil/ecclesiastical authorities) was the governmental form of the established Church. Was it to be episcopal or reformed in the direction of the presbyterian model? Just under the surface of this question lay a more delicate and secular question as to the sphere of the Queen's perogative; for any attack on the Church's structure was ultimately an affront to royal supremacy. These are indeed the questions that are usually focused upon by most historians, but, as important as they are, it could lead to a failure to recognize what J.F.H. New calls the "teleological acts of the Puritan's program"[148] -- that is, the Puritans' attempt to make practice conform to a preconceived philosophy/theology. Was the controversy an issue of Church polity alone? Pearson states that "Cartwright's quarrel with the English Church was not a theological one."[149]

In the midst of the furore that Cartwright had created at Cambridge, he was ejected from his Chair (at the end of 1570) and withdrew to Geneva, where his reception implied "recognition as the representative and leading English neo-Calvinist."[150] Theodore Beza was the head of the Genevan Church as the successor of

John Calvin. That Beza could say that "the sun did not shine on a more learned man than Cartwright"[151] gives a clear indication of Beza's respect which resulted in his offering Cartwright a position on the faculty at the Genevan University. Cartwright lectured in theology until the bubonic plague struck a lethal blow to much of Geneva in July of 1571. The severity of the pestilence caused the closing of the school for a time and in one of Beza's letters to Bullinger he suggests that even Cartwright "was beginning to languish."[152] By the winter of 1571 the disease abated, but the school had not yet re-opened.

Cartwright wrote to his friends in England that he was eager to be restored to his homeland; yet he delayed his plans at their urging in order that he might gain a greater insight into the presbyterian system before returning. To obtain this insight first hand Cartwright asked Beza's permission to observe the Geneva Consistory in action. His attendance at this usually closed meeting demonstrated that the Council showed not only a willingness to accept Cartwright as a sincere presbyterian, but also an awareness that Cartwright wished to transplant Geneva's consistorial practices into the Church of England.[153] Such becomes apparent when Cartwright returned to England in 1572 bringing with him a lucid system of church government to supplement his theological views set forth in his lectures on Acts two years earlier. The tour in Geneva accorded Cartwright broad recognition as a puritan leader which in turn granted him credibility as a presbyterian spokesman in the Admonition Controversy that was soon to erupt.

B. "Reading is not feeding..."

There was a biased bill of 1571 pending in Parliament seeking subscription to the stipulations in Elizabeth's Thirty-Nine Articles to which there was no Puritan objection. This Puritan influence in Parliament would result in those unpopular, anti-Puritan articles being omitted. Elizabeth promptly refused her consent to a measure that would "mutilate the formularies in this fashion."[154] The final results were the "Canons of 1571" which like the "Advertisements" were considered authoritative by the Ecclesiastical Commission and made it plain that "preachers would subscribe to the entire set of articles."[155] It was becoming more and more apparent to the Puritans that the Bishops would now be able to proceed against them with a firm hand, strengthened by the Queen's command that "none should suffer to decline either on the left or on the right hand from the direct line limited by the authority of our said laws and Injunctions."[156]

The leader of this Puritan drive in parliament was William Strickland. In a speech of April 5, Strickland asked that all things be brought "to the purity of the primitive church." Thomas Norton then asked that the Reformation of Ecclesiastical Laws drawn up under Cranmer and recently published be considered for implementation. On April 14 Strickland brought in a bill to reform the 1559 Prayer Book, abolish the use of copes and surplices, baptism in private houses, kneeling at communion, use of the ring at weddings and other superstitious practices. After its first reading the Queen intervened as supreme head of the church to prevent Strickland from attending the House. Strickland returned after a fuss, but the bill was dropped.[157]

But the debate was by no means over. Just a few days before Parliament rose in June, 1572 the authorities were taken aback by the appearance of a small, anonymous tract entitled An Admonition to the Parliament. This little pamphlet has been called "the first open manifesto of the puritan party; it marks the point at which puritanism began to be a hostile force, determined to do away with the existing system of polity and worship in the English Church."[158] A large part of the impact of this tract on the Bishops and Parliament was due to what Knappen called its "shrewd application of the New Testament golden-age standard to the current establishment."[159] The authors, John Field and Thomas Wilcox, citing numerous Scripture references, had penned a crisp, inflammatory attack on what they saw as the remaining "Roman abuses" in the English Church. The heart of their Puritan cause is succinctly put in the tract itself:

> The outwarde markes wherby a true christian church is knowne, are preaching of the worde purely, ministring of the sacraments sincerely, and ecclesiastical discipline which consisteth in admonition and correction of faults severelie... Either must we have right ministerie of God, & right government of his church, according to the scriptures ...or else there can be no right religion...
>
> By the word of God, it is an offyce of preaching, they make it an offyce of reading: Christe said goe preache, they in mockerie give them the Bible, and authoritie to preache, and yet suffer them not, except that they have newe licences. So that they make the cheefest part preaching, but an accessorie that is as a thing without which their offyce may and doth consist. In the scriptures there is attributed unto the ministers of God, the knowledge of the heavenly misteries, and therfore as the greatest tooken of their love, they are enjoined to fede Gods Lambes, and yet with these, suche are admitted and accepted, as onely are bare readers that are able to say service, and minister a sacrament. And that this is not the feding that Christ spake of, the scriptures are plain. Reading is not feeding, but it is as evill as playing upon a stage, and worse too. For players yet learne their partes wythout booke, and these, a manye of them can scarcely read within booke. These are emptie feeders, darcke eyes, ill workemen to hasten in the Lordes harvest messengers that cannot call, Prophets that cannot declare the wil of the Lorde, unsavery salte, blinde guides, sleepie watchmen untrustie dispensers of gods secretes, evil dividers of the worde, weake to withstand the adversary, not able to confute, and to conclude, so farre from making the man of God perfect to all good works, that rather the quite contrary may be confyrmed.160

The support for their arguments rested upon what they saw as a glaring contrast between the present Church of England and the New Testament Apostolic Church. This led to a call for abolition of the episcopacy and the establishment of a presbyterian form of Church government.

John Field would translate several of Calvin's sermons such as the Foure Sermons (1579) and Beza's treatise attacking bishops (1580) which Lord Glamis of Scotland obtained as a letter from Beza in August of 1575. This De triplici episcopatu circulated in Field's translation as The Judgement of a most reverend and learned man from beyond the Seas, concerning a threefolde order of bishops. John Bridges' Defense of the government established in the Church of England (1585) refuted in part Beza's attack on the divine right of bishops.

Cartwright was indeed very sympathetic to the theology and polity that was advocated by Field and Wilcox. He shows his solidarity in that he did not "scruple to express his sympathy, to visit (Field and Wilcox) in prison, and to support their arguments."[161] The authorities seemed to be convinced that Cartwright was the chief instigator of the controversy, but they had no direct evidence with which to begin a prosecution against him. But Whitgift, still in power at Cambridge, was able to take steps against Cartwright. In 1572 Whitgift deprived Cartwright of his fellowship at Trinity on a statute technicality (not taking priest's orders within the prescribed time period) hoping to curb his influence. Whitgift's efforts had but little effect for "(Cartwright's) sphere of influence was now far wider than the courts of Cambridge college."[162] Both the appearance of the Admonition and the personal confrontation between Cartwright and Whitgift ignited the literary dual which was inaugurated by Whitgift's Answer and Cartwright's Replye to this challenge of the Admonition.

The Puritans believed that the Church of England had accepted the primacy of the Scriptures in its doctrinal statements (the Thirty-Nine Articles of 1571 were certainly Reformed), but that it had not followed the Scriptures in either its form of church order or in its worship, both of which seemed to retain too many of the traditions of Roman Catholicism. One of the major issues of the Admonition had been the doctrine that the Scriptures "contain the complete plan for the edification and building of God's Church."[163] Cartwright maintained that "the word of God contains the direction of all things pertaining to the church, yea, of whatsoever things can fall into any part of a man's life."[164] Cartwright desired a positive approach in the use of Scripture to determine polity practices. "It is necessary," Cartwright wrote, "to have the word of God go before us in all our actions... for that we cannot otherwise be assured that they please God."[165] Cartwright's primary concern is that the Scriptures be consulted as the first and foremost guide in any decisions the Church makes, be they concerned with salvation, ethics, or polity.

Whitgift answers Cartwright's assertion that the authority of Scripture must be comprehensively applied by agreeing that "nothing ought to be tolerated in the Church as necessary unto salvation, or as an article of faith, except it be expressly contained in the Word of God, or may be manifestly thereof be gathered;"[166] but he also draws the corollary, "Yet do I deny that the Scriptures do express particularly everything that is to be done in the Church."[167] For Whitgift there are aspects of Church polity and worship that are not expressly regulated in Scripture. As John Bridges says in his _Defense of the Government Established in the Church of England_, Conformists can readily admit that the Puritan program is based on Scriptural authority if what is understood is simply that "it is agreeable, or not contrary to God's holy word."[168]

This double negative, "not contrary to" Scripture, becomes the rallying cry of the established Church and when Whitgift makes a special point of using this double negative Cartwright objects. Whitgift glosses a quotation from Augustine, "'That if anything be universally observed of the whole church' (not repugnant to scriptures), for he so meaneth, 'not to keep that, or to reason of that is madness'." But Cartwright protests: "Concerning your gloss ('if it be not repugnant to the scripture'),... it is not enough, because it must be grounded by the scripture."[169] Whitgift sees no logical difference between a double negative and a positive agreement with Scripture: "In matters of order, ceremonies, and government, it is sufficient if they 'be not repugnant to the scripture.' Neither do I think any great difference to be betwixt 'not repugnant to the word of God,' and 'according to the word'."[170]

It becomes clear that both parties are approaching the question of Biblical authority from similar epistemological assumptions but with quite different preoccupations. Whitgift (later more clearly stated by Hooker) wants to give human reason a place alongside the Scriptures and then to rely on Reason as a compliment to the message of the Bible with specific practical concerns (such as church government and discipline) which are not expressly detailed in the text. By contrast, Cartwright held that the Bible was the "revealed will of God from end to end, through and through,"[171] and he believed it to be authoritative in all manner of ecclesiastical life without the need of aid from Reason or any other source. One must not forget that the conflict between Whitgift and Cartwright was not an academic debate alone, but, rather, a struggle for survival. The Admonition was soon available in Oxford where it seems that a few were aroused by the Whitgift/Cartwright Answere to the Admonition. Arthur Wake of Christ Church used a Paul's Cross sermon of August 1573 to confirm what Cartwright set down in writing. But Wake left Oxford soon after and was quickly deprived of his living at Great Billing.[172]

The efforts of the authorities to censure Cartwright and his publications during this time led to a warrant for his arrest issued in December of 1573 by the Ecclesiastical Commission. This preceded his itinerant journey to Germany and matriculation at Heidelberg University where most of the faculty espoused Calvinistic principles. But upon the death of the German Calvinist sympathizer, Frederick III, and the accession of Ludwig VI (a decided Lutheran), Cartwright became one of "those divines who had ruled for so long in the spirit of the Old Testament and the Roman Inquisition"[173] and had to vacate Heidelberg along with the more established Protestants.

Before he had been forced to leave Heidelberg, however, he traveled to Basel where in the company of Walter Travers he wrote a preface to Travers' Disciplina Ecclesiastica in 1574. Cartwright on his own admission is known to have written the preface, for in a letter to Christopher Hatton about 1580, after referring to his own writings on the subject of church discipline, he says: "If yt may seems to longe, lett the trial be, by the ecclesiasticall discipline written in Laten, whiche as it handleth the same matter, so by a preface sett before itt, I have testified my agreement therewith."[174] He also translated Travers' handbook into English under the title A Full and Plaine Declaration of Ecclesiastical Discipline owt of the Worde of God and off the Declininge of the Church of England from the Same. The treatise soon became "the most authoritative English account of the Calvinist scheme of Church order"[175] because of its appeal to the general public. It is interesting to note that after the voluminous replies and answers issued by Cartwright and Whitgift that it was this "slight pamphlet of twenty-two pages, not a learned tome" which became the accepted standard primer of presbyterian puritanism in England.[176]

Cartwright's career, sees him turn up in Middelburg, Holland, where he is employed as a sales supervisor for the English Merchant Adventurers, who were strong supporters of further purification of the Church.[177] During this period (1577) he completed The rest of the second replie of Thomas Cartwright agaynst Master Doctor Vuhitgifts (sic) second ansvver, touching the Church discipline. This work is a watershed for the English Puritan movement. It marks out a decisive rift between Cartwright's Puritanism and those dissenters of a more radical persuasion. The Rest deals primarily with "popish apparel" an issue reminiscent of the Vestiarian question of the previous decade. Cartwright advocates compromise if a minister must choose between either losing his preaching position or wearing the surplice. He feels quite strongly that these "secondary issues" should not lead to succession from the Church.

Cartwright returned to England in 1598 and lived out his life in Warwick. But even in his late years he was often sought out as a presbyterian spokesman and was to have spoken at the Hampton Court Conference, but his death in December, 1603, prevented his serving. His funeral sermon was preached by John "Decalogue" Dod. His papers were left to Dod and Hildersham including A Treatise of Christian Religion (1616) with its appended "short Catechisme." The Catechisme appended to the several editions of Dod and Cleaver, Ten Commandements is this short form by Cartwright. The question, "What is praier?" is answered alike in the Treatise of 1616 and Dod/Cleaver where it reads as follows:

> It is a calling vpon God in the name of Christ, for the more ample and full fruition of the good things wee have need of.177

Chapter 12) A Rustie Talent

The Elizabethan Puritan bishops shared with the presbyterian classical reformers and the congregational puritans a common concern to purify the Church of England which was begun in King Edward's day, delayed under Mary and continued under Elizabeth. Their institutional means to achieve that goal varied though a common ideological core sustained their sundry efforts. One ought to shift the focus from the diocesan level through the regional level down to the local level. How did faithful pastors carry out the puritan program at the parish level and how did the auditors respond to preaching from the scriptures? Richard Greenham, Richard Rogers and Thomas Shepard are three whose diverse parish experience from the sixteenth to the seventeenth century and from Cambridge in Old England to Cambridge in New England can document that level of reform.

Congregational puritans such as Robert Browne and Henry Barrow will come into the next chapter on English separatism rather than occupy our attention just now. As a transition from the classical puritans such as Cartwright to the parish preachers like Greenham one might pause to read a 1574 response to Master Cartwright. The anonymous Defense of the Ecclesiastical Regiment in Englande (1574) is a skillful rejection of Cartwright's "precision" position on the status quo ante. The author betrays his own position when he says on page 107:

> And so doubte I not a whit, but under the rounde cappe of one Precision, lurketh more deadly poyson than under the Rochettes of four and twentie Bishops.

Three different comments from this Defense will summarize the intensity of feeling about Puritans in 1574. In so doing our taxonomy will experience the challenge of a contemporary discussion. The first comment provides a simile of a ship and its mast in which the precisions are the enemy.

> euen as in skirmishe upon the seas, the toppe gallant is stricken downe before the shippe be sunk: euen so in the perilous waues of this unstable worlde, they whiche only bend themselues to make shipwracke of the Churche of Christe, (to make sure work) strike downe the maste of all authoritie, from whence the Byshops, who in respect of their vocation are moste fifty termed watchmen in the Scripture, may discouer a far off the fleete of Sathan our professed enimie, and either stryke sayle for feare of daunger, or prepare themseues for a fierce encounter. (p.5)

Secondly, our writer worries about the rhetoric of rebellion which calls Whitgift "Linsey Woolsey Bishop, Pope of Lambeth" (p.92). His response is often in kind:

> The case is harde, when euery saucie iacke, discoursing of diuinitie upon his bench at home, dare presume upon his owne bare worde, to controll both Prince and state (p.32).

Finally, after complaining about Cartwright's inconsistency in attacking bishops while wearing robes in the very Cambridge colleges founded by episcopal largesse (pp. 97-98), our intrepid commentator calls these precisions meddlers in other men's affairs.

> If they be the children of Abraham, let them trace their fathers steppes: if they be Eagles, let them not forsake the body, which is the Churche of Christ. Practise muste be lynked with preaching, and the time not wasted in vayne and childishe questions: let them not be curious in trifles, and recklesse in more wayghtie causes. They must beware of enquiring after other mens affayres, and negligent in discharge of their own vocation. They must acknowledge a duetie to their superiours, and presume not too farre of their rustie talent.178

A. Kent and Suffolk

1. Cranbrook

Cranbrook in County Kent reflects the tensions which puritan clergy introduced into the parish structure, even if its puritan tendancies were held by a tenacious minority.[179] A recent portrait sketched from Sussex wills together with Cranbrook records gives the reader a miniature view of puritan impact at the parish level.[180]

Cranbrook was one of the largest parishes in Kent, measuring eight miles by six with three hundred households containing 1500 communicants in 1557 and at least 2000 by 1597.[181] A genuine protestant ministry began at Cranbrook in October 1561 with the admission of Richard Fletcher, whose residency was as remarkable as his religion.[182] It was a puritan place in the sense of sustaining a puritan minority not to be confined to any particular class of society. The practice of worship seems protestant rather than puritan since Fletcher wore the surplice throughout the 1560s and 1570s, and communion was received while kneeling in the chancel: 1563, "Payd for mattes to laye in the quyre to knele on"; 1563: "Payd for 12 yardes of matttynge for the communyon place."[183]

Between 1575 and 1585 Fletcher employed three curate preachers in succession who were puritans. John Stroud ran the clandestine puritan press of the early 1570s; Thomas Ely (Hely) was a leading Sussex nonconformist; Dudley Fenner, who arrived in 1583, was the prodigious and erudite puritan spokesman. The press was provocative, for Stroud was well known to the ecclesiastical courts of London and Rochester to the south-east.[184]

Stroud was inflammatory in his denunciation of bishops as "ungracious knaves" and active in his support of conventicles. Fletcher's son was recruited to defend his father at Cranbrook, while a dozen ministers and 138 people petitioned Archbishop Edmund Grindal to reinstate Stroud as a preacher.[185] Amongst other concerns Stroud argued that,

> It is a common thinge now for euery pragmaticall prentice to have in his hand and mouthe the gouernment and

> reformation of the Churche. And he that in exercise can speak thereof, that is the man. Euery artificer must be a reformer and a teacher, forgetting their state thei stand in bothe to be taught and to be reformed.186

Dudley Fenner introduced peculiar baptismal names to Cranbrook in March 1583 with the baptism of Joyagaine Netter and Fromabove Hendly, as well as his own daughter Morefruit in the end of that year. Fortunately, John Bigg's son Smallhope, was still alive and well in 1615.[187] Fenner (1558?-1587) matriculated at Peterhouse, Cambridge on June 15, 1575 as the scion of great wealth in Kent. After a few months in Cranbrook, Fenner followed Cartwright to Antwerp. In 1583 Fenner returned to Cranbrook only to find that the new Archbishop John Whitgift insisted on three symbols of conformity; the Queen's supremacy, authority of the prayer-book and the thirty-nine articles. Fenner and seventeen Kentish ministers refused to subscribe, for which action Whitgift suspended their licenses to preach. Fenner was apprehended after the Queen's council did not interfere. He languished in prison for several months before he subscribed so that he could go abroad. Fenner took charge of the reformed church at Middelburg where Cartwright had settled. There he died at the end of 1587.[188] One of Fenner's most impressive works is the 1587 Defence of the godlie Ministers, against the slaunders of D. Bridges.

2. Dedham

If Cranbrook is a microcosm of parish concerns in Kent, Suffolk mirrors magisterial involvement in the puritan agenda. Professor Collinson describes the particularities of place in his delightful essay on Suffolk written to honor Geoffrey Nuttall.

Samuel Ward of Ipswich delivered his 1618 sermon on Jethro at Bury St. Edmunds. In this portrait of the biblical prince and priest, Collinson finds a puritan pattern of magistracy --and-- ministry cooperating to promote God's glory akin to the agenda outlined under Edward VI. It was Bucer's De Regno Christi which struck the notes of such mutuality. Ward cites Bucer to underline the minister's task to encourage the magistrate. Four separate editions of this sermon in 1618, 1621, 1623 and 1627 as well as its inclusion in collections of 1623, 1626 and 1636 gave wide circulation to such sentiments in Jacobean times.

> And what is our office that are ministers, but as God's trumpets and drummers to encourage, hearten and put life in these that fight his battles and doe his work.[189]

In the 1570s, as Collinson points out, Suffolk came closer to approximating the godly commonwealth than any other part of England at any other time. John Knewstub was the most famous of these Suffolk preachers and resided at Cockfield from 1579 to 1624. Bury St. Edmunds was a center of activity where regular combination lectures were given on Mondays and whose school sent many a son on to Cambridge such as Richard Sibbes.[190] The most scholarly Reformation version of scripture was the Tremellius Bible which circulated amongst the ministers. Sir Robert Jermyn's sister provided for ten copies of the Bible to be given to Suffolk ministers including Knewstub.[191]

Knewstub's Lectures Upon the Twentieth Chapter of Exodus are an example of the learned reflection which mirrors obedience for such magistrates. As a Cambridge man (B.A. 1564) and Cartwright supporter as well as a member of Field's central committee, Knewstub took an active role in the Presbyterian Puritan movement. He was one of the four puritan spokesmen at Hampton Court in 1604.[192] The Lectures went through four printings from 1577 to 1584.[193] The preface of the 1578 edition speaks of just such obedience:

> When we shall have profited in drawing near unto Christ, and making much of his mercy by an often and true sight of ourselves in the law, there is yet remaining another use and fruit to be taken by it of no less profit than the former, which is, that when we shall have taken comfort in the mercies of Christ and decreed to walk in the obedience of his will to declared our thankfulness thereby, the law will stand us in good stead to quicken us thereunto...
>
> And who is he then, that seeing what duties are to be performed both to the Lord and to his brethren, and in what manner of affection (for it is the end of Christ's

> death and the purchase of his passion, to have a number not only given, but zealously given unto good works (cf. Tit. 2:14)) remembering withal what an enemy he hath at home of his own nature, if there be any fear of God in him, that shall not be occasioned hereby more plentifully to practice the means of his salvation -- especially knowing that those who are ingrafted into the body of Christ must die unto sin and rise up into these fruits of righteousness?[194]

Dedham was the home of the Lewkenor family and their ministers Robert Pricke and his son Timothy whose successive pastorate ran the full course of sixty years from 1577 to 1638. Professor Collinson who used the Dedham classis in Essex as the central example of his 1967 Elizabethan Puritan Movement[195] returns a decade later to Dedham as the model of a puritan commonwealth.[196] The pastors who took the alias Oldmayne and the Lewkenor family cooperated in bringing the gospel to the tiny hamlet. Martha Hignam spent her last thirty-five years at Dedham where she acquired the former monastic property of the Abbots Dedham and built a house. Martha who was the mother-in-law of Lewkenor left a will of 1593 which sets forth a series of evangelical legacies. She left her Geneva Bible to the parish church, endowed a scholarship at Emmanuel College, Cambridge and left £40 to provide a parsonage which still exists.[197]

Lewkenor sat in every parliament save that of 1601 from 1571 until his death in 1605. He was there to advance the precision cause. When he spoke up for the extreme measures in Anthony Cope's presbyterian bill of 1587, he was sent to the tower for such clandestine activity. In one parliamentary speech Lewkenor referred to the bishops as "rather deformers than reformers."[198] The Lewkenor papers (British Library MS. Add. 38492) show all but 13 of the sixty-five items connected with the national campaign for reformation.

Robert Pricke supported his patron who loaned him many books. One such list of nine items include works by Beza, Danaeus and Pierre du Moulin.[199] Pricke exhorted Lewkenor that sin not sully his service for Jesus Christ.

> We cease not hear in our smale measure to lift up our unworthie eies and handes... both in confessing of our sinnes and striving with his majestie by humble requestes for all necessarie blessing upon you and the rest of your worthie yokefellowes in the service of Jesus Christ...200

Thomas Beard's Theatre of Gods Iudgments collected examples of those who thwarted God's will and so were punished. Pharaoh was one such example "where he surprised and ensnared him, overthrew and violently ouerturned the wheeles of his chariots, and put his whole armie to a hurliburly..."[201] These in Dedham were surely supporting actors in their own puritan theater of England lest similar punishment catch them in a torrent of their own making. Beard became Oliver Cromwell's teacher at Huntingdon where no doubt he passed on such sentiments to the next generation of Puritan gentry.

B. "Dark Corners of the Land"

The former Master of Balliol College, Oxford wrote a delightful book about seventeenth-century England which he called The World Turned Upside Down. Christopher Hill explores the puritan insistence on inner discipline as a response to the unsettled condition of society. New men were to create a new order, even if their masterlessness meant societal freedom for many rather than security of conscience for some. Beneath the surface stability of rural England Professor Hill describes the seething mobility of forest squatters, strolling players, pedlars and vagabonds.[202] In the dark corners of the land puritan types created pockets of inner repose. Wales was one such corner where the evangelical response sought to briddle the brigands.

When opposition to Henry VIII's divorce came from the North and West of England, the Pilgrimage of Grace and Cornish Rising of 1549 indicated dissatisfaction with the protestantism of the capital. In 1551 six traveling ministers were appointed to tour Wales, Lancashire, Yorkshire, the Scottish Borders, Devon and Hampshire in rotation. John Knox and Edmund Grindal were among their number. John Penry sought help for Wales from Queen and Parliament, saying in 1587 that for one parish with a quarterly sermon which was the Elizabethan standard, twenty had none. There was not a solitary parish in "the most barren corner of the land" these past 29 years where a godly minister had executed a learned ministry for six consecutive years.[203] In 1567 even the bishops concurred that 90% of the North Wales clergy were unable to preach. Bishop Bayly's report on Bangor of 1623 contains these observations: "But two sermons... this twelvemonth;" "no sermon... this five or six years;" "no sermons at all."[204] The protection of popery and popular superstitions assisted by landed gentry gave the authorities qualms about the loyalty of these areas. Robert Parsons told Philip II of Spain in 1585 that "all Wales would rise up to assist a Spanish invasion."[205]

Literature was crucial to this crusade, including a Welsh Bible. The Hampton Court Conference discussed such dark corners of the land. James announced the intention to place preachers in Wales. The Book of Homilies appeared in Welsh in 1606 to match the 1551 Welsh Epistles and Gospels and the entire New Testament and Prayer book of 1567.

Richard Davies who was elected bishop of St. Davids in 1561 was a member of Grindal's circle whom Edmund Spenser commemorated as "Diggan Davie" in the Shepherd's Calendar.[206] His 1567 preface to the Welsh New Testament was an Address to the Welsh Nation. Davies shared with Archbishop Matthew Parker the legend that Joseph of Aremathia introduced Christianity to Britain, which the Augustine mission via Canterbury desecrated and Romanized. Protestantism was not alien to Wales which accepted "the faith of Christ and the word of God, which it had receiued before all the islands of the world."[207] Davies translated I Timothy, Hebrews, James and I-II Peter. The Welsh of this literate translation was difficult for the common folk to read and own who had only an expensive folio printed in 1588 by William Morgan of Llandaff and St. Asaph. Not until 1630 did two London merchants of Welsh origin pay for printing a handy size edition which, "for the first time brought the Scriptures to the homes of those... who could read."[208]

An example of the benefit from this concern over Wales is the subsequent activity of Morgan Llwyd who received his education at the free school at Wrexham and then became a chaplain(?) during the Civil War. He seems to have been vicar at Wrexham from 1646 and founder of a chapel for nonconformists. He became an appointee to preach under the February 2, 1649 act for the propagation of the gospel in Wales. His works have a purity of diction which put them in the first rank of Welsh prose, especially Llyfr y Tri Aderyn (The Three Birds) of 1653 which is in the form of a dialogue between an eagle (Cromwell), a dove (Puritan) and a raven (Archbishop Laud?).[209]

Llwyd was converted under the ministry of an Oxford trained puritan, one Walter Cradock (1606?-1659). After going down from Oxford, Cradock served two parishes in Wales as curate. The Bishop of Llandaff deprived Cradock of his curacy for his puritanical views after which Cradock appeared in Wrexham for a year. After a stint in Herefordshire, he became preacher of a congregational church and Allhallows-the-Great, London. By his death in 1659 Cradock produced some works remarkable for their clarity and piety. Among these are a sermon of 1646, The Saints Fulnesse of Joy; Gospel-Libertie (1648); and Gospel-Holinesse, or, the saving sight of God (1651).[210] The first was a sermon on I John (1:3); the second, I Corinthians (10:23); and the third, Isaiah (6:5).

There was a note of joy in Cradock's preaching because the gospel "is only good newes, there is not one word of bad newes... but only glad tidings, sweet and good newes to the heart of the worst of sinners."[211] In Gospel-Holinesse he laments a heathenish desire of holiness as a legal faith. Ordinary professors, i.e. believers, find too much corruption and so little grace. But God would have us trust Him before he will trust us.

> I have seen poore women in the mountaines of Wales... they haue been so poor that when they have come to a house to beg a little whey or butter-milke, they have been faine to beg the loane of a pot... to put it in. So... we cannot carry one graine of grace home, unlesse

> God give us spirituall buckets. As that woman said, John 4, Here is water, but where is the bucket to draw? So God may say, thou wantest grace, but where is thy bucket? saith the humble soule, Lord I have none, thou must both give the water and lend the bucket to carry it home.212

Morgan Llwyd used to preach at Pwllheli on market days, and his custom was to walk through the market with his hands on his back, holding his Bible in one of them; "and the people would retreat before him, as though a chariot were rushing through the streets."[213] Such an 1820 description of Welsh Puritan personality is vivid indeed. Morgan Llwyd held that "flesh is the will and mystery of man" and included sermons among those secrets. The journey inward through the transient to the eternal brings one to God the creator. At the same time Isaiah 45:15 reminded Llwyd that no human mind can entirely comprehend God.[214] At least one can travel to the fringes of revelation. The Spirit of God takes one to the chamber of the heart to converse with God. In Gwaedd Ynghymru he says, "Oh man, God has shown you what is good. He has set a candle within you to light your way."[215]

To read the book within does not mean in Llwyd's language to discard other books, but rather to remove the rust from what is written. In Gair O'r Gair Llwyd writes as follows:

> If you haue read the letter, haue you understood the Spirit in it after all your reading? ...choose to listen to God's Word and you shall live.216

In 1652 Llwyd wished his hearers to avail themselves of spiritual substance in God's Word which fans the candle of the heart. Llyfr y Tri Aderyn uses the symbol of a rose springing up to flower as a sign of union with Christ. "Take heed," he answers, "lest your candle go out on the earth, so that there be no light in you to show you your destiny when you die."[217] Professor Jones points to Llwyd's influence through his books, which, in their concern for the reality of sin and forgiveness, were read by the leaders of Welsh revival in the eighteenth century. That corner of the land may have been dark, but one small candle at least lighted the pathway to the God of Heaven who resides in human hearts.

How fitting that Llwyd's congregation in Wrexham were called "New Lights."[218]

Llwyd is neither a slave of Jacob Boehme, whose works he translated into Welsh, nor a Quaker, though he uses the word "quake" to describe the work of God. The voice of the Spirit is not to be found in carnal animosity, certainly not in the whirlwind nor the bloodshed of civil war (cf. I Kings XIX).

> When the true shepherd speaks, and a man hears him, the heart burns within, and the flesh quakes, and the mind lights up like a candle, and the conscience ferments like wine in a vessel, and the will bends to the truth: and that thin, heavenly, mighty voice raises the dead to life, from the grave of himself, to wear the crown, and wondrously renews the whole life to live like a lamb of God.219

Llwyd was also a fine poet who once wrote a poem called The order of Christs remote poore and despicable Churches in Wales. There he wrote of the fellowship of the saints and the sanctity of obedience.

> No honest soules kept out
> their presence we desire,
> no new engagement, no new bonds
> do we at all require.
> But wellcome saincts as saincts,
> of all we make but one,
> exhorting one another more
> to live to christ alone. 220

C. Old English Puritans

1. Richard Greenham

In 1646 John Geree published his pamphlet called, The Character of an old English Puritane, or Non-Conformist. The old Puritan before the parliamentary problems of Laudian England was a man devoted to God's word and to prayer.

> He was a man of good spiritual appetite, and could not be content with one meal a day. An afternoon sermon did relish as well to him as one in the morning.221

By common wisdom none fit that pattern better than Richard Greenham of Pembroke College, Cambridge, who was rector of Dry Drayton some seven miles west of Cambridge. Henry Holland collected Greenham's writings to which he added a description of this faithful pastor. "That most rare graces of Gods spirit did shine in him," wrote Holland in his preface "all tempered as with faith vnfained vnto Christ, so with... compassion and loue towards men."[222]

As a Fellow from 1566 to 1570 of Pembroke and a Cartwright supporter, Greenham would come under suspicion. One day he responded to the Bishop of Ely that the fault for discontent over conformity "might lie on either side, or on neither side: For (said he) if they loued one another as they ought... it lay on neither side."[223] During two decades Greenham rose at four to prepare "the verbal bread of life to his rural parishoners." After the morning sermon he tramped the fields to converse with his parishioners at the plow. On his way into Cambridge he seldom failed to cast alms to the Castle prisoners. His home was childless but often visited by clerical companions like Cambridge dons or country parsons such as Richard Rogers. He left Dry Drayton heartsick that but one family benefited from his preaching.[224] Three years in London ended when the plague took his life in 1594.

One of Greenham's works bears the title, Godly Treatises of Divers Arguments, Tending Principally to comfort and cure santes afflicted. Treatise number three gives the "markes of a righteous man." The dedicatory epistle summarizes the notes of an upright man as follows: 1) true righteousness is imputed after one feels naked of righteousness because of sin, 2) One must desire to leave sin and escape its punishment; 3) One must commit himself by faith unto Christ and trust in his all sufficient merits for full reconciliation with God; 4) such a justified and reconciled person is also sanctified sufficiently to walk upright before God; 5) This uprightness has four special notes.

Those four special notes of uprightness (Hebrew Yashar) form the central thrust in Greenham's ministry, which as both Holland and Thomas Fuller testify was one of consolation for bruised consciences. There is nothing here of the practical syllogism of

Beza or Perkins, but nonetheless a sensitive treatment of Yashar as the ability to discern the intent of obedience to God's law while freed from obstacles. Thus the intensive or piel form of the verb in Proverbs 3:6 which directs a person's course is supported by Greenham's pastoral advice; i.e., "in all your ways acknowledge Him, and He will direct your paths." The third and fourth marks underscore this very well indeed.

> The third marke is euen to proceed on, in euery good grace & in al obedience not to stay in the beginning, or to slide back, when we are gone somewhat forward. And here yet Gods children may both linger and fall: but they mislike and mourne for their lingering & if they fall, they take better hold of Christ in a new repentance: and because by their fall they haue left much ground, they run the faster & cheerfuller in the rest of their rase. The fourth note of a righteous man is to loue righteous maners, and righteous matters, as well in others as in our selues: wee must loue our superiours before vs, to follow them; our equals to confirme them, and to bee confirmed by them; our inferiours to instruct them, and to helpe them forward in the waies of godlines.225

Thomas Fuller, whose father was well acquainted with Greenham, recounts the lack of response at Dry Drayton to his preaching, hence the verses:

> Greenham had pastures green,
> But sheep full lean.226

2. Richard Rogers (1550?-1618)

Richard Rogers matriculated at Christ's College, Cambridge in November of 1565, and graduated B.A. in 1570/71. Rogers became lecturer at Wethersfield, Essex, about 1577. Apart from a suspension of eight months in 1583, Rogers preached at Wethersfield until his death in 1618 (April 21). He was the author of Seaven Treatises (1603), often reissued in abbreviated form as The Practice of Christianity (1618) as well as a contributer to A Garden of Spiritual Flowers (1612). Rogers preached and lectured on Judges which became a commentary (1615) and left the best known Puritan diary[227] whose purpose seems to express that articulated by John Carter: "to cast up his accounts with God every day."[228]

Edward Dering and other fellows made Christ's College in the decades before Emmanuel College "the greatest Puritan seminary of them all." In addition to Dering and Rogers there were Laurence Chaderton, William Perkins and John Milton. One forgets that students slept in trundle beds at their tutors' feet, so that if proximity ever influenced theology it happened in Cambridge colleges. Dering was a university student during Mary's reign (born 1540), defended Jewel against Harding in the 1560s and was a successful Greek tutor at Christ's. Such tutors toughened the resolve of godly pastors to see royal arms and courtly hearts shepherd England's parishes with skillful hands. John Field edited Dering's Workes as the first (1590) of the Puritan posthumous collections. His letters of spiritual counsel may have likewise been the first such collection to circulate.

On February 25, 1570 Dering preached a remarkable sermon before the Queen which Collinson sees as a turning point.[229] Dering chose Psalm (78:70-72) as his text where David was brought from tending sheep to be the shepherd of his people: "And David shepherded them with integrity of heart; with skillful hands he led them." (N.I.V.) God had chosen the Queen and if she were "as an untamed and unruly heifer," God could unmake her.[230] Elizabeth must keep back the ignorant from the ministry by removing authority from the bishops. They are not to make ministers in their closet of whomever they please. If they claim to be learned and yet do not preach, they "are dumb dogs and will not bark, briddle at the least their greedy appetites. Pull out of their mouths those poisoned bones that they so greedily gnaw upon."[231]

Life for Rogers was "a continual fret" in Porter's words, because though he studied ten hours a day he still worried about "what heavenly books lie by me unoccupied and unsearched."[232] Rogers' time was often compromised even though he resolved to rise early enough to reflect on an hour's reading before meditation and prayer. Winter mornings and domestic concerns combined to reduce the hour in half.[233] So in 1588 one reads the following entry.

> Dec. 21, 1588. I finde small comfort as yet after my coven[ant], for partly by thincking of our placeinge in an other house, and heareinge that after our travaile we are like to be disapointed, I was constrained to attende about that, and partly, not rizeinge early of late, and then lookinge after the boyes, I have been much unsetled and my time taken from study...234

Rogers' record is a delicate balance between success and failure in meeting self-imposed standards of growth in grace and lapses from love. But then, that over-the-shoulder-glance for a sight of the evil one seems to be characteristic for many an Elizabethan Puritan for whom God himself was to be seen by faith. One wonders if the introspective view of life as a constant struggle does not create the impression of a self-fulfilling prophecy as in the following diary entrees for 1588:

> One day this while I was sodianly overtaken with hardnes of hart because of the ra[in]. I held from murm[uring], but I could not lik nor be contented with it nor bringe my hart to it. This went to my hart when I saw what rebel[lion] was in me. I was then to study for my sermon, and nether could I goe about that with such unsetlednes of hart, and yet not to goe about it, my sorow was the more to be idle. I purposed to bewail my sin at more leisure, and for that time to proceed in my study, and so did. The next day I had harty detest[ation] of my sin, and so retourned againe to my god... And thus may be partly seen my poore course in this pilgrimage.235

> Then the weather, being heavy, troubled me againe, as before, and unsetled me at study for the good part of the day, and that for thincking that thinges would be deare, which, by a chapter of eccle[siastes], 5:9, I saw with harty shame tha I should thus roave after profit, who had so litel cause, and for many yeares togither had litle used so to doe. I was ashamed of it hartily that night, and so doe still continue this morne[ing]. It is wonderful that ever such mistes should be cast before ones eyes, as to be so excessivly caryed after earthly th[ings], and yet not to see it a fault nor ones selfe unsetled.236

If one were depressed by rain, England would be a difficult site for ministry. The frequent rains after all were responsible for creating England's green and pleasant land. Would Rogers complain of spiritual dryness during a drought?

Rogers' Seven Treatises (1603) does sound a positive note in its preface, that though one were "sad and heauie in heart" for sin and abominations of the land, it should so be "yet without discouragement, or dumpishness: resting and belieuing in God... without dreadfull and deadly desprayring."[237] Rogers' purpose was to discount Robert Parson's Directory as well as Jaspar Loarte, Exercise of a Christian Life. These tie men to a ridiculous daily task of reading some part of Christ's passion and recital of daily prayers. After a lengthy dismissal of that Catholic piety, Rogers goes on to write of the "freedome and libertie we may haue by faith."[238]

The third corrected edition of Seaven Treatises adds several duties of daily living. Rogers thanks the Queen for her support of the gospel which alleviates the famine of hearing God's word (Amos 8:11-12). One of these new duties is to visit the sick as a pastoral command.[239] The privileges of the true Christian are God's gracious helps: prayer, watchfulness, reviewal of the past day, and belief that God will bless these means.[240] The 1630 fifth edition is a reprint of this 1610 third edition.

That the spiritual interacted with the temporal authority can be seen in Rogers' Commentary On Judges (1615), dedicated to Sir Edward Coke, Lord Chief Justice of England. One of Rogers' reasons for publishing these 103 sermons in commentary form was to support the church and commonwealth, "both compast with one wall, and both yeelding mutual aids & defences each to other."[241] The civil sword must back and authorize the ministry of the word "against them, who profanely cōtemne the word..."[242] Though the courage of those ancient magistrates was matched by the forlorne times in which they lived, even so did the Lord give them the sword to fight against" forreine enemies... and then... against the intestine adverseries (no lesse hurtfull) of God, his Gospell, and our common peace. For this sword rusteth not, nor losseth her edge with time."[243] Rogers has interpreted the hard to obtain commentary of Peter Martyr on Judges for the simpler hearers' benefit and to teach preachers how to instruct their folk "plainely and pithily as may be for their best edifying." This Rogers is eager to do in his commentary because "some fill their Sermons with the froth of their own braines..."[244] No rusty sword indeed...!

The positive tone of Rogers on Judges comes in comments such as those on the necessity of gratitude as a biblical response to God's offer of grace. "Christians should have two bookes," writes Rogers, "in the one to record their faults and falles, in the other to register Gods benefits... he that is thankful is a good Christian."[245] That thankfulness should extend to the blessing of God on the wealthy, since "God alloweth wealthy men to occupie and prosper in their calling... and teacheth, that the diligent hand maketh rich... for the Lord allows that men should encrease rather than diminish that which they have..."[246] It is a great favor of God that people have access to markets and fairs to purchase their needed commodities, but never on the Sabbath! In all these and by small means God works great things for his own people. He removes the pain of extreme illness, prevented the Gun-powder treason and caused thousands to respond by subduing their stony hearts. That "Fruit of the Gospell" is why all these are to be remembered so as to "foster praise among us."[247]

Chapter 13) Thomas Shepard: Colonial Pastor

Thomas Shepard was born in 1605 at Towcester, Northamptonshire. Shepard states that he was born on "powder treason day" at "that very hour of the day wherein the Parliament should have been blown up by Popish priests," and his father named him Thomas on that account because he could hardly believe that such wickedness could be attempted against such a "religious and good Parliament."[248] That seems to fix the date at November 5, 1605, a day also know as "Gunpowder Day" or "Guy Fawkes Day." His father was William Shepard, an apprentice to a grocer named Bland. William Shepard married the grocer's daughter, and Thomas was the youngest of their nine children.

A plague came to Towcester when Thomas was three, and he, "being the youngest and best beloved" of his mother,[249] was sent to live with his grandparents in the nearby town of Fossecut, and later to live with his uncle in Adthrop. By the time he returned home, his mother had died, though not of the plague. His father remarried, and he wrote, she "did let me see the difference between my own mother and a stepmother: she did seem not to love me but to incense my father often against me..."[250]

Thomas was sent by his father to a Welshman, Mr. Rice, who kept the Free School in Towcester, but he wrote, "he was exceeding curst and cruel and would deal roughly with me and so discouraged me wholly from the desire of learning that I remember I wished oftentimes myself in any condition to keep hogs or beasts rather than to go to school and learn."[251] His father died when Thomas was ten, leaving two children by his second wife.

A. Cambridge Convert

Thomas' brother, John, rescued him from his stepmother who was neglecting his education. He was returned to school where he learned some Latin and Greek under a new schoolmaster, William Cluer, a graduate of Emmanuel College in Cambridge and "an eminent preacher." When he was fifteen, his brother made arrangements for him to be admitted as a pensioner at Emmanuel College, which he entered on February 10, 1619/20.[252] He later reflected:

> ...I have oft thought what a woeful estate I had been left in if the Lord had left me in the profane, ignorant town of Towcester where I was born, that the Lord should pluck me out of that sink and Sodom, who was the least in my father's house, forsaken of father and mother, yet that the Lord should fetch me out from thence by such a sweet hand.[253]

At Emmanuel College Thomas tried the ways of the world. One day he became dead drunk, and was carried to a "scholar's chamber" where he awakened the next morning in shame and confusion.

It being a Sabbath, he spent the day lying in a cornfield reflecting on his life. That seemed to be the beginning of his conversion experience. When Dr. Preston became Master of the College, his preaching particularly affected Thomas. He was often convicted through sermons and conversations with godly individuals. He frequently went into the fields for meditation, and took with him a little book in which he would record those things the Lord showed him. The three things that seemed to trouble him the most were lack of conviction, pride, and doubt. One day while walking in the fields, the Lord gave him this thought - "Be not discouraged therefore because thou art so vile, but make this double use of it: 1) bother thyself the more; 2) fell a greater need and put a greater price upon Jesus Christ who only can redeem thee from all sin."[254] In due time his struggle ended and he wrote, "The Lord made me see that so many as receive him, he gives power to be the sons of God (John 1:12), and I saw the Lord gave me a heart to receive Christ with a naked hand, even naked Christ, and so the Lord gave me peace."[255]

Thomas received his B.A. degree in 1623/24 and his M.A. degree in 1627. Six months before he received his M.A. degree, he went to live with Mr. Thomas Weld, vicar of Terling, who later became pastor at Roxbury in Massachusetts Bay. While there, he also enjoyed the preaching of Mr. Thomas Hooker who was preaching in Chelmsford, Essex, and later ministered at Newton in Massachusetts Bay before moving to Hartford in 1636. These men became his friends and counsellors and assisted him in setting up a lectureship in Earle's Colne in Essex for three years. Shortly after he received his M.A. degree, he took orders of the Bishop of Peterborough, Bishop Dove, which he later considered sinful. Shepard wrote concerning his time spent in Cambridge:

> But this I have found: the Lord was not content to take me from one town to another, but from the worst town, I think, in the world to the best place for knowledge and learning, *viz;* to Cambridge, and then the Lord was not content to give me good means but the best means and ministry and help of private Christians, for Dr. Preston and Dr. Goodwin were the most able men for preaching Christ in this latter age. And when I came from thence

> the Lord sent me to the best country in England, viz; to Essex, and set me in the midst of the best ministry in the country by whose monthly fasts and conferences I found much of God. And thus the Lord Jesus provided for me of all things of the best.256

B. English Pastor

While Thomas Shepard was at Earle's Colne, he sought to accomplish three things in his preaching: 1) to show the people the misery of their sinful state; 2) to show them the remedy in Christ Jesus; and 3) to show them how they should walk having been redeemed by Christ. It was not long before he was being accused of being a "Nonconformable man," though he, himself, was not yet sure. When the three years were ended, the people urged him to stay on, which he did. However, it was only six months later that Bishop Laud came, and he was silenced on December 16, 1630. The scene was later described by Shepard as follows:

> I was inhibited from preaching in the diocese of London by Dr. Laud, bishop of the diocese. As soon as I came in the morning, About Eight of the clock, falling into a fit of rage, he asked me what degree I had taken in the University. I answered him, I was a Master of Arts. He asked me, Of what College? I answered, Of Emmanuel. He asked how long I had lived in his diocese. I answered, Three years and upwards. He asked who maintained me all this while, charging me to deal plainly with him, adding withal that he had been more cheated and equivocated with by some of my malignant faction than ever was man by Jesuit, at the speaking of which words he looked as though blood would have gushed out of his face and did shake as if he had been haunted with an ague fit, to my apprehension by reason of his extreme malice and secret venom. I desired him to excuse me. He fell then to threten me and withal to bitter railing, calling me all to naught, saying, You pratin coxcomb! Do you think all the learning is in your brain? He pronounced his sentence thus: I charge you that you neither preach, read, marry, bury, or exercise any ministerial function in any part of my diocese, for if you do, and I hear of it, I will be upon your back and follow you wherever you go, in any part of the kingdom, and so everlastingly disenable you. I besought him not to deal so, in regard of a poor town. Here he stopped me in what I was going on to say. A poor town! You have made a company of seditious, factious Bedlams, and what do you prate to me of a poor town? I prayed him to suffer me to catechise in the

> Sabbath days in the afternoon. He replied, spare your breath; I will have no such fellows prate in my diocese. Get you gone, and now make your complaints to whom you will! So away I went, and blessed be God that I may go to him.257

After Shepard was silenced, the Harlakendens at Earle's Colne took him into their home and he stayed with them for six months of intensive study. Bishop Laud again summoned Shepard to appear in the Court of Reldon, and charged him to leave Earl's Colne. He and Mr. Weld later went to confront Bishop Laud, but he was forced to flee on horseback. Just prior to this third incident with Bishop Laud, he received an invitation to go to Buttercrambe, Yorkshire to serve as tutor and chaplain in the family of Sir Richard Darley, and he now decided to accept the offer. "Arriving at Buttercrambe Hall on a wet Saturday night he was astounded to find that some members of the family were playing at dice and backgammon."[258] Shepard concluded that this was indeed a profane house. While preaching at a wedding he met Mistress Margaret Tauteville, a cousin of Darley's whom he later married in 1632, and wrote:

> ...he then gave me her who was a most sweet humble woman, full of Christ, and a very discerning Christian, a wife who was most incomparably loving to me and every way amiable and holy and endued with a very sweet spirit of prayer... And thus I did marry the best and fittest woman in the world unto me...259

Soon after his marriage, he accepted a call to Heddon, near Newcastle, Northumberland. Because of the strong influence of Bishop Laud, Bishop Morton of Durham forbade him to preach publicly, and so he preached in the country. Many of his friends had by now left, or were planning to leave for New England. Shepard wrote, "And, so, seeing I had been tossed from the south to the north of England and now could go no farther, I then began to listen to a call to New England."[260] After his first son Thomas was born, he disguised himself and left Newcastle in June, 1634 for Ipswich. By this time his wife was pregnant again, and they resolved to go to New England that year on the "Hope of

Ipswich." After a delay of several weeks, they set sail at the beginning of winter only to be driven back by a severe storm in which they nearly lost their lives. This experience was keenly remembered and Shepard wrote, "I desire this mercy may be remembered of my children and their children's children when I am dead and cannot praise the lord in the land of the living anymore."[261] They did not entirely escape tragedy, for their son became sick with vomiting and died. It was of great grief to them that Thomas could not attend his son's burial for fear of being discovered.

C. Setting Sail

Their second son named Thomas was born on April 5, 1635, in London, and on August 10, 1635 they set sail for the second time. Again there were storms at sea -- the ship, the "Defense," was old and sprung a leak. Mrs. Shepard was tossed about and struck her head on a bolt with her infant son in her arms. Though later she became ill with a severe cold, they finally came in sight of the New England shore on October 2, 1635.

The Shepards arrived in Boston on October 3rd, some five years after the Winthrop fleet had arrived, accompanied by Thomas' brother Samuel, and Mr. Harlakenden. The Shepards arrived in Boston just as Thomas Hooker was preparing to leave Newtown for Connecticut territory. In Edward Johnson's Wonder-Working Providence, Johnson wrote:

> These people and Church of Christ being thus departed from New-towne, the godly people who came in their roomes, gathered the eleaventh Church of Christ, and called to the Office of a Pastor, that gratious sweet Heavenly minded, and soule-ravishing Minister, Master Thomas Shepeard, in whose soule the Lord shead abroad his love so abundantly, that thousands of souls have come to blesse God for him, even at this very day, who are the Seale of him Ministrey, and hee a man of a thousand, indued with abundance of true saving knoledge for himselfe and others... His natural parts were weake, but spent to the full.262

Johnson is also frequently quoted as saying that Shepard was a "poor, weak, pale-complectioned man."

The church pastored by Thomas Shepard in Newtown began with a group of friends, most of whom had come over on the "Defense." They entered into fellowship at Newtown on February 1, 1636. This church was the first to invite neighboring churches to send their elders to assist a new congregation, a practice which became regular in New England. Perhaps for this reason John Winthrop gave special attention to the proceedings in his Journal.

> Mr. Shepherd, a godly minister, come lately out of England, and divers other good Christians, intending to raise a church body, came and acquainted the magistrates therewith, who gave their approbation. They also sent to all the neighboring churches for their elders to give their assistance, at a certain day, at Newtown, when they should consitute their body. Accordingly, at this day, there met a great assembly, where the proceeding was as followeth:
>
> Mr Shepherd and two others (who were after to be chose to office) sate together in the elder's seat. Then the elder of them began with prayer. After this, Mr. Shepherd prayed with deep confession of sin, etc., and exercised out of Eph. V. - that he might make it to himself a holy, etc.; and also opened the cause of their meeting, etc. Then the elder desired to know of the churches assembled, what number were needful to make a church, and how they ought to proceed in this action. Whereupon some of the ancient ministers, conferring shortly together, gave answer: That the scripture did not set down any certain rule for the number. Three (they thought) were too few, because by Matt. xviii. an appeal was allowed from three; but that seven might be a fit number. And, for their proceeding, they advised, that such as were to join should make confession of their faith, and declare what work of grace the Lord had wrought in them; which accordingly they did, Mr. Shepherd first, then four others, then the elder, and one who was to be deacon, (who had also prayed,) and another member. Then the covenant was read, and they all gave a solemn assent to it. Then the elder desired of the churches, that, if they did approve them to be a church, they would give them the right hand of fellowship. Whereupon Mr. Cotton, (upon short speech with some others near him,) in the name of their churches, gave his hand to the elder, with a short speech of their assent, and desired the peace of the Lord Jesus to be with them. Then Mr. Shepherd made

> an exhortation to the rest of his body, about the nature of their covenant, and to stand firm to it, and commended them to the Lord in a most heavenly prayer. Then the elder told the assembly, that they were intended to choose Mr. Shepherd for their pastor, (by the name of the brother who had exercised,) and desired the churches, that if they had any thing to except against him, they would impart it to them before the day of ordination. Then he gave the churches thanks for their assistance, and so left them to the Lord.263

During this same month of February, Margaret Shepard died of consumption which followed the cold she had contracted on the ship.

D. New England Converts

In his first year in New England Thomas Shepard was faced with the two major conflicts of the early colony - the antinomian controversy and the Pequot War. The earliest known documents of the antinomian controversy are the letters that Thomas Shepard and John Cotton exchanged sometime before June, 1636 when Thomas Hooker left for the Connecticut. Shepard expressed dismay at some of the themes of Cotton's sermons and asked him to explain his views more fully. This exchange of letters served only to clarify their disagreements. Eventually the Synod of Cambridge was called, opening on August 30, 1637 to examine the antinomian questions. Thomas Shepard opened the synod with prayer, and the synod proceeded to condemn some eighty "erroneous opinions." In Shepard's view, the principle point of the antinomians which he found objectionable was:

> ...that a Christian should not take any evidence of God's special grace and love toward him by the sight of any graces or conditional evangelical promises to faith or sanctification, in way of ratiocination (for this was evidence and so a way of works), but it must be without the sight of any grace, faith, holiness, or special change in himself, by immediate revelation in an absolute promise. And because that the whole scriptures do give such clear, plain, and notable evidences of favor to persons called and sanctified, hence they said that a second evidence might be taken from hence but no first evidence.264

The final result of the controversy was that the principal protagonists from among the antinomians were removed from the colony.

Chief among them was Anne Hutchinson. It is significant, though, that in spite of Mr. Shepard's unswerving condemnation of the antinomians, and his sharp rebuke of Anne Hutchinson, John Cotton could report in The Way of Congregational Churches Cleared concerning Anne Hutchinson's attitude toward the elders that "of them shee esteemed best of Mr. Shepheard."[265]

Since Thomas Shepard reported that preaching during this time largely centered on the antinomian questions, it is of particular interest to note the content of his own preaching. During these years he was preaching his series, The Parable of the Ten Virgins Opened and Applied. This work was not only to become a transatlantic devotional classic after it was published posthumously, but it was used extensively by Jonathan Edwards in preparing his Treatise on Religious Affections.

Thomas Shepard also blamed the Pequot War on the Pequots, and especially their chief sachem, Sassacus, "a proud, cruel, unhappy, and headstrong prince," who "slew nine or ten men, women, and children at unawares and took two maids prisoners, carrying them away captive to the Pequot Country."[266] He viewed this war as a judgement from God, for as the antinomian controversy heated up, the war broke out, but as the controversy became settled, victory in war was also achieved. It must be said that Shepard showed a constant interest in the conversion of the Indians, and assisted John Eliot in establishing the first Indian mission in Cambridge. He provided the English for John Eliot's The Indiane Primer, and wrote The Clear Sun-Shine of the Gospel breaking forth upon the Indians in New England.

With both the antinomian controversy and the Pequot War behind them, the magistrates of the colony could turn to other matters. As early as October 28, 1636 the General Court of Massachusetts Bay voted to give a certain sum to establish a school or college. That act has become the traditional date for the founding of Harvard, but the Pequot War and the Hutchinson heresy delayed further progress. Several towns vied for the college, but Newtown (which from now on would be called Cambridge) became the chosen site largely because it had remained relatively free from the antinomian influence. Thomas Shepard became a member of the first Board of Overseers. He is also generally recognized as the one who founded the tradition of scholarships in America. John Winthrop wrote in his Journal:

> Mr. Shepherd, the pastor of the church in Cambridge, being at Connecticut when the commissioners met there for the United Colonies, moved them for some contribution of help towards the maintenance of poor scholars in the college, whereupon the commissioners ordered that it should be commended to the deputies of the general courts and the elders within the several colonies to raise (by way of voluntary contribution) one peck of corn or twelve pence money, or other commodity, of every family, which those of Connecticut presently performed.[267]

This benevolent spirit was also evident to the members of Shepard's congregation. He encouraged them to be hospitable to newcomers to the Colony, and also to share among themselves according to need. Samuel Eliot Morison gives an interesting list of some of the acts of benevolence recorded in the records of the church dating back to Shepard's time.[268]

In 1637, Thomas Shepard married Joanna Hooker, the eldest daughter of Thomas Hooker. They had four sons, two of whom died in infancy. Samuel and John survived their father. Thomas Shepard seemed to be blessed with good marriages, for he wrote of his second wife:

> She was a woman of incomparable meekness of spirit, toward myself especially, and very loving, of great prudence to take care for and order my family affairs, being neither too lavish nor sordid in anything, so that I knew not what was under her hands. She had an excellency to reprove for sin and discerned the evils of men. She loved God's people dearly and studious to profit by their fellowship, and therefore loved their company. She loved God's word exceedingly and hence was glad she could read my notes which she had to muse on every week. She had a spirit of prayer beyond ordinary of her time and experience.[269]

Their fourth son, John, was born on April 2, 1646, and Joanna died three weeks later. On September 8, 1647, Thomas married Margaret Boradel, who bore him one son, Jeremiah.

During these latter years, the major business of New England was the development of a public confession of faith and a plan of church government. Thomas Shepard took an active part in this process which resulted in the Cambridge Platform of 1648. This became a part of the laws of the Commonwealth of Massachusetts and a platform for Congregational Churches in America. So did Bishop Laud's actions deprive England of Shepard's godly ministry and provide New England with one of its more impressive theologians.

Samuel Eliot Morison has written two especially good paragraphs which give insight into the mind of Thomas Shepard, gathered, it seems, from his writings.

> Compared with his brethren on the frontier, the lot of Thomas Shepard was cast in pleasant places. Harvard College was established at his door; Boston could be visited in the course of a day;... Yet life never came easy to Shepard, so exalted was the standard that he set for himself. Although reputed the most successful pastor of his day in leading lost souls to God, he was never satisfied... He could never get his sermons prepared in time, but would meditate and procrastinate until there was left only the fag-end of Saturday night and early Sunday morning. In the breathless, oppressive dog-days, when the meeting-house was a damp oven, Shepard could not catch the divine spark... in late winter, after the cold had got into every plank and nail of the building, when snow sifted through cracks in the clapboards, the congregation shivered in their thickest woolens, and the sacramental bread froze so hard that it "rattles sadly" when broken into the paten.
>
> Shepard spent too much time in his study, to the neglect of his family... family prayers never seemed to hit the mark; and there were times when he felt that the Romans had the right idea, and Christ's ministers should celibate... Want of power to deliver Christ's message was his constant infirmity, so Shepard imagined; "Yet so searching was his preaching," said one of his flock, "and so great a power attending, as a hypocrite could not easily bear it, and it seemed almost irresistible."270

In the summer of 1649 at the age of forty-three Thomas Shepard caught a sore throat while riding home from a church council in Rowley. He developed a fever, and died in Cambridge on August 25th. Thomas Shepard was a very loving man who took seriously the care of his flock. This Shepard was a true shepherd of the Lord.

One way to sense the ideological committment of Shepard's congregation is to browse in the recent edition (1981) of his Confessions. To make sure of life eternal "without which all our time here is worse than lost" is the main design of Shephard's reformed ministry.[271] The confessions of fifty-one persons applying for church membership at Cambridge were recorded in a small leather notebook measuring 5-3/4 by 3-7/8 inches now in the possession of the New England Historic Genealogical Society.

Nathaniel Eaton, first head of Harvard College, took his education in England at Westminster School, and in 1629 at Trinity College, Cambridge. In 1639 he made his confession before the Church at Cambridge in New England. While at Trinity, Eaton discovered his hidden corruption in the context of sabbath breaking and company keeping. In London a sermon from Amos (4:12) caught him by the hooks since he was not then prepared to meet his God.[272] God worked on Eaton's spirit which gave him reason to see the "freeness of his love in Christ."[273] When Eaton saw from I Samuel (12:22) that the Lord had chosen him amongst those to be his people, then he was persuaded that the sowing of scripture in his life would bear fruit to eternal life.[274]

John Trumbull singles out Puritan preaching as the agent provocateur in his conversion. His confession of 1637 singles out both Arthur Dent's Plaine Mans Path-Way to Heaven and the sermons of Obediah Sedgwick, Puritan trained at Queen's College, Oxford. Sedgwick showed Trumbull that repentance was a reality.[275]

Nicholas Wyeth (1595-1680) emigrated from Suffolk around 1638. His confession is even more explicit about Puritan preaching. Every sabbath day for a year Wyeth went four miles to hear Robert Selby preach at Bedfield near Ipswich. He then heard Jeremiah Burroughes who was a graduate of Emmanuel College, Cambridge preach at Bury St. Edmunds. Burroughes preached on Galatians (6:7) -- "as a man sows so shall he reap." This text so inspired Wyeth that he went twenty miles to hear Mr. Rogers preach on Colossians (3:1) -- "if risen seek things which are above."[276] Several questions arose since Wyeth's arrival in New England which steeled his resolve to "enjoy the society of God's people" -- questions such as:

> Did the Lord ever give you any assurance of His love in Christ? Answer. The Lord let me see if not born again I could not enter into Kingdom of God. Question. What supports your heart with hope? Answer. Nothing but free grace in Christ.277

The biblical references in these confessions are widely scattered throughout the Old and New Testaments. There are 544 total citations in the fifty-one confessions, 226 of which are to the Old Testament and 318 to the New. 12.7% are to Isaiah and 26.8% are to the synoptic Gospels. Six per cent are to Psalms and 7.4% are to St. John's Gospel. Jeremiah has a surprising 15 references (2.8%) while Exodus and Deuteronomy together form only 4% of the total. For a covenant people such confessions are more individualistic than a reading of the sermons themselves would indicate. Deuteronomic history may well be assumed as a puritan axiom, but in these confessions they form 4% of the total while the Isaiah-Jeremiah-John continuum has 22.9%.[278] What appears in printed puritan sermons is one source of information for assessing the puritan mentality; what is recalled from auditors such as these New England immigrants is of like significance as these confessions bear witness. They are a paradigm of puritan response to the priority of preaching.

The first monograph to discuss these confessions stresses the geographical discontinuity of these new world expressions with a solitary seventeenth century account printed in England. For Caldwell, the members who deliver these confessions before Shepard's congregation are speaking "New Englandly" from the moment of their arrival.[279] Their geographical relocation rather than their theological reorientation provides a key to these confessions which Caldwell sees as... The Beginnings of an American Expression. Several of these confessions incorporate a vivid sense of time and place in Old England as they speak of travel to hear sermons in English parish churches and markets. That distance which they travelled before embarkation to the colonies was as great a moral adventure as the voyage across the North Atlantic.[280] The distance from sin to grace in these accounts was as great as the journey from Bristol to Boston.

My hesitation is also based on Edward Taylor's account of his sea voyage in which there are no overt religious comments. If Caldwell were correct, Taylor's account should place the sea voyage in a theological grid as she claims these confessions place a moral journey in a geographical one. The geographical references to England are more numerous than those to New England, leading one to feel that the insular references are as normative as the colonial ones. In spite of this reservation about Caldwell's account, her study in the end recognizes the conversionist character of these confessions.

The significance of these confessions as theological travelogues needs to be stressed along with their geographical setting. For the sense of sin and the gratitude for grace are the commmon threads which stitch together these confessions which cloak transcontinental sinners newly resident in the colonial wilderness. Caldwell attributes the sense of sin as psychological disorientation, attributing such comments to their authors' geographical dislocation. But if the interpretation is to turn on a geographical point, the reader should note that travel in England to hear sermons is ignored in favour of relocation in colonial North America. These confessions, however, endorse the validity of those walks across the English countryside which are geographical comments tied to a certain purpose -- to hear the Word of God in its canonical shape as preached by the Puritans. Those confessions make the point that wilderness of soul is more dangerous than any physical trek and that the drama of grace secures them against the "things that go bump in the night."

Governor Thomas Dudley after but nine months in Massachusetts sent advice to the countess of Lincoln that "if any come hether to plant... for spiritual [ends]... he may finde here what may well content him."[281] Spiritual advantages, notes Anderson, were all they were promised. It seems that Shephard's confessors testify to just such an adventure which Anderson so impressively documents.

END NOTES to SECTION IV

[1]Thomas Stapleton, A Fortresse of the faith first planted amonge vs english men, and continued hitherto in the vniversal church of Christ (Antwerpe: Ihon Laet, 1565), sig.Ll2^{r}. Collinson, Elizabethan Puritan Movement (London: Jonathan Cape, 1967), p.86 claims John Stow in 1567 as the first to use this 'sobriquet.' William Ringler of The Huntington Library called to my attention B.L.Ms.Add.33,974,fol.50^{v} (c.1550s) where Francis Stacy claims "And purytans here in thys tyme/Who to the highest sence to clym."

[2]Thomas Cartwright, A reply to an answere... of... Whitegift (London, 1574), p.172.

[3]Leonard J. Trinterud, editor, Elizabethan Puritanism (New York: Oxford Univ. Press, 1971), p.213.

[4]Ibid., pp.213-214. Compare A Brieff discours off the troubles begonne at Franckford (1574), letter of William Kethe for the congregation of Arrow [Aarou]. "Praised be God through oure lorde Jesus Christe whiche pulled downe marie that did persecute/and hathe set vpp the godly lady Elizabeth Queene off Englande/to restore and maintaine there/the pure preachinge off his word." January 16, 1559 - sig. Aaiv^{r}.

[5]C.M. Dent, Protestant Reformers in Elizabethan Oxford (Oxford: The Univ. Press, 1983), p.180.

[6]Peter Lake, Moderate Puritans and the Elizabethan Church (Cambridge: The Univ. Press, 1982), p.3.

[7]Christopher Hill, "Occasional Conformity," pp.201-202 in R. Buick Knox, editor, Reformation Conformity and Dissent (London: Epworth Press, 1977).

[8]Paul Christianson, The Reformers and Babylon (Toronto: Univ. Press, 1978), p.99.

[9]William Hunt, The Puritan Moment (Cambridge, Mass/London: Harvard Univ. Press, 1983), pp.91-92, 114.

[10]Patrick Collinson, "The Church and the New Religion," p.171 in Christopher Haigh, editor, The Reign of Elizabeth I (Athens: Univ. of Georgia Press, 1985).

[11]Ibid., p.172.

[12]John Manningham, Diary (1602/03), cited by Patrick Collinson, "A Comment: Concerning the Name Puritan," Journal of Ecclesiastical History 31 (1980), p.487.

[13]Barnaby Rich, The honestie of this age, p.28 [S.T.C. 20986-20988.5]. Above reported in Carl Bridenbaugh, Vexed and Troubled Englishmen 1590-1642 (New York: Oxford Univ. Press, 1968), pp. 195-196.

[14]Philip Stubbes, THE ANATOMIE/OF ABUSES:/(London: Richard James, 19 May 1583), sig. 5^{v}.

[15]Ibid., sig. $Eviii^{r-v}$.

[16]Oliver Ormerod, THE/PICTURE/of a Puritane:/(nineteen lines)/(London: E.A. for Nathaniel Fosbroke, 1605), sig. $A2^{v}$ passim.

[17]Ibid., sigs. $E3^{v}$-$F1^{r}$.

[18]J.T. Cliffe, The Puritan Gentry (London: Routledge & Kegan Paul plc., 1984), pp.185-189. See review by Patrick McGrath, Journal of Ecclesiastical History 36 (1985): 126, "out of the list of 123 families... only 24 qualify as puritans..."

[19]Collinson, op.cit., pp.484-485. The latest discussion seems to be in Michael G. Finlayson, "Historians and the idea of 'Puritanism'," Historians, Puritanism and the English Revolution: The Religious Factor in English Politics before and after the Interregnum (Toronto: Univ. of Toronto Press, 1983), pp.42-76.

[20]Ibid., p.485, Cartwright is discussed in John Morgan, Godly Learning. Puritan Attitudes Towards Reason, Learning, and Education, 1560-1640 (Cambridge: Cambridge Univ. Press, 1986), pp.114-115. On Martyr see Patrick Collinson, "England and International Calvinism, 1558-1640," p.214 in Menna Prestwich, editor, International Calvinism 1541-1715 (Oxford: Clarendon Press, 1985).

[21]Nicholas Tyacke, "Popular Puritan Mentality in Late Elizabethan England," The English Commonwealth 1547-1640 Essays in Politics and Society, edited by Peter Clark, Alan G.R. Smith and Nicholas Tyacke (New York: Barnes & Noble, 1979), p.77.

[22]Ibid., p.78.

[23] *Ibid.*, p.80.

[24] *loc.cit.*

[25] *Ibid.*, p.92.

[26] *loc.cit.*

[27] Percival Wilbrun, *A checke or reproofe of M. Howlet's untimely schreeching* (1581), fol. 15^{v}, cited in Patrick Collinson, *The Elizabethan Puritan Movement* (London: Jonathan Cape, 1967), p.27.

[28] Collinson, *op.cit.*, p.24.

[29] S.T. Bindoff, *Tudor England* (London: Penquin Books Ltd., 1962), pp.226-227.

[30] ENGLISH PVRITANISME/CONTAINE-/ning./The maine opinions of the rigidest/sort of those that are called Puritanes/In the Realme of England./(quotations Acts 24:14 and Acts 28:22)/(London: 1605), sig. B3^{r}.

[31] Rosemary O'Day, *The English Clergy. The Emergence and Consolidation of a Profession 1558-1642* (Leicester: Leicester Univ. Press, 1979), p.86.

[32] Cliffe, *op.cit.*, p.26.

[33] Thomas Tymme, A SILVER/watch-bell./(14 lines)/(London: William Cotton, 1606), sig. P3^{r}.

[34] Ralph Houlbrooke, "The Protestant Episcopate 1547-1603: The Pastoral Contribution," *Church and Society in England: Henry VIII to James I*, edited by Felicity Heal and Rosemary O'Day (London: MacMillan Press, 1977), p.79.

[35] James Gairdner, "Bishop Hooper's Visitation of Gloucester," *English Historical Review* XIX (1904), p.99. See W.P.M. Kennedy, editor, "Bishop Wakeman's Visitation Articles for the diocese of Gloucester, 1548," *English Historical Review* XXXIX (1924), 253-254 and F.D. Price, "Gloucester Diocese under Bishop Hooper 1551-1553," *Transactions of the Bristol and Gloucestershire Archaeological Society* LX (1938), 51-151. See Hooper's Injunctions in *Later Writings of Bishop Hooper* (Cambridge: At the Univ. Press, MDCCCLII), pp.130ff.

[36] John Strype, *Ecclesiastical Memorials* (Oxford: 1822) III. 11:389-413.

[37]R.B. Walker, "Lincoln Cathedral in the Reign of Queen Elizabeth I," Journal of Ecclesiastical History XI (1960), p.186. See also J.W.F. Hill, Tudor and Stuart Lincoln (Cambridge: At the Univ. Press, 1956).

[38]Ibid., p.187

[39]Ibid., pp.188-189. Compare R.V.H. Burne, "Chester Cathedral in the Reigns of Mary and Elizabeth," Journal of Chester and North Wales Architectural Society XXXVIII (1951): 41-94.

[40]See Chapter VI: "The Old Episcopate and the New" in Henry Norbert Birt, The Elizabethan Religious Settlement (London: George Bell and Sons, 1907), pp.207-252. The best account which is superior to many of the D.N.B. articles on these bishops is in F.O. White, Lives of the Elizabethan Bishops of the Anglican Church (1898).

[41]James Pilkington, Works (Parker Society), p.586. On the struggle of Robert Horne with the Hampshire conservatives and William Paulet, lord treasurer and first marquis of Winchester, see Ronald H. Fritze, "The Role of Family and Religion in the Local Politics of Early Elizabethan England: the Case of Hampshire in the 1560s," Historical Journal 25 (1982): 267-87.

[42]M. Rosemary O'Day, "Thomas Bentham: A Case Study in the Problems of the Early Elizabethan Episcopate," Journal of Ecclesiastical History XXIII (1972), p.139. Now see Rosemary O'Day, The English Clergy (Leicester: Leicester Univ. Press, 1979), pp.38-48.

[43]Joel Berlatsky, "Thomas Bentham and the Plight of Early Elizabethan Bishops," Historical Magazine of the Protestant Episcopal Church XLIII (1974), p.328.

[44]See Gina Alexander, "Bishop Bonner and the Parliament of 1559," Bulletin of the Institute of Historical Research LVI (1983), pp.171-178.

[45]Ibid., pp.329-330. See Rosemary O'Day, "Cumulative Debt: The Bishops of Coventry and Lichfield and their Economic Problems c. 1540-1640," Midland History III (1976), 76-90.

[46]"The Letter-Book of Thomas Bentham, Bishop of Coventry and Lichfield, 1560-1561," edited by Rosemary O'Day and Joel Berlatsky, Camden Miscellany XXVII (1979), p.131.

[47]O'Day, op.cit., p.142.

[48]Public Record Office E 135/9/6.

[49]Thomas Bentham, Letter Book 1560-1561, p.175.

[50]W.H. Frere, Visitation Articles and Injunctions of the Period of the Reformation (London: Alcuin Club, 1910) III (1559-75), p.166. See Peter Clark, "The Alehouse and the Alternative Society" in Donald Pennington and Keith Thomas, Puritans and Revolutionaries (Oxford: Clarendon Press, 1978), pp.47-72.

[51]Berlatsky, op.cit., p.340.

[52]Felicity Heal, Of Prelates and Princes (Cambridge: At the Univ. Press, 1980), "The resources of the Elizabethan bishops," p.266.

[53]Ibid., p.327.

[54]"Jewel, John," Dictionary of National Biography X: 815.

[55]M. Anderson, Peter Martyr: Reformer in Exile, pp.527-528.

[56]John Jewel, The Apology of the Church of England (London: J. Beale, 1635), sig. H12^{r}.

[57]Ibid., sig. K8^{r}.

[58]Ibid., sig. M7^{r}.

[59]Ibid., sig. M10^{r}.

[60]loc.cit.

[61]See Marvin O'Connell, Thomas Stapleton and the Counter Reformation (New Haven: Yale Univ. Press, 1964), pp.125-130.

[62]Thomas Cartwright, A reply to an answere... of...Whitegift (London 1574), p.172.

[63]Norman L. Jones, Faith by Statute. Parliament and the settlement of religion 1559. (London: Royal Historical Society Studies in History 32/Swift Printers, 1982).

[64]M. Anderson, Peter Martyr: Reformer in Exile, pp.224-225.

[65]Norman L. Jones, "Elizabeth's First Year: The Conception and Birth of the Elizabethan Political World," pp.31-33 in Christopher Haigh, editor, The Reign of Elizabeth I (Athens: Univ. of Georgia Press, 1985). C. M. Dent, Protestant Reformers in Elizabethan Oxford (Oxford: Oxford Univ. Press, 1983): 17-43. Winthrop S. Hudson, The Cambridge Connection and the Elizabethan Settlement of 1559 (Durham: Duke Univ. Press, 1980), pp.43-89.

[66]Both variants of the 1576 edition with line 5 ending either 'col-' or 'volumen' are at Oxford, the first at Worcester College and the second at All Souls.

[67]Letter to Cooke of October 15, 1558 is in the British Library, Add. Ms.29549:12 (f.16^{r}-16^{v}).

[68]Zurich Letters II: 13 and 76.

[69]See Chapter I. "Prologue: The Infusion of Protestantism In The Reign of Edward VI" in C.M. Dent, Protestant Reformers In Elizabethan Oxford (Oxford: Oxford Univ. Press, 1983), pp.4-16.

[70]Jewel, op.cit., sig A2^{v}.

[71]Ibid., sig. A3^{v}.

[72]Philip M.J. McNair, "Peter Martyr in England," Joseph C. McLelland, editor, Peter Martyr Vermigli and Italian Reform (Waterloo: Wilfred Laurier Univ. Press, 1980), p.97.

[73]"Harding, Thomas," Dictionary of National Biography VIII: 1223.

[74]John Jewel, "A Sermon Preached at Paul's Cross," Works, edited by John Ayre for The Parker Society (Cambridge: At The Univ. Press, MDCCCXLV), p.11.

[75]John Jewel, Works, "The Reply to Harding's Answer," p.330.

[76]Ibid., p.331.

[77]loc.cit.

[78]Ibid., p.334.

[79]loc.cit.

[80]Ibid., p.335.

[81]Ibid., p.337.

[82]John Jewel, Works, The Second Portion (MDCCCXLVII), p.806.

[83]Ibid., pp.807-808.

[84]A.J. Carlson, "The Puritans and the Convocation of 1563," Theodore Rabb and Jerrold Siegal, Action and Conviction in Early Modern Europe (Princeton: Princeton Univ. Press, 1969), p.134.

[85]John Parkhurst, Iniunctions exhibited by John...in his first visitacion beginning the second date of Maye...[1561] (S.T.C.2 10286).

[86]Carlson, op.cit., p.136.

[87]Ibid., p.141 from Petyt MS. 538/47 fols.581-584 reprinted in Strype, Annals I, Bk.I, 507-512.

[88]Ibid., p.142.

[89]Ibid., pp.145-146.

[90]Ibid., p.148.

[91]Ibid., p.153 M.76.

[92]Ibid., p.150.

[93]Ibid., p.152.

[94]William P. Haugaard, "John Calvin and the Catechism of Alexander Nowell," Archiv für Reformationsgeschichte 61 (1970), 50-65.

[95]Ibid., pp.53-55.

[96]Ibid., p.62.

[97]Patrick Collinson, Archbishop Grindal 1519-1583 The Struggle for a Reformed Church (Berkeley: Univ. of California Press, 1979), p.127.

[98]Claire Cross, review of Collinson, Archbishop Grindal, English Historical Review XCV (1980), p.843.

[99]Patrick Collinson, "The Reformer and the Archbishop: Martin Bucer and an English Bucerian," Journal of Religious History VI (1971): 305-30.

[100]Cross,op.cit., pp.843-844. Collinson, Archbishop Grindal, pp.79-82.

[101]A. Gordon Kinder, Casiodoro De Reina Spanish Reformer of the Sixteenth Century (London: Tamesis Books Limited, 1975), p.119.

[102]Paul J. Hauben, Three Spanish heretics and the Reformation (Geneve: Librairie Droz, 1967), p.87.

[103]Collinson, Archbishop Grindal, p.145.

[104]Ibid., pp.149-150.

[105]Kinder, op.cit., p.78.

[106]Hauben, op.cit., p.57: Strype: Parker II; 403.

[107]Collinson, op.cit., pp.234-235.

[108]Ibid., p.237.

[109]Stanford E. Lemberg, "Archbishop Grindal and the Prophesyings," Historical Magazine of the Protestant Episcopal Church XXXIV (1965), pp.88-89.

[110] *Ibid.*, p.101.

[111] *Ibid.*, pp.102-103.

[112] Collinson, *op.cit.*, p.240.

[113] Edmund Grindal, *Remains,* edited by William Nicholson for the Parker Society (Cambridge: At The Univ. Press, MDCCCXLIII), p.389.

[114] Patrick Collinson, "The downfall of Archbishop Grindal and its Place in Elizabethan Political and Ecclesiastical History," in Clark, Smith and Tyacke, *The English Commonwealth 1547-1640*, pp.39-57.

[115] "Hutton, Matthew," *Dictionary of National Biography* X: 357.

[116] Lambeth MS. 1138, No.3, cited in M.M. Knappen, *Tudor Puritanism* (Chicago: Univ. of Chicago Press), p.302 m.55.

[117] *D.N.B.* X: 357.

[118] Public Record Office State Papers Domestic 12/48/41 Hutton to Burghley, 31 November 1568. Cited by Peter Lake, "Matthew Hutton--A Puritan Bishop?" *History* 64 (1979), p.184.

[119] *Ibid.*, p.186.

[120] *Ibid.*, p.192.

[121] *loc.cit.* British Library Lansdowne Mss. 983, fol.57 13 October 1595.

[122] *Ibid.*, p.197.

[123] *Ibid.*, p.199.

[124] *Ibid.*, p.200.

[125] Patrick Collinson, "Sir Nicholas Bacon and the Elizabethan Via Media," *Historical Journal* 23 (1980), p.268.

[126] *Ibid.*, p.269. See Wilfrid R. Prest, "Preachers, puritans and the religion of lawyers," pp.187-219 in his *The Inns of Court under Elizabeth I and the early Stuarts 1590-1640* (London: 1972).

[127] A.F. Scott-Pearson, *Thomas Cartwright and Elizabethan Puritanism, 1535-1603*, (Gloucester: Peter Smith, 1966), p.4.

[128] *Ibid.*, p.5.

[129] Leslie Stephen and Sidney Lee, *The Dictionary of National Biography*, Vol. 3: Brown - Chaloner, (London: Oxford Univ. Press, 1950), p.1135.

[130]Sir George Paule, Life of Whitgift (London: Thomas Snodham, 1612), pp.9-10.

[131]Pearson, Thomas Cartwright, p.11.

[132]Ibid., pp.12-17

[133]Patrick Collinson, The Elizabethan Puritan Movement (Berkeley: Univ. of California Press, 1967), p.112.

[134]W. Horton Davies, Worship and Theology in England: From Cranmer to Hooker, 1534-1603 (Princeton: Princeton Univ. Press, 1970), p.46. (See n. 16 for Mss. reference)

[135]H. Gee and W.J. Hardy, Documents Illustrative of English Church History (London: Macmillan and Co., 1914), p.471.

[136]John Knox, Works Vol. II, edited by David Laing, (New York: AMS Press, 1966), p.174.

[137]Pearson, Thomas Cartwright, p.18.

[138]Ibid., p.19.

[139]D.N.B. III: 1136.

[140]Pearson, Thomas Cartwright, p.19.

[141]E.H. Emerson, English Puritanism: From John Hooper to John Milton (Durham: Duke Univ. Press, 1968), p.66.

[142]Pearson, Thomas Cartwright, p.24.

[143]Pearson, Thomas Cartwright, p.26.

[144]D.N.B. III: 1136.

[145]Pearson, Thomas Cartwright, p.28.

[146]Ibid., pp.28-29.

[147]Knappen, Tudor Puritanism, pp.224-5.

[148]J.F.H. New, "The Whitgift-Cartwright Controversy," Archiv für Reformationsgeschichte 59 (July-December, 1968): 203.

[149]Pearson, Thomas Cartwright, p.407.

[150]Collinson, Elizabethan Puritan Movement, p.113.

[151]Pearson, Thomas Cartwright, p.48.

[152]Ibid., p.49.

[153]Ibid., pp.50-3.

[154]J.R. Neale, "Parliament and the Articles of Religion," English Historical Review 67(1952): 180.

[155]P.M. Dawley, John Whitgift and the English Reformation (New York: Charles Scribner's Sons, 1954), p.87.

[156] Ibid., p.87. (from Parker Correspondence)

[157] J. Neale, Elizabeth I and Her Parliaments I: 195ff.

[158] W.H. Frere and Rev. C.E. Douglas, Puritan Manifestoes (New York: Burt Franklin, 1972), p. vii. See Patrick Collinson, "John Field and Elizabethan Puritanism" in S.T. Bindoff, J. Hurstfield and C.H. Williams, editors, Elizabethan Government and Society (London: The Athlone Press, 1961), pp.127-162.

[159] M.M. Knappen, Tudor Puritanism (Chicago: Univ. of Chicago Press, 1939), p.234.

[160] Frere and Douglas, Puritan Manifestoes, pp.9 & 22.

[161] D.N.B. III: 1137.

[162] Dawley, Whitgift, p.90.

[163] D.J. McGinn, The Admonition Controversy (New Brunswick: Rutgers Univ. Press, 1949), p.49.

[164] J. Ayre, John Whitgift: Works (Cambridge: Parker Society, 1851-3), Vol. I, p.190.

[165] J.S. Coolidge, The Pauline Renaissance in England: Puritanism and the Bible (Oxford: Clarendon Press, 1970), p.11.

[166] Ayre, Whitgift's Works I, p.180.

[167] Ibid., p.191.

[168] Coolidge, Pauline Renaissance, p.7.

[169] Ayre, Whitgift's Works I, p.238.

[170] Ibid., I, p.239-40.

[171] Davies, Worship and Theology, p.53.

[172] C.M. Dent, Protestant Reformers in Elizabethan Oxford, pp.45-46.

[173] Pearson, Thomas Cartwright, p.135.

[174] S.J. Knox, Walter Travers: Paragon of Elizabethan Puritanism (London: Methuen and Co. Ltd., 1962), p.29.

[175] Collinson, Elizabethan Puritan Movement, p.249.

[176] Ibid., p.296.

177John Dod and Robert Cleaver, A Plaine and Familiar Exposition of the Ten Commandements (London: Felix Kyngston for Thomas Man, 1614), sig.Bb4^{v}.

[178] A DEFENSE/ of the Ecclesiasticall/Regiment in Englande,/ defaced by T.C. in his/Replie agaynst D./VVhitgifte (London:

Henry Bynneman for Humfrey Toy, 1574), p.193. The Cambridge Univ. Library copy assigns the text to Lord Henry Howard.

[179]Patrick Collinson, "Cranbrook and the Fletchers: Popular and Unpopular Religion in the Kentish Weald," in Reformation Principle and Practice, edited by Peter Newman Brooks (London: Scolar Press, 1980), pp.171-202.

[180]Patrick Collinson, "Magistracy and Ministry: A Suffolk Miniature" in Reformation Conformity and Dissent: Essays in Honour of Geoffrey Nuttall, edited by R. Buick Knox (London: Epworth Press, 1977), pp.70-91. See also Paul Seaver, "Community Control and Puritan Politics in Elizabethan Suffolk," Albion 9 (Winter 1977): 297-315 and on Sussex see Jeremy Goring, "The Reformation of the Ministry in Elizabethan Sussex," Journal of Ecclesiastical History 34 (1983): 345-366. On Essex see the Barrington Family Letters 1628-1632, edited by Arthur Searle (London: Royal Historical Society), Camden Fourth Series 28 (1983). Sir Francis Barrington who was the cousin of Sir Francis Hastings employed Ezekiel Rogers, the son of Richard Rogers, as his chaplain for a dozen years from 1610. Roger Williams wrote to Lady Joan Barrington on May 2, 1629 (pp.65-68) while Arthur Hildersham sent her his commentary on John (4) in March of 1629 (p.62).

[181]Collinson, "Cranbrook," p.174.

[182]Ibid., p.180.

[183]Ibid., p.190 n.97.

[184]Ibid., p.191.

[185]Ibid., p.193.

[186]Ibid., p.192.

[187]Ibid., pp.197-198.

[188]"Fenner, Dudley," Dictionary of National Biography V: 1181.

[189]Collinson, "Magistracy and Ministry," p.72.

[190]Ibid., p.76.

[191]Ibid., p.77.

[192]Patrick Collinson, "The Jacobean Religious Settlement: The Hampton Court Conference," in Howard Tomlinson, editor,

Before The English Civil War (London: Macmillan Press, 1983), pp.27-51 and Frederick Shriver, "Hampton Court Re-visited: James I and the Puritans," Journal of Ecclesiastical History XXXIII (1982), 48-71.

[193]S.T.C.2 15042-15045.

[194]John Knewstub, "Epistle Dedicatory," The Lectures upon the Twentieth Chapter of Exodus (London: Lucas Harrison, 1578) in Leonard J. Trinterud, editor, Elizabethan Puritanism (New York: Oxford Univ. Press, 1971), p.317.

[195]Patrick Collinson, The Elizabethan Puritan Movement (London: Jonathan Cape, 1967), 220-227 etc.

[196]Collinson, "Magistracy and Ministry," pp.79-91.

[197]Ibid., p.82.

[198]J.E. Neale, Elizabeth I and her Parliaments, 1584-1601, pp.145-66.

[199]Collinson, op.cit., p.85.

[200]Ibid., p.86.

[201]Thomas Beard, THE THEATRE/of Gods Iudgments:/Or,/A COLLECTION OF HISTO-/ries out of Sacred, Ecclesiasticall, and pro-/phane Authours, concerning the admirable Iudge-/ments of God Vpon the transgressours/of his commandements./(two lines and device)/(London/Printed by Adam Islip./1597), sig. C2^{v}.

[202]cf. P. Clark and P. Slack, Crisis and Order in English Towns, 1500-1700 (1971) and Christopher Hill, The World Turned Upside Down (New York: Penguin Books, 1976), pp.47-49.

[203]Christopher Hill, Change and Continuity in 17th Century England (Cambridge: Harvard Univ. Press, 1975), p.7.

[204]Ibid., p.8. Maurice Kyffin translated Jewel's Apology into Welsh (1595). Only thirty books were published in Wales in the sixteenth century. See Glanmore Williams, "Religion and Welsh Literature in the Age of the Reformation," Proceedings of the British Academy LXIX (1983), pp.373-90.

[205]Ibid., p.10.

[206]P. McLane, "Diggan Davie again," Journal of English and Germanic Philology XLVI (1947), 144-149.

[207]Glanmor Williams, Welsh Reformation Essays (Cardiff: Univ. of Wales Press, 1967), p.213.

[208]Ibid., p.16.

[209]"Llwyd, Morgan," Dictionary of National Biography XII: 3-4.

[210]"Cradock, Walter," Dictionary of National Biography IV: 1363.

[211]Geoffry Nuttall, The Welsh Saints 1640-1660 (Cardiff: Univ. of Wales Press, 1957), p.24.

[212]Ibid., pp.33-34.

[213]R. Tudor Jones, "The Healing Herb and the Rose of Love: The Piety of Two Welsh Puritans," Reformation Conformity and Dissent, p.165.

[214]Ibid., p.167.

[215]Ibid., p.170.

[216]Ibid., p.172.

[217]Ibid., p.177.

[218]Geoffry Nuttall, The Holy Spirit in Puritan Faith and Experience (Oxford: Basil Blackwell, 1946), p.51.

[219]Ibid., p.140.

[220]Ibid., p.42. See also "Walter Cradock (1606?-1659): The Man and his Message" in Nuttall, The Puritan Spirit: essays and addresses (London: Epworth Press, 1967): 118-129.

[221]Cited in Barrington R. White, editor, The English Puritan Tradition (Nashville: Broadman Press, 1980), p.11.

[222]Henry Holland, "To The Reader," The Works of...M. Richard Greenham (London: Felix Kingston, 1599), sig A5^{v}.

[223]Samuel Clarke, The lives of Thirty-Two English Divines (1677), p.13.

[224]H.C. Porter, Reformation and Reaction in Tudor Cambridge (Cambridge: At the Univ. Press, 1958), pp.217-218.

[225]Greenham, Works, sig. Q1^{r}.

[226]Thomas Fuller, The Church History of Britain (London: Thomas Tegg and Son, 1837), III: 133. On Greenham's educational activity see K.R.M. Short, "A Theory of Common Education in

Elizabethan Puritanism," *Journal of Ecclesiastical History* XXIII (1972): 31-48.

[227]"Rogers, Richard," *Dictionary of National Biography* XVII: 138.

[228]Porter, *op.cit.*, p.220.

[229]Patrick Collinson, *A Mirror of Elizabethan Puritanism, The Life and Letters of 'Godly Master dering'* (London: Dr. Williams Trust, 1964), p.15.

[230]*Ibid.*, p.17.

[231]Trinterud, *Elizabethan Puritanism*, p.160. On the wider implications of all this now see Peter Lake, *Moderate Puritans and the Elizabethan Church* (Cambridge: At the Univ. Press, 1982), pp.16-24.

[232]M.M. Knappen, *Two Elizabethan Puritan Diaries* (Chicago: American Society of Church History, 1933), p.84.

[233]*Ibid.*, p.27.

[234]*Ibid.*, p.82.

[235]*Ibid.*, p.78. July 16, 1588.

[236]*Ibid.*, p.79. July 31, 1588.

[237]Richard Rogers, SEVEN/TREATISES (London: 1603), sig. A5^{v}.

[238]*Ibid.*, sig. A8^{v} and sig. B2^{r}.

[239]SEAVEN/TREATISES (London: 1610), sig. Mmm1^{v}.

[240]SEAVEN/TREATISES (London: 1604), sig. Ccc6^{v}.

[241]Richard Rogers, A/COMMENTARY/Upon the whole/Booke of Ivdges./(10 lines)/Heb. 12.1 (between lines) in 4 lines. London: Felix Kyngston for Thomas Man, 1615. Sig. B1^{r}.

[242]*loc.cit.*

[243]*Ibid.*, sig. B1^{v}-B2^{r}.

[244]*Ibid.*, sig. B4^{r} and B5^{r}.

[245]*Ibid.*, sig. Y1^{v}.

[246]*Ibid.*, sig. Z3^{v}.

[247]*Ibid.*, sig. Aa1^{r-v}.

[248]Thomas Shepard, "The Autobiography," in *God's Plot, The Paradoxes of Puritan Piety, Being the Autobiography & Journal of Thomas Shepard*, Michael McGiffert, editor, (Univ. of Massachusetts Press, 1972), p.37.

[249]Ibid., p.38.

[250]loc.cit.

[251]loc.cit.

[252]According to Samuel E. Morison, 1/4 of the 134 university alumni who are known to have emigrated to New England before 1650 had their education at Emmanuel, a Puritan stronghold. See Builders of the Bay Colony (Boston: Houghton Mifflin Co., 1930), pp.107-108.

[253]Shepard, op.cit., p.40.

[254]Ibid., pp.45-46. See Samuel Ward's positive comments about Emmanuel College in M.M. Knappen, Two Elizabethan Puritan Diaries by Richard Rogers and Samuel Ward, pp.107-129.

[255]Ibid., pp.56-57.

[256]Ibid., p.47.

[257]Ibid., p.49. For others silenced in Essex see Victoria County History, Essex ii, 51-53.

[258]Cliffe, op.cit., p.142.

[259]Shepard, op.cit., p.53.

[260]Ibid., p.55.

[261]Ibid., p.61.

[262]Samuel Eliot Morison, Builders of the Bay Colony, pp.111-112.

[263]John Winthrop, Winthrop's Journal, History of New England, 1630-1649, Vol. I, in Original Narratives of Early American History, James Kendall Hosmer, ed. (New York: Charles Scribners Sons, 1908), pp.173-174.

[264]Shepard, op.cit., p.65.

[265]John Cotton, "The Way of Congregational Churches Cleared" in The Antinomian Controversy, 1636-1638, A Documentary History, David D. Hall, ed. (Middletown: Wesleyan Univ. Press, 1968), p.413.

[266]Shepard, op.cit., p.67.

[267]Winthrop, op.cit., Vol. II, p.223.

[268]Morison, op.cit., p.130.

[269]Shepard, op.cit., pp.70-71.

[270]Morison, op.cit., pp.132-133.

[271] Two exchanges on the significance of these confessions appeared in the _William and Mary Quarterly_ XLI (1984). See George Selement, "The Meeting of Elite and Popular Minds at Cambridge, New England, 1638-1645," pp.32-48 and David D. Hall, "Toward a History of Popular Religion in Early New England," pp.49-55.

[272] _Thomas Shepard's Confessions_, edited by George Selement & Bruce C. Woolley (Boston: The Colonial Society of Massachusetts, 1981), p.54.

[273] _Ibid._, p.56.

[274] _Ibid._, p.57.

[275] _Ibid._, p.109: Perhaps John Sedgwick.

[276] _Ibid._, p.194.

[277] _Ibid._, p.195.

[278] _Ibid._, p.213.

[279] Patricia Caldwell, _The Puritan Conversion Narrative_ (Cambridge: At the Univ. Press, 1983), p.41.

[280] _Ibid._, pp.129-130.

[281] Virginia DeJohn Anderson, "Migrants and Motives: Religion and the Settlement of New England, 1630-1640," _New England Quarterly_ 58 (1985), pp.374-375. See also Aviku Zakai, "The Gospel of Reformation: The Origins of the Great Puritan Migration," _Journal of Ecclesiastical History_ 37 (1986): 584-602.

SECTION V. SCRIPTURE AND SOCIETY

Chapter 14) Pre-critical Commentaries

A. Latin Culture/Latin Commentaries

William Bradford concluded his narrative of the events of September 6, 1620 with a series of references to Psalm 107, confessing like the Psalmist the loving-kindness of God. The sons and daughters of Plymouth Plantation found that such expressions were appropriate to describe their religious views and those motives which led them to the wilderness of colonial North America.

> What could now sustain them but the Spirit of God and His grace! May not and ought not the children of these fathers rightly say: "Our fathers were Englishmen which came over this great ocean, and were ready to perish in this wilderness; but they cried unto the Lord, and He heard their voice and looked on their adversity." When they wandered in the desert wilderness out of the way, and found no city to dwell in, both hungry and thirsty, their soul was overwhelmed in them. Let them confess before the Lord His loving kindness and His wonderful works before the sons of men.1

Recently Patricia Caldwell has analyzed the anxiety of several confessions which future migrants made before Thomas Shepard's congregation in New Town. They had learned to speak "New Englandly" from the moment of their arrival in the Bay Colony. Bradford finds comfort in the words of Psalm 107 while Caldwell senses immense anxiety in the scattered geographic comments of these Puritan confessions. Bradford's confidence amidst the physical dangers of colonial North America stands in stark contrast to Caldwell's linguistic concern over these highly edited clerical compilations.

Two recent studies of Puritan scriptural language describe these concerns as those of a Pauline Renaissance and the presence of the godly in Stuart England. Neither it seems cite the range of printed and manuscript primary sources which would help us sort out these matters in a rational fashion. Coolidge cites no biblical commentaries of this period while McGee omits all mention of Dod and Cleaver, Exposition on the Ten Commendements, whose nineteen editions between 1603 and 1638 undermine his principle contention. Dod and Cleaver refuse to separate the first four sayings on the moral law from the final ones on ceremonial matters, thereby contradicting McGee's precise distinction beteen Puritans on the one hand and Anglicans on the other.[1]

A more precise use of Puritan biblical commentaries can enrich our understanding of a consensual Calvinism whose inner logic William Hunt labels as "the code of redemption." By consensual Calvinism is meant that amalgam of continental reform derived from Bucer, Bullinger, Beza, Peter Martyr and Calvin which found alternate if not overlapping expression in Episcopal, Presbyterian, Congregational and Separatist forms in the English Church from 1560-1640. Peter Lake's term, moderate puritanism, would be this author's preferred taxonomy to the Anglican/Puritan pattern adhered to by Richard Greaves, John New, John Coolidge and J. Sears McGee. More satisfactory is the brilliant recent (1986) Cambridge study by John Morgan whose title Godly Learning is a superb match for Collinson's Godly People. That future study of Puritan thought, i.e., Godly Thinking, must incorporate the huge repository of manuscripts which J. T. Cliffe, The Puritan Gentry has sampled and which Collinson complains is missing from a body of North American writing on Puritanism "which neglects manuscript evidence and tends to feed upon itself" (Journal of Ecclesiastical History 31 (1980): 486). There are shelves of full and partial biblical commentaries/sermons/lectures listed in William Crowe's, Exact Collection of our English Writers on the Old and New Testament (1663/1668) which scholars should no longer ignore. To turn away from such available texts can impoverish our understanding of a common biblical culture in Old England which Bradford and others transported to New England. To the extent such massive textual evidence is cited in scattered fashion, to that extent scholars of Tudor and Stuart Puritanism demonstrate how unfamiliar they are with the primary documents of English protestant thought. It is necessary to approach these printed sources afresh to sense the nuances of the puritan theological corpus which contains considerable social and intellectual data in its biblical commentaries. If one widens one's perspective to include these multiple sources, a fresh discovery emerges. Though these migrant's fathers were Englishmen, their intellectual ancestors were the continental divines whose Latin folios inspired the Marian exiles in their own wilderness trek from Frankfort to Geneva and Zurich. Were not the marginalia of their Geneva New Testaments covered with the practical syllogism of Theodore Beza -- and their libraries well stocked with the Latin commentaries of Peter Martyr and Rudolf Gualter? Patrick Collinson finds the theological centre of gravity in the Elizabethan Church in one author and one book, not Calvin's Institutes but the Common Places of Peter Martyr.

Professor T.H.L. Parker's survey of Calvin's New Testament Commentaries broadens the spectrum to include all of the New Testament save the Apocalypse,[2] whose special use shows up in several recent studies.[3] The Old Testament has been less well described, though a fresh study of Hebrew scholarship in Tudor England narrows that gap a bit.[4] Parker's new edition of Calvin's Latin commentary on Romans (Leiden: 1981) as well as the appearance of several Latin versions of the Bible in the sixteenth century remind us that the Puritan commentator lived in a culture for whom the circulation of Latin commentaries was crucial.[5] From the Erasmian Latin text of the New Testament in which Thomas Bilney found a personal source of renewal[6] to Sebastian Munster's 1537 text; from the Latin version of Leo Jud and Bibliander of 1543 or Castellio of 1551 to Robert Estienne's 1557 Geneva tome with Beza's fresh Latin New Testament, and on to Tremellius/Junius (1580), Piscator (1602-1610) and the London Polyglot of 1655-57, one recalls the impact of the Latin Scriptures on English reformers.[7] In fact a glance at North American colonial library lists shows 215 Latin commentaries and 96 in English, a ratio of 2.24/1 fifteen decades after the Wittenberg lectures of Luther and Melanchthon.

One should note the commerce in biblical commentaries and their continental connection via Zurich and Geneva. Calvin's commentaries circulated widely and several were translated by the Puritans. The Zurich connection meant the exchange of students[8] as well as Latin commentaries such as those of Peter Martyr who taught at Oxford from 1548 where his lectures on I Corinthians and Romans were delivered. These Latin commentaries went to four (I Corinthians) and seven (Romans) editions between 1551 and 1613. John Day issued an English version of Romans in 1568. In Zurich after a three year stint at Strasburg where Martyr lectured to the Marian Exiles on Judges, Vermigli completed his commentaries on Judges (1561) which Day issued in a 1564 translation. Then in succession came learned folios on Samuel (1564), Kings (1566) and Genesis (1569) after his death. The Psalms (1564) also appeared in English in 1569. The Judges saw five editions by 1609, the Samuel four by 1595, Kings five by 1599 and Genesis three by 1606. Three Latin editions of the Psalms by 1604 mean that English Puritans had access to thirty-one Latin and three English commentaries by this Florentine humanist early in the seventeenth century.[9]

The Puritan divine Richard Rogers in his Seven Treatises (1603) suggests that reading is a means of sustaining a godly life. First one must read "the booke of God... and then other sound and godly bookes." One should not read superstitious pamphlets nor "Machiavels blashemies," but rather "Calvin's Institutions, Peter Martyrs Common places, Beza's Confession ..."[10] The Common Places (1583) was a massive folio translation of the loci or extracts from Martyr's commentaries which together with treatises and letters was printed in thirteen Latin editions between 1576 and 1656. The presence of Martyr's volumes in English libraries, from the 102 copies in Oxford Collegiate libraries to the 100 copies in Cambridge colleges, as well as those in the English Cathedral libraries indicate the impact of Cranmer's associate throughout the Puritan period. Peterborough Cathedral library has 24 Martyr editions now on permanent loan in the Cambridge University Library. Ely Cathedral dispersed some and transferred two additional copies to the Cambridge University Library.

Martyr's commentaries sold in the provincial bookshops, as can be seen from John Awdley of Hull whose inventory of 1644 lists Vermigli's Common Places (1583),[11] and John Foster of York who in 1616 had Martyr's Latin commentaries on Kings and on Samuel for sale as well as the Oxford eucharistic Disputatio.[12] John Wilkins in 1646 compiled a list of commentaries for pastors to use. In his own Ecclesiastes Wilkins suggested Martyr on Genesis, Judges, Samuel, Kings, Lamentations, Romans and I Corinthians. Calvin shows up ten times on the Old Testament list and four times for the New. This is the earliest detailed tally of commentaries in the seventeenth century known to me. It occupies signatures $D4^{r}$-$F3^{v}$ in this 1646 commentary, published at London by M.F. for Samuel Gellibrand.

The Zurich connection is strengthened by the commentaries of Rudolf Gualter, whose contact with England involved his own family[13] -- Gualter had visited England for a few months in 1537 and his son studied at Cambridge and then Magdalen College, Oxford from July 1573 for a year. His personal friendship in Zurich with Martyr during the Florentine's six year residence from 1556 should not be forgotten, nor that Martyr thanked Gualter in 1551 for assisting his I Corinthians through the Zurich press of Froschover.[14] At least forty-three separate editions of Gualter's Latin commentaries are extant in Cambridge libraries, from the Johannine Epistles of 1553 to the Pauline Epistles of 1609.[15] Even more copies are extant in Oxford collegiate libraries.[16] Even though current copies reflect the gifts to Oxford colleges over several centuries, one should not hesitate, short of a minute inspection of contemporary catalogues, to assume that this Zurich literature was in fact available and read in sixteenth century Oxford.

The Acts was translated and published in 1572,[17] while three separate Old Testament English commentaries on four of the Minor Prophets appeared in 1573, 1580, and 1582. Their short titles are Certaine godlie homelies or sermons vpon the prophets Abdias and Jonas (S.T.C.2 25010), The homilies or familiar sermons vpon the prophet Joel (S.T.C.2 25012) and The sermons of master Ralfe Gualter vpon the prophet Zepheniah (S.T.C.2 25014).

A glance at the Joel will give the reader the flavour of this Zurich commentator whose study of the Minor Prophets obviously circulated amongst the scholars of Tudor and Stuart England.[18] Gualter dedicated his commentary to Eberhard of Broich, Lord Friddeburge on August 17, 1560. Gualter urges patience in sermon five of Joel where he reflects on "A day of darkness" and the land as "desolate wilderness" wherein "the heavens shall shake... and the Starres shall withdrawe their shining."[19] The sermon ends with a consolatory word:

> Let us acknowledge therfore his prouidence, which extendeth it selfe euen unto Sparrowes and the heyres of our heade, & let us know it to be his hand, if at any time wee bee afflicted: againe, let us take it paciently, and turning unto him embrace his sauing health, which hee offreth unto us in his sonne Jesus Christe...20

Lanhydrock House in Cornwall has a library with a remarkable collection of continental commentaries. At the opposite end of England from Hull, its three Martyr volumes and nineteen by Gualter form the nucleus of a Puritan lending library.[21] The Martyr copies are a Latin Romans (1559), English Romans (1568) and Latin Kings (1599). The Gualter collection includes an Isaiah of 1595, Matthew I (1609), Matthew II (1614), Luke (1601) and Acts of 1599, none of which are in Cambridge or the British Library.

These Zurich commentaries demonstrate the continuous market for continental divinity amongst academic theologians in Tudor and Stuart England. Together with the Renaissance editions of the Hebrew and Greek scriptures, they and the Latin versions of the Bible are the quarry for many a Puritan sermon which mined this rich deposit for coals to warm the household of faith.

B. Peter Martyr on Romans 8 (1558/1568)

Peter Martyr lectured on Romans while in Strasbourg with Martin Bucer. One student writes about those classes at the

College of St. Thomas which had reached Romans (12) by March of 1546.[22] At Oxford Martyr lectured again on Romans, beginning in 1550 from 9 to 10 A.M. He revised these in 1552 for publication.[23] The Latin edition came from the Basle press of Pietro Perna in 1558 and the Elizabethan translation in 1568 from John Day.[24] McLelland has explored Martyr's views on predestination and I have briefly touched on chapters three to nine and eleven to twelve.[25] Romans (8) calls for more detailed analysis if one wishes to observe at first hand Martyr's method of textual analysis. This commentary had a permanent attraction for the European Reformed community between 1545 as lectures at Strasbourg, the 1550s as Oxford grist for Cranmer's reforming agenda and in the seven Latin and one English printed editions between 1558 and 1613.

Romans (8) is a paradigm of Martyr's exegetical procedure. It is a mean between the extremes of Calvin's lucid brevity and Bucer's pious prolixity. Martyr knew Bucer, Bullinger and Melanchthon on Romans as well as Erasmus, Chrysostom and Calvin.[26] It seems best to compare Calvin's comments with Martyr at crucial points in a verse-by-verse analysis. Calvin's 1540 Romans was expanded in a 1551 edition and again in 1556.

Martyr first of all analyzes Romans (8) under six headings. Then he introduces his theological method of law/gospel and attacks scholastic philosophy. Martyr sees chapter eight as the other side of chapter seven, viz.:

> And euen as before he aboundantly entreated of the violence and tyranny of sinne, which it useth against us being unwittinge and unwilling thereunto: so now on the other side he teacheth, what the spirite of christ worketh in the saintes... for a godly man consisteth of his owne corrupt and vitiate nature, and also of ye spirit of christ: & because we haue before learned, what ye corruption of nature, that is, sinne, woorketh in us, and now is declared, what benefites of christ we obtayne by his spirite.27

Martyr sees six items occupying St. Paul's mind in describing the invincible safeguard which the elect have in Christ.

1. Paul removes every condemnation which is taken away as the Apostle says by the law of the spirit of life. This spirit is obtained by the benefit of Christ's death "For they which seperate themseules from Christ, can not be pertakers of his benefite."28
2. By this spirit the faithful partake not only of Christ's death but also of his resurrection.29
3. St. Paul amplifies this state obtained by the spirit of Christ. "We are moved by this spirit, and made strong against aduersaries, & to suffer all afflictions."30
4. St. Paul confutes those who object to the state in which the faithful live. "As yet we haue not obteyned an absolute regeneration nor perfect saluatio: for we haue it now but only in hope, which when time shall serve, that is, in the end of the worlde, shall be made perfect."31
5. In spite of evil closing in on every side, our saluation is sure "for the prouidence of God, whereby we are predestinate to eternall felicity can neither be chaunged, nor yet in any poynte fayle."32
6. "Lastly, he sayth, that ye loue of God towards us is so greate, that by no creature can it be plucked from us. Hereby it is manifest, of how greate force the spirite of adoption is, wherewith we are sealed so long as we wayte for the perfection of our felicity. And these things serue wonderfully to proue, that our iustification consisteth not of workes, but of fayth, and of the meare and free mercy of God."33

John Calvin begins his exposition of Romans (8) with a warning based on verse one. Even though St. Paul has said there is no condemnation for those in Christ Jesus who walk after the spirit, Calvin warns "and this last verily is added, least any upon a vaine opinion should boast himselfe, as though hee were freed from the curse, whiles in the meane time he doth securely cocker his fleshe."[34] Martyr's introduction strikes all the positive notes without Calvin's suspicion, 'can this really be so?'

Verse two tests considerable differences between Erasmus and Martyr on the one hand and Calvin on the other. The text is different for Erasmus than Calvin. The Vulgata read "Liberabit me a lege peccati, & mortis." Erasmus translated 'a lege' by 'a iure'.[35] Calvin in the 1556 edition interjects a sober note on this change: "I had rather keepe the name of law, then with Erasmus to translate it right or power: because Paule did not without cause allude unto the lawe of God."[36] Bullinger is brief on verse two saying simply, "This is why the faithful are freed from the terror of condemnation... we know that through Christ will be our gifts -- life, redemption and sanctification."[37]

Martyr unlike Calvin sees no danger that those led by the Spirit will fail. A godly man to be sure consists of his own corrupt nature and the spirit of Christ. Martyr says St. Paul entreats of the Spirit's help and benefits "least any man should thinke with himselfe, that not all manner of Christians enioye this excellente help of God, but onelye certaine principall and excellent men, such as were the Apostles."[38] We need to believe the pardon which is offered unto us, "if we desire to have the fruition of this so great a benefite."[39] Where Calvin in chapter eight of Romans warns his audience of the flesh's frailty, Martyr is content to leave that warning in Romans seven while rejoicing with St. Paul in chapter eight over the freedom of Christ's benefits. As the exposition unfolds, this difference of tone remains between Calvin's 1540 Romans and Martyr's 1550/51 commentary. One ought to keep in mind the probable impact of John Chrysostom on Vermigli at this point and/or Philip Melanchthon.

Martyr takes verse two and the phrase "a iure peccati & mortis" to mean freedom "from the guiltiness, or bond, whereby we were bound unto sinne, and unto eternall death. And when this bond is taken away there then remaineth nothing, why we should feare condemnation."[40] Martyr follows Chrysostom that the Greek text does not allow law to be called "the law of the spirite, and the law of life."[41] The distinction between law and gospel has a patristic content in Martyr's commentary not to be found in Bucer (1536), Bullinger (1537), or Calvin (1540).

> The Gospel, so long as it doth but outwardly only make a sound, neither is the holy ghost inwardly in the hartes of the hearers, to moue and bowe them to beleue, so long (I say) the Gospell hath the nature of the killyng letter, neyther differeth it any thyng from the lawe, as touchyng efficacye unto saluation. For althoughe it conteyne other thynges then the Lawe dothe, yet it canne neyther geue Grace, nor remission of synnes unto the bearers. But after that the holy ghost hath once moued ye harts of the hearers to beleue, then at the length

> the Gospell obtayneth his power to make safe. Wherefore the lawe of sinne, and of death, from which we are deliuered, is it, whereof before it was sayd, that it leadeth us captives, and rebelleth against the lawe of the minde. 'In this fight (saith Chrysostome) the holy ghost is present with vs, and helpeth and deliuereth vs, that we runne not into dammation [sic.]. He crowneth vs (saith he) and furnishing vs on euery side with stayes and helpes bringeth us into the battayle.' Which I thus understand, that we are counted crowned through the forgeuenes of our sinnes: and holpen with succors, when we are so holpen with free and gracious giftes, and with the strengt of the spirite, and instrumente of heauenly giftes that we suffer not this lawe of naturall corruption to raigne in us.42

Not only does Martyr provide a longer comment on verse two than Calvin or Bullinger, but he also employs Chrysostom and adopts Erasmus' 'a iure' in place of Calvin's defense of the Vulgata 'a lege'. Apart from this initial difference, Martyr also compares delivery from the bond of sin to the Exodus motif. Then Martyr cites Augustine, De Nuptiis 1:32 on the forgiveness of sins.[43] Martyr utilizes a homily by Chrysostom, De sancto & Adorando spiritu written against Arius and Eunomius. These ancient heretics would have the holy ghost be a human servant rather than equal to God. Only in the latter case would the spirit be free and the author of our freedom from sin.[44] Verse three reflects agreement between Calvin and Martyr. Calvin criticized Chrysostom who understood that sin itself was slain.

> Chrysostom & diuers after him, understand it some more hardly: namely, that sin was condemned of sin, because it slewe Christ uniustly & unworthily.45

Martyr concurrs, "But that interpretation which Chrisostome and Ambrose have, is fare more strange: for they thynke that sinne it selfe was condemned of Christe for sinne."[46]

Romans (8:28-30) elicits a terse definition of predestination. Martyr again has used Augustine, this time from De corruptione & gratia. Now he cites Romans (9) that election might be according to the purpose of God, Ephesians (1) that we have been predestined according to purpose and grace, and II Timothy (1) "Which hath called us wyth his holy calling, not according to our works but according to purpose and grace."[47]

Martyr notes that Paul distinguishes between certain callings, one which is outward by holy scripture and sermons, the other which is inward both temporary and permanent.[48] Vermigli then defines predestination in an extended comment on verse 29 by selecting three passages from Romans (9), Ephesians, and I Timothy. Martyr goes on to define the term 'purpose' which he claims Paul, Ambrose & Chrysostom all relate to God and not the predestinate. Then Martyr makes several distinctions.

1. Neither the will of believing nor the counsel to live a holy life spring from the elect. God predestines them to eternal life and to holy works.49
2. Enquiry into why God gives such good purpose or works to one man and not another is fruitless.50
3. Good works are the means whereby God brings us to eternal life and are not causes.51
4. These works are not always seen in the predestination of God. Infants for example die before they can perform good works.52

Martyr proceeds to deny a fond device of the schoolmen which says only the damned and reprobate are foreknown. He cites Origen to the effect that scripture nowhere mentions wicked men who are foreknown of God.[53] Martyr concludes with a classical reference.

> It is the point of ungodly men and of scorners to say, that God is deceived in his counsels. For so dallieth Lucianus in Timone, that when the temple of Castor and Pollux was smitten with lightening, it erred much, for that otherwise it was sent of Iupiter upon Anaxagoras. Wherefore a godly mind ought to be persuaded of two thinges: First that the predestination of God cannot erre from his ende appointed: Secondly, that we assure ourselues, tht we pertayne unto the number of the predestinate. Which thing although it cannot be comprehended by naturall knowledge, yet it may be holden by the certainty of hope and of fayth.54

Martyr likes very well the saying of Chrysostom that all violence is excluded. "For the election of God bringeth no violence either unto the predestinate or unto the reprobate."[55] Martyr also quotes Augustine, De Corruptione & gratia that the power of God cannot be overcome by our sin.

Vermigli's non-violent view of predestination taken from Romans (8:28-30) in comparison with Romans (9), Ephesians & I Timothy is intriguing in its support from a selective use of Augustine, Chrysostom and Origen. The patristic focus of Marytr's Romans commentary sets it apart from those of Bucer, Bullinger, Calvin and Melanchthon. Even a cursory survey of Romans (8) reflects Martyr's independent judgement and skillful collaboration with the protestant exegesis he mentions in the preface.

On the final verses of Romans (8) St. Paul asked, "If God be on our side, who can be against us?" Martyr found that at Romans (8:13-39) Chrysostom expressed St. Paul's concern for God's elect better than anyone else.

> Chrisostome in this place sayth: Why asketh thou O Paul, who can be Agaynst us? The whole worlde ryseth up agaynst us: the Deuill, tyrannes, they of our owne householde, our kinsfolkes, our citizens, and the flesh. It is true (saith he) that all those thynges fight agaynst us, but they shall not preuayle: yea rather they shall aduance our saluation. Iob was by temptations, by hys wyfe & friends, by the Chaldeans, wyndes, and fire from heauen made of more fame then he was before.56

One must incorporate into one's discussion of Puritan attitudes toward predestination the widely circulating patristic nuances of this Romans commentary, striking as it does an independent line from both Calvin and Bullinger.

English Puritan commentaries seem to be derivative at best when one compares them with Martyr's Romans or Calvin's Isaiah (1609). Calvin on Ephesians is based on sermons while his I Corinthians has a different approach. The point to be made is that the continental commentaries seem more directly textual with the theological comments sorted out in loci as with Vermigli or separated into the Institutes as with Calvin. English commentaries by comparison lean toward the sermonic in many cases.

C. Pre-Critical Exegesis

Latin commentaries from continental sources and for sale in regions of sixteenth century England counterbalance the usual concentration on English language texts of major Puritan figures such as Ames and London preachers like Sibbes or Preston.[57] These several Latin volumes present a variety of approaches to biblical exegesis in a period which bears the lable of "pre-critical." That should provoke a brief reflection on the use of scripture in England before 1700.

Coolidge's The Pauline Renaissance in England provides additional comment on the practice of exegesis in which another antimony is present in Puritan biblical comments, subtle but radical. The sense of response to God's word and a rational conformity to God's truth led these scriptural types to find in the Epistles of Paul a reconciliation of these twin senses of obedience. Reading of the scriptures led these later disciples (1549-1662) to know Christ as did the original ones by His bodily presence and St. Paul by special apparition: "...the writing of the Apostles do point him out truly, and nothing but him."[58]

Recently Hans - Joachim Kraus has pointed to the nuances which need to be presented in a more precise discussion of the reformers.[59] The starting point for Calvin as an example is a new knowledge of scripture in which the basis for its authority is the character of the divine speaker. As Calvin said in the Institutes (II, ii, xxi), "we are incapable of understanding the mysteries of God any further than we have been illuminated by divine grace." Kraus makes a telling point about the failure to be precise about the reformers' use of scripture. The direct participation of the reformers in the battle for the gospel, the seriousness with which they exhort, comfort and instruct -- all of this leads Kraus to contend for the "kerygmatic analogies which made a direct impression on the exegete" and which in turn ought not to be dismissed as interpretations.

To find that reality which is identical with God's sequential dealing with men in the Puritan period, one might turn to John Knox the Scottish Reformer. The Scots Confession (1560) which was drawn up by Knox and others established the identity of first century Pauline churches in Corinth and Ephesus with those in sixteenth century Scotland. Their rationale was the teaching in the Scottish churches which was contained in the written word of God, "to witt, in the buikeis of the Auld and New Testamentis."[60] The nuances called for by Kraus are present in most sermons of master John Knox. His sermon of 19 August 1565 on Isaiah (26:13-21) is a paradigm of narrative exegetical procedures.

Isaiah (26:13) reads as Knox knew it in the Geneva Bible (1560): "O Lorde our God, other lordes beside thee have ruled us; but we will remember thee onely, and thy Name." The tyranny that the Israelites sustained in captivity called forth this litany. To better understand this complaint, says Knox, we must observe two things. First one must observe the source of all authority and then to what end God appoints powers.[61] There is no power but God as the Apostle says! The sword is committed to the powers to punish "wycked doers, and unto the praise of such as do well."[62] The stubborn disobedience of God's ancient people brought prophets among them, rising early, desiring them to turn to God and mend their wicked ways (II Kings 17).

> "Now so it is," said Knox, "that God by that Great Pastor our Lorde Jesus, nowe manifestly in his worde calleth us from all impietie, as well of body, as of mind, to holynesse of life, and to his spirituall service..."[63]

Here John Knox makes the extraordinary claim that the words of Isaiah (26) are addressed to the citizens of Edinburgh and are reinforced by II Kings (17) and Romans (13). Knox does not split apart the historical context and its intended narrative reference. To do so would be to escape the implications of the narrative for the life of the interpreter by the use of historical/critical exegesis. So then the corporate life of those who listened to the Bible in Knox's audience is a commentaire vécu on the Bible itself, assimilating the antimonies of the world into which Christ came. The Scots heard afresh a recital of their dilemmas and paradoxes in the conditions of Edinburgh on a Sunday in August of 1565.

One should not imply that Knox had popular support for his reform in Edinburgh. The city catholics held a mass in Holyrood Chapel on August 8, 1563 which provoked a riot. Two protestant activists stirred up the populace during the following week. Their presense at the mass was viewed by Knox as "picheting," though each had a pistol and was tried for disturbing public order. Knox's lack of success at their trial "casts considerable doubt on the amount of popular support he was able to draw on in Edinburgh itself."[64]

Chapter 15) Sermons and Society

A. Lectures by Combination

Quarterly sermons were compulsory in all English parishes as the Tudor age dawned. Royal injunctions of 1559 tripled the number of parish homilies by mandating one sermon each month. In 1587 sixteen sermons were required each year (33% increase per annum) and by 1604 incumbants by law must preach each Sunday. Over forty-five years sermonic instruction increased by 433% in each parish. Fifty-seven sermons or series of sermons were printed in the year 1623 alone.[65]

In London which had ninety-four incumbants in 1560, forty-four were University graduates. In 1577 of these ninety-seven, fifty-five were graduates and by 1595 sixty-nine of ninety-six were well educated. Not only did the frequency of sermons increase, but the theological preparation of ministers intensified over thirty-five years from 46.8% in London parishes to 71.8% by 1595. Clearly Puritans were ministers of sacred scripture. When one adds to this amalgam that godly laity such as the Puritan Earl Henry Hastings appointed such candidates in their corner of the land, can one wonder that a dream of a godly ministry in the parish had not yet vanished at the local level? A godly corps of Puritan pastors together with a cadre of aristocratic supporters still would seek to rebuild Jerusalem in England's verdant land. Not all were eager to listen to the increased volume of sermons. Its effectiveness in Elizabethan times has been questioned on the grounds that what transpired in London did not go down so well in Lancashire and even the "city" sermons were often social rather than spiritual occasions. Christopher Haigh points to several instances where noted preachers caught their parishioners slighting the sermons and even worse. John Angier of Denton complained that "some sleep from the beginning to the end, as if they come for no other purpose but to sleep... Hell was made for sermon-sleepers."[66]

Where Haigh speaks of results, Collinson reports the intent via some eighty-five locations for Combination Lectures which reflects a market for preaching on the local level.[67] In Chester diocese, for example, the Lancashire clergy were required to attend the prophesyings held at Easter, midsummer and Michaelmas at the market town of Preston from 1582. In fact, they were held in five centers where in Puritan areas they continued up to the Civil War. In all there were fourteen centers with usually four moderators at each, marking some fifty-three in all for the 1580s.[68] Furthermore, thirty-nine of the puritan clergy in the diocese of Chester were educated at Oxford with fourteen from Brasenose College. The earliest of these was Christopher Goodman and included Richard Mather for a time in 1618.

George Gifford mirrors the concern of a large segment of society when in 1582 he articulated the eschatological dimensions of this Puritan agenda in Essex. "Through want of a sincere ministry of the Word... there is a flood of ignorance and darkness overflowing the most part of the land..."[69] Essex mirrors the struggle between parish renewal and episcopal control. When Archbishop Whitgift issued fresh articles which "required subscription to the Thirty-Nine Articles and assent to the entire contents of the book of Common Prayer, at least forty-three Essex ministers were suspended for their refusal to comply."[70] Twenty-seven ministers petitioned the Privy Council while in Colchester godly laity enlisted Sir Francis Walsingham against Sir Thomas Heneage, the burough's patron and knight of the shire.[71] At Maldon in Essex came a lengthy petition in favour of George Gifford. The argument here shifted away from the specific details of vestments and church polity to stress the contribution of Gifford to social order, the creation of a godly discipline and obedience to the moral consequences of the Pauline renaissance. Preaching of that sort was a prerequisite for political stability. Gifford put the godly in terror of their very lives.[72]

One way around the strictures which the crown placed on prophesying, as in the famous suspension of Archbishop Grindal, was the practice in London of parish lecturers for hire. Sermonophile citizens set up lecturing positions in at least three parishes during young King Edward's reign.[73] Though the Marian interlude interrupted protestant preaching, under Elizabeth London parishes such as St. Antholin engaged a trio of preachers to read lectures. After Parker's purge in 1566 the number grew from a handful to thirty-three by 1589. Almost one-third of all the London parishes supported extra Sunday and weekday sermons, while one out of every two parishes established such a voluntary position sometime during this period.[74] Indeed from 1566 when the vestments controversy forced the crackdown of episcopal authority until 1583, when for the first time all lecturers were checked by episcopal visitation, such lectureships were loopholes for clerical puritanism in London. St. Stephen Coleman Street was a notable example of this practice which in 1600 paid John Dod £30 per annum, well beyond the annual endowment of £11 since the fifteenth century.

Lecture duties varied from parish to parish. A lecturer might preach four times a week or meet the average of once on Sunday and once in midweek. Instruction in the catechism might even involve textual exposition to a mixed audience of adults and children. St. Antholin was the most heavily endowed parish which drew from lecturers' estates as well as legacies to employ three lecturers throughout most of the Elizabethan period.[75] Such weekday activity revitalized parish life in the capitol. It also affected more diligent sermon preparation. St. Botolph's parish may have set an example when at Aldgate the lecturer preached eight consecutive sermons on Matthew (27:2-11) and devoted twenty-four hours over a year's time to that chapter. Any incumbant need inspect his Sunday text with care as he crafted a sermon to match that attention to scripture during the week.[76]

St. Bartholomew's by the Exchange is a clear example of lay patronage, situated next to St. Stephen, Coleman Street. Late in the sixteenth century the Puritan parishioners obtained the right to appoint a lecturer from special funds. The Haberdashers' Company whose hall was in Maiden Lane supported this lectureship through their liveryman William Jones who established it in 1615. The preacher was the noted Puritan John Downame who would be rector of All Hallows the Great from 1630 to 1652 and was in the neighboring parish of St. Margaret Lothbury since 1602. Not only did Downame deliver the weekly Haberdashers' lecture but he also consulted regularly with the Company's Court of Assistants on appointments of preachers, lecturers and schoolmasters. All in all, "for virtually thirty-five years, a weekly Puritan lecture was given at an important church situated in the the financial heart of the city."[77]

Professor Collinson has traced combination lectures which respond to similar expectations in the seventeenth century. A combination lecture or exercise typically called for thirteen ministers each to preach quarterly in order of seniority in the weekly market town lecture. As few as three or as many as twenty might so combine to preach in rotation, followed by a conference among the ministers before or after a dinner.[78]

Bury St. Edmunds sustained such combination lectures and exercises from 1572 to 1636. Bishop Matthew Wren confirmed two single lectures in 1636 to be preached on Wednesday and Friday as well as a lecture on Monday's market day. Wren allowed fifty ministers to participate in this pattern which seems to be the continuation of the "godly exercise" which Parkhurst had allowed in 1573. Perhaps predictably enough, Wren's successor Edmund Freke came into confrontation with the preachers and the Puritan gentry of West Suffolk over this matter of lectures by combination.[79] Collinson would use "collegiality" to describe these exercises rather than "presbyterian."[80]

The diocese of Norwich gave nine reasons for such lectures in the reign of James I. These arguments speak of an English church still quite secure in both its structure and its integrity.

1. First, the propagation of the Ghospell and edefieng of the church.
2. Incouraging of the meaner sorte of preachers.
3. Exciting of sluggards to the studie of divinitie by means whereof their owne parishes also shallbe the better served.
4. Increase of love and acquaintance amongst preachers.
5. Increase of religion and learning, by meetinges and conference.
6. Varietie will more delighte the people's attention.
7. Advauncement to the clergie man, when their guiftes shalbe knowne.
8. People wanting preachers shall or maye be there taught.
9. Benefit also to the inhabitauntes for their markett by concurse of people.81

B. Funeral Sermons

Elizabethan Puritans in their conferences and exercises reflect much human and social experience. They learned from the mirror of God's word as well as religious biography. Professor Collinson points to Foxe's Actes and Monuments at one end (1570 complete) and Samuel Clarke at the other (1652). Owen Watkins explores a full range of Puritan literature in his study of the Puritan Experience which he subtitles "Studies in Spiritual Autobiography."[82] Watkins describes power, feeling and enjoyment as the key words in Puritan descriptions of spiritual experience.[83] The pattern of Puritan experience, whether autobiography as in Bunyan's Grace Abounding or early seventeenth century funeral sermons, builds a structure of suspense. The self-deceived sinner is humiliated by the requirements of the moral law which suspends him between hope and despair. As he seeks assurance of salvation, the second self-deception then intrudes as one postpones the comforts available in the righteousness of Christ. Continual temptations face the new saint in this conversion model.[84]

Collinson explores funeral sermons as the raw material for Samuel Clarke's Marrow of ecclesiastical historie. In so doing he discovers a striking departure from the conversionist chronicle so familiar among introspective Puritans.[85] These funeral sermons were cuckoos in the protestant nest, "hatched from the dubious egg of the classical panegyric, which was not laid by Luther or Calvin, nor yet by St. Paul."[86]

Some seventy separate funeral sermons between 1600 and 1640 distinguish between panegyrick and preaching as in Thomas Cartwright's complaint to Archbishop Whitgift that the oratory of Gregory of Nazianzus "savoured of the manner of Athens, where he was brought up."[87] To test Collinson's hypothesis that funeral sermons undergo a transformation from a conversionist milieu to litanies of praise, we turn to an analysis of one such sermon preached in 1615. Emmanuel Utie was a fellow of St. John's College, Cambridge who preached his funeral sermon to Dudley Fenner's parishioners of St. Stephens Walbrooke.[88]

The sermon choses Matthew (10:3) as its text where Matthew says he was a publican, i.e., a sinner. Two conclusions follow from the first part: 1) That we are not to account ourselves good, for the good things we have done;[89] 2) To Christ belongs a feast for his Mercy, to us a gospel to record that thankfulness.[90] The second part points to the significance of the biblical scribe as a publican:

> This is the truth: That the holy Ghost in the Scripture doth finger out the faults of his owne children, and makes them be the penmen of their own shame.91

Utie's contemporaries excuse the sins of Old Testament patriarchs such as Noah, whose drunkeness is called "weaknesse of age." Lot's incest is labled "good nature" and Adam's weakness toward Eve is called "tendernesse."[92] A sin must not be concealed; therefore one must label malefactors in the congregation for what they are -- publicans![93]

The sermon goes on for thirty-six pages before it mentions the deceased.

> One sinne he had, you that haue lesse, write him in your Table-bookes to be a sinner... And so let me set him as it were in a ship: He hoizt up the saile and turn'd it which way it pleased him; the deuill he blew the winde, but I hope God sate at the Rudder, and steer'd him the best course vnto heauen:94

That sin which Utie excused was gluttony while at the same time he warned the departed's friends not to be caught in their cups of drunkeness like Belshazzar of old. The sermon fits Collinson's typology as tightly as possible.

C. Plague Sermons (1563-1667)

During the last forty years of Tudor rule, three severe plagues struck London-in 1563, again in 1593 and one with a higher mortality in 1603. In 1563 plague deaths were 25% of London's population. In 1593 Shrewsbury calculates some 14.4% of recorded deaths were plague induced. In 1603 the death totals mounted to 16.1% of London's population as the numbers who died in London increased with each major incidence of the plague.[95]

In Norwich the plague broke out in 1580, 1583, 1590 and especially in 1602/03 when one-fourth of the population died.[96] Colchester especially suffered high mortality in 1579, 1586, 1597 and 1603.[97] There is good evidence to label 1579 a smallpox epidemic because of its seasonal incidence (December 1578/August 1579). The first mention of organized relief is found in Colchester. The Assembly Book reads for 28 November 1603:

> At this assembly it is ordered that the double collection for relief of the infected sick people shall be from henceforth continued until Christmas Day next.98

If that would not suffice, then monies paid in by the towns were to be dispersed.

The Plague struck London with a vengeance in 1625, 1636 and 1665/66. Shrewsbury gives the London deaths in 1626 as 16.4% of the 250,000 population.[99] In 1665/66 17.25% of London's 400,000 population succombed to the plague.[100]

Cambridge excavations in 1952 on Midsummer Common unearthed a number of human skeletons, remains of plague victims who occupied as many as forty plague huts on the commons.[101] In 1625 the King and Privy Council closed Sturbridge Fair near Cambridge the University suspended sermons at Great St. Marys. Letters sent by post were fumed. Residents needed a certificate from the Mayor and University Vice-Chancellor in order to leave the city.[102]

Shrewsbury records that one-fourth of Norwich died in the plague of 1602/03. There an extant civic mortality bill from October 1665/October 1666 reports 2,251 of 3,012 deaths as plague deaths.[103] That 11% mortality rate led Thomas Corie to lament that "most of our chefest shopkeepers in the market ar gon and ther shopes shut up."[104]

Colchester lost nearly half its inhabitants to the 1665/66 plague. Caution must be exercised about establishing any long term effects of the plague since the population rapidly recovered. Ship fines suggest that economic activity slowed very little.[105] Ipswich by contrast lost but 1071 of its 8000 population during 1665/66.[106] Pest accounts of four Ipswich parishes survive which together with the Royal collection proclaimed on 6 July 1666 and those of the two Alms Houses totaled £640.15.7 for poor relief.[107]

1. Religious Response (1563-1667)

Few modern studies of Puritan England mention the plague, let alone describe its impact on theological reflection. One solitary set of sermons from the North of England has been combed for its literary excellence[108] while a recent survey of this period links up increased societal mobility with the weakened social fabric.[109] Wilson's literary analysis coupled with Dyer's use of four additional clerical responses hardly exhausts the available sermonic corpus. Analysis of more than thirty additional religious discussions of the plague should fill in the gap created by the notable lack of attention given to this genre in recent accounts of Puritan thought.[110]

The reading of religious plague literature should begin with a litany, i.e., that prepared by Edmund Grindal, Bishop of London.[111] _A Fourme Twyse Aweke_ (1563) ordered a public fast every

Wednesday. The preface calls for repentance so that God might aside his deserved wrath and deadly visitation on the populace.

> It hath ben thought meete to set foorth by publique order, some occasion to excite and stirre up all godly people within this Realme, to pray earnestly and hartely to God, to turne away his deserved wrath from us...112

Alexander Nowell's Homily printed with the Fourme compares the sixteenth century plague with the calamities visited on the Jews as recorded in Leviticus (26) and Deuteronomy (28). The Homily urges repentance so that "lyke punyshmants and plagues" not be visited in Tudor times.[113] The tone has been set for the next century in England that the plague like the Turk on the continent is an instrument used by God for judgment of his people and their repentance.[114] In 1596 the Puritan preacher George Gifford added the Turks to his list of calamities and plagues.[115]

Authorities issued a standard prayer of thanksgiving in 1625. Its rhetoric is a standard clerical response to the plague.

> Almightie and eternall God, which strikest and healest, bringest downe to death, and quickenest againe, who in thy just Judgement for our sinnes diddest lately sore plague us with great sicknesse and mortalitie;... We most humbly acknowledge... from the bottome of our hearts this thine exceeding gracious goodnes... toward us most vile and wretched sinners.116

William Kemp put a theological twist on causes for the plague. The primary cause is a supernatural one in which Satan is the agent. As in Poland and Germany even now in England witches sometimes cause the plague.[117] Though sin causes the pestilence, Kemp appeals secondly to nature which 'breeds' the plague by corrupting the air. Then Kemp multiples his list of natural causes by turning to stars and planets, solar and lunar eclipses, comets, excessive heat or rain. All of these natural causes breed plague which fear and imagination help to spread.[118] If there are more flies than usual, a great increase of frogs or an extraordinary growth of mushrooms, then the plague is stalking the land.[119]

From the pulpit Englishmen were told why catastrophic disease was a regular feature of their daily lives. It was difficult for parishioners to sort out the primary cause which was the God of the Old Testament from the secondary causes which were emblazoned in the sky or sins all about their land. The strident sermons and their Old Testament texts competed with a host of astrological predictions.[120] A rough count of biblical references from several plague sermons indicates the following frequencies of citation: Psalms, 18; Deuteronomy, 8; II Samuel, 5; I & II Chronicles, 4; and Numbers, 3. The most frequent texts cited were Psalm (91), Psalm (106:30), Deuteronomy (28) and II Samuel (24).

Continental plague treatises were translated from works by Andreas Osiander, Theodore Beza and Johann Ewich which also included sections of Luther's 1527 Plague Letter. These continental authors appear in English translation between 1537 and 1583. Luther's letter represents a surprising omission in this list.[121]

Miles Coverdale translated Andreas Osiander's 1533 sermon on Psalm 91.[122] It was printed in 1537, twice in 1538, and reset in 1603.[123] Osiander describes the terror which the plague aroused in his comment at Psalm (91:5) on the "horror of nyght."

> Then goeth ther one astray another loseth hys coloure, ye thyrde falleth sycke, ye fourthe is become crocked, the fythe goeth out of hys wyt. And so men thynke, that the devell hath done it...124

Osiander permits flight in plague seasons if one does not abandon belief, God's command, his own vocation or the love of a neighbor. Those sessions of the plague are the result of human error as Deuteronomy (28:21) states: "The Lord shall make the pestilence cleave unto thee, until he have consumed thee from off the land, whither thou goest to possess it." Others, says Osiander, dissent from the view that their sins are responsible and point to the influence of stars, working of comets and unseasonable weather, "out of the South windes, out of stincking waters, or out of foule mistes of the grounde."[125] One ought not fear the arrow by day nor the terror of night since the more dangerous the plague, the more excellent the promise.[126]

Theodore Beza wrote his De Peste in 1579 which Vignon reprinted at Geneva in 1580. It also appeared at Leiden in 1581 and 1655.[127] John Stockwood's preface to his translation is a concise summary of the question whether by taking flight one sins against ones neighbor or by tarrying provokes God.[128] Beza worries that some cite scripture which calls the plague 'God's Hand' (II Samuel 24), the 'Sword of God' (I Chronicles 21) and 'Arrows' (Psalm 91) to deny its infectuous nature. Those hold that the sin which provokes God to stir up inferior causes against men is the cause of all disease, and use this as an excuse to forsake their christian duty.[129]

Others seek to escape by sudden flight. Beza argues that if the plague itself is not good, it still leads to a good end by causing repentance. Those who flee the plague flee that means by which God brings a good end to pass.[130] Beza asks himself who and when may one obey the ancient motto, "Quickly, A far of, Long ere you return"?[131]

In the light of these two questions Beza sets down three general plague precepts:

I. 'Thou shalt not kill' means never rashly to place lives in danger of infection.

II. One ought not to forget one's Christian duty in times of plague.

III. The sickly and those with children should leave plague infested sites.

> Let man helpe man, Citizen Citizen, that needeth any helpe of his, according too his power... And for faithfull Pastors to forsake but one poore sheepe at that time when as he most of al needeth heavenly cofort, it were to shameful, nay too wicked a part.[132]

This most practical pastoral advice from the Genevan leader was reprinted at the time of the 1665 London plague.[133] Beza's De Peste in Latin editions as well as in the collected Tractationes speak of a wider circulation of these ideas in England than for Osiander's German text.

Luther's 1527 letter on the plague was not translated though several sections of it show up in Johann Ewich's Duty of a Magistrate (1582).[134] Luther is quoted in extenso on the care of one's neighbor. Luther argued that God created medical science so that every man could take care of his body. One who does not use "physick" is a murderer before God. So, too, one who despises meat, drink, clothing and shelter presumes on God's care. There is no greater folly, wrote Luther, than that which despises a remedy against the plague. Such negligence is that:

> which he may hurt and infect others also through this his negligence, who peradventure, if he had suffered himselfe to have been looked unto, had remained unhurt and alive.135

The London minster William Warde gave two sermons on the plague in 1607. The text on the title page is Deuteronomy (32:23): "I will spend plagues upon them; I will bestow mine arrowes upon them."[136] The first sermon quotes Deuteronomy (28:59) to argue that the more stubbornly a people resist God the more severe and permanent the plague would become. Even Pilate, claimed Warde, would rise up in judgment against those who curse "And tosse that dreadfull Name of God in their mouthes, as a football is tossed too and fro on the plaine ground."[137]

Warde's second sermon on "God's Arrowes" lists specific sins which provoked the plague. Warde laments that less than half attend their parish church on a Sunday and that trust in national might is a form of idolatry.[138]

> The plague then is Gods hand, and his providence is in it... It is a blowe of his hand, and it is one of Gods Arrowes. It hittes where it pleaseth God to levell it ...If thou flee into the uttermost part of the earth, thou art not free from this Arrow of God.139

James Godskall comments in The Kings Medicine (1604) that Psalm (7:12) as well as Psalm (91:5) warns Godskall that the Avenger God "ordayned his arrowes for them that persecuted him."[140] Godskall chooses several targets for "God's Arrowes," directing them against blasphemers of God's majesty and those who adulterize their neighbors and play the whore against themselves. These are linked together in an anti-catholic tirade.

> traitors by conviction, locusts, come from the bottom-lesse pit of hell, spued foorth from the sea of Rome and Rhemes in heapes... as uermins, being come out of the high Oke tree of Rome, seek to destroy the green Olive tree in the house of the Lord.141

When William Gauge spoke of God's three Arrows of plague, famine and the sword in his triple sermon of 1631 he selected as his text Ezekiel (6:11). The remedy for the plague in the Gouge sermon was a confession of twelve personal and national sins to escape the thick cloud of the papacy.[142]

2. Sins of Society

Three proverbs emerge from the sermonic plague literature of 1563-1667 in England. The first is the ancient advice,"Quickly, A far of, long ere you return." A second and common advice was to focus on those sins which were the targets for Arrows of the Almighty. In the third place yearly Almanacs contained a third bit of advice for a plague weary society: to scan the starry skies for signs of healing.

Those who followed the ancient dictum often fled at the expense of their poor neighbor. Benjamin Spenser complained that ministers, physicians and traders abandoned London during the 1625 plague. "The one would help me being soule-sick, the other being body-sicke, the third being belly-sicke."[143] Local and Royal collections were levied to alleviate the resultant misery.

An astrologer like Robert Anton defended his science against "Gypsy fumblings." Anton's Dialogue betwixt Nature and Time presents nature as "the verie Hospitall of all theyr diseases."[144] His seven "Satyrs" attack humorists who mock the ancient art," like the Maior of some Puritan towne, spic'd with austeerest schisme; that scarce will see A Maypole to be nearer heauen than hee."[145]

Like the astrologer the theologian who pointed to sins rather than the stars held that God was the primary cause of plague. They argued about the secondary causes, accusing one another of fatalistic thoughts. William Kemp for one held that human sin moved the supernatural to cause the plague.[146] The societal defects which these sermons catalog are quite specific.

William Warde commences his catalog of secondary causes with the affront of feminine charms and excessive pride in dress. Warde complains:

> and is ther not many a cursed Iesabell, that delight in nothing so much as in paynting their faces, and hiding Gods handyworke, spending time (which is so precious)... or practising with their looking glasses to see if all be well without, but never looke into the glasse of Gods word, to see if all be well within.147

James Godskall turned to Genesis (6 and 7) for the cause of the plague. In his Arke of Noah (1607) Godskall lamented that the same sins that deluged the world in Noah's day now inundate England. Self security, disobedience, fornication, cruelty and corruption moved God to send the plague into the land.[148] Godskall reminds his readers that those who repented of their sins would be rescued, more in fact than the eight persons were saved in the Old Testament flood story.[149]

John Featly is less allegorical than Godskall when he links six sins with biblical passages. His Tears in time of Pestilence (1665) contemporized the agony of ancient Israel's national scandals. Jehovah now passes a just sentence when He responds with the plague to:

1) A land populated by Adulterers (Jeremiah 23:10)
2) Idolatry openly flaunted (Micah 1:5)
3) People no longer set apart (Ezra 10:1)
4) Women's pride which destroys men as daughters walk with wanton eyes and mincing gait (Isaiah 3:16)
5) Herbs and flowers which suffer (Jeremiah 12:4 and Psalm 119:36)
6) Falsified market balances and social justice begging in the streets (Amos 8:5,8).150

Mathew Mead's Solomon's Prescription (1666) collects more specific sins than any other plague sermon. If pestilence grips a nation, argues Mead, it is a sign of interior plague in people's hearts, "some such wickedness which provok'd God to pour out his Wrath upon them."[151] Mead adds some fresh sins to the list such as sodomy, going on to condemn licentious stage plays and apparel. Drunkeness and gluttony swell the list to which also should be added crafty professors who dabble at popery. These are the most crafty of all in a society which condons murder and neglects public worship. They profane the Lord's Supper as well.[152]

> Oh happy Plague that befell us in 1665, which discovered to the Inhabitants of England this Plague of their own hearts, their uncharitableness and animosities one against another, and cur'd them...153

Thomas Swadlin (1600-1670) adds some color to the catalog of national sins by blaming the plague on schismatics and heretics, "Papists and Anabaptists." Using Zepheniah (1:10) Swadlin berates the "Gulles, and Gallants, and painteed Iezzabels... Crane-paced, level-toes, that walke with stretched-out neckes."[154] To catalogue clerical foibles among societal sins, listing particular faults of merchant, magistrate or minister with cries for social justice had the net effect of placing every English person on common ground before the justice and mercy of a democratic deity. These plague sermons in the end represent radical statements of common sin and particular grace. These sermons might be labled as jeremiads for their lament of national foibles.

The standard response to catastrophe continues for another century in the sermons preached after the 1755 Lisbon earthquake. Then Charles Chauncy of Colonial Boston ignores his theological differences with Jonathan Edwards to strike this common theme in a sermon titled, Earthquakes A Token of the Righteous Anger of God.[155] Sacvan Berkovitch contrasts the European jeremiad with that of the American Puritan. The latter turned sermonic threats into consolation. Our English plague sermons contain a measure of consolation which makes one hesitate to make such a sharp delineation between English and Colonial Puritan rhetoric.[156] The covenant which God maintained with His elect people would be the implicit assumption undergirding most if not all of these plague homilies.[157]

Robert Sanderson's sermon on Psalm (106:30) circulated more widely than any other plague sermon, circulating in nineteen editions in seventy-two years. The sermon was preached on 4 August 1625 to the magistrates in Lincoln. The text reads,"Then stood up Phinehes, and executed judgement: and the plague was stayed."[158] This was a rich example for all magistrates to urge them to execute justice with zeal. Sanderson comments on the lack of swift justice in Caroline England.

> Our heavy oppression of our brethren at home, in racking the rents, and cracking the backes, and grinding the faces of the poore: our cheape and irreverent regard unto Gods holy ordinances of his Word and Sacraments, and Sabbaths, and Ministers: our Wantonesse and Toyishnesse of understanding in corrupting the simplicity of our Christian Faith, and troubling the peace of the Church with a thousandniceties... and... that universal Corruption which is... in those which... wee call the Courts of Iustice, by sale of offices, enhauncing of fees...159

The most explicit political piece is Edmund Staunton's sermon to the Lords on 30 October 1644. Staunton selects the same text as Sanderson to urge revolution. Staunton perceives four bars to justice which a seventeenth century Phinehas should remove: the iron bar of fears, the golden bar of hopes, the fleshly bar of civil relationships and the "effeminite barre of groundless pitie."[160] Staunton's summary call for revolutionary justice asks that blood flow in the streets.

> There is a fire of ciuill war kindled in England, still burning in the bowels of it... but two bloods will quench it, the blood of Christ and of his desperate enemies.161

To all of these political alarms ringing from the plague passages of the Old Testament comes a not unexpected censure of political catholicism. Thomas Darling uses Ezekiel (9:1-2) to warn London against the Jesuits. The city had been the sink of sin, a cloister for atheists and papists as well as the home of "gallants, forsooth, and miscreants fraught with affections of all lewednesse... Atheisticall politicians... Matchiauill himselfe will not serve ...poisoning Iesuites... which have so long cloyed the noualists of the city, so full of sugred words."[162]

The litany of secondary causation based on public and private sins comes from such diverse quarters as Henry Holland who prints a prayer of Richard Greenham -- the paragon of a Puritan pastor, and Robert Sanderson, protegee of Archbishop Laud and member of the 1661 Savoy Conference. One hesitates to identify plague sermons with any special interest group whether Puritan or papist. A common discontent which ignored warnings of preachers and astrologers alike was well stated by the poet George Wither:

> This land hath some sense of what she ayles,
> And uery much, these evill times bewayles:
> But, not so much our sinnes do we lament,
> Or mourne, that God for them is discontent,
> As that the Plagues they bring disturb our pleasure,
> Encrease our dangers, and exhaust our treasures.[163]

3. Stars or Sins?

The theological issue which emerges from a reading of English plague sermons in this period is part of the formal discussion over predestination.[164] In fact these sermons and the almanac literature give one an excellent perspective on the discussions over fate and providence. Richard Leake, for example, touched on just that issue in one of his 1599 sermons by claiming that illness of body or mind proceeds from sins as the first occasion and disease proceeds from the "foredecreed counsell of the highest..."[165] Thomas Doolitell utilizes sixteen Old Testament passages to make the same point: Leveticus (26:25); Deuteronomy (28:21); Amos (4:10); Jeremiah (24:10, 14:12); II Samuel (24:15); Exodus (9:15); Numbers (25:8-9); Ezekiel (33:27); Psalm (106:29); Numbers (11:33); Numbers (14:27); Ezra (5:12); Numbers (16:47-50); Jeremiah (29:17-18) and Exodus (5:3).[166]

Astrologers like John Gadbury talk about "God not contradicting the course of second causes."[167] James Bowker in 1668 wrote that "The Heavens a Book, The Stars be letters fair, God is the Writer, Men the Readers are." John Calvin made some careful distinctions about students of the stars in his Advertissment contre l'Astrologie judiciare (1549) which appeared in English translation in 1561. There Calvin lamented the "foolishe curiositie to judge by ye stars of all things what should chaunce unto men."[168] Though God has not revealed in Calvin's time the sincere truth of his gospel, yet he will punish those whose pride manifests itself in such a foolish abuse as Astrology.[169] Astrologers cloak their science as mathematics and so deceive many.

Calvin distinguishes astrology from sorcery whe he observes Moses who said that God made the Sun, moon and stars which govern tilling of the earth and civil policy. The common folk sense this when they perceive that days are shorter in winter than summer,"that it is whotte in sumer and colde in winter." They notice effects while astrology declares the causes.[170] Calvin calls the former 'naturall' and the latter "judicialle Astrologie."[171] In his Genesis (1:16) comment Calvin defends as useful those clever astronomers who prove Saturn larger than the moon.[172]

Calvin does not argue against seeking "in the heavenly creatures the begynning and cause of the accedentes which are sene here in the earth."[173] This is not the first cause but an inferior means to accomplish God's will. In the Institutes I.XVI.8 Calvin cited Deuteronomy (28:2,15) and in I.XVI.9 he goes on to mention secondary causes and the treatment of disease. At Institutes I.XVI.8 Calvin states:

> But if the misfortunes and miseries that oppresse us, doe chaunce without the worke of men, let us remember the doctrine of the Law: whatsoever is prosperous floweth from the fountaine of Gods blessing, and that all aduersities are his cursings.174

There is then in Calvin's view a certain agreement between earthly pestilence and the influence of the stars. Yet when David chose the pestilence as the rod of God by which he was to be chastened, Calvin will not admit that the stars had caused this. Calvin does not deny that God uses natural agents to chasten men,"but must we saye that this is done by a continuall order even as the starres are thereunto prepared? No."[175]

Calvin felt that no good science was contrary to the fear of God.[176]

> I wyll wyllyngly agree with them in thys poynte that when it pleaseth him he doth applie the nature and propertie of the starres to his service. Onely I say this that neither famines, pestilences, nor warres, come at any tyme by the disposition of the starres.177

Peter Baro challenged the Genevan orthodoxy at Cambridge. His 1579 dispute on providence and predestination argued that God's purpose does not take away the liberty of man's corrupt will. Baro's Two Theames went on to state that "secondary causes are not enforced by Gods purpose and decree, but carried willingly and after their own nature."[178] Baro thought that absolute necessity made God the author of sin. The liberty of man's will avoids such a decree of God "whereby God himselve should be so tyed and bound, that he neither would, nor could change any thing in it. It were more tolerable for mankind if destiny were dependant on the stars and God remained free above them ever ready to be moved by human prayer."[179]

A Special Treatise of Gods Providence appeared with Baro's disclaimer at the same time that theologians considered the meaning of strange diseases like the plague. Andreas Hyperius wanted for the sake of the godly and all men "to gather some furnitures of comfort and consolation." Hyperius challenged predestination of Calvin's kind because he worried about "so universal a plague & pestilence, so many strange kinds of diseases farre surmounting the skill and conning of ye phisitions."[180]

Hyperius cites the medieval Rabbi David Kimhi who states that as in Psalm (107) nothing is done by chance or fortune, for the wicked are afflicted through God's providence for their sins and again set at liberty by God's mercy to sing his praises.[181] Providential questions held pastoral implications for Englishmen who sought explanations for and consolation in times of catastrophic illness.

Luther and Beza both touch on christian duties in catastrophic times. Some would argue that sin had provoked God to send the plague against a disobedient people. Two trends followed from this observation that all things happened in the created order by the will of the Creator God. First of all, Beza dissented from the conclusion that it was useless to flee because God's vengeance was the cause of the plague. Beza argued that this became their excuse to forsake all the duties of christians toward humanity.[182] They used this theological opinion to deny the contagious nature of catastrophic disease.[183] The other conclusion was that such a view made God the author of sin. It would be an act of pastoral concern to deny such a cruel view of God. This concern motivated Hyperius and Baro to question Calvin's view of providence.

Beza's _De Peste_ encouraged pastors to serve their people in times of plague. Luther had refused to flee Wittenberg during 1527, choosing instead to minister to the needy. Osiander's sermon on Psalm (91) warned against abandonment of faith, vocation or neighborly love. John Squier, the grandson of Bishop Aylmer and the son of Adam Squier, Master of Balliol College, Oxford, preached at St. Leonard's, Shoreditch in Middlesex from 1612 to 1643.[184]

Squier's text for his _Thanksgiving Sermon_ (1636) was Psalm (50:15): "Call upon me, in the time of trouble; I will heare thee, and thou shalt praise me."[185] The results of such preaching were dramatic, claimed Squier, since in the week after the first parish fast on October 26 burials in his parish decreased by 190. The second week burials declined by 139, the third by 80, the fourth by 197, the fifth by 165, the sixth by 61 and the seventh by 61.[186] As colder weather of November and December, 1535 arrived, frost as well as fast reduced the plague in Squire's parish.

James Balmford (Bamford) gives an extended comment on pastoral duty during plague seasons. Balmford's _A Short Dialogue_ (1603) was reprinted in 1625. _A Short Dialogue_ alternates between the comments of a professor and a preacher. The professor reminds the preacher that ministers forbade persons from church attendance who lived in infected houses or who had plague sores. These are they who sought comfort for their souls. He worries that in so denying them spiritual comfort ministers abandon both piety and charity.[187] The preacher responds:

> What? Is this Pietie, with an high hand to breake godly Orders of a gracious Prince set downe for preservation of life? Is this Charitie, presumptuously to hazard the lives God knoweth of how many? Is this either Pietie or Charitie, wilfully to runne our selves into mortall daunger?[188]

The professor asks for scriptural proof that princes may do this. The preacher responds that "Neighbour, you stille begge the question."[189]

Balmford's professor retains his doubts about turning away plague victims from the church. He marvels that preachers who should be examples of love and faith so flatly speak against the express words of Christ "who will judge my charity and visiting or not visiting the sicke."[190] The preacher is troubled by the professor's definition of pastoral care as love for the sick in catastrophic times. "O neighbor," he complains, "you now lay an loade."[191]

> Now if they visite everyone that is sicke, how can they attend unto reading, and follow Christ in the most proper and necessarie worke of the ministrie? ...But I cannot find where Christ prescribed visiting of the sicke, as a ministers dutie.[192]

The professor quotes St. James who called for the Elders-Ministers to pray with the sick. "I never," he concludes, "heard of this matter doubted before."[193] The preacher in turn worried about who would be left to prepare sermons if too many clergy died of the pest. No doubt he meant to ask who would prepare plague sermons. Balmford's Dialogue sums up many of the concerns circulating in the writings of Luther, Beza, and Osiander. The plague precipitated a crisis in pastoral care.

D. Plagues and Puritanism

Alan Dyer suggests that the plague "encouraged the marked religious feeling of the period, and especially nonconformity and Puritanism."[194] Analysis of the context of the above sermons finds no evidence for such a conclusion. Greater incidence of the plague in the fourteenth century did not lead to more nonconformity than in the sixteenth and seventeenth centuries. Dyer's point is well taken, however, if he means that the breakdown of authority was assisted by the flight of parish ministers in plague times.

Margaret Spufford marshalls impressive local evidence that by 1676 dissent in Cambridgeshire villages had spread as a function of manorial subdivision in a parish. There was a coincidence between parishes containing single manors, and conformity. Spread of dissenting opinion cannot be determined by these economic units alone, which may have been merely a by-product of settlement size. Spufford concludes that "no single social background is common to all the communities which were deeply affected by dissent... No determinism, economic, social, educational or geographical, will fully account for the existence of religious conviction, which is as it should be."[195]

Very helpful is David Stannard's comment in The Puritan Way of Death in which he argues for the omnipresent spectre of disease and starvation. "It was a world in which the nights were blacker, the days more silent, and the winters more terrifying and cold than most men of the twentieth century can even begin to imagine."[196] Our burden has been to observe plague sermons which depend on arguments from providence. Puritan orthodoxy mitigated divine retribution through arguments that repentance avert stay the arrows of the Almighty.

One plague sermon by John Donne adds an image of resignation even though repentance might not resist disease. His text was Exodus (12:30): "For there was not a house where there was not one dead."[197] The first house is Pharaoh's in Egypt where all the firstborn died. "The next is, our own house, our habitation, our family" so that we who have divested our immortality might understand our mortality.[198] The third house is of clay or the body where the windows are the eyes, the timber our bones, the foundation our feet and the roof "but this thatch of hair."[199] The fourth house is God's house or that church and grounds in which scarce one day has passed but that sad eyes see one or more dead. These four houses are so many 'spiritual Pesthouses', "into which our sins had heaped powder, and Gods indignation had cast a match to kindle it."[200]

London was in Donne's mind as he lamented how "there is an Egypt in every Goshen, neasts of snakes in the hand of God fell upon thousands in this deadly infection..."[201] God has sifted his Church in a fire of tribulation so that its members shall receive the consolation of their immortality. Donne continues:

> Clocks and Sun-dials were but a late invention upon earth; but the Sun it self, and the earth it self, was but a late invention in heaven. God had been an infinite, a super-infinite, an unimaginable space, millions of millions of unimaginable spaces in heaven, before the Creation. And our afternoon shall be as long as Gods forenoon; for as God never saw beginning, so we shall never see end...202

In conclusion, five common themes arise from these sermons which derive from several segments of the English clergy. They demonstrate Professor Collinson's view that the religion of Protestants between 1559 and 1625 was conservative and in contact with a view of reality which had continuity with the concerns of several decades. These themes are as follows:

1. Plague sermons use Old Testament texts such as Psalm (91:5) and Deuteronomy (28) to identify ancient catastrophe with contemporary chaos.
2. Questions about providence emerge as a pastoral issue in Puritanism.
3. Astrologers and theologians argue over secondary causes for catastrophic disease.
4. Continental plague literature focuses attention on pastoral duty in times of the plague.
5. The urban poor suffered as minister, magistrate and merchant fled into the countryside. This left them without pastoral care, law and order, or food in the markets.

In the end whether the English fled the pest or stayed, blamed the stars or their sins for the plague, one biblical passage more than any other became their consolation. Retribution and repentance merged into the familiar lines of Psalm (91) from Coverdale's Bible:

> For he shall deliver thee... from the noisome pestilence. Thou shalt not be afraide for any terrour by night: nor for the arrow that flieth by day. For the pestilence that walketh in darknes: nor for the sicknes that destroyeth in the noone day... neither shall any plague come nigh thy dwelling.203

Plague sermons offered just such a consolation, built as they were upon the care of the Creator God for His own creatures. It made no difference whether the minister was Puritan or not, occupied a rich living or a modest village pulpit. When catastrophe struck, English sermons sounded a common theme, whether preached in 1563 or 1666. The standard pulpit rhetoric, whether applied to earthquakes, plague or comets, still assumed that God controlled the destiny of His people. As He had no beginning, so shall they have no ending.

It is clear at this point of our narrative that English society was polarized by its religious minorities, whether they be Catholic recusants or Puritan migrants. Margaret Spufford cites the Jesuit prisoner William Weston who could observe large groups of Puritans from his prison in Wisbeck Castle in the Isle of Ely. His famous account of 1588 speaks of "vast crowds of them flocking to perform their practices - sermons, communions and faasts."[204] Often they would argue amongst themselves "about the meaning of passages from the Scriptures - men, women, boys, girls, rustics, labourers and idiots - and more often than not, it was said, it ended in violence and fisticuffs."[205]

More recently Christopher Haigh picks up this theme and traces the endogamy which created those divisions whereby 'parish anglicans' gadded to dances as well as sermons and would have their clergy join them. Their model minister was not the godly preacher but rather he who read devout services, resolved parish conflict "and joined his people for 'good fellowship' on the ale bench."[206] Despite the growing professionalism of the lower clergy and the fraternity created by their "tribal" lectures and prophesyings, there remains a factor that exiled these moderate Puritans in their own land. So long as two-thirds of their reading was based on Continental Reformed orthodoxy, paranoia would continue to arise from those, whether Laudian or not, whose preference was for peace rather than conflict in the parish.

To take several steps beyond Haigh's observation and contend that the protest against Rome obscured the more critical dissent within the English Church does not seem to account for the continuous polemical nature of the Puritan reliance on faith as God's radical intervention in Christ. The Baro/Barrett query at Cambridge is neither the normative dissent some would make it out to be nor was Cambridge itself the necessary focal point of inimical and irreconcilable tensions within the Elizabethan protestant establishment which surfaced in those debates over predestination and providence. Though Richard Hooker appeals to reason as the principal instrument supporting institutional authority, the Puritans were not without their own varieties of rationality even after Perkins lined out its epistemology in the 1590s. Regional studies are too far advanced to permit one time and one place to determine why Puritanism should fall short of its axiomatic agenda to purify the parish structure.

Some fifty years after Weston's account of Puritan fisticuffs over Scripture, an anonymous broadsheet signed W.G. is a symbol of that inner exile which theological conviction continued to press from continental models. A Mappe of the Man of Sin (1622/23) depicts the progress of a sinful man from 'A' depicted as the Antichrist attired like a bishop blinded by the sun, on to a road which leads to the New Jerusalem. The route passes cathedrals collapsing about simoniacs who in turn are gathered around the Pope. All this is illustrated by scriptural analogues. Sixty lines of verse explain this pictorial broadside first listed in a 1984 Sale Cataloque.[207] The verse is explicit whoever the archpuritan W.G. might be:

> K. and though Romes sectaries erect strict Rites/
> In Holy Counted Cloysters full delights/
> Are their sole aime: but those alas soone
> turne/When these that ioy, shall sodly sit
> and mourne...
>
> T. Gods Citty is resured for such as trust/
> not in their owne works but on Christ the just.

And were not the English Separatists those who transferred their verbal sparring across the North Sea to the Netherlands in the 1590s or to New England in the decades which followed? John Winthrop's "City on a Hill" was "reserved for such as trust/not in their owne works but on Christ the Just." The central conviction which drove these puritans out of the parish structure of Stuart England into the wilderness of Colonial North America was precisely that trust in Christ the just with all its implied anti-catholic rhetoric. It was not predestination alone which was the central theological issue in Stuart England with Melanchthon on occasion used by the Laudians to counter Calvin. Trust in Christ ties into the early English reformation which affirmed that in Christ God has provided both a righteous judge and gracious saviour. He alone was the elect Son whom the Father God chose to save His people from their sins. Those who alone trusted in Christ as their high priest were willing like Abraham of old to leave the comforts of Egypt or England to seek a city whose builder and maker was God (Hebrews 11:10). They were also convinced that no pestilence would stalk them in the dark nor plague destroy them at midday.

END NOTES to SECTION V

[1]Alan Heimert and Andrew Delbanco, editors, The Puritans In America (Cambridge: Harvard Univ. Press, 1985), p.58. Bradford's note is to Psalm 107:1-5,8. John S. Coolidge, The Pauline Renaissance In England: Puritanism and the Bible (Oxford: At the Univ. Press, 1970), and J. Sears McGee, The Godly Man in Stuart England (New Haven: Yale Univ. Press, 1976).

[2]T.H.L. Parker, Calvin's New Testament Commentaries (Grand Rapids: Wm. B. Eerdmans, 1971).

[3]Richard Bauckham, Tudor Apocalypse (Appleford: Sutton Courtenay Press, 1980); Katherine R. Firth, The Apocalyptic Tradition in Reformation Britain 1530-1645 (Oxford: At the Univ. Press, 1979); Paul Christianson, The Reformers and Babylon (Toronto: At the Univ. Press, 1979).

[4]G. Lloyd Jones, The discovery of Hebrew in Tudor England: a third language (Manchester: At the Univ. Press, 1983).

[5]William Crashawe (1572-1626), Puritan preacher at the Middle Temple, offered his 4000 volume library for sale. St. John's College, Cambridge obtained 1000 volumes by 1626. Crashawe, who edited Perkin's Of the Calling of the Ministrie (1605), had scarcely any English books in what seems to have been the largest Puritan library of the time--more than 90% Latin. See P.J. Wallis, "The library of William Crashawe," Transactions of the Cambridge Bibliographical Society II (1956), p.227 and R.M. Fisher, "William Crashawe's Library at the Temple 1605-1615," The Library, Fifth Series 30 (1975): 116-124.

[6]Now see John F. Davis, "The trials of Thomas Bylney and the English Reformation," Historical Journal 24 (1981): 775-790 and J.Y. Batley, On A Reformer's Latin Bible (Cambridge: Deighton, Bell Co. Ltd., 1940).

[7]In Oliver Payne's Sales Catalogue (1731) of Defoe and Farewell's libraries, three Latin Bibles, two Latin New Testaments and one Greek/Latin New Testament were for sale, i.e., Tremellius & Junius of 1585, 1593 and 1608, Beza's Latin New Testament of 1624, a Greek/Latin New Testament of 1582 by Beza and a Cambridge

1642 Latin New Testament. Helmut Heidenreich, The Libraries of Daniel Defoe and Philips Farewell (Berlin, 1970), nos. 293, 17, 11, 1243, 2 and LO 64. See also The Contents of Scripture (London: Adam Islip for R. Jackson, 1596) which is a collection from Tremellius, Junius, Beza, Piscator and others in English.

[8]Clair Cross, "Continental Students and the protestant Reformation in England, in the sixteenth century," Derek Baker, editor, Reform and Reformation: England and the Continent C.1500-C.1750 (Oxford: Basil Blackwell, 1979), pp.35-38.

[9]John Patrick Donnelly, "Short Title Bibliography of the Works of Peter Martyr Vermigli," in Robert M. Kingdon, The Political thought of Peter Martyr Vermigli (Genève: Librairie Droz, 1980), pp.172-176.

[10]Richard Rogers, SEVEN TREATISES,/(five lines)/practise of Christianitie/(eleven lines & device)/(London: Felix Kyngston for Thomas Man and Robert Dexter, 1603), sig. Ee 4^{r-v}.

[11]C.W. Chilton, "The Inventory of a Provincial Bookseller's Stock of 1644," The Library, sixth series, I (1979), p.131.

[12]Robert Davies, "John Foster, of York, Stationer," A Memoir of the York Press (Westminster: Nichols and Sons, 1868),pp.342ff.

[13]C.M. Dent, Protestant Reformers in Elizabethan Oxford, pp.75-77. See also Paul Boesch, "Rudolf Gwalters Reise nach England im Jahr 1537," Zwingliana VIII/8 (1947): 433-471.

[14]Marvin Walter Anderson, Peter Martyr A Reformer In Exile (1542-1562) (Nieuwkoop: B. DeGraaf, 1975), p.143.

[15]H.M. Adams, Catalogue of Books Printed on the Continent of Europe, 1501-1600 in Cambridge Libraries I (Cambridge: At the Univ. Press, 1967), nos. 1359-1414. Aberdeen Univ. Library has three more Gualter editions and the British Library has another three. With the New Castle upon Tyme Thomlinson collection showing a Matthew (second edition of additional part (1596), fifty editions at least were printed in the sixteenth century.

[16]Paul Morgan, Oxford Intercollegiate Catalogue (1979), Duke Humfrey's Room, Bodleian. One could add as well that Oecolampadius' commentaries were read as well on Genesis, Job, Daniel, Isaiah, Jeremiah, Ezekiel, Hosiah, Haggai, Zachariah, Malachi and

all the Minor Prophets. See now N.R. Ker, "Merton College Inventory 1556" and "Books at Christ Church, 1562-1602" in T.H. Aston, History of Oxford III, James McConica, editor, The Collegiate University (Oxford: Clarendon Press, 1986), pp.487-519.

[17] S.T.C.2 25013.

[18] THE/Homilies or famil-/ar Sermons of M. Ro-/dolph Gualther Ti-/gurine upon the/Prophet Ioel/(three lines plus device)/ (London: Thomas Dawson for William Ponsonby, 1582), sig. D8^{v}-E1^{r}.

[19] Ibid., sig. D8^{v}-E1^{r}. (Joel 2:2-10).

[20] Ibid., sig. E8^{v}.

[21] David J. Keep, "Zurich Theology in a Gentleman's Library," Zwingliana XIV/4 (1972), pp.222-223. Gualter on Romans, Galatians, Hebrews and the Psalms show up as well in the 1613 Inventory of John English at Oxford. See W.C. Costin, "The Inventory of John English, B.C.L., Fellow of St. Johns College," Oxoniensia xi and xii (1946-47), nos. 70, 170, 383.

[22] Phillip Denis, "La Correspondance d'Hubert de Bapasme, refugié lillois à Strasburg," Bulletin Historique et Littéraire de la Societe de l'Histoire du Protestantisme francais CXXIV (1978), p.104.

[23] Marvin Anderson, "Peter Martyr on Romans," Scottish Journal of Theology 26 (1973), p.402.

[24] Other Latin editions are 1559, 1560, 1568, 1570, 1612 and 1613.

[25] Anderson, op.cit., pp.406-418. J.C. McLelland, "The Reformed Doctrine of Predestination According to Peter Martyr," Scottish Journal of Theology 8 (1955): 255-271. See also my Reformer In Exile, pp.146-147 and 344-346.

[26] See my Peter Martyr A Reformer In Exile, pp.330-334.

[27] Romanes (1568), sig. Mmv^{r}.

[28] Ibid., sig. Mmiiii^{v}.

[29] loc.cit.

[30] loc.cit.

[31] loc.cit.

[32] loc.cit.

[33] loc.cit.

[34]A/Commentarie Vpon the -/pistle of Saint Paul to the Ro-/manes, written in La-/tine by M./Iohn-Caluin, and newely transla-/ted into Englishe by Chri-/stopher Rosdell/preacher. (Imprinted at London for Iohn/Harison [Thomas Dawson] and George Bishop./1583), sig. M5[r]. This is a translation from the 1556 expanded edition.

[35]NOVVM TESTA-/MENTVM IAM QVINTVM AC POSTRE-/MUM ACCURATISSIMA CURA RECOGNITUM/ a DES. ERASMO ROTERODAMO cum Annotatio-/nibus.... (BASILEAE: HIERON. FROBENIUM ET NICO=/LAVM EPISCOPIVM ANNO M.D.XLII), sig. E3[v]

[36]Calvin, Romanes (1583), sig. M5[v].

[37]IN OMNES APOSTO=/LICAS EPISTOLAS, DIVI VIDELICET/PAVLI XIII. ET VII. CANONICAS, COMMENTARII/Heinrychi Bullingeri, ab ipso iam recogniti, &/nonnullis in locis aucti. (TIGVRI APVD CHRISTOPHORVM FRO=/shouerum, Anno M.D. LVIII.), sig. f. 4[r]. First printed 1537 and reprinted in 1539, 1544, 1549, 1558, 1582 and 1603.

[38]Romanes (1568), sig. Mmv[r].

[39]Ibid., sig. Mmv[v].

[40]Ibid., sig. Mmv[r-v].

[41]Ibid., sig. Mmv[v].

[42]Ibid., sig. Mmvl[r].

[43]Ibid., sig. Mmvl[r-v].

[44]Ibid., sig. Mmvl[v].

[45]Calvin, Romanes (1583), sig. M7[r].

[46]Martyr, Romans (1568), sig. Nniii[r]. See R.J. Schoeck, "The Use of St. John Chrysostom In Sixteenth-Century Controversy: Christopher St. German and Sir Thomas More in 1533," Harvard Theological Review 54 (1961), p.22 n.3: Martyr owned the Verona 1529 Greek edition in three volumes and brought at least one manuscript with him from Italy.

[47]Martyr, Romans (1568), sig. Ssiii[r].

[48]Ibid., sig. Ssiii[r-v]. So too Calvin: "And this testimony consisteth not in the sole eternall preaching, but it hath the efficacie of the spirit coupled." Romanes (1583), sig. O5[v].

[49]Ibid., sig. Ssiii[v].

[50]Ibid., sig. Ssiii^{r}.

[51]loc.cit.

[52]loc.cit. Note the reluctant critique of Chrysostom.

[53]Ibid., sig. Ssiiii^{v}.

[54]loc.cit.

[55]Ibid., sig. Ssiiii^{r}.

[56]Ibid., sig. Tti^{r}.

[57]On Sibbes see Jon R. Knott, Jr., The Sword of the Spirit (Chicago: At the Univ. Press, 1980), pp.42-61.

[58]John Coolidge, The Pauline Renaissance, p.142.

[59]Hans - Joachim Kraus, "Calvins exegetische Prinzipen," Zeitschrift für Kirchengeschichte 79 (1968), p.329. The same point has been made by the Strasbourg scholar Bernard Roussel in "Histoire de L'Eglise et Histoire de L'Exegese au XVIe siecle," Bibliotheque D'Humanisme et Renaissance 37 (1975), pp.181-192.

[60]"The Confession of the fayth and doctrin beleued and professed by the Protestantes of the Realme of Scottland... authorized as a doctrin grounded upon the infallable wourd of God," in David Laing, The Works of John Knox (New York: AMS Press, 1966): II, 110-11.

[61]Knox, Works VI, 235.

[62]Ibid., p.236.

[63]Ibid., p.241.

[64]Michael Lynch, Edinburgh and the Reformation (Edinburgh: John Donald, 1981), p.104.

[65]Judith Simmons, "Publications of 1623," The Library, 5th series, XXI (1966), pp.211-212.

[66]Christopher Haigh, "Puritan evangelism in the reign of Elizabeth I," English Historical Review XCII (1977), pp. 47-48.

[67]Patrick Collinson, Godly People: Essays on English Protestantism and Puritanism (London: Hambledon Press, 1983), "A Gazetteer of Combination Lectures" in Appendix: 563.

[68]R.C. Richardson, Puritanism in north-west England, pp. 63-66.

[69]George Gifford, The Country Divinity (1582).

[70]William Hunt, The Puritan Movement (Cambridge: Harvard Univ. Press, 1983), p.97.

[71]Ibid., pp.97-98.

[72]Ibid., p.98.

[73]H. Gareth Owen, "Lecturers and Lectureships in Tudor England," Church Quarterly Review CLXII (1962), p.63.

[74]Ibid., p.65.

[75]Ibid., p.69. See Ian Green, "'For Children in Yeeres and Children in Understanding': The Emergence of the English Catechism under Elizabeth and the Early Stuarts," Journal of Ecclesiastical History 37 (1986): 397-425.

[76]Ibid., p.76 note 93. Guidhall Library Ms. 9234/5.

[77]Dorothy Williams Whitney, "London Puritanism: The Haberdashers' Company," Church History XXXII (1963), p.312. Account taken from pp. 309-312.

[78]Patrick Collinson, "Lectures by combination: structures and characteristics of church life in seventeenth-century England," Bulletin of the Institute of Historical Research XLVIII (1975), pp.183-184.

[79]Ibid., p.192.

[80]Ibid., p.212.

[81]loc.cit.

[82]Owen C. Watkins, The Puritan Experience (New York: Schocken, 1972).

[83]Ibid., p.98.

[84]Dean Ebner, Autobiography In Seventeenth-Century England (Paris: Mouton, 1971), p.103.

[85]Patrick Collinson,"'A Magazine of Religious Patterns': An Erasmian Topic Translated in English Protestantism," in Derek Brewer, editor, Renaissance and Renewal In Christian History (Oxford: Basil Blackwell, 1977), p.241.

[86]Ibid., p.243.

[87]Ibid., p.243: Works of Whitgift, Parker Society (1851): 3 p.375.

[88]Emmanuel Utie, Matthew the Publican./A FVNERALL/SERMON,/ Preached in St. Stephens/Walbrooke the 11. of March/1615. (Lon-

don: Edward Griffin for Nathaniel Butter, 1616), sig. $A2^v$, margin.

[89] *Ibid.*, sig. B3r.

[90] *Ibid.*, sig. $C4^{r-v}$.

[91] *Ibid.*, sig. $D3^r$.

[92] *Ibid.*, sig. $E2^r$.

[93] *Ibid.*, sig. $E4^r$.

[94] *Ibid.*, sig. $F3^r$-$F4^r$.

[95] J.F.D. Shrewsbury, *A History of Bubonic Plague in the British Isles* (Cambridge: At The Univ. Press, 1970), pp.192, 227 and 267. On page 487 he gives them as 25%, 12.5% and 19% of London's population in 1563, 1593 and 1603.

[96] *Ibid.*, pp.221, 235, 245 and 272.

[97] I.G. Doolittle, "The plague in Colchester 1579-1666," *Transactions of the Essex Archaeological Society* 4 (1972): 134-145. (Essex Archaeology and History 4 (1972).)

[98] *Ibid.*, p.139.

[99] Shrewsbury, *op.cit.*, pp.333 and 487.

[100] *Ibid.*, pp.459 and 487.

[101] Raymond Williamson, "The Plague in Cambridge," *Medical History* I (1957), p.59.

[102] *Ibid.*, pp.60-61. See also C.P. Murrell, "The Plague in Cambridge, 1665-1666," *Cambridge Review* (1951), pp.375-6 and 403-6.

[103] Shrewsbury, *op.cit.*, p.272. Bill in *Calendar of State Papers, Domestic, 1666-1667*, no. 108 (p.188).

[104] Penelope Cornfield, "A provincial capital in the late seventeenth century: The case of Norwich," *Crisis and Order in English Towns 1500-1700*, edited by Peter Clark and Paul Slack (London: Routledge & Kegan Paul, 1972), p.268. The latest study has but five brief references to the plague. See John T. Evans, *Seventeenth-Century Norwich Politics, Religion, and Government 1620-1690* (Oxford: Clarendon Press, 1979).

[105] I.G. Doolittle, "The Effects of the Plague on a Provincial Town in the Sixteenth and Seventeenth Centuries," *Medical History* 19 (1975), pp.333-341.

[106] A.G.E. Jones,"The Great Plague in Ipswich 1665-1666," *Proceedings of the Suffolk Institute of Archaeology* XXVIII (1961), p.88.

[107] *Ibid.*, p.87.

[108] Edward M. Wilson, "Richard Leake's plague sermons, 1599," *Transactions of the Cumberland and Westmorland Antiquarian and Archaeological Society* LXXV (1975): 150-173.

[109] Alan D. Dyer, "The Influence of Bubonic Plague in England 1500-1667," *Medical History* 22 (1978): 319-326.

[110] Entry under 'Plays, players' but not 'plague' in A.G. Dickens, *The English Reformation* (New York: Schocken, 1964); Patrick Collinson, *The Elizabethan Puritan Movement* (London: Jonathan Cape, 1967) has a general entry 'preaching'; Keith Thomas, *Religion and the Decline of Magic* (New York: Charles Scribner's Sons, 1971), has a section on "Astrology and Religion" which concentrates on the period after 1640 (pp.358-385); J. Sears McGee, *The Godly Man in Stuart England* (New Haven: Yale Univ. Press, 1976) has an entry on the 'Poor' but not the Plague; Irvonwy Morgan, *The Godly Preachers of the Elizabethan Church* (London: The Epworth Press, 1965) has no plague entry at all; Richard Greaves, *Society and Religion in Elizabethan England* (Minneapolis: Univ. of Minnesota Press, 1982) has no entry under plague or disease; Patrick Collinson, *The Religion of Protestants* (Oxford: At the Univ. Press, 1982) has nothing on the plague. Paul Slack, *The Impact of Plague in Tudor and Stuart England* (London: Rutledge & Kegan Paul, 1985) appeared after this chapter was completed. On religious response to the plague see pp. 228-254.

[111] Patrick Collinson, *Archbishop Grindal 1519-1583 The Struggle for a Reformed Church* (London: Jonathan Cape, 1979): 163-165.

[112] A FOURME/to be used in Common/prayer twyse aweke, and al=/so an order of publique fast,/to be used every Wednesday/in the weeke, durying this/tyme of mortalitie,and/other afflictions, wher=/with the Realme at/this present is/visited./XXX Julii. 1563./Rycharde Jugge and John Cawood. Sig. Aii^{r-v}.

[113]*Ibid.*, sig. Diii^{v}. Collinson assigns the homily to Nowell. See *op.cit.*, p. 164.

[114]*How Preachers Should Exhort The People to Repentance and Earnest Prayer against the Turk* in John W. Bohnstedt,"The Infidel Scourge of God," *Transactions of the American Philosophical Society* 58 (1968), p.51.

[115]George Gifford, *Sermons upon the whole booke of the Revelation* (London: 1593), p.173. This and other references given in Richard Bauckham, *Tudor Apocalypse* (Appleford, Abingdon: Sutton Courteney Press, 1978), pp.96-99.

[116]A short Forme of/Thanksgiving to GOD/For staying the conta-/gioys sicknesse of/the Plague:/To be vsed in Common/ Prayer, on Sundayes,/ Wednesdayes, and/Frydayes. London: Bonham Norton and John Bill, 1625. Sig. Ci^{v}.

[117]William Kemp, A BRIEF/TREATISE/of the/Nature, Causes, Signes,/Preservation From,/And Cure of/THE/PESTILENCE. London: D. Kemp, 1665. Sig. B3^{r-v}.

[118]*Ibid.*, sig. C1^{r-v}.

[119]*Ibid.*, sig. E1^{v}.

[120]On almanacs now see Bernard S. Capp, *Astrology and the Popular Press English Almanacs 1500-1800* (London: Faber and Faber, 1979).

[121]man//fur dem Ster//ben fliehen muge (Wittenberg: Hans Luft, 1st part of November, 1527). Benzing shows four Luft printings of 1527 and one each at Magdeburg, Zurich, Hagenau, Augburg, Nürnberg and Marburg all in 1527. Joseph Benzing, *Luther bibliographie Verzeichnis Der Gedruckten Schriften Martin Luthers Biz zu Dessen Tod* (Baden-Baden: Verlag Librairie Heitz, 1966), nos. 2424-2433.

[122]Andreas Osiander, *Wie und wohn ein Christ die grausamen Plag der Pestilentz fliehen soll* (Nuremberg: J. Petrecus, 1533). Wellcome Library Copy. 1543 Nuremberg edition in British Library.

[123]A/GODLY AND/LEARNED SER-/MON, VPON THE/91. Psalme./ Declaring how, and to what/place, a Christian man ought to/flie in the daungerous time of the/Pestilence, for his best saftie and de=/liuerence. London: Edward White, 1603. Emmanuel College,

Cambridge copy used by permission of the Librarian. Textual varients from 1538 edition are restricted to spelling.

124 Andreas Osiander, HOW/and whether a/Christe ma ought/to flye the horryble/plage of the Pestilence./A SERMON OUT/of the XCI Psalme/Qui habitat in adiuto=/By Andrewe Osiander./Translated out of hygh Almayne into Englyshe./Southwark: James Nicolson (1538). Sig. G1^{v}. Pembroke College, Cambridge copy used by permission of Gilbert Stephenson M.A., Assistant Librarian.

125 A GODLY AND LEARNED SERMON (1603), sig. A3^{v}. Identical wording in HOW and whether (1538), sig. EVIII^{r}.

126 Ibid., sig. B7^{v}.

127 De Peste Quaestiones Duae Explicatae: Una, Sitne Contagiosa: Altera, an & quatenus sit Christionis per secessionem vitanda (Genevae: Eustathius Vignon, 1579).

128 Theodore Beza, A shorte learned and/pithie Treatize of the/Plague, wherein are handled these/two questions: The one, whether the/Plague bee infectious, or no: The other,/whether and howe farre it may of/Christians bee shunned by going aside./A discourse very necessary for this/our tyme, and country;to sa-/tisfie the doubtful con=/sciences of a great/number://5 lines// London: Thomas Dawson for George Bishop, 1580. Peterborough Cathedral Library copy. Sig. 3^{v}-4^{r}.

129 Ibid., sig. A7^{r}.

130 Ibid., sig. C4^{v}.

131 Ibid., sig. C8^{r-v}.

132 Ibid., sig. D2^{r-v}.

133 A learned treatise of the plague: wherein... whether or no: and whether, and how farr it may be shunned of Christians, by going aside? Are resolved. London: T. Ratcliffe for E. Thomas, 1665.

134 De Officio fidelis et prudentis magistratus tempore pestilentiae rempub. A contagio praeseruandi liberandique libri duo (Neapoli Nemetum: 1582). Cambridge Univ. Library copy.

135 Johann Ewich, OF/The duetie of a faithfull and/Wise Magistrate, in preser-/uming and deliuering of the common/wealth from infection, in the time/of the plague or pestilence:/Two

Bookes. trans. John Stockwood. London: Thomas Dawson, 1583. Sig. G8^{v}. See Carl J. Schindler, translator, "Whether One may flee from a deadly plague," Luther's Works American Edition 43: Devotional Writings II (Philadelphia: Fortress Press, 1968), pp.131-132.

[136]William Warde, GODS/ARROWES,/OR,/Two Sermons, concerning/ the visitation of God by/the Pestilence. London: Henry Ballard, 1607. Text from Geneva Bible.

[137]Ibid., sig. C2^{v}.

[138]Ibid., sigs. D7^{r} and E5^{r}.

[139]Ibid., sig. F7^{v}. Reference is to Psalm (139:8).

[140]James Godskall, THE KINGS MEDI-/CINE FOR THIS PRE-/sent year 1604. prescribed by the/whole colledge of the spirituall ply-/sitions, made after the coppy of the carpo:/rall kings medicine.... London: Edward White, 1604. Sig. A3^{v}.

[141]Ibid., sig. A5^{r-v}.

[142]William Gouge, GODS/THREE/ARROWES:/PLAGUE, FAMINE,/SWORD, /In three treatises. London: George Miller for Edward Brewster, 1631. Sig. F8^{r}.

[143]Benjamin Spenser, VOX CIVITATIS/OR/LONDONS Complaint/ against her Children in the/COVNTREY./London: Printed by I.D. for Nicolas Bourne, 1625.

[144]Robert Anton, THE/PHILOSOPHERS/SATYRS,//4 lines and device//London,/Printed by T.C. and B.A. for Roger Iackson,... 1616. Sig. b3^{r}. Emmanuel College, Cambridge copy.

[145]Ibid., sig. E4^{r}.

[146]See above, note 210.

[147]William Warde, GODS ARROWES (1607), sig. E6^{r-v}.

[148]James Godskall, THE ARKE/of NOAH,/FOR/The Londoners that remaine i the Cittie/to enter in, with their families, to be preserued/from the deluge of the Plague./London: Thomas Creede, 1603. Sig. A4^{r}.

[149]I Peter (3:20).

[150]John Featley, Tears in time of Pestilence:/or,/A SPIRITUAL/ANTIDOTE/Against the/PLAGUE. London: W. Godbid, 1665. Sigs. C5^{v}, C6^{v}, C8^{v}, D1^{v}, D3^{r-v}, D4^{r}. See also Featley's, A/

DIVINE ANTIDOTE/against the Plague:/OR/Mourning Teares,/IN/ Soliloquies and Prayers. (London: Thomas Mabb, 1665). Wellcome Library copies cited by permission.

[151]Mathew Mead, SOLOMON'S PRESCRIPTION/For the Removal of the/PESTILENCE:/OR,/The Discovery of the PlAGUE of our/Hearts, in order to the Healing of/that in our Flesh. London: (n.p.), 1666. Sig. $B4^r$. Wellcome Library copy.

[152]Ibid., sigs. $C4^r$-$G1^r$.

[153]Ibid., sig. $G1^v$. See also Mathew Mead, AN/APPENDIX/TO/ SOLOMON'S Prescription/for the Removal of the PESTILENCE. London: (n.p.), 1667. Sigs. $G1^v$-$G8^v$.

[154]Thomas Swadlin, SERMONS, ME-/ditations and/Prayers, upon the Plague. 1636./by T.S./London: N. & Jo. Okes for John Benson, 1637. Sigs. $B2^v$-$B3^r$.

[155]Charles Edwin Clark,"Science, Reason, and an Angry God," New England Quarterly xxxvii (1965), pp.355-57.

[156]Sacvan Berkovitch, The American Jeremiad (Madison: Univ. of Wisconsin, 1978), p.8.

[157]Michael McGiffert,"William Tyndale's Conception of Covenant," Journal of Ecclesiastical History 32(1981), p.169.

[158]Robert Sanderson, TWELVE/SERMONS/PREACHED/1. AD CLERUM III./2. AD MAGISTRATUM III./3. AD POPULUM VI./London: Aug. Math. for Robert Dawlman, 1632. Sermon on sigs. $Dd3^r$-$Hh4^v$. Text from Geneva Bible.

[159]Ibid., sig. $Gg4^r$.

[160]Edmund Staunton, PHINEHAS'S ZEAL/IN EXECVTION/OF IVDGEMENT./OR,/A DIVINE REMEDY FOR/ENGLANDS MISERY//ten lines//London: I.L. for Chritopher Meredith, 1645. Sigs. $D1^v$-$D2^v$.

[161]Ibid., sig. $D4^v$.

[162]Thomas Darling, A/POTION/FOR THE/HEART-plague,/as a soveraigne/remedie for/the other:/set downe in a letter sent/unto the humble/in spirit./AT LONDON/Printed by Arnold Harfield/for Simon Waterson./1603. Sigs. $A6^v$-$A7^r$. S.T.C. 20132.5 entered under POTION but prefaced signed Thomas Darling. Bodleian copy Vet. A2f.-282(2).

[163]George Wither, Britains remembrancer (1628), sig. $Z8^v$.

[164] See now Dewey Wallace, Puritans and Predestination: Grace in English Protestant Theology, 1525 to 1695 (Chapel Hill: Univ. of North Carolina Press, 1982).

[165] Richard Leake, FOURE/SERMONS,/PREACHED AND PUB/LIKELY TAUGHT BY Richard/Leake, Preacher of the word of God.... London: Felix Kingston, for Thomas Man, 1599. Sigs. $E8^{v}$-$F1^{r}$.

[166] Thomas Doolitell, A/SPIRITUAL/ANTIDOTE/Against./Sinful Contagion./A Cordial for/BELIEVERS/Upon their Death-Beds./With/A CORROSIVE/FOR/The Unconverted. Second edition, corrected. London: R.L. for Tho. Passenger, 1667. Sigs. $A6^{r}$-$A8^{v}$.

[167] John Gadbury, London's Deliverance predicted (1665), titlepage.

[168] John Calvin, AN AD/monicion against/ASTROLOGY IVDICIALL/ and other curiosities, that raigne now/in the world: written in the french/tonge by IHON CALVINE/and translated into En/glishe, by G.G.//eleven lines//London: Roland Hall, 1561. Sig. Av^{r-v}.

[169] Ibid., sigs. Av^{v}-Avi^{v}.

[170] Ibid., sig. $Avii^{r}$.

[171] Ibid., sig. $B1^{r}$.

[172] Calvin: Commentaries, Library of Christian Classics, edited by Joseph Haroutunion (London: SCM Press Ltd., 1958), p.356.

[173] John Calvin, An Admonicion (1561), sig. $C1^{v}$.

[174] John Calvin, THE/Institution of Christian/Religion, written in Latine/by M. John Calvine, and Tran-/slated into English according to the/Authors last edition, with sundry Tables//ten lines//London: Arnold Hatfield for Bonham Norton, 1599. Sig. $H4^{r}$.

[175] Calvin, An Admonicion (1561), sig. Cii^{r}.

[176] Ibid., sig. Eviii.

[177] Ibid., sig. $Ciii^{v}$.

[178] H.C. Porter, Reformation and Reaction at Tudor Cambridge (Cambridge: At the Univ. Press, 1958), p.377.

[179] Peter Baro, Fower Sermons/and two Que-/stions./As they were Ut-/tered and disputed at Cle-/rum in S. Maries Church/and Schooles in/Cambridge./London: John Woolfe, 1588, sig. $Kkvii^{r}$. Printed in continuous signatures with A special Treatise of Gods

Providence. S.T.C.2 11760. See Peter Lake, "The Case of Peter Baro," Moderate Puritans and the Elizabethan Church (Cambridge: At the Univ. Press, 1982): 227-242.

[180]Andreas Gerhard Hyperius, A speciall Trea-/tise of Gods Providence,/and of comforts against all/kinds of crosses & calami-/ties to be fetched from/the same. London: John Wolfe (1588?), sig. A4^{r}. Wolf reprinted this in 1602. Translation from the Basle Varia opuscula Theologica (1580), pp. 94-363.

[181]Ibid., sig. SViii^{r}.

[182]Theodore Beza, A shorte learned and pithie Treatize of the Plague (1580), sig. Al^{v}.

[183]Ibid., sig. A7^{r}.

[184]John Venn, Alumni Cantabrigiensis, Part I to 1751 (Cambridge: At the Univ. Press, 1927): IV, p.140.

[185]John Squier, A/THANKES-/GIUING,/FOR THE DECREASING,/and hop of the removing of the/PLAGUE./Being a Sermon Preached at St. PAULS/in London, upon the 1. of January, 1636./...London: B.A. and T.F. for John Clark, 1637. Second edition revised.

[186]Ibid., sigs. D3^{v}-D4^{v}.

[187]James Bamford, A SHORT DIA=/LOGUE CONCER-/NING THE PLAGUES/INFECTION./Published to preserve blood,/through the blessing of God./London: Richard Boyle, 1603. Bodleian copy of S.T.C.2 1338. Sig. Bl^{v}.

[188]Ibid., sig. B2^{v}.

[189]Ibid., sig. B3^{r}.

[190]Ibid., sig. Cl^{r-v}.

[191]Ibid., sig. Cl^{v}.

[192]Ibid., sig. C2^{r}.

[193]Ibid., sig. C2^{v}.

[194]Dyer, op.cit., p.326.

[195]Margaret Spufford, Contrasting Communities English Villagers in the Sixteenth and Seventeenth Centuries (Cambridge: At the Univ. Press, 1979), p.352. See tables 19 and 20.

[196]David Stannard, The Puritan Way of Death (Oxford: 1977), pp.38-39.

[197]"The First Sermon After Our Dispersion, by the Sickness," The Sermons of John Donne, edited by Evelyn M. Simpson and George R. Potter (Berkeley/Los Angeles: Univ. of California Press, 1962): VI, p.349. Sermon 18 in XXVI. Sermons (1661). Donne's division follows the traditional literal, allegorical, anagogical and tropological catagories.

[198]Ibid., pp.351 and 354.

[199]Ibid., p.356.

[200]Ibid., pp.357 and 358. A Litanie (1633) XXII, line 5 calls the plague "thine Angell".

[201]Ibid., p.359.

[202]Ibid., pp.363-364.

[203]Psalm (91:3,5,6 and 10). The Booke of Common Prayer (1627), sig. F2^{v}. See also Henry Holland, SPIRITUALL/PRESERVATIVES/against the Pestilence./OR/SEVEN LECTURES ON/the 91. Psalme. London: T.C. for John Browne and Roger Jackson. 1603. Sig. d7^{r-v}. Corrected copy of 1593 edition.

[204]Margaret Spufford, Contrasting communities, p.263.

[205]loc.cit.

[206]Christopher Haigh, "The Church of England, the Catholics and the People" in Haigh, The Reign of Elizabeth I (Athens: Univ. of Georgia Press, 1985), p.219.

[207]Four Centuries of English Books from Bernard Quaritch XVI-XIX. Catalogue 1043 (London: Robert Stockwell Ltd., 1984), no. 77 [S.T.C. 1151.2]. Pictured.

SECTION VI. TRANSCONTINENTAL PROTESTANTS (1532-1683)

Chapter 16) The Shadow of Servetus

A. From Geneva to London

In January of 1553 a Spanish physician published a book called the Restoration of Christianity which he had ready in manuscript for some years. Some two decades before as a secretary to the Emperor's Spanish chaplain, Michael Servetus lived in Basle where he published a book with the title Seven books on Errors about the Trinity. When he left Basle to take up residence in Strasbourg, Bucer who was troubled by Servetus asked him to leave. On his return to Basle, the magistrates ordered Servetus to retract the errors in his book. Servetus wrote a new book called Two Books of Dialogues on the Trinity which retracted nothing from the other book. When the Spanish Inquisition ordered his arrest, Servetus dropped from sight to reappear in Paris as Michael Villeneuve, mathematics lecturer. Now as a brilliant student of medicine, he wrote a popular work on medicinal syrups (1537).

"Servetus left Paris to practice medicine in the provinces."[1] After 1540 he transferred residence to Vienne, a suburb of Lyons, where he spent a dozen or so tranquil years. His patron was the Archbishop of Vienne and the firm of Trechsel employed him as an editor.[2]

In January 1553 the Restoration of Christianity was ready. The title Restitutio is a deliberate attack on John Calvin's Institutes. The full title was an announcement of an entire agenda, i.e., "The Restoration of Christianity. A Calling of the whole Apostolic Church to make a fresh start, restored completely in the knowledge of God, the faith of Christ, our justification, regeneration, baptism, and the Lord's Supper, Our restoration finally in the kingdom of heaven, with the loosing of the captivity of ungodly Babylon and Anti-christ and his own destroyed."[3]

Book Five of the first section on the Trinity contains the first printed description of the lesser circulation of the blood through the lungs.

Calvin did not wait until 1553 to attack the anti-trinitarian views of Servetus. In the mid-1530s Calvin set a rendevouz in Paris which Servetus missed. Calvin refers to Servetus as a "Wonderful rascal" in a 1539 addition to the Institutes.[4] At Institutes II. XIV. 8 (1559) Calvin refers to his 1554 refutation of Servetus' "grosser deceptions" in the Defense of the Orthodox Faith, going on to call him "a foul dog."[5] In his commentary on I John (1:1) Calvin disproves the "senseless cavil of Servetus" that the nature and essence of deity became one with the incarnation as the means whereby the Word was transferred into flesh.[6] In his Harmony of the Gospels at John (1:1) Calvin attacks Servetus' ancestry:

> Servetus, a haughty scoundrel belonging to the Spanish nation, invents... that this eternal Speech began... when he was displayed in the creation of the world...7

The I John reference comes from 1551 and the Harmony from 1553.

Servetus sent a copy of his Restitutes to Calvin who knew very well that Servetus was suspect. Servetus now did a foolish thing, for though he had been condemned in absentia at Vienne "to be burned alive in a slow fire until his body becomes ashes," he attended Calvin's sermon in Geneva where he was recognized and arrested. After a series of hearings before the Syndics from August 14, Servetus was burned at the stake in 1553 at Geneva.[8]

Before one considers the storm of controversy over the execution of Servetus, one should ask about the nature of his "heresy." Jerome Friedman labels this person as a "total heretic" in his 1978 study and in chapter eleven especially delineates the glossary of heresy, recording Servetus' proclivity towards unconventional statements about the Christian tradition.[9] A central concern emerges in the Restitutes where Servetus complains that the orthodox Church Fathers" said the flesh is made the Word, not the Word flesh."[10] He saw Protestantism as the ancient Gnostic error reborn.[11] One of Servetus' allies in this crusade against tri-theism was the late medieval Jewish exegete Rabbi David Kimchi, whose tract Answers to Christians was used to oppose the traditional Christian interpretation of Psalm (2:7): "Thou art my Son, this day I have begotten thee." The Psalmist spoke of David, not of Christ![12]

Elizabeth Hirsch more recently explores the Neoplatonic tradition to explain Servetus' total rejection of traditional Christological statements. Calvin states the substance of Servetus' error in the Institutes II. XIV. 8 where God is said to will from the beginning to begat a Son which was effected by his actual formation, i.e., a shadowy son which was at length begotten by the Word described as a seed.[13]

Servetus had two goals in mind. The first was to bring God into the world so that man could know him. How could man conceive of God before his visible appearance? Through the incarnation of Christ this was all changed so that our abstract knowledge of God is concrete.[14] The second goal was an optimistic view of man, for since through Christ one has full access to the divine spirit, it is incumbant to make the spirit of Christ one's own. Calvin objected that such a transformation of Christ's human body "deprives us of the Son of David, the promised redeemer."[15]

Calvin was shocked at Servetus' denial of the preexistence of Christ as well as the overly optimistic view of human potential. Human nature achieved its own deification through the response of man to the splendor of Christ. Both the new vision of God and the new vision of man's divine capabilities vanished in the flames of Geneva. It was only an accident of Servetus' folly that Geneva was the place of burning and not Catholic France or Lutheran territory. Total heresy of that sort which redefined the New Testament view of Christ and man met complete rejection in the Christian Europe of 1553.

Sebastian Castellio mounted a serious attack on Calvin in his small treatise of March 1554 under the title On Heretics and those who Persecute them. The pen name Martinus Bellius did not hide the principal author's identity from Calvin and Theodore Beza. Sebastian Castellio (1515-1563) had crossed Calvin's path earlier as a schoolmaster and an able scholar hired in 1543. He resigned as principal of the College after quarrels over his French translation of the New Testament which Calvin reviewed too slowly for Castellio's liking. He applied for admittance to the Company of Pastors but was rejected for not holding to the literal clause of the Creed, 'he descended into hell' and for believing that the Song of Solomon was a lascivious and obscene poem. Castellio then attacked his former colleagues at the Congregation on May 29, 1544 for their drunken whoremongering actions.[16] Castellio had to leave Geneva. He became a Greek professor at Basle.

In 1551 Castellio published his Latin translation of the Bible. The preface to King Edward VI of England defends tolerance of heretics.

> What times do we live in?...We are becoming bloodthirsty killers out of zeal for Christ, who shed his own blood to save that of others.17

The mention that tares should grow until the Judgement Day reminds one that the parable in Matthew (13) became a proof text for religious liberty.[18]

Castellio observed that burning heretics over dogmatic subtleties means that persecutors forget how to live as Christians. The preface is a moving address to Christ, that while on earth none suffered injury more readily than he, yet "thou didst pray for those who inflicted those insults and injuries on thee." If Christ does not command these things in the present, they are "done by the command and the instigation of Satan."[19]

Castellio annotated a 1553 edition of Calvin's Institutes with comments about human knowledge to the effect that "Calvin dissents from Augustine."[20] The 1554 On Heretics cites from the relevant texts of the Church Fathers. He then cites his own opinion under the pseudonym of George Kleinberg as a commentary on II Timothy (3:12): "All that will live godly in Christ Jesus, shall suffer persecution." The sheep can only endure with weakness. The Christian has the weapons of the spirit, however, with which Basil Montfort (Sebastian Castellio) attacks the false prophets of the new Israel. Castellio concludes with I Corinthians (4:5) not to judge before the time when the Lord will come "who will bring to light the hidden things of darkness."[21] Against that light the execution of Servetus cast a very long shadow indeed.

Servetus cast his long shadow along the Thames in Elizabethan England. Italian refugees were distressed at the news of 1553. Lelio Sozzini wrote from Basle to a Genevan friend that "Abel's blood cries to heaven, and Cain will have no more rest on this earth."[22] Major treatises by Italians on toleration were published at Basle between 1563 and 1577. The first is the Thirty Dialogues of Ochino, whose 28th dialogue treats of toleration. Another is a 1577 continuation of Castellio's complaint written by Mino Celsi, whose second edition (1584) included a letter from Beza to Dudith (June 1570) with Dudith's reply of August 1570 on the suppression of heresy.[23]

Jacob Acontius lived in England from 1559 until his death in 1567. As a naturalized citizen and military engineer, Elizabeth gave him a pension.[24] Acontius' first literary work was on Method, which when used to study the sciences first attains a just spirit. Method then searches for the truth and for its exposition. As W.K. Jordan put it, such a fearless approach to persecution and toleration was like a breath of fresh air, doing for persecution what Machiavelli did for politics.[25] This work of 1558 published in Basle was followed by personal intervention in the Dutch Church's affairs in London.

Bishop Edmund Grindal had excommunicated the pastor, Adriaan van Haemstede, for harboring certain Anabaptists without renouncing their error. Acontius urged that doctrines not essential to salvation should not be imposed upon Christians and from 1559 until 1562 Acontius took Haemstede's side.[26] In 1565 Acontius published The Strategies of Satan at Basle in which he claimed that nothing furthers Satan's cunning policy better than religious hatred. Man seeks personal triumph rather than the triumph of truth.[27] One sure way Satan operates is to exploit personal ardour in studying Scripture by letting it degenerate into violent disputes.[28] Unlike Castellio, Acontius eschews all reference to tradition.

This Elizabethan engineer used Castellio's argument and the defense of London Anabaptist opinions to argue for toleration. How radical were the types whom the Thirty-Nine Articles label Anabaptists? Were there continental radicals resident in Grindal's diocese or was "Anabaptist" a generic term to catch all dissidents from Lollards to Dutch parishioners? Answers to that question will determine one's understanding of the Dissenting Tradition from 1532 until the Toleration Act of 1689.

Irwin Horst argues that probably in 1532 several English and Flemish persons were taken into custody for imparting and distributing an Anabaptist book. One John Clarke had 44 copies in his possession and John Raulings had distributed 40 additional copies. The confession of which no extant copy is known was an English translation of the Schleitheim Confession (1527), or so Horst posits.[29] Unfortunately for Horst's case, no copy of the Anabaptist Confession has survived nor can he demonstrate the physical presense of Anabaptists in England. The closest Horst comes is to assume that the missing 1530s confession is Anabaptist and that the controversy in the 1540s among the Stranger's Churches was an Anabaptist quarrel because it dwelt on the question of Christ's celestial flesh.[30] Horst does demonstrate that however much contact there was between continental anabaptists and English radicals, Lollardy shaped English non-conformity from 1530 to 1558. "Perhaps the time is ripe for a more comprehensive account of Lollardy during the early English Reformation."[31]

Two recent studies assist one to comprehend Lollardy with John Pykas of Colchester and John Hacker of London in 1528 to Robert Cooche, friend of William Turner and John Knox in the

1550s. J.F. Davis points to the combination of dissent amongst several segments of English society which indicates that Lollardy combined with the "hotter" sort of protestants to produce further reformation.[32] Christopher Clement explores radical tendencies in English theology only to conclude that a person like Robert Cooche belonged to the final generation of Lollards who maintain the doctrine of free will in a tenuous existence during the early years of Elizabethan reform.[33]

Bishop Tunstall of London discovered in 1528 that one John Hacker was the sustainer of Lollard cells in London, Berkshire and Essex. The London Conventicles centered on Coleman Street: heretical books were distributed from All Saints Honey Lane, and the Cambridge reformers took up pulpits here, such as Hugh Latimer at St. Mary Abchurch. In 1532 reforming congregations gathered here at Bow Lane in a warehouse, on the same street used by the Marian underground in 1555. When John Field, Thomas Wilcox and Robert Crowley held cures in the same quarter of London during Puritan times they were found at St. Giles Cripplegate and All Hallows Honey Lane.[34]

John Hacker's Lollard connections were strong at Colchester where John Pykas learned his heresies from Wycliffite scriptures and Tyndale's New Testament. Half of the 200 heretics listed in Foxe who abjured between 1527 and 1532 came from the city and half from Essex including Colchester and Steeple Bumpstead.[35] The latter was the home of John Tyball who exchanged his Wycliffite New Testament for Tyndale's at Robert Barne's suggestion in 1527.[36]

The more direct connection was made by the Christian Brethren, a wing of Lollardy which had printing presses and middle-class components. The first solid evidence comes from 1531 when a Carthusian priest learned about the Brethren's activities against the eucharist. They had clerks in London in their pay, whom they sent all over the realm, using auditors to keep track of funds raised for that purpose. Newdygate's report asked Sir George Parker how the king and lords viewed his attacks. Parker answered that the king as well as the dukes of Norfolk and Suffolk were hot against it. Parker than responded that they already had two thousand books in circulation against the sacrament as well as books on other subjects.[37] Davis compares this edition with the £1,850. 10d spent on 50,000 copies of the New Testament and other books by John Tyndale and Thomas Potmore. Dickens links up Humphery Monmouth as a member of the Christian Brethren, so that it is plausible that Tyndale's agent and brother assisted the Brethren in circulating some sixty-four thousand copies of Tyndale's 1526 New Testament.[38]

Another probable link was the publisher John Gough who reprinted Wycliffite tracts and supplied Thomas Garret at Oxford with Tyndale's New Testament. He with another Lollard publisher John Mayler published the works of Thomas Becon.[39] Lollard ideas seem to gain respectibility with the evangelism of a Thomas Bilney, the New Testaments of Tyndale and the preaching of the Cambridge reformers. Davis traces these contacts to places like Steeple Bumpstead where Lollards and Cambridge men seem to meet. Richard Fox, curate of that place, urged his parishioners to use The Wycket and persons like John Tyball and Thomas Hiles cooperated with the Cambridge coterie.[40] Dickens labels this amalgam 'neo-Lollard'.[41]

Horst wrestles with the specifics of Anabaptism during Edward's reign. 'Anabaptism of the Melchiorite connection' was the leading type of nonconformity during 1548-1553 in Horst's point of view.[42] Joan Bocher was burned on May 2, 1550 for her views of the incarnation:

> That you beleue that the word was made fleshe in the virgyns belly, but that Christe take fleshe of the virgyn you beleue not; because the flesh of the virgyn being the outward man synfully gotten, and bourne in synne, but the worde by the consent of the inward man of the virgin was made flesh.43

Horst takes details of her trial and burning as probably information about an Anabaptist sect with centers in London and Kent.[44] Robert Cooche and Henry Harte are further examples of isolated and community identity with Anabaptism. Horst accepts the testimony of "out-groups" that this was so, such as the writings of William Turner, i.e., A preseruatiue or triacle, agaynst the poyson of Pelagius, lately reued, & styrred upe agayn, by the furious secte of the Annabaptistes. He then turns to John Bradford who exchanged letters with Hart over the issue of Pelagianism raised by Turner's Preseruative. Finally Horst uses a pamphlet by Harte to argue that "it is strongly reminiscent of the writings of anabaptist authors such as Menno Simons."[45]

Clement has subjected this circumstantial evidence to a fresh critique in his 1980 Cambridge thesis. His analysis agrees more nearly with Davis than with Horst. What then should one think of Robert Cooche and Henry Harte? Robert Cooche left one bit of writing to Rodolf Gualter in Zurich on August 13, 1573. In this letter Cooche praises Gualter's commentary on I Corinthians for its sensible explanation of the "manner and method of the supper and the table."[46] Parkhurst thought Cooche was verbose to an extreme,[47] while William Turner describes him as tall, single and musical.[48] Martyr knew Cooche personally as did Turner and John Knox.[49]

Several theological issues surface as Cooche with access to the Court discusses infant baptism with Martyr, predestination with Knox and the Lord's Supper with Gualter. Martyr's letter of 1 December 1550 mentions their prior oral discussion about Bishop Higinus whom Cooche thought instigated infant baptism (A.D. 140), and Tertullian, whose rigorous views are ancillary at best because (says Martyr) he fell to Montanism though flourishing about A.D. 210. Cooche cited Origen out of his Romans Commentary and Homilies on Numbers and Leviticus. At best, Martyr argues, Origen refers to many who were admitted to baptism "of ripe yeares." Now if Cooche held that infants possessed original sin, Origen cannot support his case for denying them baptism.[50]

Turner's Preseruative cites from Cooche's book which used Erasmus and Vives to deny infant baptism. Turner in turn is based on Henry Harte's publications of 1548/49, i.e., A Godly

Newe short treatyse (S.T.C. 12887) and A Godlie exhortation to all suche as professe the Gospell (S.T.C. 10626) as well as A Consultorie for all Christians (S.T.C. 12564). Harte was a leader of the conventical which met at the house of Robert Cole in August of 1550. It is clear that Cooche's book attacking infant baptism circulated among this group.[51] Baptism is only for the repentent who have by faith received the gift of God's salvation in Christ. Turner cites Cooche:

> none ought to receiue it but such as haue not only heard the good promises of God: but haue also thereby receyued a syngular consolation in their hartes through remission of synne whiche they by fayth haue receyued.52

Cooche's arguments use none of Melchior Hofmann's or Marpeck's evidence. There are English books on baptism such as the 1514 treatise recorded by Thomson (pp.88-89).[53]

When John Knox published his 1560 Answer to a great nomber of blasphemous cauillations, it seems to be directed against Robert Cooche.[54] Knox links his opponent's challenge to predestination with "your Master Castalio... for ye are manifest liars..."[55]

> Therefore, it is suggested [concludes Clement] that Robert Cooche was no eccentric individualist, neither was he an aristocrat with Protestant humanist sympathies. Rather, he was a leading member of that final generation of Lollards which maintained the doctrine of free-will and which continued to maintain a tenuous, but distinctive, existence first without, and then within, the established Church of England.56

Henry Harte was the leader of the Free Will group during Edward's reign.[57] Martin concludes that "neither do the authorities label Harte and his followers 'Anabaptists' nor do they hold to the technical doctrines which would so identify them."[58] Harte and Sussex radicals such as John Trewe and Christopher Vitells do not give evidence that believers' baptism was practiced prior to 1559 in England.[59] Horst overstates his case for labeling these radicals as anything other than Lollards who became Free-Will men in the 1550s, might join the Family of Love and even end a longish life as Brownists in the 1580s.[60]

When William Bradford in far off New Plymouth produced his first Dialogue in the year 1648, young men questioned their elders whether Robert Browne was "the first inventor and beginner of this way?" The answer was, "No verily... in the days of Queen Elizabeth there was a Separated Church whereof Mr. Fitz was pastor; and another before that in the time of Queen Mary of which Mr. Rough was pastor or teacher..."[61] This London Protestant congregation had five ministers during Mary's reign, one of whom, Edmund Scambler, became Bishop of Norwich and another, Thomas Bentham, Bishop of Litchfield and Coventry. Rough had been but a month in London when he was arrested on December 12, 1557 and executed shortly after. Two of his letters sent from prison appear in Foxe's Actes and Monuments (1563) to the effect that "It was no time, for the loss of one man in the battle for the camp to turn back."[62]

The Privy Church of which Rough was pastor in Queen Mary's day was organized for worship under persecution. It provided a model for later Separatists to meet in defiance of the laws of the realm. In 1567 two other such congregations surfaced in London known as the Plumber's Hall congregation and the Privy Church of Richard Fitz.

On June 20, 1567 seven of these separatists were examined by the authorities under Grindal's interrogation. Grindal complained that one hundred of them ministered the sacraments among themselves. John Smith replied that "the book and order of preaching, ministering of the sacraments and discipline "which they held was the same as used in Geneva and London in Queen Mary's days.[63] Robert Hawkins voiced their chief criticism of the Elizabethan Church.

> You preach Christ to be priest and prophet, but you preach him not to be king, neither will you suffer him to reign with the sceptre of his word in his church alone.[64]

This reference to Matthew (18:15-17) was the locus classicus for the dissenters of 1567/69.

Grindal by June of 1568 knew of some 200 other Londoners who had withdrawn from their parish churches. The church of Holy Trinity in the liberty of the Minories, not far from the Tower, was the core and bridge of this movement. Crowley and Gough were its more radical preachers and the duchess of Suffolk gave her patronage.[65] Crowley's preface to Piers Plowman which he published in three separate quarto editions in 1550 sets the tone.

> In [this] tyme it pleased God to open the eyes of many to se hys truth, geving them boldenes of herte, to open their mouthes and crye out agaynste the worckes of darcknes, as dyd John Wicklefe, who also in those dayes translated the holye Bible into the Englishe tonge...66

In 1567 he published The Opening of the Wordes of the Prophet Joell which complained of the compromise under Elizabeth.[67] Owen comments that "the names of the preachers active in its pulpit between 1567 and 1570 read like a roll-call of the giants of contemporary Nonconformity."[68] Coverdale's last recorded sermon was there on 23 October 1568.

Crowley had long supported protestant reform with his rhetoric. He cited Peter Martyr against Archbishop Parker during the vestments controversy.[69] A decade before the Marian reaction he praised God for raising up William Tyndale "the fyrst true Apostle of Christ after Johan Wyclef the verye manne of God."[70] The burning of bibles enflamed Crowley's rhetoric against the conservative bishops:

> ranke rable of Romishe russelers in theyr syde swepynge gownes/theyr shauen crownes/cappes/and typettes/Speciallye wode Wynchestre/lewd London/lurkynge Lyncolne/dreamynge Durham/Yorke without wytt/ chatteringe Chychestre/ smylynge Salisburye/fleryng fryer wattes/and that double faced trayter Wilson/namyng it full of errours and uerye yll translated. Oh idell ydyotes and abhominable hypocrites, Shame ye not at all so euidentlye to lye and so baldelye to blasheme?71

Burrage prints some documents from the Plumber's Hall congregation and the Richard Fitz separatist "privy church." The first is a list of prisoners taken on March 4, 1567/68. One notices the forty-two streets of localities for the seventy-seven persons, places such as 'Bred Strete' (2), 'Aldersgate strete' (6) and 'St. Androwes Vndershafte' (3) or 'Dysstafe Lane' (4).[72] 'Brede strete' was the site of a vital conventicle during Marian times as witnessed by a tract published in Strasbourg by Thomas Sampson in the form of A letter to the trew professors of Christes Gospell inhabitinge in the Parishe off Allhallowis in Bredstrete in London.[73] Bredstrete and Aldersgate street are a quarter mile apart and both are within a mile of the Minories! Smithfield street is less than one fourth of a mile from Aldersgate and not one half mile from Bredstrete. All are adjacent to the River Thames whose warehouses and inns were part of the network of London dissent for scripture men.[74] Three of the seventy-seven give their address as Smithfield. All of these were within a thirty minute walk of Holy Trinity in the Minories whose modern section of London is EC 1.

The Fitz congregation has been documented in Burrage as a separatist gathering of those who wished to have the "Glorious worde and Euangell preached, not in bondage, and subjection, but freely, and purelye."[75] The first of three documents printed in Burrage gives the true marks of the church as free preaching, pure ministry of the sacraments, and discipline only, "not the fylthye Common lawe."[76]

The second is a covenant in nine parts to abstain from "idolatrouse trash" preached by them that bear the "markes of the Romysh beast." One will suffer danger for not coming to the parish church because among other reasons:

> 3. I will not beautifie with my presence those filthy ragges, which bryng the heauenly worde of the eternall our Lorde God, in to bondage, subiection, and slauerie.77

The third document reflects the reasons for withdrawal to meet twice a week, on the sabbath day in houses and on the fourth day to pray and discipline according to Matthew (18:15-18). It is in the form of a petition to the Queen in the 13th year of her reign (1571). The signators urge the monarch

> that her highnesse may send forth princes and minsters and geue them the booke of the Lord, that they may bryng home the people of god to the purity and truthe of the apostolycke churche.78

The same prayer appears a decade later in a Puritan work by Robert Browne. Thus the memory of the Fitz congregation of 1571 with its links to privy and public concerns of the previous two decades is perpetuated in Robert Browne's 1581 True and Short Declaration.[79]

These heirs of Marian London protestantism kept alive their congregational discipline and denial of Elizabethan parish worship which for them was disfigured by popish practices. London dissent was alive and well in the decades from 1551 to 1581. It remains to describe the believers' church which rose like a phoenix from the ashes of Smithfield and the gallows of Elizabeth. The shadow of Servetus cast its image on those Englishmen whom the authorities thought to be fit for hanging -- men like Greenwood and his crew.

Professor Elton has recently explored the status of John Foxe and his contribution to religious toleration in this period. Olsen's 1973 chapter on "The Church and Toleration" has been evaluated by Elton who notes the two prefaces which Foxe contributed to Special and Chosen Sermons of D. Martin Luther (1578: S.T.C. 16993) and Luther's Commentary on Galatians (1575: S.T.C. 16965). Elton finds in both prefaces "the tone of moderate reason... as Foxe's characteristic note."[80]

Foxe comments in the Galatian preface that Luther learned his divinity not from the devil, but from Paul.

> Vnlesse we had ben exercised with violence, and craftie assaultes by tirannes & heretikes, and in our heart with terrors and fiery dartes of the devill, Paule had bene to us no lesse obscure, than he... is to this day to our adversaries the papistes, the Anabaptistes and other our adversaries: And therefore the gifte of knowledge of the scripture and our studies through such inward and outward conflictes, open vnto us the minde of Paule and of all the Scriptures etc. [sig. *vir-v]

Foxe who drew the line at toleration for Jews, argued that the state had no right to burn anyone. The act de haeretico comburendo: 2 Henry IV c.15 had no force since the Commons had never given its assent. Foxe ignored the fact that "drastic changes in the structure, records and standing of parliament... fulfilled all the conditions of legal validity applicable at the time of its making."[81] What Foxe got right was the lack of statutory authority in 1575 for burning heretics handed over by the spiritual arm. That More called for the stake but Foxe for toleration are equally remarkable events, given that the latter pled for Campion and Anabaptists alike.[82] Elton concludes that one real difference between More and Foxe was that of a common dictate of humanity. "So long as the Church of Rome adhered to its determination to rule all Christians, only protestantism offered a hope of an end to persecution."[83]

B. A Believers Church (1580-1593)

John Taylor claimed to have discovered a swarm of sectaries when he pilloried their preaching in 1641. Taylor's A Swarme of Sectaries, and Schismatiques calls these lower class types "vermin" who "swarm like caterpillars/And hold conventicles in barns and cellars."[84] Their preachers included women, against which a rhymster warned in 1641: "When women preach and cobblers pray, the fiends in hell make holiday."[85] Taylor reserved his invective for the preachers when he wrote the following lines:

> A preachers work is not to geld a sow,
> Unseemly 'tis a judge should milk a cow,
> A cobbler to a pulpit should not mount,
> Nor can an ass cast up a true account.86

Though these lines were written sixty years after Browne's "buggery," they describe the Tudor age which was not yet Christopher Hill's World Turned Upside Down. In the Second Admonition To The Parliament, which Thomas Cartwright crafted in October 1572, a complaint is entered about persecution.

> What talke they of their being beyond the seas in quene Maries dayes because of the persecution, when they in queene Elizabethes dayes, are come home to raise a per-

> secution. They bost they followe the steps of good maister Ridley the martir: let them followe him in the good, and not in the badde.87

Robert Browne (1550?-1633?) is acknowledged as the leader of English separatism who broke with Puritan concerns when in 1580 he formed a separatist church in Norwich with its own liturgy and covenant. Robert Harrison who had been a Cambridge man joined Browne in this act of nonconformity. They were called Brownists. By 1582 Robert Browne took the final step toward separatism when he published his Treatise of Reformation Without Tarrying for Anie.

Robert Browne came from a prominent family in Rutland. The family had been settled at Stamford in Lincolnshire where since the fourteenth century they had amassed considerable wealth and created influence. John Browne built the church of All Saints, Stamford, at his sole expense. Robert Browne's great-great grandfather of Tolethorpe, John Browne's son, was high sheriff for the county of Rutland in the reign of Henry VII. Robert Browne was connected through both his parents with some of the most influential families in England. Cecil, Lord Burghley, was one such kinsman who gave Browne protection on several occasions.[88]

Browne took his B.A. in 1572 from Cambridge where he finished in residence at Corpus Christi College. Browne went down to London, returning to his parental home at Tolethorpe because of the London plague of 1578. Browne soon left for Cambridge where he came under Richard Greenham's direction at Dry Drayton. Greenham encouraged Browne to preach in the villages around (such as Maddingley and Hardwick?) without a license from the Bishop of Ely. Browne was so well received that St. Benét's parish in Cambridge called him as curate. He refused the necessary license which his brother obtained for him to preach, lashing out at the parochial system. "The Kingdom of God was not to be begun by whole parishes," Browne thundered, "but rather by the worthiest, were they neuer so few."[89]

When his friend Robert Harrison visited Cambridge, Browne left Cambridge to join Harrison who was Master of Old Mews Hospital in Norwich.[90] Though more than 100 persons were in Browne's conventicles at Norwich, he was sent to prison when bishop Edmund Freke took action against the Brownists. On April 19, 1581 the bishop forwarded articles of complaint to Lord Burleigh, who sent a prompt excuse that Browne had been guilty more "of zeal rather than malice."[91] Browne was by then in Suffolk at Bury St. Edmunds.[92] Lord Burleigh would intervene again in 1584/85 to release Browne from prison for publishing books in the summer of 1584.

Browne went to Middelburg in Zeeland with his congregation where he published a number of works attacking the English parish structure, while defending his view against Cartwright that a true church was a voluntary gathering of true believers bound by a covenantal subscription.[93] An idea of the covenant can be seen from that drawn up in Norwich under the title of <u>A True and Short Declaration</u>. Since there is no other as complete a description of an early English separatist congregation, it will be helpful to reproduce an extract for the modern reader. One should notice in advance of reading this 1581(?) covenant that it calls for free choice of spiritual leaders, exhortation by those who had the gift or special charge, and discipline by the congregation for abuses as well as services of thanksgiving. No bishops or elders were to rule this church which was under the reign of Christ himself, who would reveal through the scriptures those matters which would bring the church to "being better reformed" so that they might be "prospered by the good hand of God."

> so a covenant vvas made & ther mutual consent vvas geuen to hould to gether.
>
> There vvere certaine chief pointes proved vnto them by the scriptures, all vvhich being particularlie rehersed vnto them vvith exhortation, thei agreed vpon them, & pronounced their agrement to ech thing particularlie, saiing, to this vve geue our consent. First therefore thei gaue their consent, to ioine them selues to the Lord, in one couenant & fellovveshipp together, & to keep & seek agrement vnder his lavves & gouernment: and

therefore did vtterlie flee & auoide such like disorders & vvickedness, as vvas menioned before. Further thei agreed off those vvhich should teach them, and vvatch for the saluation of their soules, vvhom thei allovved & did chose as able & meete ffor that charge. For thie had sufficient triall and testimonie thereoff by that vvhich thei ahard & savve by them, & had receaued of others. So thie praied for their vvatchfulnes & diligence & promised their obedience[.]

Likevvise an order vvas agreed on ffor their meetinges together, ffor their exercises therin, as for praier, thanckes giuing, reading of the scriptures, for exhortation and edifing, ether by al men vvhich had the guift, or by those vvhich had a speciall charge before others. And for the lavvefulnes off putting forth questions, to learne the trueth, as iff anie thing seemed doubtful & hard, to require some to shevve it more plainly, or for anie to shevve it him selfe & to cause the rest to vnderstand it. Further for noting out anie speciall matter of edifing at the meeting, or for talcking seuerally there[t]o, vvith some particulars, iff none did require publique audience, or if no vvaightier & more necessarie matter vvere handled of others. Againe it vvas agreed that anie might protest, appeale, complaine, exhort, dispute, reproue c. as he had occasion, but yet in due order, vvhich Vvas then also declared. Also that all should further the kingdom off God in them selues, & especiallie in their charge & household, iff thei had anie, or in their friendes & companions & vvhosoeuer Vvas Vvorthie. Furthermore thei particularlie agreed off the manner, hovve to Vvatch to disorders, & reforme abuses, & for assembling the companie, for teaching priuatlie, & for vvarning and rebukeing both priuatly & openlie, for appointing publick humbling in more rare judgementes, and publik thankesgeuing in straunger blessinges, for gathering & testifing voices in debating matters, & propounding them in the name off the rest that agree, for an order of chosing teachers, guides & releeueres, vvhen thei vvant, for separating cleane from vncleane, for receauing anie into the fellovveship, for presenting the dalie successe of the church, & the vvantes thereof, for seeking to other churches to haue their help, being better reformed, or to bring them to reformation, for taking an order that none contend openlie, nor persecute, nor trouble disorderedly, nor bring false doctrine, nor euil cause after once or tvvise Vvarning or rebuke.

Thus all things vvere handled, set in order, & agreed on to the comfort of all, & see the matter vvrought & prospered by the good hand of God ...94

In 1582 Browne published a volume at the Schilders press with three treatises:

1) A Treatise of Reformation without Tarrying for Anie.
2) A Treatise upon the 23. of Matthewe.
3) A Booke which Showeth The life and manners of all true Christians.

These three documents under the general title Life and Manners of All True Christians all foster spiritual development by separation from an inclusive parish church. Browne broke with the Puritans over the role of the civil magistrate in accomplishing this goal. The full title of the first treatise makes this plain, i.e., and of the wickednesse of those Preachers which will not reforme till the Magistrate commaunde or compell them. Browne is explicit on restricting the magistrate to civil control, i.e., "but to compell religion, to plant churches by power, and to force a submission to Ecclesiastical gouernment by lawes and penalties, belongeth not to them."[95] The essence lies in the covenental agreement as the Treatise of Reformation states:

> Wherefore are we called the people of God and Christians? Because that by a willing Couenaunt made with our God, we are vnder the gouernement of God and Christe, and thereby do leade a godly and Christian life.[96]

The middle treatise deserves some attention for its Old Testament references and appeal to the halycon days under Edward VI which were purified by the Marian purge. A Treatise Vpon the 23. of Matthewe has 120 references to the Old Testament and 158 references to the New Testament. These 278 explicit biblical references are framed by an attack on logic and syllogisms at the front and ecclesiastical benefits at the conclusion.

The attack on logic asks whether it is "good foode for the sheep." Could Ezra in Nehemiah (8:8) give understanding to the people without syllogisms? "Did he digge out such stuffe from Cambridge horned capps."[97] Colossians (2:8) is taken by Browne to condemn philosophy and vain babblings in a triple sense of false doctrine, false knowledge and false logic. In this Browne dissents from Beza, who restricts the Pauline warning to "speculation, custome and worship of the law."[98] Furthermore, when Job disputed with his friends, "did the faces of three Moodes out of Aristotle, fraye them with their frowninges?"[99] Such logic is in Latin terms which if translated, one need not go to Cambridge to learn.[100] Solomon's wisdom is contrasted with the Aristotelian four fold causation, citing Ecclesiastes. One need not spend seven years at Cambridge in the study of Aristotle or the sciences before pondering the wisdom of the scriptures. Such are foolish disciples of heathenish "wiserdes."[101]

Browne's conclusion attacks the comfortable living of the bishops who "love the fleece and think on the fatte, and this is their inward calling."[102] The outward calling is ambition, which Browne pillories as much as pride which is their inner spirit.

> The popes olde house was destroyed in Englande, and they are called to builde him a newe. In the time of King Edward the 6. they began such a building. They had gotte the Popishe tooles, but they coulde not holde them. God was mercifull by the rodde of Queene Marie, and dyd beate such euill weapons out of their handes, yet these haue gotte againe the false popish gouernment, and by it they will blesse vs from all euill sicknes and plagues. Haue they not knowledge and skil sufficient, as another inward calling? Haue they not the whole worlde in their heades to be sure of the church? Let vs welcome wise Gentlemen: they toke in hand to build the Lords house, and now moe then xx. yeeres are past in studying for the groudwork. O perfect work, when shal it end, which is so long in beginning... Thus we see their inwarde calling. Nowe let vs come to their outwarde. How got they their roumes, Benefices and liuings? Did we send for such guesse to Rome, or to Louane, for they get into the sheepfolde thoughe the dores be shut aganst them. Came they not in at the windowes, trowe ye. Doethe not the Torche of Ambition shewe them a windowe? Be not Cambridge degrees an high ladder to go vp? Be not their bribes of flatteries, or vaunt of thier learning, a ladder to goe either vp or downe, And is not the fauour of some Patrone or Bishoppe, or worldly man, the strength of these ladders? Did they not finde out a liuing before they foud out meete people for their calling?... They haue looked vs in the face, and haue stolen away our libertie. They tooke vs by the hande, as though they would leade vs, but they haue bounde our handes behind vs. For when we looked to chuse them for Pastours, they came vpon vs by

> force, and yoked vs to their parishes, and snared vs with inioyings, and did beate vs with penalties. O worthie outward calling... Kneele downe ye Preachers, that the Bishoppe may ordayne you sitting in his chayre. His holie handes shall blesse you. They are washed from blood as was Pilates, and as the nose of a Wolfe whiche will rauen no more. Then must you take you Licenses in parchement, and paye well for them. Prepare a Boxe for your waxe, printe your message therein, and keepe touche with the Bishoppe, least he open your Boxe, and your calling flye awaye.103

Such a two-pronged attack goes deeper than the usual ecclesiological distinctives assigned to Browne as the protoseparatist according to a congregational pattern. The attack probes episcopal rights to ordain when it turns a searchlight on the Ramist dialectic practiced in Cambridge.[104]

Robert Harrison published in 1583 A Little Treatise on Ps. 122 which warned against the "liuings of the Lordlie overrulers of many churches" whose "wormewoode dregges of Antichrists cupp" must be rinsed from the bottom by the civil magistrate.[105] In Harrison's more substantial critique one reads about the bishops, deans and chancellors who were the "pope's bastards," whose minsters were "dumb dogges" and whose authority came from anti-Christ.[106] Browne quarreled with Harrison and was expelled from the Middelburg church in 1583. Thereafter he submitted to Archbishop Whitgift in 1594 after Lord Burghley's intervention. After a brief stint preaching in Northampton in 1586, Browne was elected master of Stamford grammar school. After five years he resigned in 1591 to become rector of a church in Northamptonshire. There he resided for over forty years in the parish which Lord Burghley gave over for his kinsman.[107] Meantime, Robert Harrison's death in 1585 left leadership for the separatist agenda in the hands of persons like John Greenwood and Henry Barrow.

Bishop Cox was anxious over the intransigence of these prophets as he wrote to Rudolph Gualter at Zurich. Cox defends the Prayer Book which those excellent men, master Bucer and Peter Martyr advised in Edward's reign. When they were exiles at Frankfurt, Peter Martyr wrote that "I find nothing in that book contrary to godliness."[108] Now these prophets have stirred up the people.

> By the vehemence of their harangues haue so maddened the wretched multitude... that they now obstinately refuse to enter our churches, either to baptize their children, or to partake of the Lords Supper, or to hear sermons... they seek bye paths; they establish a private religion, and assemble in private houses, and there perform their sacred rites, as the Donatists of old, and the Anabaptists now; and also our papists...109

John Greenwood (d. 1593) replaced Harrison at his death in 1585 as the leader of the Brownists. Greenwood matriculated at Corpus Christi College, Cambridge on 18 March 1578 and graduated B.A. in 1581. After ordination as deacon and priest, Greenwood was employed to say service at Rochford to Lord Robert Rich, Earl of Warwick, an Essex leader of the Puritans. The Earl of Warwick would nominate Halbeach on John Preston's recommendation as headmaster of Felstad School. This school educated four sons of Oliver Cromwell as well as Henry Mildmay, son of Sir Henry Mildmay of Grace's Hall in Essex.[110]

Greenwood became a friend of Henry Barrow and was arrested for holding a private conventicle in London in the autumn of 1586. Barrow was also arrested when he visited Greenwood in the Clink on November 19, 1586. After examination they were released only to be committed this time to the Fleet on July 20, 1588. Greenwood was kept in prison over four years until his release in 1592. Greenwood then joined Francis Johnson in forming a congregation in Nicolas Lane, London (half-way between the Minories and Bread Street). Johnson and Greenwood were arrested on December 5, 1592, indicted on March 21, 1593 and Greenwood and Barrow were hanged on April 6, 1593 at Tyburn.[111]

The March 1589 conferences with Archdeacon Hutchinson at the Fleet were printed in _A Collection of certaine Sclavnderous Articles_, while his refutation of George Gifford's charge of Donatism was issued in March of 1591 as _A Briefe Refutation of Mr. George Giffard_. These two works will repay a careful reading. The setting of the _Collection_ is the decision to use forty-two clergy and scholars to hold conferences with the fifty-two separatists held in six prisons. The first substantial pamphlet to appear in print was the 56 page tract, about May of 1590, entitled A Collection of Certaine Sclavnderous Articles. There are seven different divisions to this work. Item seven is under discussion here, i.e., "A Brief Answeare..."

The "Brief Answeare" has twelve sections which delineate the beliefs of the "newe sectories" as they were labled. The first three reject the prayers of the English parish church; four, five and twelve speak against the Church of England as a member of Christ's Church; six and seven deny the validity of baptism and Lord's Supper; eight and nine deny to the Queen authority over the church; and ten and eleven call for reform by the people without royal permission. The Queen may be excommunicated by the presbytery or eldership for cause if no reformation is seen after her admonition.[112]

The eleventh section is quite remarkable, for the Queen was the source of law who pronounced excommunication. The key phrase appears in the lines, "The prince also if he wilbe held a member of Christ or, of the Church, must be subject to Christ's censure in the church."[113] There was to be no exception of persons for such discipline is the means of salvation for princes as well. Such pastoral concern was not well received by the head of the Church. Actually, the manuscript which had circulated before November of 1588 defines the church as a company of faithful people in which Christ alone is king, priest and prophet.[114] In The True Church and the False Church the Separatists take up each of these categories. The English Church is false since:

1) Christ is not received as king; instead they stand under the "antichristian yoake of their papish gouernment."
2) Christ is not their priest; they prophane his name with their idolatrous admission of the wicked to the Lord's Supper.
3) Christ is no prophet for them; obedience is not give to his word which they use to cover their sin "rather than as a rule whereby to direct thier lives."[115]

The Briefe Answeare was followed by A Brief Refutation. George Gifford had joined the classis movement in Essex and was suspended as vicar at Maldon. In 1590 Gifford published A/Plaine Declaration/that our Brownists be full Dona-/tists, by comparing them together/from point to point out of the wri/tings of Augustine (London: Toby Cooke, 1590).

When Gifford concludes his Declaration, he notes that the Donatists in Augustine's time suspended the rules of logic. So in sixteenth century England Browne has likewise abandoned the rules of logic. Gifford concludes that the Brownists "charge the students of the Universities, as trained up in vaine and curious Artes... they would not haue their matters tried by the rules which make manifest which is truth, and which is falsehood."[116]

Greenwood responds that his cause differs from the Donatists in that they are persecuted by the clergy with the civil power in one person, "contrarie to the lawe of God."[117] Such a separation of clerical from civil function is necessary to keep Christ in his office (Greenwood states this negatively). He concludes that their tyranny pulls husband from wife and father from children, which calls them away from their "lawful callings and trades."

> "If we diserve death, let us dye in due execution, if banishment, banish us; but first by order convince us of some crime or error worthie therof, if you will cleare your selves."118

For all of the above sentiments Greenwood and Barrow were held to be fit for hanging. They were executed for sedition. They had been tried under an anti-Catholic act of 1581, for Parliament in 1593 considered a bill which would extend that statute against failure to come to church or speaking against the established government. A letter writer said that "the execution proceeded through the malice of the bishops to the Lower House."[119] Such polarities were intensified by the Puritan/Catholic conflict in counties such as Elizabethan Sussex and centers like Ipswich.[120]

Chapter 17) Radical Puritans (1593-1625)

A. The Pain of Separation

Professor Collinson says that the preaching and assimilation of primary Protestant doctrines set up processes "which were calculated to divide and even dissolve the parish." There was a popular protestantism in Elizabethan times not subject to preachers whose popular character tended toward congregational independancy.[121]

The interrogation of Barrowist prisoners from the London congregation of 1592 underlines the influence of Puritan ministers of the radical wing. In the congregation of which Francis Johnson was elected pastor there were several credited preachers and writers such as Laurence Chaderton, Egerton, Cooper and Sparkes.[122] As Dr. White put it, "for many the step from Puritanism into Separatism was often but the step between yearning and fulfilment."[123]

For a quarter century Francis Johnson led that congregation which the authorities forced Henry Barrow to abandon. Johnson took his B.A. at Cambridge (Christ's College) where he became a Fellow of his college in 1585. By January 1589 he was in trouble with the University authorities for preaching militant puritan sermons at Great St. Mary's in which they accused Johnson of wanting elders equal in authority to govern the church.[124] After a stint in prison, Johnson next appeared as a minister of Walter Traver's and Thomas Cartwright's congregation at Middelburg in the Netherlands. While there he surprised the printers of Barrow's <u>A plaine refutation</u> and had the entire printing burned to ashes under his eye. But Johnson saved two copies which, when he read them, so troubled his conscience that he crossed the seas to confer with the authors who were soon to be executed.[125]

In the early autumn of 1592 the congregation which met at Nicholas Lane elected Johnson as their pastor. He was arrested in October and again on December 5, though his interrogation was delayed until April 5, 1593 which led to his exile. By July 1593 some Nicholas Lane congregational members were in Amsterdam. When the consistory insisted that all unlicensed assemblies should cease, Reformed authorities warned other centers in the Netherlands. Francis Johnson remained in London prisons for a further four years.[126]

Information about the inner life of the congregation stems from George Johnson's disgruntled account of 1603 called A discours of some troubles. George called his brother Francis "bewitched and besotted" over his wife, who was Tomasine Boys, the widow of Edward Boys. Her fashionable dress was a bone of contention when her husband was in prison facing death.[127] George Johnson would be excommunicated over this issue of décolletage after discussions in 1599 over who could control social conduct in the congregation.

On the positive side, Johnson's congregation grew to 300 members by the time William Bradford knew it in 1609.[128] In 1596 a Confession of Faith appeared which saw a Latin edition in 1598 and a retraction by Francis Junius of Leyden in the first two months of 1599. A third letter of 1602 from Junius indicates the circulation of his letter of 9 January 1599 in England. This correspondance indicates an unusual reluctance to debate with sectaries. The English alliance with the Dutch may explain that reticence on the part of one whose notes to Revelation gave him credibility with the readers of the Geneva Bible. The Confession was printed in the English version with Junius' letters in 1602 and again in 1604.[129] The exiles had their own press which published nearly forty books between 1604 and 1622. The first was Henry Ainsworth and Francis Johnson, An Apologie of...Brownists (S.T.C.2 238).[130]

The forty-five articles of the Confession of Faith start with a traditional trinitarian affirmation, but soon take up the theme of hypocrisy (article XVII) and discipline (article XXV). Article XXV is succinct on the subject of censure.

> Euery member of each Christian congregation, how excellent, great or learned soeuer, ought to be subiect to this censure & judgment of Christ.[131]

What appears as the first complaint in the prefatory letter is the dissent from a national church planted through the Elizabethan settlement. When that Church received "the whole land" as members, then it included those who professed the Gospel in King Edward's day, shed the blood of martyrs in Queen Mary's days and now stand "in this fearful sinfull state, in Idolatry, blyndnes, superstition, and all manner wickednes, without any professed repentance."[132]

Articles XXIX (which rejects the present hierarchy) and XXX (which calls these offices 'Popish') lead on to Article XXXIII. There the true believers are to "come forth of this Antichristian estate unto the freedom and true profession of Christ..."[133] It seems therefore that the concern against idolatry and the rule of Christ over his church prompt the separation from the Ecclesia Anglicana. The clarion call is for a believers' church which is a free church.

B. "Hasty Puritans"

Henry Jacob is acknowledged as the architect of a fresh start for English Separatism when the "hasty Puritans" [which White labels Barrow, Johnson, Robinson and Smyth] lost momentum inside England and turned to the New World as exiled separatists.[134] Before one traces that exile across the Atlantic, Jacob's career shouuld be explored as a middle way between Amsterdam and the perception of religious anarchy.[135]

When Jacob founded the Southwark congregation in 1616, he established "the first continuing Congregational Church on English soil."[136] More recently Von Rohr has admitted that Jacob moved toward separatist views.[137] Henry Jacob was born in 1563 in the parish of Cheriton, Kent. At age 18 he went up to St. Mary Hall, Oxford, matriculating on 27 November 1581. After taking a B.A. (1583) and M.A. (1586), Jacob entered Corpus Christi as a precentor.[138]

Jacob seems to have visited Francis Johnson sometime in 1596 while Johnson was imprisoned in the Clink. A four year controversy ensued which can be followed in Jacob's A defence of the churches and ministry of Englande (1599) and Johnson's An answer to Maister H. Jacob (1600). In 1603 Jacob was in London where by June he joined a puritan campaign to curry favour with James I.[139] Jacob spent some time in the Clink but was released on his subscription of April 4, 1605. That document promised that Jacob would not "speak against ye Church gouernment orders now among vs established by Law," that is, while he was on bail. If in six months it appears to be "well grounded on Gods word" then he would speak for its defence.[140] During September of 1603 Jacob traveled south to meet with Puritans in Sussex. The Privy Council was not pleased.[141] By 27 September he was back in prison. The subscription is the last notice of Jacob for the next five years.

The preface of Jacob's The divine beginning and institution of Christs true visible or ministerial church is dated "from Leyden. Decemb. 20. Ano. 1610. The Stinton MS records that Jacob "discoursed much with Mr. John Robinson."[142] The Stinton MS also records that Jacob was back in London in 1616 to help form the Southwark congregation which chose and ordained him pastor.[143] Jacob remained pastor at Southwark about eight years before he sailed to the Jamestown Colony where he died in late 1623 or early 1624.

Stephen Brachlow has argued that Jacob linked ecclesiastical obedience with salvation in his writings of 1604-1616. Plausable reasons for this may lie not in Robinson's influence so much as the Hampton Court Conference of 1604 where James I dashed the hopes of Puritan reformers. In any event one can trace with Brachlow this shift in emphasis from Puritan moderation (1599) to a separatist mentality by 1616.[144] Jacob now believed that personal salvation depended on more than doctrinal orthodoxy.

> Whosoever denyeth Christ the Saviour to be our intire and perfect Prophet and spirituall King (by taking away from him som [viz., the ecclesiastical] parts of his Propheticall and Kingly Offices, and ascribing the same vnto Men) he diminisheth the honor & dignitie of Christ, he impugne the Foundation of saving faith, and is contrarie to Gods word.145

Throughout the body of Jacob's writings from 1604-1616, the idea that assurance was linked to the practice of a true church order was a primary theme. The opening sentence of Reasons was a call for reformation "for the safety of our soules."[146] In 1610, he claimed that "the first and waightiest matter in Religion that can concerne vs" was "to be assured that we are in a true Visible & Ministeriall Church of Christ: for out of a true Visible Church ordinarily there is no salvation."[147] Three years later he maintained that ecclesiastical obedience "is plainly the way to heaven."[148] By 1616, the theme had become a major preoccupation for Jacob who from the first page of the Confession, all the way through A collection of sundry matters, traces the idea that "the onely sure way for the comfort of our soules is the practise of Gods ordinances for his visible Church."[149]

Jacob's concern to link ecclesiastical obedience with salvation is to be found in the soteriological framework which he inherited from puritan circles. From 1604, Jacob tended to view the bible as an ecclesiastical law book that contained an extensive set of "absolute and immutable" rules about church order prescribed by Christ, the Mosaic "Lawgiver" of the new covenant.[150] His theological rationale for believing that salvation was tied to keeping these ecclesiastical laws was explained in his Exposition of the 2d. commandement. There Jacob said that saving faith was to be understood from two perspectives. From the perspective of God, salvation depended entirely upon grace so that "no works of ours can justify vs." But from the human perspective, true faith was to be "considered simply as it is a worke a duty for vs to doe." From man's vantage point, works were not to be considered in opposition to faith, but rather "the Law of Faith" was to be viewed as something "contained in the Law of works," i.e. the Decalogue. For the believer, true faith was to be understood as nothing less than faithfully performing the duties of the Mosaic Law. Because matters of ecclesiology were included under the second commandment, ecclesiastical obedience was a duty of faith and a necessary ingredient for acquiring assurance.[151]

Another text to which Jacob appealed was II Peter 1:10 which, within the puritan tradition of William Perkins and others, was generally understood to mean that assurance of saving faith could be gained through obedience to all God's commandments. That is how Jacob understood the passage,[152] but with his overriding concern for churchmanship, Jacob gave it an ecclesiological twist when he explained that by it believers were commanded to make their "calling, and election sure, (viz.) by walking in the true outward way; to observe the 2. Commandement in all the parts of it, a maine part whereof under the gospell is this forme of a visible Church, and government."[153]

Exactly why Jacob shifted grounds between 1599 and 1604 will probably never be known for certain. There is the possibility that he had been influenced by contemporary separatists, since his new position looked very similar to the one taken by separatists who alone among radicals after 1590 emphasized the soteriological value of true churchmanship. While late Elizabethan puritans minimized the importance of ecclesiology and concentrated almost exclusively on the development of individual piety, Jacob came to ask, as Barrow had asked Gifford in 1590, if those who thought ecclesiology indifferent could:

> give assurance to mens consciences? nay, it can not be. At least, men standing in such state, will often doubt and make question whether the spirituall blessings and graces of God in Christ bee promised, or may bee instrumentally wrought in them... This doubt, I say, at least, will and must needes arise from the opinion of our adversaries. And it can not but weaken the faith of many, if in the end it do not wholy subvert it.[154]

Jacob believed the same was true of "those [puritans?] who do professe acknowledge that Christ... hath instituted... a certain perpetuall forme of... Church Government" yet fail to "vse and practise that which they do professe to be from Heaven." They "truly seeme to destroy the conscience & faith of the people, not vnlike to the other."[155] For Jacob, as for the separatists, the practice of biblical churchmanship became the favored cure for spiritual weakness and doubt -- "the onely true complete meanes," as he put it, to "get assurance of salvation to our soules, which otherwise we for our parts cannot find."[156]

If, in fact, he learned to think along these lines through the influence of separatists, his encounter with Johnson between 1596-1600 would have been the likely occasion. Von Rohr, at least, concluded that "the victor's laurels for this debate went to Johnson, for by 1604 Jacob had begun to change his mind," and move toward a consensus with Johnson.[157] But from a remark made by Jacob during the debate, it seems likely that he was not being entirely forthright about his personal convictions when he argued the case for non-separation with Johnson. This, at least, seems to be the implication from Jacob's reply to Johnson's first attack: "You charge an vnconscionable vntruth on mee [when you said]... <u>that I should graunt and cannot deny, that all outward ceremonies and gouernment, are arbitrary at mans pleasure</u>: I onelie said, that our state holdeth that generall opinion, Not that I myselfe held it."[158] In fact, in his original statement, Jacob had not said "our state holdeth" but "we hold," though he did admit that "one or two amongst hundreths or thousands may think otherwise."[159] From his reply to Johnson, however, it appears that privately Jacob was inclined to favor the minority position while publicly condemning it.[160]

So the change in 1604 was probably not so much a change of mind as a public stand on what had previously been only a private conviction.[161] In that case, Johnson would not have been the source of his new convictions. The fact is, that Jacob did not have to turn to Johnson or any other separatist for the convictions he expressed in 1604, because the same concepts had been articulated just as clearly by Elizabethan puritans in the 1570s and 1580s. That, of course, is where Johnson and most separatists themselves traced their ecclesiological pedigree.

In 1613 Jacob quoted Cartwright's dictum that matters of church government are "of Substance of the Gospell; and that the kinde of government is a matter necessary to salvation and of faith."[162] The reason, then for the change between 1599 and 1604 was more likely tied up with the change in the puritan hopes and dissappointments that occured as a result of the accession of James I, rather than his confrontation with Johnson. While the death of Elizabeth and accession of the Scottish king at first kindled puritan hopes, the failure of Hampton Court and the subsequent deprivations may well have bred a strong radical reaction among the more extreme puritans. Jacob, at least, was one of those distressed by the failure of the four puritan representatives at Hampton Court whom he suspected of conspiring with the bishops.[163] Whatever the reason, the fact remains that a change did occur in Jacob's public stand regarding ecclesiology, the Bible and salvation.

C. Pilgrim Pastor

John Robinson has been the subject of denominational history for his double status as a founding father of Congregationalism and as first pastor of the Pilgrim Fathers whose Mayflower adventure of 1620 brought them to the New World. Robinson's farewell address has been often cited with its final sentence seen as founding an American civilization or advocating an individualism which places him outside of the Genevan orthodoxy within which he toiled.[164]

> In the next place, for the wholesome counsel Mr. Robinson gave that part of the Church wereof he was Pastor, at their departure from him to begin the great work of Plantation in New England. Amongst other wholesome instructions and exhortations, he used these expressions, or to the same purpose: We are now, ere long, to part asunder; and the Lord knoweth whether ever he should live to see our faces again. but whether the Lord had appointed it or not; he charged us, before God and his blessed angels, to follow him no further than he followed Christ; and if God should reveal anything to us by any other Instrument of his, to be as ready to receive it, as ever we were to receive any truth by him Ministry. For he was very confident the Lord had more truth and light yet to break forth out of his holy word.[165]

Both George and Brachlow underscore the identity of Robinson within the Separatist tradition and trace it to the early conventicles in Marian and Elizabethan times, articulated in the writings of Browne and Barrow and enshrined in the 1596 Confession which Robinson and his congregation adopted as their own.[166]

Robinson's Cambridge connection includes four years at Corpus Christi College where he took the B.A. in 1596, followed by the M.A. and a readership in Greek. Robinson resigned his fellowship on 10 February 1604, five days prior to his marriage.[167] On August 5 of 1603 Robinson had preached in Norwich at St. Andrews on Psalms (118:24-26). The report of 9 August 1603 labels Robinson as a radical Puritan for his factious sermon.[168] Though this parish since Marian days had a history of dissent, any doubts Bishop Jegan had about Norwich radicalism were cleared away as he read this and other reports about Robinson.

Brachlow finds it impossible to answer when Robinson took the final step to separatism, though Joseph Hall believed that after Jegan's suspension in 1605, Robinson went north to Lincolnshire.[169] Then there are three encounters with puritans which caused Robinson to ask whether separation was not necessary. The first was an "exercise" in Cambridge where the Master of Emmanuel, Lauwrence Chaderton, argued on the basis of Matthew (18:17) that the power for church discipline resided in the body of the assembly. The second took place on the same afternoon as Paul Baynes expounded Ephesians (5:7-11) against the lawless consort of the godly with the wicked. The final encounter took place in 1606 at the Coventry home of Sir William Bowes with notables such as Arthur Hildersham present.[170]

Shortly after the Coventry conference Robinson observed the ritual of covenant-taking at Scrooby manor which was administered by William Brewster.[171] This Scrooby group met every sabbath for a year until the new Archbishop of York delivered a sermon at Bowtry near Scrooby on the north. Archbishop Toby Matthew then took action against the "Brownists" by prosecuting their lay patrons. Richard Brewster and Richard Jackson were fined £20 and summoned to court. A warrant for their arrest was issued on their failure to appear. Thomas Helwys and his wife were jailed at York Castle. The Scrooby church choose exile and arrived in Amsterdam. When Hall charged Robinson's separation as spiritual matricide, Robinson retorted that though the Church of England is our mother, "so may she be, and yet not the Lord's wife!"[172]

When the Scrooby Separatists arrived in Leiden late in the Spring of 1609, Robinson entered the main stream of Dutch intellectual life. He disputed publically with the Arminian theologian Episcopius and pastored a flock of nearly 300 at its height. When the decision to move to New England came, Robinson gave a farewell address based on Ezra (8:21) that by a fast "wee might humble ourselves before our God and seek of him a Right way for vs and our children."[173]

In his major work of 1610, Robinson argued for A Justification of Separation from the Church of England (Amsterdam: G. Thorp). At a crucial point in the argument, Robinson uses the triple office of Christ as King, Priest and Prophet. Each of these offices corresponds to acts of worship, i.e., government, prayer and preaching. Thus disciplining was central as well as prophecy.[174]

Congregational discipline based on the power of the keys in Matthew (18) lay at the heart of the Separatist quarrel with the English parish church. The purpose was positive, not only that more light might break forth from God's Word, but that God's people might experience as pilgrims and strangers on the earth what the writer of I Peter (2:9-12) penned.

> 9 But ye are a chosen generacion, a royal Priesthode, an holie nacion, a peculiar people, that ye shulde shew forthe the vertues of him that hathe called you out of darkenes into his maruelious light,
>
> 10 Which in time past were not a people, yet are now the people of God: which in time past were not vnder mercie, but now haue obteined mercie.
>
> 11 Derely beloued, I beseche you, as strangers and pilgrems absteine from fleshlie lustes, which fight against the soule,
>
> 12 And haue your conuersacion honest among the Gentiles, that they which speake euil of you as of euil

> doers, maye by your good workes which they shal se, glorifie God in the day of the visitacion.

The Geneva Bible (1560) on the definition of royal priesthood and holy nation appends to verse nine the comment: "That is partakers of Christes Priesthode and kingdome." By 1620 one would read the fresh note by Beza in Tomson's translation at verse 10:

> A reason why we ought to liue holily, to wit, because we are citizens of heauen, and therefore we ought to liue according to the Lawes not of this world, which is most corrupt, but of the heauenly citie, although we be strangers in the world."

D. English Baptists

John Robinson pastored the Scrooby body as they migrated from the lower Trent valley to Amsterdam and Leyden. Another group nearby at Gainsburough chose John Smyth as their pastor while yet in England and followed him to Amsterdam in 1608. Smyth had been a student of Johnson's at Christ's College, was elected to a fellowship and in 1600 was appointed a lecturer by the corporation of Lincoln. Because of his outspoken sermons Smyth was dismissed in October 1602.[175]

These sermons were published as The bright morning starre (1603) and an exposition of Psalm (22). In spite of his troubles with the authorities, Smyth was no separatist as late as March of 1606. Sometime between November 1606 and early autumn of 1607 Smyth was both pastor of the Gainsborough congregation and a separatist.[176] He was present at the Coventry home of Sir William Bowes together with John Robinson and Arthur Hildersham. At the start Francis Johnson and his views were the model for the Scrooby-Gainsborough groups who did not separate from the Amsterdam group until they were in the Netherlands. John Dayrell, a friend of Arthur Hildersham, published a 1617 Treatise of the Church in which he testifies to the identity of these groups.

> And here my dear countrymen, who lately are gone out from us, and become Anabaptists, I beseech you, consider of this one thing with me. When you first separated from the Church of England, did you not highly esteem and reverence the Church of Amsterdam, even as the dear

> spouse and body of Christ? would not you then gladly have had communion with them if possibly you could, when you refused the same with us? Did not then all of you assure your own souls that that way which then and still we call Brownism, was the only way to life, whereupon in that way you would needs walk, come on it what would, imprisonment or banishment, life or death? Did not some of the chief of you in my hearing magnify Mr. Francis Johnson, and their books specially the Apology above all books next to the Holy Bible?177

John Smyth (?1570-1612) published his first Separatist treatise in 1607. Principles and inferences concerning the visible Church speaks of a mututal covenant "betwixt God and the saints."[178] In 1608 Smyth separated from Johnson's congregation over the use of scripture, for as Johnson's group had taken away all the books of prayer, Smyth had taken away the scriptures even in the time of prophesying and singing. The central concern is the covenant, for which Smyth argued in terse language:

> Unto whom the covenant is giuen to the body of the Church... Therefore the power of binding and loosing is given to them.179

Smyth broke with the Separatist circle in 1609 when he published The Character of the beast and first baptised himself, Thomas Helwys and then the rest of the congregation by pouring water over the face.[180] Smyth was to die of consumption in August of 1612, but not before he divided his own church over application to join the Waterlanders, a Dutch Mennonite congregation in Amsterdam. To do this he must undergo a third baptism, and did in fact reject Calvinism. Thus in 1610 Smyth denounced original sin and double predestination. Watts holds the Mennonites responsible for this break with Calvinism, whereas others argue that Smyth knew of Peter Baro's challenge at Cambridge in the 1590s and the views of Jacob Arminius who died at Leiden in 1609.[181]

Smyth's actions so divided his church that Thomas Helwys and seven or eight others seceeded from it.[182] Helwys published A Declaration of Faith (1611) which repudiated the Arminianism of the Waterlanders and their refusal to take oaths or hold office.

Helwys rejected double predestination as well, for "God would have all men saued."[183] Lumpkin calls this document the first English Baptist confession of faith. Smyth's short confession in twenty articles announced the power of excomunication for the church, a theme which A Declaration speaks of in article seventeen.

> That Brethren impenitent in one sin after the admonition of the Church, are to bee excluded the communion off the Sainets. Mat. 18.17. I Cor.5.4.13. & therfore not the committing off sin doth cut off anie from the Church, but refusin to heare the Church to reformacion.184

In 1612 Helwys and his band returned to England where at Spitalfields they founded the first General Baptist Church on English soil. Helwys pled with James I for toleration, asking in the Mistery of Iniquity that men's religion "is betwixt God and themselues."[185] By 1616 Helwys was dead and his congregation entered on a shadowy existence for the next quarter century.[186]

The intent of exploring the Separatist tradition is not to seek for genetic explanations to justify sectarian concerns. Professor Collinson has rightly pled for a broader understanding of the dissenting tradition. When the varieties of concerns and vagaries of exile are all acounted for, one persistent concern surely remains: The Church of England was a false church. Thomas Cooper defended the English Church in his Admonition to the People of England (1589) with an appeal to recent memory.

> As touching the Gouernment of the Church of England, now defended by the Bishops, this I say. When God restored the doctrine of the Gospell more sincerely and more abundantly than ever before, under that good young Prince, King Edward 6, at which time not the governors onely of this Realme under him, but a nomber of other nobelmen & Gentlemen, were well knowen to be zealous in the favour of the trueth by consent of all the States of this Land, this maner of government that now is used, was by Lawe confirmed as good and godly. The Bishops and other of the clergie that gave their advise and consent to the same were learned and zealous, Bishop Cranmer, Ridley, Latimer, and many other, which after sealed their doctrine with their blood, all learned, grave and wise in comparison of these young sectaries which greatly please themselves.187

Stephen Bredwell, physician and eye-witness to many of Browne's activities, nicknamed him "Troublechurche Browne," one of whom it may be said that while "Browne is sound, his braine is sick."[188] The persistent charge against the Separatists was that they were schismatic. William Gilgate who joined Ainsworth's congregation and then defected from it, speaks in 1621 of suffering shipwreck in the gulf of separation. He was saved from drowning in those waves off Amsterdam "by Gods gracious hand."[189] A similar charge occurs in the 1607 Considerations by John Sprint, answered by Ainsworth in Counter poyson.

B.R. White has recently illuminated the shadows of English Baptist History from 1612 to 1644 and Tolmie has described the Triumph of The Saints prior to the Civil War.[190] It seems best therefore to proceed directly to 1644 when the seven churches of London known as Particular Baptists for their Calvinism, issued a public Confession of Faith in October 1644.

The Confession of Faith was signed by representatives of seven London separatist congregations. The first to sign were William Kiffin and Thomas Patience, representing the nucleus of those who in March had formed a church by withdrawing from Jessy's church. Henry Jessy was the third pastor of the Jacob church whose second pastor was John Lathrop, a Cambridge graduate who had become pastor in 1624. Henry Jessy was the successor to Lathrop, being offered the position in 1637.[191] Jessy's memorandum is part of the Stinton MS which transcribed the Jessy, Kiffin and Knollys memoranda in the eighteenth century.[192] Kiffin launched his career on October 17, 1642 by disputing baptism with Daniel Featley. Thus by 1642 the indigenous Puritan congregation founded by Henry Jacob gave rise to six separate churches in London.[193]

The title page of the 1644 Confession says "which are commonly (though falsely) called Anabaptists." Dr. White points out that twenty-six of the fifty-three articles restate the corresponding sections of the 1596 Confession often with small verbal changes.[194] Three new features are believers' baptism, less stress on ministry and absense of stated links between church and state.[195]

A fourth new feature was the section of twelve articles (XXI-XXXII) on the life of believers as God's elect. These twelve articles imply the five points of Calvinism defended at the Synod of Dort and mark these seven congregations as Calvinistic Baptists. Article 21 states "That Christ Jesus by his death did bring forth salvation and reconciliation onely for the elect, which were those which god the Father gave him." Article 22 says that "Faith is the gift of God wrought in the hearts of the elect by the Spirit of God..."[196] The entire Confession of 1644 moved to the left of its 1596 Separatist model, however, when it rejected any link with the State, weakened the authority of the ministry in the congregation and severed the children of members from any organic link with the disciple community.[197]

The second Confession came forth in 1646 as Featley's The Dippers Dipt passed through three editions by the end of 1645. The Baptists were upset over the range of associations given by Featley, with the engraved title-page of Libertines, Adamites, Melchiorites, Muncerians and Catharists among others. A revised Confession responded to Featley against the backdrop of an intellectual defense of a national Reformed church practicing believer's baptism as articulated by John Tombes. While Tombes supported the Baptist cause, millenarians like Thomas Kilcop transported it to a future second coming, urging that Robert Maton's writings be read. Paul Hobson set forth a mystical vision in three pamphlets bordering on bliss for the baptised. A Garden Inclosed of 1647 spoke of such souls as those "who from the enjoyment of a Christ within, is made able to belieue a Christ without."[198]

The second Confession was seized by the serjeant-at-Arms when on January 26, 1646, Samuel Richardson and Benjamin Cox handed copies to members as they entered the House of Commons. The Puritan clergy recognized its orthodoxy yet were sceptical that this handful spoke for the thousands of new Anabaptists who agreed more with German Anabaptism than this London Confession. So wrote Stephen Marshall in his A Defense of Infant-Baptism (1646): 75-76.

Finally, in 1651 thirty congregations presented a General Baptist statement in seventy-five articles.[199] Sixty-one authors drew up this document which speaks of "free grace" (article 37), "peace of conscience" (article 42), poor relief (article 57) and excommunication (article 68). The Fenstanton congregation responded to the disaster of one of its members in the spirit of article 57 of the 1651 confession. When John Wilson lost his barns, hay and buildings with grain in a fire of 1654, the congregation which discovered the loss to be £30 urged each church to send two messengers to Cambridge on December 8. It pledged £6 itself for restoring Wilson's property. These hearty Baptists responded to fires in the countryside as well as the flames of the Spirit in their concern for the poor of England.[200]

Chapter 18) Pilgrim Existence

A. John Bunyan (1628-1688)

> His whole life hee accounted a warfare, wherein Christ was his Captaine, his armes, prayers and teares. The Crosse his Banner, and his word vincit qui patitur.201

"He conquers who endures" describes well the career of John Bunyan, the tinker of Bedford, whose Puritan allegory like John Downame's Christian Warfare adopts that military metaphor as the controlling theme of an evangelical guide book. Pilgrim's Progress without a doubt is the best known piece from the pen of a seventeenth century English Separatist. It was a rare talent indeed that could turn Grace Abounding into the Anglo-Saxon style of Pilgrim's Progress. The similitudes of which he speaks on the title page of the first edition provides one with a biblical source for those images which God provides. Bunyan's text is taken from Hosea (12:10):

> I spoke to the prophets
> gaue them many visions
> and told parables through them. (N.I.V.)

Bunyan's vision is that of the living Christ, told in such powerful symbols that one must include his witness in a narrative which covers seventeenth century England.

John Bunyan was God's Englishman for non-conformist believers in seventeenth century England. His life from 1628 to 1688 spans a turbulent era in national political and religious life. Well known to his countrymen as an historian, poet and divine, Bunyan wished to be called simply a Christian. He excelled as a preacher. One wintry weekday morning twelve hundred came at 7:00 A.M. to hear him. The learned Dr. John Owen could entertain this tinker with a sigh to King Charles I that he would give up all his learning for the tinker's power to reach the heart.[202] That power to inspire devotion to Jesus Christ produces a flood of pamphlets and monographs each year on the lay preacher of the Bedford meeting house. They can be summed up in a phrase, a life of devotion.[203]

The Baptist Bibliography gives eight pages of entries to those works of Bunyan published by Baptists. Several hundred other cards are on file. Among Bunyan's many works most cited are the Puritan allegory Pilgrim's Progress and the spiritual autobiography Grace Abounding to the Chief of Sinners: Or, A Brief Relation of the exceeding mercy of God in Christ, to his poor Servant John Bunyan. The preface to the 1666 edition of Grace Abounding urges readers to remember the Word of Grace which first laid hold upon them. Hope permeates this simple relation of God's mercy to His servant John Bunyan. It concludes with these haunting words:

> The milk and honey is beyond this wilderness. God be merciful to you; and grant that you may not be slothful to go in to possess the land.204

Bunyan's England was a political and spiritual wilderness. Born at Elstow near Bedford in 1628, Bunyan died in 1688. Between his birth in the days of Parliamentary rumblings to his end in the year that Mary of Modena dashed Protestant hopes by presenting the Catholic James II with a son, Bunyan labored in prison, preached in parishes all over central England and wrote much about his spiritual pilgrimage. In the popular work of 1688 The Jerusalem Sinner Saved Bunyan went to the heart of the matter when he wrote:

> Thou hast experience of God's love, for that he has opened thine eyes to see thy sins: and for that he has given thee desires to be saved by Jesus Christ. For by thy sense of sin thou art made to see thy poverty of spirit, and that has laid thee under a sure ground to hope that heaven shall be thine hereafter.[205]

In 1199 William Buniun owned land a mile from Elstow and in 1327 William Boynon lived nearby. Little was left to pass on to John Bunyan's father except a cottage. John was the first child of a second marriage. His father mended pots and made kettles at Elstow. Whether a brazier as his father wished to be known or a tinker as John Bunyan described himself, both father and son were of humble though ancient origin in the Elstow parish of Bedfordshire. Bunyan called his descent, "most despised of all families of the land." He was never a gipsy. What little Bunyan learned at school with poormen's children never included Aristotle or Plato. Until his conversion Bunyan read the ballads and chapbooks which his peer group consulted, even showing the possible effect of that reading from works like Bevis of Southampton with its "ugly Gyant thirty foot in length and a foot between his eyebrows." At age sixteen he enlisted in 1644 in the parliamentary army, perhaps because his mother died in that year to be replaced in two months by a stepmother.[206]

The House of Commons presented Charles I with the Petition of Right in 1628, the year of Bunyan's birth. Charles claimed to owe no one but God alone an account of his actions. Existing liberties found their confirmation in the Petition, but for the King no new rights may be found in its four clauses. First of all, no man could after 1628 be taxed or otherwise support the Crown apart from an Act of Parliament; secondly, no free man could be imprisoned without shown cause; thirdly, soldiers and sailors might not be billeted without an owner's permission; finally, martial law for special commissions should be revoked. The House hoped to guard private property by prohibiting arbitrary arrest and taxation, to re-establish Justices of the Peace in local shires, and to prevent the monarch from building a standing army. Charles mulcted his citizens nonetheless by myriad schemes to balance the budget.

Foreign policy fueled political dissent, for if the Hapsburgs won the Thirty Years' War in Europe a generation of Englishmen who had read John Foxe's <u>Book of Martyrs</u> would fear for their religious liberties in England as well as civic unrest. In 1637 Popery seemed to encroach on protestant liberties when a papal agent was received at court for the first time since the days of the Catholic Queen Mary Tudor.

Charles I so alienated the propertied classes that in 1639 tax payers went on strike. All awaited the Parliament of 1640 which at once impeached Archbishop Laud and the Earl of Strafford who was executed in May, 1641. The profits from the Earl's public career as much as his Spanish policy led to his fall. The first battle of the Civil War came on October 23; the Irish rebellion broke in November, 1641; then the New Model Army replaced the ill-advised and indecisive forces. A young leader in the Easter Association helped Parliament to win with Scottish aid at the Battle of Marston Moor in July 1644. Oliver Cromwell rose to lead the New Model Army as Parliament executed Archbishop Laud in January, 1645. The distraught young Bunyan entered public life as a soldier in the New Model Army in 1644.

Radical religion swept the English countryside. Millennial preachers used social unrest as a platform to advance their strange futuristic views at the expense of a guillable laity and for their own personal profit. Turmoil swept over England as first political waves then economic storms and at last the intellectual hurricane of Copernicus battered men's minds. In 1640 this resulted in two desires; that liberty might replace tyranny and godliness supplant idolatry.

At the end of the 1640s came the Levellers and their radical communistic cousins, the Diggers. After liberty came the godly Fifth Monarchists, combining economic and religious fervour in a haze of quasi-biblical millennial dreams.[207] After the execution of Charles I in 1649 Oliver Cromwell himself followed these evangelical political revolutionaries until 1653. These Fifth Monarchists seemed to be on the threshold of political power in the Parliament of 1653.[208] Their use of the Old Testament Book of Daniel to predict the millennial advent of the Messiah satisfied the enthusiasm and rampant anti-intellectualism of free congregations unhappy with rigid worship and ordained clergy. Barred from the pinnacles of society, perhaps these millennial dreamers found a spiritual superiority in their non-conformist theology. At any rate it did compensate for their material frustrations, though in many cases the air of superiority when breathed too deeply made these saints light and empty-headed indeed. Still, such visions of the planet earth which had held hope for the disenchanted Jews in the revolt of 165 B.C. as well as for modern American cults cannot always be dismissed as irrational.

In the religious realm of what Cohn called The Pursuit of the Millennium, none have matched John Bunyan's prose since 1656, and the year of his first work titled, Some Gospel Truths Opened. The political, economic and social schemes of Levellers, Diggers and Fifth Monarchists met a different response from the Quakers. Bunyan's first work tried to silence these quietists whose mysticism seemed to Bunyan to ignore scripture. Some Gospel-truths Opened (1656) goes on in its full title to say that it answers several questions by "those blustering storms of the Devils temptations, which do at this day, like so many Scorpions, break loose from the bottomless pit, to bite and torment those that have not tasted the vertue of Jesus by the revelation of the Spirit of God."[209]

trary promised his Boston saints a new world of Christ's kingdom, not the old world of Adam's Eden preached in Shepard's Newtown.[250]

Williams cared much for the Indians of New England. Though his letters to Winthrop chart the movements of hostile tribesmen, Williams also began to learn their languages in order to preach Christ among them. Internal problems of Rhode Island came to a head in 1643 over a land association and four separate settlements. Williams answered such legal questions by seeking an English charter for a new colony. That year Parliament faced the agony of civil war and the relationship of church to state. On board ship headed to England Williams wrote his Key into the Language of America, the first study printed in English of Indian customs.

> Boast not, proud English, of thy birth & blood,
> Thy brother Indian is by birth as Good.
> Of one blood God made Him and Thee and All,
> As wise, as fair, as strong, as personal.
>
> By nature wrath's his portion, thine no more
> Till Grace his soule and thine in Christ restore
> Make sure thy second birth, else thou shalt see,
> Heaven ope to Indians wild, but shut to thee.251

With the help of Sir Henry Vane, Williams gained a charter for Rhode Island. In the midst of debate, travel and stay in England, Williams published his celebrated tract, The Bloudy Tenent of Persecution (1644). It was aimed at John Cotton. A key phrase occurs where Williams writes:

> In vain have English Parliaments permitted English Bibles in the poorest English houses, and the simplest man or woman to search the Scriptures, if yet against their soules perswasion from the Scripture, they should be forced (as if they lived in Spaine or Rome it selfe without the sight of a Bible) to beleeve as the Church beleeves.252

What right impelled the Puritans to deny liberty of conscience to seekers after God's truth in the Bible? Cotton could claim that Williams saw the scriptures wrongly. Mysteriously a 1636 letter by John Cotton appeared in London shortly before Williams answered it in 1644. This Mr. Cottons Letter Lately Printed, Examined and Answered raised the issue of biblical interpretation. Williams refuted Cotton's exegesis. The church of the Jews in the Old Testament type and the Christian church in the New Testament antitype "were both separate from the world."

The testy response to Williams which Cotton called The Bloudy Tenent washed, and made white in the bloud of the Lambe (1647) led to Williams' rejoinder of 1652, The Bloody Tenent yet more Bloody by Mr. Cotton's endevour to wash it white in the blood of the Lambe, etc. One should turn to the Bloudy Tenent to sample the argument for himself. One such example responds to arguments that "soule-killers" should be cut off by civil magistrates. Williams objects that on the contrary,

> The Soules of all men in the World are either naturally dead in Sin, or alive in Christ. If dead in sinne, no man can kill them, nor more than he can kill a dead man: Nor is it a false Teacher or false Religion that can so much prevent the means of Spirituall life, as one of these two; either the force of a materiall sword, imprisoning the Soules of men in a State or Nationall Religion, Ministry or Worship; or secondly, Civill warres and combustions for Religion sake, whereby men are immediately cut off without any longer meanes of Repentance.253

Roger Williams' orthodoxy shone through the Bloody Tenent when he wrote that four foundations supported Christian faith in the New Testament. The cornerstone is Christ on whom all persons, doctrines or practices depend. The church is built on ministerial foundations of the Apostles and Prophets. Thirdly, future rejoicing in the fruits of obedience and finally, correct doctrine complete this quadrilateral. The doctrines are repentence from dead works, faith toward God, baptism, laying on of hands, the resurrection and eternal judgment. Williams could not himself condemn tens of thousands of true believers on doctrinal distinctions between essential and non-essential beliefs.

In the dialogue between Peace and Truth, Williams' Bloudy Tenent returns to distinctions between type and anti-type. Former types of the land in Old Testament times were spiritual governors, not civil magistrates. The "top of the tedious discourse" comes when Truth bursts out:

> Deare Peace, Habacuck's Fishes keep their constant bloody game of & Persecutions & in the World's mighty Ocean; the greater taking plundring, swallowing up the lesser: O, happy he whose portion is the God of Iacob! who hath nothing to lose under the Sun, but hath a State, a House, an Inheritance, a Name, a Crowne, a Life, past all the Plunderers', Ravishers', Murtherers' reach and fury!254

Habakkuk (1:13) laments that evil men prey on the righteous and swallow them up. Verses 14-17 describe the Neo-Babylonians of C. 600 B.C. who catch men in their nets and slay nations continuously (vss. 15-17). Here the type is that of secular persecutors. The antitype would be the English civil magistrate who is likewise evil. That was bold exegesis indeed. Williams extends this pattern to Christ when he writes:

> I adde, God will take away such stayes on whom Gods people rest, in his wrath, that King David, that is, Christ Iesus the Antitype, in his own Spirituall power in the hands of the Saints, may spiritually and for ever be advanced.255

John Cotton used scripture and historical precedent to reject the arguments for toleration advanced in the Bloudy Tenent. One can even understand why Cotton's grandson Cotton Mather rejected Williams in his 1702 Magnalia Christi Americana. What prompted such fierce defense of Puritan privilege?

John Cotton (1584-1652) arrived at Trinity College, Cambridge in 1597 as Queen Elizabeth still rejected Calvin's polity but permitted his doctrine. John Cotton learned two lessons at Trinity, one political and the other religious. When he matriculated at age thirteen it was a cautious time for reformers. Compromise with the establishment even aided poor students in parish placement on graduation. This political lesson Cotton learned well.

The religious lesson came from William Perkins who taught the awesome penalty of the law against sin even under the covenant of grace. Conversion by grace alone stirred young Cotton.

A fellowship at Emmanuel made him a Puritan. In 1612 John Cotton began his first pastorate in Lincolnshire where his reputation as a preacher grew for twenty years. At Boston in southern England his fame spread so much that he was invited to preach the farewell sermon to the largest body of colonists yet to sail for America. The new governor John Winthrop was there to hear Cotton preach from II Samuel (7:10).

> Moreover I will appoint a place for my people Israell, and I will plant them, that they may dwell in a place of their owne, and move no more.

The passengers on the Arbella learned that their going was holy and that they must cling to true religion. By this Cotton meant to warn against separatism.

Small wonder that when Cotton himself came to new Boston (1633) he would debate with Roger Williams. In his initial letter of 1636 Cotton pressed the point that Williams had banished himself. The previous year Cotton had received a letter from England asking him to comment on a treatise which was the first part of William's Bloudy Tenent. In answering the biblical argument Cotton claimed that whilst the field of wheat and tares in the parable of Matthew (13) was the church, the tares were hypocrites but not heretics. The sum of his historical refutation appealed to Calvin who had Servetus executed for persistent heresy.

John Cotton could not defend either liberty of conscience or democracy. If one were a heretic he was sinning against his own conscience; if the people were governors, who then should be governed? Only just cause could permit the parallel structure of the State to interfere in matters of religion. One such cause was the need to save heretics from their vices, while Roger Williams sought to save the saints from their virtues. Williams argued first that predestination prevented the elect from either falling into heresy or being compelled by the state to remain in the church. Williams forced Cotton to defend a theology in which some were outwardly purified and others inwardly sanctified.

Apostasy would then arise as men fell away from the former; orthodoxy, as men adhered to the latter.

That Williams ranted against the Quaker George Fox shows him not indifferent to doctrine. When Fox visited Providence with his inner-light doctrine, Williams was cordial. Later in 1676 he wrote a fiery tract against three Quaker apostles. In George Fox, Digg'd out of his Burrows, as in his support of the Indian wars, one can see that Williams was no pacifist. Then, too, the Quaker Christ was but half a Christ to Williams, an image in the mystical sense only. To set up an inner Christ to replace the external problems of life or the mental furniture of theologians was to empty the faith of meaning.

Williams asked Fox whether the Christ who suffered at Jerusalem was the same inner Christ of mystical experience. Is the outer Christ the real person who died a literal death on a material cross in a real Jerusalem? The hermeneutical question which Williams raised is crucial to his thought. Fox is like the Jesuit whose cousins are the Quakers. Both hedge about scripture with spiritual, allegorical and mystical illusions. When Williams argued for toleration in religious matters he was not thereby indifferent to theological questions.

Williams in the Bloudy Tenent and in other writings argues four clear theses: (1) the Church is fallen; (2) Christ will restore the Church; (3) the American aborigine needs the Gospel; (4) nature and grace are to be clearly separate. Williams in all of these issues would seem to argue that civil power belongs to the people. Williams belongs to seventeenth century English Puritanism and Separatism in which his intellectual courage set him apart from other men. Though we may praise Williams for our religious liberty, his tribute and greatness lie in his robust mind. "He dared to think."

B. Taxonomy of Toleration

Religious toleration meant the support of persons like Anne Hutchinson and Samuel Gorton. One should look briefly at each to ascertain the diversity of religious pluralism which Williams sets with his typological arguments for toleration. New England Puritans convened often to look into their souls.[256] Lay participation in these exercises was granted legal protection in both Massachusetts and Connecticut Colonies and was supported by prominent clergy such as John Cotton, Thomas Hooker and John Eliot.[257]

Though John Cotton delighted at Mrs. Hutchinson's proficiency at helping the saints, her message soon enough criticized the clergy and their sermons. What was honed in private exercises was turned on the indulgent clergy. Winthrop did accuse her of creating the uproar through the conferences.[258] Antinomian as a term used to describe this uproar is a loose label to apply to those so completely transformed by saving grace as to style themselves "white raiment Christians."[259] The English Antinomians were Eatonites, self-styled disciples of John Eaton, sometime vicar of Wickham Market in Suffolk. His followers such as John Eachard and John Traske kept this message of "free justification" alive in the 1630s.[260] The key seems to have been a high view of baptism which bestowed saving grace. This direct contact with the Holy Ghost denigrated the legal faith of the non-mystical Puritan spiritual brotherhood.

Others charged Mrs. Hutchinson with Grindletonian tendancies imbibed from that Yorkshire perfectionist group under the direction of Robert Brierley during the late 1620s. Winthrop went so far as to accuse her of belief in a "naked Christ" who so filled the soul that lustfull thoughts were crowded out. In his Short Story (1645) he said her's was a desperate cry:

> Here is a great stirre about graces and looking to hearts... I seeke not for sanctification, but for Christ, tell me not of mediation and duties, but tell me of Christ.261

Christopher Hill observes that such religious radicals "thought that sin had been invented by the ruling class to keep the poor in order."[262]

The counter-offensive suspected that such "free justification" was an offer of conversion without fear and trembling, sainthood without suffering and enthusiasm with eccentricity, especially among naive women.[263] The crisis over Anne Hutchinson was especially virulent.[264] During her examination before the General Court, Hutchinson charged that the minsters were teaching the letter and not the spirit, were preaching a covenant of works and not of grace and that they "had not the seal of the Spirit."[265] Cotton appears to be a crypto-sectary in this matter.[266] Cotton's preaching in the year of 1633 touched off a religious revival in Boston which lasted until 1636.

Anne Hutchinson stood before the Boston congregation to join its renewed membership on November 1, 1634. She had come across the Atlantic on the Griffin from Lincolnshire where her husband was well esteemed.[267] Born in 1591, Anne was the daughter of an Anglican pastor (Francis Marbury) in Alford in Lancaster. In 1605 the family moved to London where Anne married William Hutchinson from Alford in 1612. They returned to Alford where for twenty-two years they lived near Boston where John Cotton preached at St. Botalph's. Nearby at Bilsby John Wheelwright who married Anne's sister-in-law preached a similar message to that of Cotton, reinforcing the growth of conventicles in which dark places of the scripture were debated and sermons repeated.[268]

Clashes began in 1635 with the General Court moving against John Wheelwright in March of 1637 and banishing him in November. Finally it was Anne's turn to be banished and in March of 1638 she was tried for heresy in the Boston Church and excommunicated. She and some followers moved to Aquidneck Island where a town they built became Portsmouth. Samuel Gorton arrived to trouble the sectarians and was himself banished. Winthrop summed up the hearing of October 1637 by saying that the divisions among them were the result of "the vanity of some weake minds."[269] At the climax of her trial, Anne Hutchinson responded in eloquent words about her experience under the sermons of Cotton and Wheelwright in old England.

> When I was in old England, I was much troubled at the constitution of the Churches there, so farre, as I was ready to have joyned to the Separation, whereupon I set apart a day for humiliation by my selfe, to seeke direction from God, and then did God discover unto me the unfaithfulnesse of the Churches, and the danger of them, and that none of those Ministers could preach the Lord Jesus aright, for he had brought to my mind, that in the I John 4.3. Every spirit that confesseth not, that Jesus Christ is come in the flesh, is the spirit of Antichrist; I marvelled what this should meane... then it was revealed to me that the Ministers of England were these Antichrists, but I knew not how to beare this, I did in my heart rise up against it... after I had begged this light, a twelve moneth together, at last he let me see... how I did turne in upon a Covenant of works and did oppose Christ Jesus.270

During the excommunication hearings Anne recanted her errors of expression but not errors in judgement. When she was commanded to withdraw as a leper out of the Congregation, Anne turned at the door to reject her accusers' power:

> The Lord judgeth not as man judgeth, better to be cast out of the Church than to deny Christ.271

Samuel Gorton stands as a second example of the types which toleration under Roger Williams would let loose on the theological horizon. Born around 1592 in Gorton near Manchester, Samuel Gorton made his way to London as a clothier.[272] In 1637 he arrived in Boston at the height of the Hutchinsonian furor. Gorton quickly moved to Plymouth where charges of mutiny and heresy soon surfaced.

The wife of Ralph Smith, the colony's minister, frequented Gorton's home for daily prayer. The familiar scenario from Boston was being presented in Plymouth: lay preaching, private scenes and female discussion of sermons. Plymouth banished Gorton to Aquidneck (1639) where the Hutchinsons were settled. He was so swiftly repudiated there that he went to Providence where even Williams complained about his "poyson" and "bewitching and bemadding poor Providence."[273] Because this letter seems inconsistent with Williams' witness for toleration it may not be authentic. Winthrop intervened as Gorton barely if at all restrained himself in an immoderate reply. Gorton moved south to what became Warwick where he purchased land.

Gorton published his theological views on his return to England in the mid-1640s. Gorton belonged to the culture of Antinomians as did William Dell, William Edbury and John Saltmarsh.[274] The latter's 1646 work Free Grace contrasted the oldness of the Letter with the newness of the Spirit, while Dell spelled out the political implications of true saints rooting out carnal magistrates in his 1652(?) The Crucified and Quickened Christian. More recently Gura has traced links between Gurton and Thomas Lamb's General Baptist church in Bell Alley off Coleman Street. Gorton often preached there while in London.[275] Gorton also met in Sister Stag's conventicle to accord women a spiritual equality rare for the time.[276]

C. Courage and Conviction

Williams' letter of 1670 to Major John Mason when Massachusetts invaded Rhode Island sums up the quality of Williams' daring wilderness experiment. Williams reminds Major Mason that Governor Winthrop in 1637 steered him among the Indians, that Governor Winslow of Plymouth permitted him to occupy land across the Bay and that Governor Bradford confirmed that freedom which Williams repayed as an agent in the Pequot War. Then Williams urges Mason to return with his troops.

> Besides, Sir, the matter with us is not about these children's toys of land, meadows, cattle, government, etc. But here, all over this colony, a great number of weak and distressed souls, scattered, are flying hither from Old and New England; the Most High and Only Wise hath, in His infinite wisdom, provided this country and this corner as a shelter for the poor and persecuted, according to their several persuasions.277

John Cotton's biographer finds that Cotton's doctrine led to a state which was intolerable as well as intolerant. I would not agree that Williams tended to destroy any formal church gathering whatsoever. Church and State are separated in his thought and practice in order to insulate the spiritual from the secular.

Conversion of the conscience would seem to be a crucial issue at stake between the Reverend John Cotton of Boston and Roger Williams of Providence. It was more than the quarrel of two Cambridge graduates of Pembroke and Trinity colleges.

Williams sought to preserve the continuity of religious experience between Richard Greenham's godly parish at Dry Drayton near Cambridge and Providence in Rhode Island colony, as did John Cotton between the godly puritanism of Old England and the separatist colonies of New England. Neither geography nor theology can explain away the different solutions advanced to preserve that continuity. By 1662 a man could become a member of the church in two ways: through the Covenant of Grace, i.e., conversion, or through the covenant of the church, i.e., natural birth to Christian parents. As Perry Miller put the issue in The New England Mind, this duality was sure to divide and conquer puritanism. The dilemma in Miller's terms is that if works are sought after as a pattern of righteousness, man is subjected to necessity and thereby "freedom and faith are destroyed." When Roger Williams urged freedom for faith where John Cotton would enforce it, the issue took on a larger dimension.

Castellio found Calvin's Achilles heel when he attacked the execution of Servetus in Concerning Heretics. Beza showed the limits of intolerance when in 1574 he did not wish to alienate the Zurich theologians over the case of John Sylvanus in Heidelberg. When the arm of the state replaces the arm of the Almighty to purify men's lives, then the will of the Lord is frustrated. Christianity, as Williams argued cogently, is courage and conviction. His favorite biblical passage may well have been John (8:36) which neither John Cotton could enforce not George Fox could cause to evaporate into a mystical presence.

> If the Son shall make you free -- then shall you indeed be free... For where the Spirit of the Lord is, there is true liberty.

The shadow of Servetus was dispelled in Rhode Island as the comfort extended to Anne Hutchinson and the toleration for feminine prayers in Providence shone under the greater light from God's holy word.[278] Americans have learned from Roger Williams not to enforce theology by the sword and thereby quench the spirit in men and women alike. What remains is the most difficult lesson of all: theology must not be used to support the sword nor to suppress feminine believers.

END NOTES to SECTION VI

[1]Roland H. Bainton, Hunted Heretic. The Life and Death of Michael Servetus 1511-1553 (Boston: Beacon Press., 1953), p.128.

[2]Ibid., p.129

[3]T.H.L. Parker, John Calvin: A Biography (Philadelphia: Westminster Press, 1975), p.119.

[4]McNeill/Battles II. X.1 (p.429).

[5]Ibid., p.493

[6]John Calvin, Commentaries on the Catholic Epistles, translated by John Owen (Grand Rapids: Baker reprint, 1979), p.158.

[7]Baker reprint 1979, Vol. XVII of Commentaries, p.26.

[8]Philip Edgcumbe Hughes, editor and translator, The Register of the Company of Pastors of Geneva in the time of Calvin (Grand Rapids: William B. Eerdmans Publishing Co., 1966), pp.223-284.

[9]Jerome Friedman, Michael Servetus. A Case Study in Total Heresy (Genève: Librairie Droz S.A., 1978), p.113.

[10]Ibid., p.115

[11]Ibid., p.136

[12]Ibid., pp.124-125

[13]Institutes (McNeil/Battles) II. XIV.5 (p.487).

[14]Elisabeth Feist Hirsch, "Michael Servetus and the Neoplatonic Tradition. God, Christ and Man," Bibliothèque D'Humanisme et Renaissance XLII (1980), p.567. Restitutes, p.109.

[15]Institutes (McNeil/Battles) II, XIV,8 (p.493).

[16]Parker, op.cit., p.86.

[17]Joseph Le Cler, Toleration and The Reformation (London: Longmans, 1960), I: 338.

[18]Roland Bainton, "The Parable of the Tares as the proof text for Religious Liberty," Church History II (1933): 67-89.

[19]Le Cler I: 342

[20]Uwe Plath, "Sebastiani Castellionis annotationes ad Johannis Calvini Institutiones christianae religionis anno 1553 excusas," Bibliothèque D'Humanisme Et Renaissance XXXVII (1975), p.88.

[21]Le Cler I: 345 and 347.

[22]Le Cler I: 366 from Castellio's Contra libellum Calvini.

[23]P.G. Bietenholz, "Mino Celsi and the Toleration Controversy of the sixteenth century," Bibliothèque D'Humanisme Et Renaissance XXXII (1972): 31-48.

[24]W.K. Jordan, The Development of Religious Toleration in England (Gloucester: Peter Smith, 1965) I: 303-365.

[25]Ibid., p.318.

[26]Patrick Collinson, Archbishop Grindal, pp.135-137 and 151-152.

[27]"ut vincat ipse, non ut vincat veritas." Satanae Stratagemata Book VI, p.267.

[28]Le Cler I: 375.

[29]Irwin Horst, The Radical Brethren. Anabaptism and The English Reformation to 1558 (Nieuwkoop: B. De Graaf, 1972), pp.49-50. See also pp. 185-189.

[30]Ibid., pp.51-52.

[31]Ibid., p.58.

[32]J.F. Davis, "Lollardy and the Reformation in England," Archiv für Reformationsgeschichte 73 (1982), p.223. See Davis, Heresy and Reformation in the South East of England 1520-1559 (London: Royal Historical Society, 1983), p.55 for the trial and confessions of John Tewksbury before Tunstal (1527/29/31).

[33]Christopher Clement, "The English Radicals and their theology, 1535-1565," Cambridge Univ. Ph.D., 1980, p.226.

[34]Davis, op. cit., pp.224-224. On Crowley see John N. King, English Reformation Literature (Princeton: Princeton Univ. Press, 1982), pp.319-357.

[35]A.G. Dickens, The English Reformation (New York: Schocken, 1964), p.29.

[36]Ibid., p.34.

[37]Davis, "Lollardy ....", pp.228-229.

[38]Ibid., p.230. Dickens, op.cit., pp.70-71.

[39]Ibid., p.231.

[40]Ibid., pp.233-234.

[41]Dickens, op.cit., p.35.

[42]Horst, op.cit., p.108.

[43]Ibid., p.110.

[44]Ibid., p.111.

[45]Ibid., p.129.

[46]Zurich Letters (Second Series), edited by Hastings Robinson (Cambridge: At the Univ. Press, M.DDDD.XLV), p.237.

[47]G.C. Gorham, Gleanings of a Few Scattered Ears, During the Period of the Reformation in England and of the times immediately succeeding, A.D. 1533 to A.D. 1588 (London: Bell and Daldy, 1857), pp.481-482.

[48]William Turner, A Preseruative or Triacle agaynst the Poyson of Pelagius, lately renued by the furious secte of the Annabaptistes (London: S. Mierdman for A. Hester, 1551), sig. K6^{r-v}.

[49]Peter Martyr Vermilius, Common Places (1583), sig. Kkiii^{r}. John Knox, Works (Edinburgh: Ballentine Club, MDCCCLXVI) V: 222-223.

[50]Ibid., sig. Kkiii^{v}.

[51]Clement, op.cit., p.174. Cited in Turner, Preseruative, sig. M8^{r-v}.

[52]Turner, op.cit., sig. K3^{r}. Clement, p.209.

[53]Clement, op.cit., p.211

[54]Ibid., p.213.

[55]Knox, Works V: 37.

[56]Clement, op.cit., p.226.

[57]J.W. Martin, "English Protestant Separatism at its Beginnings: Henry Hart and the Free-Will Men," Sixteenth Century Journal VII (1976), p.59.

[58]Ibid., p.73.

[59]Clement, op.cit., pp.265-285.

[60]Ibid., p.312.

[61]B.R. White, The English Separatist Tradition (Oxford: Oxford Univ. Press, 1971), p.2.

[62]Ibid., p.12. Foxe VIII: 488.

[63]Ibid., p.24.

64 Ibid., p.25.

65 Patrick Collinson, Archbishop Grindal, p.178.

66 John King, English Reformation Literature, p.331.

67 Ibid., p.432.

68 H.G. Owen, "A Nursery of Elizabethan Nonconformity, 1567-1572," Journal of Ecclesiastical History XVII (1966), p.68.

69 Robert Crowley, A Briefe discourse/against the outwarde apparell/and Ministring garmen-/tes of the popishe church.

70 Henry Stalbrydge (Robert Crowley), THE EPISTLE EX=/hortatorye of an Englyshe/Christiane unto his derelye beloued con=/treye of Englande/against the pompou=/se popyshe Bysshoppes thereof/as yet/the true members of theyr fylthye fa=/ther the great Antichrist of Ro=/me. (Antwerpe, widow of C. Ruremond, 1544?), sig. Avi^{r}. Reprinted twice at Antwerp (1544) and London (1548).

71 Ibid., sig. Bvi^{r-v}.

72 Champlin Burrage, The Early English Dissenters In the Light of Recent Research (1550-1641) (Cambridge: At the Univ. Press, 1912) II: 9-11.

73 S.T.C.2 21683. See John Strype, Memorials of the Reformation VII: 66-67 for defense of justification by free grace.

74 A.G. Dickens, "The English Reformation and the English Public House," lecture of May 9, 1984 at Merton College, Oxford.

75 Burrage, II: 13.

76 loc.cit.

77 Ibid., p.14.

78 Ibid., p.18.

79 B.R. White, "A Puritan Work by Robert Browne," Baptist Quarterly XVIII (1959), p.116.

80 G.R. Elton, "Persecution and Toleration in the English Reformation," p.173 in W.J. Sheils, editor, Persecution and Toleration (Oxford: Basil Blackwell, 1984). Cf. V. Norskov Olsen, John Foxe and The Elizabethan Church (Berkeley: Univ. of California Press, 1973), pp.197-219.

81 Ibid., p. 176.

[82] Ibid., pp. 177-78.

[83] Ibid., p. 187.

[84] John Taylor, A/Svvarme/Of/Sectaries, And/Schismatiques:/ Wherein is discouvered the strange prea-/ching (or prating) of such as are by their trades/Coblers, Tinkers, Pedlers, Weavers, Sow-/gelders, and Chymney-Sweepers (London: 1641), p.7.

[85] Taylor, op.cit., p.82.

[86] LVCIFERS/Lacky,/Or,/The devils new Creature./Being/The true Character of a dissembling/Brownist, whose life is hypocriticall, instructi/ons Schismaticall, thoughts dangerous, Actions/ malicious, and opinions impious./[eight lines + ornament] (London: John Greensmith, 1641), sig. A3.

[87] Puritan Manifestoes, edited by W.H. Frere and C.E. Douglas (London: Church Historical Society, 1907/1972 reprint), p.112.

[88] "Browne, Robert (1550?-1633?)," Dictionary of National Biography III: 57.

[89] Ibid., p.58.

[90] H.C. Porter, Reformation and Reaction in Tudor Cambridge, p.244.

[91] Dictionary of National Biography III: 59.

[92] On Norwich see Albert Peel, The Brownists in Norwich and Norfolk about 1580 (Cambridge: At the Univ. Press, 1920), p.3.

[93] M.M. Knappen, Tudor Puritanism (Chicago: Univ. of Chicago Press: 1939), p.307.

[94] Burrage, Early English Dissenters I: 98-99.

[95] Williston Walker, The Creeds and Platforms of Congregationalism (Boston: Pilgrim Press, 1960 reprint), p.13.

[96] Ibid., p.18.

[97] The Writings of Robert Harrison and Robert Browne, edited by Albert Peel and Leland Carlson (London: George Allen & Unwin Ltd., 1953), pp.173-174.

[98] Ibid., p.175.

[99] Ibid., p.176.

[100] Ibid., p.177.

[101] Ibid., p.181.

[102] Ibid., p.218.

[103] Ibid., pp.219-220.

[104] Lisa Jardine, "Humanism and Dialectic in Sixteenth-Century Cambridge," in R.R. Bolger, editor, Classical Influences on European Culture A.D. 1500-1700 (Cambridge: At the Univ. Press, 1976), pp.141-154.

[105] A Treatise of the church and the Kingdome of Christ, in Peel and Carlson, pp.31ff.

[106] Ibid., pp.119-120.

[107] Dictionary of National Biography III: 60.

[108] Zurich Letters I: 235. February 12, 1571 at Ely. Martyr's letter was in response to two letters from John Fox commenting on the Frankfort fuss over the Prayerbook. Strype, Memorials (1816) VII: 151-154.

[109] Ibid., p.237.

[110] J.T. Cliffe, The Puritan Gentry, pp.80-81.

[111] "Greenwood, John (d. 1593)," Dictionary of National Biography VIII: 527.

[112] The Writings of John Greenwood 1587-1590 edited by Leland H. Carlson (London: George Allen and Unwin Ltd., 1962), pp.121-127.

[113] Ibid., p.127.

[114] Ibid., p.99.

[115] Ibid., p.99

[116] George Gifford, A Plaine Declaration (1590), sig. $K3^r$.

[117] John Greenwood, A Brief Refutation (1591) in The Writings of John Greenwood and Henry Barrow 1591-1593, edited by Leland H. Carlson (London: George Allen and Unwin Ltd., 1970), p.37.

[118] Ibid., p.37.

[119] J.E. Neale, Elizabeth I And Her Parliaments 1584-1601 (London: Jonathan Cape, 1958), p.291.

[120] Diarmaid MacCulloch, "Catholic and Puritan in Elizabethan Suffolk," Archiv für Reformationsgeschichte 72(1981), pp.267-269.

[121] Patrick Collinson, "The Godly: aspects of Popular Protestantism," in Godly People. Essays on English Protestantism (London: Hambledon Press, 1984), pp.2-3.

[122] White, *op.cit.*, p.85.

[123] *Ibid.*, p.84.

[124] Porter, *Reformation and Reaction in Tudor Cambridge*, p.142.

[125] William Bradford, *First Dialogue* in White, *op.cit.*, p.93.

[126] On the Middelburgh saga see Keith L. Sprunger, *Dutch Puritanism* (Leiden: E.J. Brill, 1982), pp.24-34.

[127] George Johnson, *A discours of some troubles*, p.95.

[128] White, *op.cit.*, p.114.

[129] *Ibid.*, p.111. AN APOLOGIE/OR DEFENCE/OF SUCH TRVE CHRISTIANS/as are commonly (but vniustly) called/Brovvnists:/[15 lines] (1604), sig. A2^{v}-D3^{r}.

[130] A.F. Johnson, "The Exiled English Church at Amsterdam and its Press," *The Library*, Fifth Series V (1951), p.225.

[131] *AN APOLOGIE* (1604), sig. C3^{v}.

[132] *Ibid.*, sig. A4^{v}.

[133] *Ibid.*, sig. B4^{v}.

[134] Murray Tolmie, *The Triumph of The Saints* (Cambridge: At the Univ. Press, 1977), pp.3-4.

[135] cf. Richard Bancraft, *Daungerous Positions and Proceedings* (London: 1593), p.183: "Beware of such sectaries, as (under their many both godly and goodly pretences) do seditiously indevour to disturbe the land."

[136] John von Rohr, "The Congregationalism of Henry Jacob," *Transactions of the Congregational Historical Society* XIX (1962), p.107.

[137] John von Rohr, "*Extra Ecclesiam Nulla Salus*: An Early Congregational Version," *Church History* XXXVI (1967), pp.117-119.

[138] *Admissions Register 1517-1647* MS. Oxford college archives.

[139] Burrage, *Early English Dissenters* II: 146-148.

[140] *Ibid.*, p.151.

[141] Roger Manning, *Religion and Society in Elizabethan Sussex* (Leicester: Leicester Univ. Press, 1969), p.208.

[142]Stinton MS, "A Repository," p.2. See B.R. White, "Who Really Wrote the 'Kiffin Manuscript?'," Baptist History and heritage I, no. 3 (1967), 3-10 and 14.

[143]loc.cit. See Tolmie, op.cit., pp.7-12.

[144]What follows is adapted with permission from Stephen Brachlow, "Puritan Theology and Radical Churchmen in Pre-Revolutionary England," unpublished D. Phil. thesis, Oxford Univ. (1979), pp.199-206. Since its incorporation here, Brachlow himself has published an updated version in the Journal of Ecclesiastical History 36 (1985): 228-54.

[145]Reasons taken ovt of Gods Word (1604), p.53.

[146]Ibid. "To the high and mightie Prince Iames," sig. A, fol. 2^r.

[147]Exposition of the 2d. commandement, sig. D, fol. 6^v.

[148]Attestation, p.151.

[149]Sundry matters, sig. B, fol. 4^v.

[150]Divine beginning, sig. D, fol. 8^v. Elsewhere he described Christ as "the Teacher and Lawgiver... of his Church... in that same respect wherein Moses was so excellent and faithful a servant" (Ibid., sig. F, fols. 1^v-2^r). Jacob, like other radicals, admitted that some ecclesiastical matters were indifferent, but these were peripheral matters (e.g. time, place, ceremonies like footwashing and love feasts) and themselves highly circumscribed by either general rules of Scripture or natural reason (Reasons, "To the high and mightie Prince Iames," sig. A, fol. 2^r., and pp.11-12). For Jacob, as indeed for most radicals, there would be very little room for variety among biblically organized churches.

[151]Exposition of the 2d. commandement, sig. B, fol. 1^{r-v}., and sig. E, fol. 7^r.

[152]Jacob's attraction to the theology of Perkins can be seen most visibly in the fact that much of his catechism of c. 1605 (Burrage, II, 153-61) was copied verbatim from an earlier catechism published by Perkins.

[153]Confession, sig. D, fol. 3^{r-v}.

[154] Attestation, pp.155-56.

[155] Divine beginning, "To the Christian Reader," not paginated.

[156] Confession, sig. D, fol. 3^r.

[157] "Extra Ecclesia, Nulla Salus," p.119; see also Watts, Dissenters, pp.51-52.

[158] Defence of the chvrches of Englande, p.15.

[159] Ibid., pp.11-12.

[160] This would be entirely within Jacob's character. It should be remembered that in 1605, when Jacob subscribed to the document prepared by the Bishop of London, he was being less than candid about his personal views.

[161] It could, of course, also have been a rather immoderate use of evasive tactics often employed by the radicals, viz. when arguing with someone to the left, one adopts one line, while quite another when attacking those to the right.

[162] Attestation, p.193.

[163] Collinson, Elizabethan Puritan Movement, p.455-62.

[164] Timothy George, John Robinson and the English Separatist Tradition (Macon: Mercer Univ. Press, 1982), p.92.

[165] Ibid., p.91. From Edward Winslow, Hypocrisie Vnmasked (London: 1646), pp.97-98. See also W.W. Fenn, "John Robinson's Farewell Address," Harvard Theological Review 13 (1920), 236-251.

[166] Ibid., p.241. Stephen Brachlow, "More Light on John Robinson and the Separatist Tradition," Fides et Historia XIII (1980), p.14-15.

[167] Brachlow, op.cit., p.7

[168] Ibid., p.8.

[169] Joseph Hall, A common apologie of the Church of England (London: 1610), p.115 as cited by Brachlow, p.9.

[170] Brachlow, op.cit., pp.9-10. George, op.cit., p.83 confuses this conference with another at which John Dod attended.

[171] George, op.cit., p.85.

[172] Ibid., pp.86-88.

[173] Ibid., p.90. On Amsterdam and Leiden see Keith L. Sprunger, Dutch Puritanism (Leiden: E. J. Brill, 1982): 66-67; 134-39; 340-41.

[174] Justification (1610), p.351.

[175] Walter H. Burgess, John Smith, the Se-Baptist, Thomas Helwys and the first Baptist Church in England (London: James Clarke and Co.: 1911), pp.51-52

[176] B.R. White, The English Separatist Tradition, p.121.

[177] Ibid., p.124. On the continuing generic charge of Anabaptism see Oliver Ormerod, the/Pictvre/of a Puritane:/Or,/A Relation of the opinions, qualities,/and practises of the Anabaptists/in Germanie, and of the Puritanes/in England./VVherein is firmely prooued, that the/Puritanes doe resemble the Anabap-/tists, in aboue fourescore seuerall/thinges./By O. O. of Emmanuel./Wherunto is annexed a short treatise, entituled, Pu/ritano-papismus: or a discouerie of Puritan-/Papisme./...[4 lines] (London/Printed by E.A. for Nathaniel Fosbroke, and/are to be solde at his Shop, at the West end/of Paules: 1605).

[178] Ibid., p.125.

[179] Ibid., p.129.

[180] Michael Watts, The Dissenters, p.45.

[181] Ibid., p.46. See L.D. Kliever, "General Baptist Origins," Mennonite Quarterly Review XXXVI (1962), pp.316-17.

[182] Burgess, op.cit., pp.182-184.

[183] W.L. Lumpkin, Baptist Confessions of Faith (Chicago: Judson Press, 1969), p.118.

[184] Ibid., p.121.

[185] Watts, op.cit., p.49.

[186] B.R. White, The English Baptists of the Seventeenth Century (London: Baptist History Society, 1983), p.28.

[187] Thomas Cooper, An/Admonition/To The People Of/England:/ VVherein Are An-/svvered Not Onely The/slaunderous vntruthes, reprochfully vt-/tered by Martin the Libeller, but also many other/Crimes by some of this broode, [six lines] (London: Deputies of Christopher Barker, 1589), pp.73-74.

[188]Stephen Bredwell, The Rasing/Of The Fovndations/of Brovvnisme./[nine lines; device] (London: John Windet, 1588), p.43.

[189]William Gilgate, Certaine Reasons Proouing the Separation, commonly called Brownists, to be Schismatiques (London: W. Stansby, 1621), preface to Reader.

[190]Now see J.F. McGregor, "The Baptists: Fount of All Heresy," pp. 23-64 in J.F. McGregor and B. Reay, _Radical Religion In The English Revolution_ (Oxford: Oxford Univ. Press, 1984).

[191]Tolmie, _op_._cit_., pp.12-19.

[192]See above, note 142.

[193]Tolmie, _op_._cit_., p.27.

[194]White, _English Baptists of the Seventeenth Century_, p.61.

[195]Lumpkin, _op_._cit_., p.162.

[196]_Ibid_., pp.61-63.

[197]B.R. White, "The Doctrine of the Church in the Particular Baptist Confession of 1644," _Journal of Theological Studies_ XIX (1968), p.590.

[198]Tolmie, _op_._cit_., p.63.

[199]Lumpkin, _op_._cit_., pp.174-187.

[200]White, _English Baptists of the Seventeenth Century_, pp.47-48.

[201]John Geree, _The Character of an Old English Puritane, or Non-Conformist_ (1646), cited in Roger Sharrock, _John Bunyan_, (London: MacMillan, 1968), p.22.

[202]John Brown, _John Bunyan (1628-1688). His Life, Times and Work_, revised by Frank Mott Harrison (London: Hulbert Publishing Co., 1928), p.336.

[203]See E. Beatrice Batson, _John Bunyan Allegory and Imagination_ (Barnes and Noble: 1984).

[204]_Grace Abounding to The Chief of Sinners_, edited by Roger Sharrock (Oxford: At the Clarendon Press, 1962), p.4.

[205]_The Jerusalem Sinner Saved; or Good News for the Vilest of Men_ (Oxford: At the Clarendon Press, 1985).

[206]"Bunyan, John," Dictionary of National Biography Roger Sharrock, John Bunyan, pp.9-12. Citation given in Margaret Spufford, Small Books and Pleasant Histories (Athens: Univ. of Georgia Press, 1982), p.7.

[207]See impressive article by K.H.D. Haley, "Sir Johannes Rothe: English Knight and Dutch Fifth Monarchist" in Donald Pemmington and Keith Thomas, Puritans and Revolutionaries (Oxford: At the Clarendon Press, 1978), pp.310-332.

[208]B.S. Capp, The Fifth Monarchy men (Totowa: Rowman and Littlefield, 1972), pp.65-75, 99-106 and 172-185.

[209]The Miscellaneous Works of John Bunyan I: Some Gospel Truths Opened, edited by T.L. Underwood & Roger Sharrock (Oxford: At the Clarendon Press, 1980), p.5. But see Anne Hawkins, Archetypes of Conversion (Lewisburg: Bucknell Univ. Press, 1985), pp.90-92 who portrays Bunyan's oscillation between progress and regress as "hope with despair and joy with fear."

[210]Ibid., p.XXXI

[211]Cited in B. Reay, "Quakerism and Society," McGregor and Reay, op.cit. p.162.

[212]Miscellaneous Works I, pp.XXXVII-XXXVIII.

[213]Ibid., p.302.

[214]Grace Abounding, pp.49-50.

[215]Ibid., pp.40-41.

[216]Ibid., p.xxxvii.

[217]See Felicity A. Nussbaum, "'By These Words I Was Sustained': Bunyan's Grace Abounding," EHL 49 (1982): 18-34. On an alternate view see Anne Hawkins, "The Double-Conversion in Bunyan's Grace Abounding," Philological Quarterly 61 (1982): 259-76. Hawkins fails to note the expansion of the text which adds the consolatory reference to Luther.

[218]The Doctrine of the Law and Grace unfolded, edited by Richard L. Greaves (Oxford: At The Clarendon Press, 1976), p.9.

[219]Ibid., p.16.

[220]U. Milo Kaufmann, The Pilgrim's Progress and Traditions in Puritan Meditation (New Haven: Yale Univ. Press, 1966), p.61.

[221] Ibid., pp.62-63.

[222] Ibid., p.79

[223] The Pilgrim's Progress, edited by Roger Sharrock (London: Penguin Books, 1982), p.69 and Hawkins, Archetypes of Conversion, p.112.

[224] Ibid., p.91.

[225] Ibid., p.99.

[226] Ibid., p.136.

[227] I.M. Green, The Re-Establishment of the Church of England 1660-1663 (Oxford: Oxford Univ. Press, 1978). Many of the clergy assented to a Prayer Book not printed in time or numbers to see before the required subscription. It appeared on August 13. cf. p.147 of Green.

[228] Ibid., p.199.

[229] Come and Welcome, To Jesus Christ, edited by Richard Greaves (Oxford: At the Clarendon Press, 1976), pp.357-358.

[230] Ibid., p.363.

[231] John Bunyan, His Last Sermon (London: John Marshall, 1725?), edition of A Discourse upon the Pharisee and the Publican, pp.159-160.

[232] John E. Pomfret, Founding The American Colonies 1583-1660 (New York: Harper & Row, 1970), p.114.

[233] Ibid., p.116. See Of Plymouth Plantation, edited Samuel Eliot Morison (New York: 1967), pp.147-169.

[234] George D. Langdon, Jr., "The Franchise and Political Democracy in Plymouth Colony," William and Mary Quarterly XX (1963): 513-526.

[235] Darrett Rutman, Winthrop's Boston: Portrait of a Puritan Town, 1630-1649 (Chapel Hill: Univ. of North Carolina Press, 1965).

[236] Pomfret, op.cit., pp.186-187.

[237] Jesper Rosenmier, "The Teacher and the Witness: John Cotton and Roger Williams," William and Mary Quarterly XXV (1968): 408-431.

[238]S.H.B., "Williams, Roger (c. 1603-1682/83)," Dictionary of American Biography (New York: Charles Scribners Sons, 1936) X: 286.

[239]Ibid., pp.286-287.

[240]Ibid., p.287.

[241]Roger Williams, The Hireling Ministry None of Christs. Writings VII: 154-155. See Hans R. Guggisberg, "Religious Freedom and the History of the Christian World in Roger Williams' Thought," Early American Literature XII (1977): 36-48.

[242]Roger Williams, Mr. Cottons Letter Lately Printed, Examined and Answered, Writings I: 40-41.

[243]Alden T. Vaughn, "Pequots and Puritans: The Causes of the War of 1637," William and Mary Quarterly XXI (1964): 256-259.

[244]Roger Williams, Letter to John Winthrop, Providence, August 24, 1637, Writings VI: 11-12.

[245]See the classic account by Charles Francis Adams, The Antinomian Controversy [Three Episodes in Massachusetts History], edited by Emery Battis (New York: De Capo Press, 1976).

[246]Jesper Rosenmeier, "New England's Perfection: The Image of Adam and the Image of Christ in the Antinomian Crisis, 1634 to 1638," William and Mary Quarterly XXVII (1970), pp.437-438.

[247]Ibid., p.439.

[248]Ibid., p.440. Thomas Shephard, The Sincere Convert (1641), p.28.

[249]Parable of the Ten Virgins (1660) I: 174.

[250]Rosenmeier, op.cit., p.449.

[251]Roger Williams, A Key into the Language of America (1643), Writings I:81.

[252]Roger Williams, The Blovdy Tenent, of Persecution, Writings III: 13.

[253]Ibid., p.208.

[254]Ibid., p.424.

[255]Ibid., p.22. See Sacvan Bercovitch, "Typology in Puritan New England: The Williams-Cotton Controversy Reassessed," American Quarterly XIX (1967), pp.166-191.

[256]Gerald F. Moran, "Religious Renewal, Puritan Tribalism, and the Family in Seventeenth-Century Milford, Connecticut," _William and Mary Quarterly_ XXXVI 1979): 236-254.

[257]Cotton Mather, _Magnalia Christi Americana_ I (1853): 357.

[258]Stephen Foster, "New England and the Challenge of Heresy, 1630 to 1660: The Puritan Crisis in Transatlantic Perspective," _William and Mary Quarterly_ XXXVIII (1981), p.630.

[259]_Ibid._, p.631. John Eachard, Public Record Office, S.P. 16/520, ff.143-144. Letter written on the trial of Samuel Pretty in 1631 before the High Commission.

[260]_Ibid._, p.633. On Traske see _S.T.C._ 24178.5: _The true gospel vindicated from the reproach of a new gospel_ (1636) and the response by Edward Norice, _The New gospel, not the true gospel_. (1638). _S.T.C._ 18645.

[261]Cited in David S. Lovejoy, _Religious Enthusiasm In the New World_ (Cambridge, Mass./London: Harvard Univ. Press, 1985), p. 71 from Hall, ed., _Antinomian Controversy_, p.246.

[262]Christopher Hill, "Irreligion in the 'Puritan' Revolution," p.200 in McGregor and Reay, editors, _Radical Religion In The English Revolution_ (Oxford: 1984). See further Hill's _The World Turned Upside Down_ (London: Penguin, 1975), pp.81-85.

[263]_Ibid._, p.638.

[264]See William K.B. Stoever, "The Nature of New England Antinomianism," _A faire and Easie Way to Heaven_ (Middletown: Wesleyan Univ. Press, 1978), pp.161-183.

[265]_Ibid._, p.166.

[266]_Ibid._, p.177.

[267]Emery Battis, _Saints and Sectaries_ (Chapel Hill: Univ. of North Carolina Press, 1962), pp.2 and 4.

[268]Francis J. Bremer, _Anne Hutchinson: Troubler of Puritan Zion_ (Huntington: Robert E. Krieger, 1981), pp.1-3.

[269]Edmund S. Morgan, "The Case against Anne Hutchinson," _New England Quarterly_ X (1937), p.649.

[270]Cited in James Fulton MacLear, "'The Heart of New England Rent': The Mystical Element in Early Puritan History," _The Mis-_

sissippi Valley Historical Review LXII (1956), p.641. See Michael McGiffert, "Grace and Works: The Rise and Division of Covenant Divinity in Elizabethan Puritanism," Harvard Theological Review 75 (1982): 463-502. Trial account is excerpted in Rosemary Ruether & Rosemary Keller, editors, Women and Religion in America, Volume 2 in The Colonial and Revolutionary Periods: A Documentary History (San Francisco: Harper & Row, 1983): 165-175.

271 Lyle Koehler, "The Case of the American Jezebels: Anne Hutchinson and Female Agitation During the Years of Antinomian Turmoil, 1636-1640," William and Mary Quarterly XXXI (1974), p.69. Koehler's charge of sexism during the trial is refuted in Ann F. Withington and Jack Schwartz, "The Political Trial of Anne Hutchinson," New England Quarterly LI (1978): 228-29.

272 John M. Mackie, "Life of Samuel Gorton, One of the First Settlers of Warwick, in Rhode Island," in Jared Sparks, editor, Library of American Biography, second series V (Boston, 1864): 317-411.

273 Philip F. Gura, "The Radical Ideology of Samuel Gorton: New Light on the Relation of English to American Puritanism," William and Mary Quarterly xxvi (1979), p.83. See Kenneth W. Porter, "Samuel Gorton, New England Firebrand," New England Quarterly 7 (1934): 405-444 and Robert Emmet Wall, Jr., Massachusetts Bay. The Crucial Decade, 1640-1650 (New Haven: Yale Univ. Press, 1972): 121-156, "Massachusetts vrs. Samuel Gorton." Now see Gura, A Glimpse of Sions Glory (Middletown: Wesleyan Univ. Press, 1984): 276-303.

274 Christopher Hill, The World Turned Upside Down, pp.99-105, 58-59 and 103-104. See Tai Liu, Discord in Zion: The Puritan Divines and The Revolution 1640-1660 (The Hague: Martinus Nijhoff, 1973), pp.97-100.

275 Philip F. Gura, "Samuel Gorton and Religious Radicalism in England, 1644-1648," William and Mary Quarterly XL (1983), p.121. On Lamb see B.R. White, The English Baptists of the Seventeenth Century, pp.32-40.

[276]Lyle Koehler, A Search for Power: The "Weaker Sex" in Seventeenth-Century New England (Urbana: Univ. of Illinois Press, 1980), pp.304-309.

[277]Roger Williams to John Mason, Providence, June 22, 1670. Writings VI: 344.

[278]Williams refers to Servetus and Beza in Bloudy Tenent. See Writings III: 52. He uses Calvin and Beza on Romans (13) to support his argument. Writings III: 154-155.

EPILOGUE: THE WILDERNESS

We have traced through three centuries the English setting of evangelical Christianity in which a conscious decision has been made to concentrate on the particularities of place. This is set forth as a mode of understanding which confers "conditional intelligibility upon the whole mass of undifferentiated human activity."[1] Such a practice of history which provides a European setting for American Evangelicals not only distinguishes them from their Fundamentalist cousins, but helps them to set a fresh agenda as they complete a three hundred year trek beyond 1683 and enter into the third millenium of the Christian era. We reject any historical research which discards that European background in favor of insights limited by the American horizon. One need only count up the impact of continuous European influence in every area of American theology to see how limited such a view can be; a point of view which does in fact foster a blurred vision of our past.

The reader might recall from the prologue the question raised by Winthrop Hudson, "How American is Religion in America?" American religious history must not continue to ignore its European foundations or it will prove Hudson's point that it does foster anti-intellectualism. Professor Hudson points us to that European soil for the proper understanding of American Evangelicalism. More recently the late Sidney Ahlstrom argued persuasively in his remarkable _A Religious History Of The American People_ that the inheritance of seventeenth century England in America had not been adequately recognized. From that transcontinental heritage of the Reformation as it penetrated the British Isles and "from this realm would come the colonial impulses... which would form the chief foundations -- political, economic, and religious -- of the American tradition."[2] The biblical commentaries described in section five influenced every level of intellectual, social, artistic and political life -- reflecting as they still do the vibrancy of lecture hall and pulpit in the golden age of English preaching. Such a continuous contribution at every level calls out for recognition as part of the social fabric of a Protestant America still affecting the perception of religion in large sections well into the twentieth century.

Section one explored the renewal of biblical study under Wyclif's inspiration while section two traced the struggle over the first printed English Bible as the hierarchy sought to control its circulation. Section three continued that story as it spoke of exiled communities who prepared fresh translations for worship and witness. Section four set forth the Puritan pastoral concern at the parish level and its impact on national life. Section five traced the scriptural support for sermons in English society from 1562-1663. A special genre of plague sermons tested that biblical base and reflected a greater consensus than expected, as tragedy continued to mold national religious reflection. Section six traced the struggle for religious liberty on the part of English separatists. From Wyclif in 1378 to Williams in 1683 we have observed the concerns of a godly people expressed through the medium of vernacular scripture, the recovery of preaching and the relation of church and state.

The American theologian Donald Bloesch calls for such a renewed vision in his recent volume on _The Future of Evangelical Christianity_ (Doubleday: 1983). He has a helpful comment about the need for our sort of narrative:

> The more prevalent failing in modern evangelicalism is to ignore the past altogether, to emphasize communication skills over the commentary on scripture in the history of the church, to downplay nurture in the faith of the church in favor of strategies for expanding the church. Some of the new evangelical schools advertise programs in church growth and electronic media studies but are strangely silent regarding their offerings in systematic theology or the history of Christian thought. Evangelicalism will be caught up and submerged in the mainstream of popular culture-religion unless it rediscovers its identity as a bona fide branch of the holy catholic church. It needs to reclaim its glorious heritage, which extends from the first century of the church onward but which was given special visibility in the Protestant Reformation of the sixteenth century and

> the evangelical revival movements of the seventeenth and eighteenth centuries.3

Karl Rahner, a leading European Catholic thinker, has also noted the contribution of the evangelical heritage. Evangelical Christianity has a positive function for the Catholic church as its seeks to be the church which extends its fundamental mission. It calls the Catholic church back to the "primary origins of Holy Scripture and all the more so of the Holy Spirit."[4] Rahner goes on to assert the permanence of this Evangelical Christianity.

> From a historical point of view the concrete reality of Catholic Christianity cannot even be imagined outside an historical situation to whose powerful historical moments Evangelical Christianity did not also belong.5

When Perry Miller chose _Errand Into the Wilderness_ for one of his titles on colonial American Puritanism, he struck a note which echoes across the Christian centuries. Cotton Mather's _Magnalia Christi Americana_ helped to weave such a theme into the fabric of colonial society. The positive image of the Wilderness through which Williams went to escape persecution and, by analogy, the turmoil which Wyclif endured or the troubles of a Tyndale and the Marian Exiles, not to speak of the Separatist agony under Elizabeth -- all of this could look to the lines of Isaiah (35:1-2,6,8):

> The wilderness will rejoice and blossom. Like the crocus it will burst into bloom. Water will gush forth in the wilderness and streams in the desert. And a highway will be there. It will be called the Way of Holiness; it will be for those who walk in that Way.

The presence of God's Word, proclamation of the Scriptures through preaching and the toleration of error in a sectarian desert are the agents of renewal for God's people as they travel through the wilderness of this life. Peter Carroll argues that the Puritans replaced the stone walls of England with the idea of God's Hedge, thereby enclosing their transplanted medieval cities in the New England wilderness with God's law. Their desire for social cohesion soon clashed with that societal dream as geographical dispersal undermined their social aspirations.[6] The

Puritan sermons which set forth the hope of renewal amidst the rhetoric of gloom were themselves transformed into a transcendental philosophy by the time of Emerson's 1838 address.

As one moves from the civic setting of the Norwich Grociers Paradise play of 1565 to Edward Johnson's Wonder-Working Providence of Sions Saviour in New England only the tone has changed. Popular approval of protestant themes can be seen in the Paradise play of 1533, a naive tale of Adam and Eve who succomb to a most wily serpent. At their expulsion they wring their hands and sing a "dullful [doleful] song." The 1565 edition is a protestant play in Genevan ideological dress which garnishes the tree with flowers, fruits and grocieries. The serpent now has a handsome painted skin and tail. Two abstract figures enter the narrative as Dolor and Misery who seize the unlucky pair to escort them out of paradise into the wilderness of a sinfilled world. The decorated tree was a delightful touch when this morality play was performed in Norwich as late as 1953.[7] It shows popular support of protestant themes in sixteenth century Norwich.

A century later Edward Johnson provided his New England readers with steel for their souls when he penned these lines for defenders of the English colony.

> In that Wildernesse, whether you are going... the Lord Christ intends to atchieve greater matters by this little handfull then the World is aware of... keepe your weapons in continuall readinesse, seeing you are called to fight the Battails of your Lord Christ...8

Whether in Norwich or New England the common ideology of solidarity in sin carries on to the nineteenth century where Melville and Hawthorne espouse a literary Calvinism whose "brotherhood of sinners" is seared in the American soul.[9]

By Emerson's 1838 Divinity School Address, a Calvinistic pessimism clashed with his transcendental view of the world fashioned by a deity who pronounced all His creation as good. Emerson, who was no evangelical, sensed that the New England orthodox clergy had so stressed the faults of humans that the goodness of God in giving His Son held small hope for those preoccupied with the propaganda of religious self-doubt. Beset as they were by Rome on the one side which tore at the fabric of scriptural authority and a Socinus whose ilk denied the eternality of their saviour, this clergy was under pressure indeed.

Even Emerson had his literary critics such as Nathaniel Hawthorne, who labled the giant of Doubting Castle 'Emerson' in his parody of Bunyan's Pilgrim's Progress. Such irony was itself an affirmation of human solidarity in sin, a literary Calvinism which lampooned Emerson's aescetic complaint. Hawthorne and Emerson alike note the unbalanced sound of the protestant pulpit, missing in many ways the first generation protestant stress that every peril of daily life was matched by the promises of Christ.

Those who trusted Christ as their alien righteousness found in Him a consolation for their sins. Luther after all had taught the bondage of the will so that the conscience might go free. Those who taught free will bound the conscience. St. Paul called such teachers "hypocritical liars" whose seared consciences could deprive the faithful. "For everything God created is good," wrote Paul in I Timothy (4:4), "and nothing is to be rejected if it is received with thanksgiving." The American Unitarian William Ellery Channing had his finger on the rapid pulse of these self-conscious Calvinists when in 1820 he wrote The Moral Argument Against Calvinism: "We desire to think humbly of ourselves, and reverently of our Creator... There is an affected humility, we think, as dangerous as pride."[10]

The point to be made is that the hyper-Calvinists of New England had departed from the sixteenth century stress on promise and redemption. The Bezan practical syllogism came unravelled as generations of reformed pastors enquired into their own consciences and those of their parishioners. Their mistake was to produce as strong a feeling of faith as of sin, indeed to elicit the former by increased stress on the latter. Edward Taylor the Colonial poet put the matter well when he meditated on John (6:51) about Christ the Living Bread as "Heavens Sugar Cake":

> Did God mould up this Bread in Heaven, and bake,
>   Which from his Table came, and to thine goeth?

Doth he bespeake thee thus, This Soule Bread take.
Come Eate thy fill of this thy Gods White Loafe?
Its Food too fine for Angells, yet come, take
And Eate thy fill. Its Heavens Sugar Cake.[11]

Those pristine reformers saw the light of the knowledge of God in the face of Christ (II Cor. 4:6), in whom were hid not only the treasures of wisdom and knowledge, but also of joy and beauty as well as hope and confidence in the life everlasting. Evangelicals sung these stanzas of wisdom, joy and hope on their trek from the Oxford of Wyclif to the Harvard of Thomas Shepard.

To tip the scale toward some theologically uncertainty principle was foreign to a Cambridge reformer like Thomas Bilney who read out Erasmus' fresh Latin of I Timothy (1:15) as 'certain' rather than the Vulgate 'faithful.' The certainty that Christ came to save him as chief of sinners inspired Bilney's affirmation of Christian hope as they burned him at the stake in 1531. The certainty of Christ as Saviour and the solidarity of those scriptures which proclaimed His gift of enemy love galvanized a national church whose medieval theologians had misled them by speculations on the sovereignty of God.

Whether it be some great Saxon Jeremiah like Luther or Calvin as a French Ezekiel -- those prophetic voices rang out the name of the Son of Man. He whom the Apocalypse calls "Word of God" speaks on behalf of His own glory which requires no human defense. This very Saviour who is also Sovereign goes forth to conquer both the kingdoms of this world and the hearts of His little flock in love.

The Evangelical experience of European Christians over those thirty decades from Wyclif to Williams was well said by Sir Walter Mildmay in retort to Queen Elizabeth. When she roared at him, "So, sir, you have founded a Puritan College", he replied, "no, Madam, but I have set an acorn which when it becomes an oak, God alone knows what will be the fruit thereof." Then from his Emmanuel College statutes he added -- "that from this seed ground the English church might have pastors which is a thing necessary above all others."[12]

Whether the oak grew in a wilderness of religious pluralism, war, urban life or conflicting ideas, one temptation remains. Those faithful sons and daughters of the Corpus Christianorum refused the temptation to live by bread alone. Their strength surged forth from the sword of the Spirit which is the Word of God. The certainty of their struggle was matched by the conviction of their victory. With Luther and Bunyan they knew that one word would slay their ancient foe. Behind these intrepid explorers of God's wilderness there stand the Cambridge Platonists, Emmanuel's men, who reminded those austere divines that the spirit of man is the candle of the Lord and the light of truth unquenchable (Proverbs 20:27). Truth was to be no cloistered virtue for these Puritan pioneers.

It was with good reason that Wyclif became known as the Doctor Evangelicus. His perception of the medieval Bishop of Lincoln, Robert Grosseteste, took root in the fifteenth century in the Lollard exegesis of John (10:14). The Lord of the Church would not refer to Himself as the Good Shepherd unless there were bad ones about. So then in the next century the spirit of the English Reformation spread that evangelical concern which A.G. Dickens has so well expressed.

> Imperfectly as the Reformers executed their task, too swiftly as they froze the living things in their minds, this desire to free man's image of God from anthropomorphism and marginal cults, to envisage the magnitude and the uniqueness of Christ's sacrifice, to cast aside misleading unessentials and accretions, to bring men nearer in love to the real person of the Founder, this type of aspiration lies at the heart of their message for our own century .... When they talk of God, or of the Son of God, fallen creatures and visible churches should at least be tentative. It needed Christ himself to interpret the world of the Spirit in the lame words of men.13

Like John Wyclif these pastors held up to their people the mirror of eternity in the Christian scriptures of the Old and New Testaments. However dim that view might seem, it reflected the image of the Christ who cares for His own flock with an everlasting love. It was that confidence which led these pastors out of the collegiate precincts of Cambridge and Oxford into the parishes of Old and New England.

In the final analysis it was the faithful shepherd who handed on that evangelical spirit in a score of ways. These were indeed pastors of great learning who were: "content to give a score of years and all they had of wisdom to the little people in small country parishes."[14]

END NOTES to EPILOGUE

[1]David Boucher, "The Creation of The Past: British Idealism & Michael Oakeskott's Philosophy of History," History and Theory XXIII (1984), p.203.

[2]Sydney E. Ahlstrom, A Religious History Of The American People (New Haven: Yale Univ. Press, 1972), p.83.

[3]Donald Bloesch, The Future of Evangelical Christianity (New York: Doubleday, 1983), p. 117.

[4]Karl Rahner, Foundations of Christian Faith (New York: Seabury Press, 1978), p.367.

[5]loc.cit.

[6]Peter N. Carroll, Puritanism and the Wilderness. The Intellectual Significance of the New England Frontier 1629-1700 (New York: Columbia Univ. Press, 1969), p.128.

[7]Ruth Harriett Blackburn, Tudor Biblical Drama, unpublished 1957 Columbia Univ. Ph.D. thesis, pp. 14-16. Text in Osborn Waterhouse, editor, Non-Cycle Mystery Plays, Early English Text Society, English Series 104 (London: 1909).

[8]J. Franklin Jameson, editor, Johnson's Wonder-Working Providence 1628-1651 (New York: Barnes & Noble, 1967), pp.33-34.

[9]Gene Bluestein, "The Brotherhood of Sinners: Literary Calvinism," New England Quarterly 50 (1977): 195-213. On Melville see T. Walter Herbert, Mobey-Dick and Calvinism. A World Dismantled (Rutgers: 1977) and on Hawthorne, Agnes McNeill Donohue, Hawthorne: Calvin's Ironic Stepchild (Kent State, 1985).

[10]David Robinson, editor, William Ellery Channing Selected Writings (New York: Paulist Press, 1985), p.109.

[11]Alan Heimert and Andrew Delbanco, The Puritans in America (Cambridge: Harvard Univ. Press, 1985), p.303.

[12]Gordon Rupp, William Bedell 1571-1642 (Cambridge: W.Heffer & Sons Ltd., 1972), pp.13-14. See H.C. Porter, Puritanism in Tudor England (Columbia: Univ. of South Carolina, 1971), p.186.

[13]A.G. Dickens, The English Reformation (New York: Schocken, 1964), p.340.

[14]E.G. Rupp, Hort and the Cambridge Tradition (Cambridge: At the Univ. Press, 1970), pp.20-21.

SELECT BIBLIOGRAPHY

I. Sources

Heimert, Alan and Andrew Delbanco, eds., The Puritans In America (Cambridge: Harvard Univ. Press, 1985).

Hudson, Anne, English Wycliffite Sermons I (Oxford: At the Clarendon Press, 1983).

Hudson, Anne, Selections From English Wycliffite Writings (Cambridge: At the Univ. Press, 1978).

O'Day, Rosemary and Joel Berlatsky, eds., "The Letter-Book of Thomas Bentham, Bishop of Coventry and Lichfield, 1560-1561," Camden Miscellany XXVII (1979).

Peel, Albert and Leland Carlson, eds., The Writings of Robert Harrison and Robert Browne (London: George Allen & Unwin Ltd., 1953).

Pollard, Alfred W., Records of the English Bible (Folkestone: Wm. Dawson & Sons Ltd., 1974).

Selement, George and Bruce C. Woolley, eds., Thomas Shepard's Confessions (Boston: The Colonial Society of Massachusetts, 1981).

Slavin, Arthur J., Thomas Cromwell On Church and Commonwealth Selected Letters, 1523-1540 (New York: Harper & Row, 1969).

Wallis, N. H., The New Testament Translated by William Tyndale 1534 (Cambridge: At the Univ. Press, 1938).

Williams, C. H., ed., English Historical Documents 1485-1558 (New York: Oxford Univ. Press, 1967).

II. Monographs

Anderson, Judith H., Biographical Truth The Representation of Historical Persons in Tudor-Stuart Writing (New Haven: Yale Univ. Press, 1984).

Aston, Margaret, Thomas Arundel (Oxford: At the Clarendon Press, 1967).

Aston, T. H., *History of Oxford* III, James McConica, ed., *The Collegiate University* (Oxford: Clarendon Press, 1986).

Batson, E. Beatrice, *John Bunyan Allegory and Imagination* (Totowa: Barnes and Noble: 1984).

Battis, Emery, *Saints and Sectaries* (Chapel Hill: Univ. of North Carolina Press, 1962).

Bindoff, S. T., *Tudor England* (London: Penquin Books Ltd., 1962).

Bridenbaugh, Carl, *Vexed and Troubled Englishmen 1590-1642* (New York: Oxford Univ. Press, 1968).

Carroll, Peter N., *Puritanism and the Wilderness. The Intellectual Significance of the New England Frontier 1629-1700* (New York: Columbia Univ. Press, 1969).

Christianson, Paul, *Reformers and Babylon* (Toronto: Univ. of Toronto Press, 1978)

Clebsch, William A., *England's Earliest Protestants* (New Haven: Yale Univ. Press, 1964).

Cliffe, J. T., *The Puritan Gentry* (London: Routledge & Kegan Paul plc., 1984).

Collinson, Patrick, *Archbishop Grindal 1519-1583: The Struggle for a Reformed Church* (Berkeley: Univ. of California Press, 1979).

Collinson, Patrick, *Godly People: Essays on English Protestantism and Puritanism* (London: Hambledon Press, 1983).

Cross, Claïre, *The Puritan Earl: The Life of Henry Hastings, Third Earl of Huntingdon 1536-1595* (London: MacMillan, 1966).

Dent, C. M., *Protestant Reformers in Elizabethan Oxford* (Oxford: Oxford Univ. Press, 1983).

Dickens, A. G., *The English Reformation* (New York: Schocken Books, 1964).

Dickens, A. G., *Thomas Cromwell and the English Reformation* (London: Hutchinson, 1959).

Friedman, Jerome, *Michael Servetus. A Case Study in Total Heresy* (Genéve: Librairie Droz S.A., 1978).

Greg, W., Some Aspects and Problems of London Publishing Between 1550-1650 (Oxford: Clarendon Press, 1956).

Gura, Philip F., A Glimpse of Sions Glory (Middletown: Wesleyan Univ. Press, 1984).

Guy, J. A., The Public Career of Sir Thomas More (New Haven: Yale Univ. Press, 1980).

Haigh, Christopher, ed., The Reign of Elizabeth I (Athens: Univ. of Georgia Press, 1985).

Holmes, Peter, Resistance and Compromise: The Political Thought of the Elizabethan Catholics (Cambridge, Mass/London: Harvard Univ. Press, 1983).

Hunt, William, The Puritan Moment (Cambridge, Mass/London: Harvard Univ. Press, 1983).

Jones, Norman L., Faith by Statute. Parliament and the settlement of religion 1559 (London: Royal Historical Society Studies in History 32/Swift Printers, 1982).

Kaufmann, U. Milo, The Pilgrim's Progress and Traditions in Puritan Meditation (New Haven: Yale Univ. Press, 1966).

King, John N., English Reformation Literature (Princeton: Princeton Univ. Press, 1982).

Knapp, Peggy Ann, The Style of John Wyclif's English Sermons (Hague-Paris: Mouton, 1977).

Lake, Peter, Moderate Puritans and the Elizabethan Church (Cambridge: The Univ. Press, 1982).

Lambert, M. D., Medieval Heresy (London: Edward Arnold, 1977).

McEvoy, James, The Philosophy of Robert Grosseteste (Oxford: The Clarendon Press, 1982).

McFarlane, K. B., Lancastrian Kings and Lollard Knights (Oxford: The Clarendon Press, 1972).

McGregor, J. F. and B. Reay, Radical Religion In The English Revolution (Oxford: Oxford Univ. Press, 1984).

Milward, Peter, Religious Controversies of the Elizabethan Age (Lincoln: Univ. of Nebraska Press, 1977).

Morgan, John, Godly Learning. Puritan Attitudes Towards Reason, Learning, and Education, 1560-1640 (Cambridge: Cambridge Univ. Press, 1986).

O'Day, Rosemary, The English Clergy. The Emergence and Consolidation of a Profession 1558-1642 (Leicester: Leicester Univ. Press, 1979).

Pearson, A. F. Scott, Thomas Cartwright and Elizabethan Puritanism, 1535-1603 (Gloucester: Peter Smith, 1966).

Porter, H. C., Reformation and Reaction in Tudor Cambridge (Cambridge: At the Univ. Press, 1958).

Reid, W. Stanford, Trumpeter of God (New York: Charles Scribner's Sons, 1974).

Robson, J. A., Wyclif and the Oxford Schools (Cambridge: At the Univ. Press, 1961).

Slack, Paul, The Impact of Plague in Tudor and Stuart England (London: Rutledge & Kegan Paul, 1985).

Spinka, Mathew, The Letters of John Hus (Manchester: Manchester Univ. Press, 1972).

Spufford, Margaret, Contrasting Communities English Villagers in the Sixteenth and Seventeenth Centuries (Cambridge: At the Univ. Press, 1979).

Thomson, John A. F., The Later Lollards 1414-1520 (Oxford: Oxford Univ. Press, 1967).

Tolmie, Murray, The Triumph of The Saints (Cambridge: At the Univ. Press, 1977).

Wallace, Dewey, Puritans and Predestination: Grace in English Protestant Theology, 1525 to 1695 (Chapel Hill: Univ. of North Carolina Press, 1982).

White, B. R., The English Baptists of the Seventeenth Century (London: Baptist History Society, 1983).

White, B. R., The English Separatist Tradition (Oxford: Oxford Univ. Press, 1971).

Youings, Joyce, Sixteenth-Century England (London: Penguin Books, 1984).

III. Articles

Almasy, R., "The purpose of Richard Hooker's polemic," Journal of the History of Ideas XXXIX (1978): 251-70.

Anderson, Virginia DeJohn, "Migrants and Motives: Religion and the Settlement of New England, 1630-1640," New England Quarterly 58 (1985): 339-83.

Aston, Margaret, "'Caim's Castles': Poverty, Politics, and Disendowment" in R. B. Dobson, ed., The Church, Politics and Patronage (Gloucester/ New York: Alan Sutton/ St. Martins Press, 1984): 45-81.

Aston, Margaret, "The Debate on Bible Translation, Oxford 1401," English Historical Review XC (1975): 1-18.

Bainton, Roland, "The Parable of the Tares as the proof text for Religious Liberty," Church History II (1933): 67-89.

Bluestein, Gene, "The Brotherhood of Sinners: Literary Calvinism," New England Quarterly 50 (1977): 195-213.

Bonini, Cissie Rafferty, "Lutheran Influences in the Early English Reformation: Richard Morison Re-examined," Archiv für Reformationsgeschichte 64 (1973): 206-24.

Clancy, Thomas, "Papist-Protestant-Puritan: English Religious Taxonomy 1565-1665," Recusant History 13 (1976): 227-53.

Collinson, Patrick, "John Field and Elizabethan Puritanism" in S. T. Bindoff, J. Hurstfield and C. H. Williams, eds., Elizabethan Government and Society (London: The Athlone Press, 1961): 127-62.

Collinson, Patrick, "The Godly: aspects of Popular Protestantism," in Godly People. Essays on English Protestantism (London: Hambledon Press, 1984): 1-18.

Davies, Richard G., "Thomas Arundel as Archbishop of Canterbury, 1396-1414," Journal of Ecclesiastical History XXIV (1973): 9-22.

Davis, John F., "The trials of Thomas Bylney and the English Reformation," Historical Journal 24 (1981): 775-90.

Duggan, Lawrence G., "The Unresponsiveness of the Late Medieval Church: A Reconsideration," Sixteenth Century Journal IX (1978): 3-26.

Eerde, Katherine S. Van, "Robert Waldegrave: The Printer as Agent and Link between Sixteenth-Century England and Scotland," Renaissance Quarterly XXXIV (1981): 40-78.

Elton, G. R., "Thomas Cromwell Redivivus," Archiv für Reformationsgeschichte 68 (1977): 192-208.

Evans, G. R., "Wyclif's Logic and Wyclif's Exegesis: The Context" in Katharine Walsh and Diana Wood, eds., The Bible in the Medieval World, Essays in Memory of Beryl Smalley (Oxford: Basil Blackwell, 1985): 287-300.

Fines, John, "Heresy Trials in the Diocese of Coventry and Litchfield," Journal of Ecclesiastical History XIV(1963): 160-74.

Foster, Stephen, "New England and the Challenge of Heresy, 1630 to 1660: The Puritan Crisis in Transatlantic Perspective," William and Mary Quarterly XXXVIII (1981): 624-60.

Guggisberg, Hans R., "Religious Freedom and the History of the Christian World in Roger Williams' Thought," Early American Literature XII (1977): 36-48.

Haigh, Christopher "Anticlericalism and the English Reformation," History 68 (1983): 391-407.

Handy, Robert T., "Wilderness experiences of Religion in America" in F. F. Church and T. George, eds., Continuity and Discontinuity in Church History (Leiden: E.J. Brill,1979): 301-14.

Hargreaves, Henry, "The Marginal Glosses to the Wycliffite New Testament," Studia Neophilologica XXXIII (1961): 285-300.

Heal, Felicity, "The resources of the Elizabethan bishops," Of Prelates and Princes (Cambridge: At the Univ. Press, 1980): 265-311.

Hudson, Anne, "A Lollard Quaternion," Review of English Studies XXII (1971): 435-42.

Hudson, Winthrop S., "How American is Religion in America?" in Jerald C. Brauer, ed., Reinterpretation in American Church History (Chicago: Univ. of Chicago Press, 1968): 153-67.

Jones, Norman L., "Elizabeth's First Year: The Conception and Birth of the Elizabethan Political World," in Christopher Haigh, ed., The Reign of Elizabeth I (Athens: Univ. of Georgia Press, 1985): 31-33.

Kaminsky, Howard, "Wyclifism as Ideology of Revolution," Church History XXXII (1963): 57-74.

Kenny, Anthony, "Church, King and Pope," _Wyclif_ (Oxford: Oxford Univ. Press, 1985): 68-79.

Kenny, Anthony, "The truth of scripture," _Wyclif_ (Oxford: Oxford Univ. Press, 1985): 56-67.

Kyle, Richard, "John Knox and the Purification of Religion: the Intellectual Aspects of his Crusade against Idolatry," _Archiv für Reformationsgeschichte_ 77 (1986): 265-80.

Lake, Peter, "The significance of the Elizabethan identification of the Pope as Antichrist," _Journal of Ecclesiastical History_ 31 (1980): 161-78.

Luoma, J. K., "Restitution or Reformation? Cartwright and Hooker on the Elizabethan Church," _Historical Magazine of the Protestant Episcopal Church_ XLVI (1977): 85-106.

McGiffert, Michael, "William Tyndale's Conception of Covenant," _Journal of Ecclesiastical History_ 32 (1981): 167-84.

McLane, Paul E., "Prince Lucifer and the Fitful 'Lanternes of Lyght': Wolsey and the Bishops in Skelton's _Colyn Cloute_," _Huntington Library Quarterly_ 43 (1980): 159-79.

Meyer, Carl S., "Henry VIII Burns Luther's Books," _Journal of Ecclesiastical History_ IX (1958): 173-87.

Nussbaum, Felicity A., "'By These Words I Was Sustained': Bunyan's Grace Abounding," _EHL_ 49 (1982): 18-34.

O'Malley, John W., S.J. "Erasmus and the History of Sacred Rhetoric: The Ecclesiastes of 1535," _Erasmus of Rotterdam Society Yearbook Five_ (1985): 1-29.

Owen, H. G., "A Nursery of Elizabethan Nonconformity, 1567-1572," _Journal of Ecclesiastical History_ XVII (1966): 65-76.

Prest, Wilfrid R., "Preachers, puritans and the religion of lawyers," _The Inns of Court under Elizabeth I and the Early Stuarts 1590-1640_ (London: 1972): 187-219.

Price, F. D. "Gloucester Diocese under Bishop Hooper 1551-1553," _Transactions of the Bristol and Gloucestershire Archaeological Society_ LX (1938): 51-151.

Raitt, Jill, "Beza, Guide for the Faithful Life," _Scottish Journal of Theology_ 39 (1986): 83-107.

Rosenmier, Jesper, "The Teacher and the Witness: John Cotton and Roger Williams," William and Mary Quarterly XXV (1968): 408-431.

Seaver, Paul, "Community Control and Puritan Politics in Elizabethan Suffolk," Albion 9 (Winter 1977): 297-315.

Selement, George, "The Meeting of Elite and Popular Minds at Cambridge, New England, 1638-1645," William and Mary Quarterly XLI (1984): 32-48.

Smalley, Beryl, "John Wyclif's Postilla Super Totam Bibliam," Bodleian Library Record VIII (1953): 186-205.

White, B. R., "The Doctrine of the Church in the Particular Baptist Confession of 1644," Journal of Theological Studies XIX (1968): 570-90.

Williams, Glanmore, "Religion and Welsh Literature in the Age of the Reformation," Proceedings of the British Academy LXIX (1983): 371-408.

Yost, John K., "German Protestant Humanism and the Early English Reformation: Richard Taverner and Official Translation," Bibliotheque d'Humanisme et Renaissance XXXII(1970): 613-25.

INDEX OF PERSONS

Abbot, George, Archbishop, 199
Abbot, Robert, Bishop, 199
Acontius, Jacob, 367-368
Ahlstrom, Sidney, 450
Aidan, Bishop, 19
Ainsworth, Henry, 388, 400
Aires, Henry, 179
Airy, Henry, 199
Alexander the Great, 161
Allen, William, Cardinal, 142, 189-195; "Angelle of darknes," 190; Cardinalate, 190; Cecil's Execution of Justice, 191; Defense of English Catholics, 191-192; Douai Seminary, 190; Gregory Martin, 193-94; Lancashire visit, 190; Oxford residence, 189; Recusant leader, 142, Rheims College, 190; Rheims N.T. (1582), 195
Alley, William, Bishop of Exeter, 237
Almasy, R., 185
Ambrose, Bishop, 198, 220, 316-317
Ames, William, 319
Anderson, Marvin W., 8
Anderson, Virginia Dejong, 290
Angier, John of Denton, 322
Anne of Bohemia, Queen, 17, 41-42
Antigonus, 161
Anton, Robert, 333
Aquinas, Thomas, 21, 40, 46,192
Arematthia, Joseph of, 267
Aristotle, 91, 381-382, 404,411
Arminius, Jacob, 398
Arthur, Thomas, 72
Arundel, Earl of, 194
Arundel, Thomas, Archbishop, 15, 17-18, 41, 49-50, 79
Aston, John, 16, 50
Aston, Margaret, 14, 18-19, 41, 50-51
Athanasius, 220
Audley, Thomas, 112
Augustine, Bishop, 26, 36, 45, 50, 198-199, 233, 257, 316-318, 366, 386
Auriol, Peter, 32
Awdley, John, 311
Aylmer, John, 225

Backus, Irena, 169
Bacon, Ann, 172, 180
Bacon, Anthony, 172, 180
Bacon, Edward, 245
Bacon, Francis, 180
Bacon, Nathaniel, 245
Bacon, Sir Nicholaus, 172, 180, 245
Bacon, Robert, 5
Bale, John, Bishop, 25-26, 75, 143, 185
Balmford, James, 340-341
Bankes, Richard, 105
Barker, Christopher, London printer, 169, 178, 186

Barlow, Bishop, 123
Barnes, Joseph, 178
Barnes, Robert, 76,87,93-95,369
Baro, Peter, 175, 339, 398
Baron, John, 179
Barrow, Henry, 260, 383-384, 386-387, 389, 392, 395
Bayly, Bishop, 267
Bayly, Lewis, 409
Bayne(s), Christopher, 226-227
Baynes, Paul, 395
Beale, Abraham, 176
Beard, Thomas, 266
Becon, Thomas, 370
Bede, Venerable, 19
Bell, Stephen, 49
Benedict II, Pope, 187
Bennett, Henry S., 176
Benroth, Gustav A., 32, 35
Bentham, Thomas, Bishop, 223-226, 238, 243-244, 373
Berkovitch, Sacvan, 335
Berthelet, Thomas, 98, 109-110
Bessarion, Cardinal, 234
Beza, Theodore, 142, 154, 159, 169-185, 191-192, 194-195, 197-198, 200,215,220, 238-241, 244-245, 252-253, 255, 265,271, 308-310, 331, 339-341, 365, 367, 381, 397,432; Ashby textbooks, 181; Bishop and Harrison printers of Beza, 176; Briefe and Pithie Summe 173-174, 178; Browne dissents, 381; Career, 171; Cartwright, 252-253; Christian Meditations, 172, 178; Codex Beza, 171; Confessio (1560), 220, 310; De Peste (1579), 331, 339-340; De Veris... Notis (1579), 175; Diduth letter (1750), 367; Queen Elizabeth,172; Fulke's defense, 198; Genevan pastor, 142; Geneva N.T.(1586), 170; Gilby translates Beza, 179; Golding translates Beza, 179; Greek N.T.(1556), 154; Greek/Latin N.T.(1565), 169; Hooker on Beza, 184-185; Latin Works, 172; Letters to London Churches, 172; Oiseleur's annotations (1574), 169; Oxford influence, 181; Penry translates Beza, 179; Poemata (1569), 180; Poissy (1561), 191; Predestination, 173,183-184; Questiones and Answeres, 174,178; Recusant complaint, 194-195; Rheims N.T. (1600), 197; de Reina letter, 240; Responsio (1558) to Castellio, 159, 175, 365; Romans (5:12), 169-170; Stubbs translates Beza, 179; Sylvanus letter (1574), 432; Theses Theologicae (1586), 175, 178; Threefold Order of Bishops, 175,241,255; Tomson version (1576), 169,182,397; Vautroullier prints Beza's

Latin texts, 177; Waldegrave prints Beza, 179
Bibliander, Theodorus, 309
Bigg, John, 263
Bilney, Thomas, 72, 158, 309, 370, 455
Bilson, Thomas, 199
Bindoff, S. T., 222
Bishop, George, 176
Bloesch, Donald, 451
Bocher, Joan, 370
Bodley, John, 168
Bodley, Thomas, 199
Boehme, Jacob, 270
Boleyn, Anne, Tudor queen, 99-100, 104
Boniface VIII, Pope, 187-188
Bonner, Edmund, Bishop, 116, 118, 124
Boradel, Margaret, 285
Bowes, Sir William, 395
Bowker, James, 337
Boynon, William, 404
Boys, Thomasine, 388
Brachlow, Stephen, 390,394,395
Bradford, John, 218
Bradford, John, 371
Bradford, William, 307-308, 372, 388, 419, 431
Bradshaw, William, 222
Braybrooke, Robert de, Archbishop, 17
Bredwell, Stephen, 399
Brenz, John, 228
Brewster, Richard, 395
Brewster, William, 395, 419
Brigden, Susan, 71-72
Bridges, John, 255, 257
Brierley, Robert, 428
Brinkelow, Henry, 87
Brinsley, John, 181
Bristow, Richard, 190, 194-196, 200
Bradwardine, Thomas, 21, 29
Browne, John, 378
Browne, Robert, 178, 260, 372, 376; Aristotle's logic, 381-382; Brownists, 386, 395; "buggery," 377; Cambridge caps and degrees, 381-382; Career, 378-379; Covenant, 379-380; Treatise Upon 23 Matthewe (1582), 381-383; "Troublechurche Browne," 399; True and Short Declaration, 379
Brute, William, 48-49
Bucer, Martin, 80,159,215,220, 231, 238-239, 244-246, 263, 308, 312-313, 315, 318, 363, 383; Cambridge, 159,245-246; Cartwright lists B., 220; Continental reform, 308; Covenant theology, 80; Cox and Book of Common Prayer, 383; De Regno Christi, 263; Grindal, 238-239; Hutton, 244; Puritanism, 215; Romans (1536), 315,318; Servetus, 363; Vermigli and Strasbourg, 312-313
Buckingham, John, Bishop 16

Bugenhagen, Johann, 83-84
Bulkeley, Edward, 199
Bullinger, Heinrich, 144, 149, 173, 176-178, 188, 215, 231, 253, 308, 313-316, 318; Apocalypse, 188; Beza's letter, 253; English translations, 173, 176-178; Jewel's Apology (1561), 231; Knox interview (1554), 144; Romans 8 (1537) 313-316, 318
Bullingham, Nicholas, Bishop, 225
Buniun, William, 404
Bunyan, John, 325, 402-419,454, 456; Apollyon, 414; Beulah land,417; Mr. By-ends, 415-416; Come & Welcome (1678), 418; Doubting Castle, 416-417, 454; Grace Abounding (1666), 325, 402-403, 409-410, 411; Grace Abounding (1672?), 410; Grace Abounding (1680), 407, 410; Hill Lucre, 416; House Beautiful, 414; Interpreter's House, 412-413; Law and Grace (1659), 411; Luther, 410, 417; Pilgrim's Progress (1678), 402, 412-419; Pilgrim's Progress (1678/79), 414; Quaker errors, 407; Sermon (1688), 418-419; Sighs from Hell (1658), 408; Some Gospel-truths Opened (1656), 406; Vanity Fair, 415; Vindication of Some Gospel Truths Opened (1657), 407
Burrage, Champlin, 374-375
Burroughes, Jeremiah, 287-288
Burroughs, Edward 405
Butterworth, Charles C., 139
Byddell, John, 109, 113
Bynneman, Henry, 177-178

Caldwell, Patricia, 288-289,307
Caligula, Emperor, 161
Calvin, John, 143-144,146,148-149,151,154,169,173,176-180, 182-183,185,192,197,220-221, 237-238,241,252,308-310,313-316, 318-319, 326, 337-338, 363-366, 425-426, 432, 455; Cardinal Allen cites, 192; Astrologie judiciare (1549), 337-338; Beza's fidelity, 182-183; Bishop and Harrison, 176-177; Castellio, 365-366,432; "Christ is end of the Lawe," 154,169; Commentaries on N.T., 309; John Cotton, 426; John Day, 176; Queen Elizabeth, 425; English editions, 173; Female rulers, 146; Frankfurt Church, 143; French Ezekiel, 455; German Catechism, 237-238; Richard Hooker, 185; Institutes, 220-221,310,319, 363,366; John Knox, 143; "Prophesyings," 241; Rheims

N.T., (1600), 197; Romans (8), 313-316,318; Servetus, 363-365
Camerarius, Joachim von, the Elder, 169
Campensis, James, 95
Campion, Edmund, S.J., 190, 192, 194, 377
Canisius, Peter, S.J., 2
Capito, Wolfgang, 105
Carlson, A. J., 235-236, 237
Carroll, Peter, 452
Carter, John, 272
Cartwright, Thomas, 172, 178, 185,199,215, 219-220,230, 245-247, 249-253, 256-259, 260-261, 263-264, 271,326, 377,379,387,393; Basle, 258; Beza, 172, Robert Browne, 379; Cambridge Disputation (1564), 247; Career,245-260; Catechisme (1616), 259-260; Defense of Ecclesiastical Regiment (1574), 260-261; Deprived of Cambridge Chair, 252, 256; Queen Elizabeth, 247; Geneva, 252-253; Gregory of Nazianzus, 220; Great St. Mary's, 149-50; Heidelberg, 258; Hildersham, 220; Ireland, 249; Henry Jacob, 393; Thomas Lever, 246; Middelburg, 387; Ormerod, 219; "Puritan," 215, 230; Replye (1572) to Whitgifts' Answer, 256-258; Second Admonition (1572), 377; second replie (1577) to Whitgifts' second answer, 259; Sermons on Acts (1570), 250; Six Articles (1570), 251; Walter Travers, 258-259
Cassander, 161
Castellio, Sebastian, 159, 175, 309, 365-368, 372, 432
Catherine, Duchess of Suffolk, 179-180
Catto, J. I., 30, 31
Cecil, Robert, 243
Cecil, William, Lord Burleigh, 144,172,179,191,227,237-238, 242-243,251-252,378-379,383
Celsi, Mino, 367
Cervicorn, Eucharius, 99
Chaderton, Laurence, 177, 216, 250, 273, 387, 395
Chadwick, Owen, 151
Chambers, R. W., 91
Channing, William Ellery 454
Charles I, Stuart King, 403-404, 405
Charles II, Stuart King, 411, 416
Charles IX, King, 181
Charles V, Emperor, 144, 152
Chauncy, Charles, 335
Cheke, Sir John, 231
Child, John, 409
Chrysostom, John, Bishop and Patriarch, 50, 119, 220, 233, 313, 315, 316-318
Cicero, 95

Clanvow, John, 48
Clarke, John, 368
Clarke, Samuel, 172, 325
Claydon, John, 53
Cleaver, Robert, 217, 308
Clebsch, William, 81
Clement VI, Pope, 22
Clement, Christopher, 369-371, 372
Cliffe, J. T., 220, 222, 308
Cluer, William, 277
Cochlaeus, Johannes, 86
Cohn, Norman, 406
Coke, Sir Edward, 275
Coke, Sir William, 420
Cole, Henry, 230, 232
Cole, Robert, 372
Cole, William, 154, 159-160
Colet, John, 71
Collett, William, 7
Collinson, Patrick, 1,2,153, 217-220, 222,238,247,263, 265,273, 308-309, 322, 324-325, 327,344,386,399
Coocke, Robert, 368-372
Cooke, Sir Anthony, 231
Coolidge, John, 307-308,319
Cooper, 387
Cooper, Thomas, Bishop, 232,399
Copernicus, 405
Corro, Antonio del, 238, 240
Cotton, John, 283-284, 420-423, 425-429, 431-432
Courteney, William, Archbishop, 15-16, 26, 33-34
Coverdale, Miles, Bishop, 75, 93-96, 100,102,104,109,113, 116,118, 122-123, 154-155, 159, 163-164, 222,228,330, 343, 374; Biblical editions, 95-96, 222; Continental visit (1528-46), 94; *Coverdale Bible* (1535), 98-104; Cromwell letter (1527), 113; *Deuteronomy* (32), 102; *Geneva Bible* (1560), 154-157; *Great Bible* (1539), 118; *Ghostly Psalms* (1539), 95; *Isaiah* (40), 103; *James* (4), 156-157; *Job* (39), 103-104; *John* (14), 156-157; John Jewel, 228; Lutheran translator, 75, 330; *Matthew* (6), 155-156; *Micah* (2:1), 159; Nicholson's editions (1537), 116; Pentateuch translation (1529), 94; Preacher (1528), 93; *Proverbs* (9), 102-103,164; *Psalm* (91), 344; *Romans* (8), 156-157; Sermon (1568), 374; *Taverner's Bible* (1539), 109; Textual varients (1540-41), 122-123; Translator's preface (1535), 100-101
Cox, Benjamin, 401
Cox, Richard, Bishop, 143, 152, 223, 225, 228, 230, 241, 383
Cradoch, Walter, 268
Cranmer, Thomas, Archbishop 95, 107-108, 114, 118-123, 141,

144, 228, 241, 399; Black rubric, 114; Canterbury convocation (1542), 122-123; Coat of Arms, 118; Cooper's Admonition (1589), 399; Defense of the True Sacrament (1550), 241; Disputation (1554), 228; Great Bible Prologue (1540), 119-122; Latin/English N.T. mandated for Clergy, 114; Letter to Cromwell (1537), 107-108; Martyrdom (1556), 141
Crespin, Jean, 153, 157
Cromwell, Oliver, 266, 384, 405-406
Cromwell, Thomas, 75,95,97-99, 104-105, 107-108, 111-114, 116-118, 122; Cranmer's letter (1537), 107-108; Episcopal letter (1538), 113-114; Grafton's letter (1537), 108; Great Bible (1539), 95, 111-112,116-118; Injunctions to Clergy (1538), 111-112; Lutheran translations, 75; Matthew's Bible (1537), 114; Nycholson's letter (1535), 99; Rochepot Affair, 117-118; Thomas Starkey, 112; Supplication (1529?), 112; Richard Taverner, 104-105; Tyndale supporter, 113; Vernacular bible proposal (1531) by St. German, 97-98
Cross, Claire, 180
Crowe, William, 308
Crowley, Robert, 369, 373-374
Cyprian, Bishop, 198, 220

Dahmus, Joseph, 16
Danaeus, Lambert, 245, 265
Danner, Dan, 151
Darling, Thomas, 336
Davies, Richard, Bishop, 267
Davis, J. F., 368, 370-371
Dawson, Thomas, 177
Day, John, English printer, 115, 176, 310
Dayrell, John, 397
Deanseley, Margaret, 39, 42
Dell, William, 430
Democritus, 5
Denham, Henry, 178
Dent, Arthur, 287, 409
Dent, C. M., 216
Dering, Edward, 273
Dickens, A. G., 112, 370, 456
Dod, John, 217, 259, 308
Dodd, Gregory, 237
Domitian, Emperor, 161,186,188
Donne, John, 37, 342-343
Doolitell, Thomas, 337
Dorley, Sir Richard, 280
Dorman, Thomas, 230
Dorne, John, 70
Dove, Richard, Bishop, 278
Downame, John, 402
Dudith (Dudicz), Andreas, 367
Dudley, Thomas, 290
Duggan, Lawrence, 2
Dyer, Alan, 341

Eachard, John, 428
Earle, 218
Eason, 170
East, Thomas, 178
Eaton, John, 428
Eaton, Nathaniel, 287
Eberhard of Broich, Lord Fridleburge, 312
Eck, Johann, 2
Edbury, William, 430
Edward II, King, 28
Edward VI, Tudor King, 140, 144-145,159,179,189,232,234, 239, 245-246, 260, 263, 323, 370,372,381-383, 388-389,399
Edwards, Jonathan, 37, 335
Egerton, 387
Eliot, John, 284, 427
Elizabeth I, Tudor Queen, 154, 172-173, 176, 189-192, 200, 215, 223, 225, 227, 230-231, 235-239, 241, 243, 245, 247-248, 253-254, 260, 273, 275, 367, 373-375, 377, 425, 455
Elton, Sir Geoffrey R., 91, 105, 112, 376-377
Ely [Hely], Thomas, 262
Emerson, Ralph Waldo, 1,453-454
Epicurus, 5
Episcopius, 396
Erasmus, Desiderius, 2-3, 69, 77-78,86,94,105,113,140,178, 181,198,313-314,316,371,455; John Brinsley, 181; Coverdale, 94; Ecclesiastes (1535), 2-3; Enchiridion (1533), 78; William How, 178; Infant Baptism, 371; Luther's Conclusions, 69; Matthew (3:2), 198, More's letter (1532), 86; Paraphrases, 140; Romans (8), 313-314, 316; Taverner translates, 105, 113; I Timothy (1:15), 455; Tyndale, 77-78
Essex, Earl of, 244
Estienne, Robert, 309
Ewich, Johann, 332

Fagius, Paul, 159, 245
Featley, Daniel, 400-401
Featly, John, 334
Felinus [Bucer], 139
Fenner, Dudley, 178,262-263,326
Fenner, Dudley, 221, 262
Field, John, 177, 179, 241, 254-256, 273, 369
Fish, Simon, 96
Fisher, John, Cardinal, 94,159
Fitz, Richard, 373-374
Fletcher, Richard, 262
Fogny, John, 195
Forshall and Madden, 39, 44-45
Foster, John, 311
Fox, George, 407, 426-427, 432
Fox, Richard, 370
Fox, Sir Richard, 93
Foxe, John, 19, 25, 51, 59, 77-79, 94-95, 112, 115, 117, 171, 185, 188, 222, 224, 325, 369, 373, 376-377, 405; Antichrist, 188; John Bale's

Image, 185; Thomas Cromwell, 112; John Day publishes Actes and Monuments, 115; Great Bible (1539), 117; Henrician heretics, 369; Luther prefaces, 376-377; John Rough, 373; Title page of A. & M., 222; Tyndale, 77-79, 94-95; Wyclif, 25
Francis I, King, 116-117
Frederick II, Emperor, 186
Frederick III, Count Palatine, 258
Freke, Edmund, Bishop, 324, 379
Frere, 220
Friedman, Jerome, 364
Fristedt, S. L., 39-40
Frith, John, 74-75, 87, 158
Fritzralph, William, Bishop, 19, 21-22, 27
Froben, John, 69
Froschover, Christopher, 159
Fry, Francis, 122
Fulke, William, 104,190,197-198
Fuller, John, 53-54
Fuller, Thomas, 271-272
Fuller, Thomas, 407
Fyll, Robert, 179

Gadbury, John, 337
Gardiner, Stephen, Bishop, 93, 123, 145, 157-158
Garrett, Thomas, 73-74,225,370
Garvais, Henry, 116
Gauge, William, 333
Gaunt, John, Duke, 15, 26, 30
Gee, John Archer, 78
George, Timothy, 394
Geveren, 181
Gheast, Edmund, Bishop, 241
Gibbons, Richard, S.J., 197
Gifford, George, 322-323, 329, 384-386, 392
Gifford, John, 410
Gilbert, George, 195
Gilby, Anthony, 149, 151, 154, 157-161, 163, 179-180
Gilgate, William, 400
Glamis, Lord, 255
Glauburg, Johann von, 152
Godskall, James, 332, 334
Golding, Arthur, 176, 179
Goodman, Christopher, 154, 322
Goodrich, Thomas, Bishop, 123
Goodrich, Richard, 231
Gorton, Samuel, 427, 429-431
Gough, John, 370, 373
Grafton, Robert, English printer, 106-108, 116-117, 119, 123, 139
Greaves, Richard, 148-149, 308
Greenham, Richard, 260, 270-272, 337, 378, 431
Greenslade, S. L., 88, 99, 102
Greenwood, John, 383-384, 386
Gregoire, Pierre, 193
Gregory I, Pope, 59
Gregory IX, Pope, 186
Gregory of Nazianzus, Bishop and Patriarch, 120, 220, 233, 326
Gregory VII, Pope, 186

Gregory XI, Pope, 27-28
Grene, Christopher, 226
Grindal, Edmund, Archbishop, 143, 172, 224-225, 227, 235, 238-244, 262, 266-267, 323, 328, 367, 373
Grosseteste, Robert, Bishop, 4, 5, 19-20, 24, 31, 456
Gualter, Rudolf, 160, 231, 311, 371, 383
Gura, Philip, 430
Guy, J. A., 98

Haaland, C. Carlyle, 96
Habson, Paul, 401
Hacker, John, 69, 368-369
Haddon, James, 143
Haemstede, Adriaan van, 238,367
Haigh, Christopher, 70, 321, 344-345
Hakluyt, William, 181
Halbeach, 384
Hall, Joseph, 395-396
Hampole, Richard [Rolle], 19
Handy, Robert, 11 (n.30)
Harding, Thomas, 193, 230, 232-234
Hargreaves, Henry, 39-46
Harlakenden, Mr., 281
Harley, Sir Robert, 220
Harmer, John, 179-180
Harrison, John, 174
Harrison, Lucas, 176
Harrison, Robert, 378, 383-384
Harte, Henry, 370-372
Hastings, Francis, 180, 182
Hastings, Lord Henry (see Huntingdon, Earl of)
Hatton, Christopher, 179, 258
Hawkins, Anne, 413
Hawkins, Robert, 373
Hawthorne, Nathaniel, 454
Heale, Felicity, 227
Heath, Nicholas, Bishop, 122
Hegesippus, 187
Helwys, Thomas, 395, 398, 399
Hemmingsen, Nels, 177
Hendley, Thomas, 221
Hendly, Fromabove, 263
Heneage, Sir Thomas, 322
Henry III, Emperor, 186
Henry VIII, Tudor King, 77,83, 85,96, 104-106,110,113, 116-118,123,139-140,158,189,266
Herbert, A. S., 140, 154, 170
Hereford, Nicholas, 16, 33, 34, 39-42, 50
Higgins, Edward, 181
Higinus, Bishop, 371
Hignam, Martha, 265
Hildersham, Arthur, 220, 259, 395, 397
Hildersham, Richard, 180
Hiles, Thomas, 370
Hill, Christopher, 216, 266, 377, 428
Hill, W. Speed, 185
Hirsch, Elizabeth, 365
Hofmann, Melchior, 372
Holland, Henry, 270-271, 337
Hollybush, John, 114
Holmes, Peter, 192-193

Hoockstraten, Johannes, Antwerp printer, 74
Hooker, Joanna, 285
Hooker, Richard, 184-185, 257, 345
Hooker, Thomas, 278, 281, 283, 285, 427
Hooper, John, Bishop, 148-149, 224
Hopkinson, William, 175, 179
Horne, Robert, Bishop, 225
Horst, Irwin, 368, 370-372
Hotman, Francis, 146
How, William, 178
Howards, 70
Howson, John, 199
Hubmaier, Balthasar, 75
Hudson, Anne, 13, 37, 40, 42-44, 46, 51, 53
Hudson, Winthrop, 1, 231, 450
Hughes, Celia, 96
Hunt, William, 217, 308
Huntingdon, Earl of, Lord Hastings, 172, 174, 179-180, 239, 321
Hus, John, 3, 4, 20, 28, 35
Hutchinson, Anne, 283-284, 421-422, 427-430, 432
Hutchinson, Archbishop, 384
Hutchinson, William, 429
Hutson, Harold H., 109
Hutton, Matthew, Bishop, 224, 242-244
Hychens [Hutchins, Hitchins]. See Tyndale
Hyperius, Andreas, 339

Ibn Ezra, Abraham (1089-1164), 159
Illyricus, Matthew Flacius, 197

Jackson, Richard, 395
Jacob, Henry, 389-394, 400
James VI and I, Stuart King of Scotland and England, 178, 189-190, 200, 238, 244, 267, 324, 389-390, 394, 399
James, Thomas, 199
Jeffary, Thomas, 124-125
Jegan, John, Bishop, 395
Jermyn, Sir Robert, 264
Jerome, 50
Jessy, Henry, 400
Jewel, John, Bishop, 180, 215, 224-225, 228-235, 238, 243-244; Ann Bacon translates Apology,180; Thomas Harding, 232-35; Merton College, Oxford, 228; Peter Martyr, 228-229, 231, 238; "Puritan" in Apologie (1562),215, 229-230; St. Paul's Cross Sermon (1559), 232
John XXIII, Antipope, 41
Johnson, Edward, 281
Johnson, Francis, 384, 387-389, 393, 397-398
Johnson, George, 388
Jones, G. Lloyd, 159
Jones, Norman L., 230
Jones, R. Tudor, 269
Jones, William, 324
Jordan, W. K., 367

Josephus, 187
Joye, George, 139
Jud, Leo, 309
Jugge, Richard, 154
Julius III, Pope, 181
Junius, Francis, 170, 185, 187-188, 388

Kaufmann, U. Milo, 412-413
Keltridge, John, 194
Kemp, David, 241
Kendall, Timothy, 180
Kethe, William, 149
Kichel, Walter, 183
Kiffin, William, 400
Kilcop, Thomas, 401
Kimchi, David, Rabbi (1160?-1235?), 159, 339, 364
Knapp, Peggy Ann, 40
Knappen, M. M., 254
Knewstub, John, 264
Knighton, William, 48
Knollys, Hansard, 400
Knowles, David, 5
Knox, John, 142-153, 157-158, 192, 223, 228, 248, 266, 319-321, 368, 371-372; Amersham Sermon (1553), 144; Answer to blasphemous cauillations (1560), 372; Apellation, 147-150; Black rubric, 144; First Blast, 146-147; Second Blast, 150; Robert Cooche, 368, 371-372; Edinburgh riot (August 8, 1563), 320-321; Queen Elizabeth, 248; English stay, 143-144; English visitation (1551), 266; A Faithful Admonition (1554),145-146; Genevan pastor, 142; Frankfurt strife, 152-153, 223, 228; Anthony Gilby, 157; Letter to Commonalty of Scotland, 148; Newcastle Sermon (1552), 143; Scots Confession(1560), 319; Sermon on Isaiah (26) [1565], 320
Kraus, Hans-Joachim, 319-320

Lake, Arthur, Bishop, 181
Lake, Peter, 216, 243-244, 308
Lamb, Thomas, 430
Lambert, Malcolm, 54
Langland, William, 71
Lathrop, John, 400
Latimer, Hugh, Bishop, 95, 141, 180, 399
Latimer, Thomas, Knight, 47
Laud, William, Archbishop, 199, 279-280, 286, 337, 405
Leake, Richard, 337
Lee, Edward, Archbishop, 114
Lefalt, John, 178
Leicester, Earl of, 179-180
Lever, Thomas, 246
Lever, Thomas, 143, 152, 227
Lewis, Clive Staples, 91
Lewkenor, 265
Lindberg, C., 39-40
Linder, Robert, 176, 178
Llwyd, Morgan, 268-269, 270

Loftus, Adam, Archbishop, 249
Lombard, Peter, 21
London, Dr., 73-74
Longland, John, Bishop, 73
Ludwig VI, Count Palatine, 258
Luft, Hans, 101
Luther, Martin, 2, 69-70,72,74-77,80,82-84,88,91-92,95-96, 101,109,168-169,173,177,180, 198,220,326,332,339-341,376, 410, 414, 417-418, 454-456; Babylonian Captivity (1520), 83; Robert Barnes,95; Bugenhagen, 84; Bunyan, 410, 417; Canon, 101, 109; I Corinthians (7), 74; Coverdale, 96; Donatism, 88; Erasmus, 69, 83; Galatians (1535), 92, 168-69, 376, 410; Timothy Kendall, 180; Law/Gospel, 80; Gregory Martin, 198; Thomas More, 69, 83; Ninety-Five Theses, 83; On The Holy Cross (1526), 83; Oxford,70; Pater Noster (1526), 82-83; Plague letter (1527), 332, 339-340; Preface to Romans, 80, 82-83; Parable of the Wicked Mammon (1528), 69, 74, 80, 83; Special and Chosen Sermons (1578), 376; Tyndale, 69, 80, 82-83; Vautroullier, 177; White Horse Inn, 95
Lyford, John, 419
Lyra, Nicholas, 32, 45, 188
Machiavelli, Niccolo, 310, 336, 367
Malden, William, 124
Man, Thomas, 178
Manning, Bernard, 39
Manningham, John, 218-219
Map, Walter, 71
Marbury, Francis, 429
Marlorat, Augustin, 177
Marpeck, Pilgrim, 372
Marprelate, Martin, 219
Marsden, George, 7
Marshall, Stephen, 402
Marshall, William, 113
Marten, Anthony, 221
Martin, Gregory, 190, 193-195, 197-198
Martin, J. W., 372
Martyr, Peter [See Vermigli, Pietro Martire]
Martz, Louis, 90
Mary Tudor, Queen, 106, 140, 145-146, 152, 158-159, 162, 179,224,118,232,235,239,246, 260, 373, 382, 389, 405
Mary, Queen of Scots, 190-191, 200
Masham, Sir William, 420
Mason, Major John, 431
Mather, Cotton, 425, 451
Mather, Richard, 322
Maton, Robert, 401
Matthew, Thomas, 106, 109, 155
Matthew, Toby, Archbishop, 395
Maunsell, Arthur, 178
Maxwell, Lawrence, 69

May, John, 251
Mayler, John, 370
McFarlane, K. B., 48
McGee, J. Sears, 308
McGiffert, Michael, 81
McLelland, Joseph, 313
McPhee, Ian, 172
Mead, Matthew, 334-335
Melanchthon, Philip, 75, 105, 177, 181, 313, 315, 318, 346
Middleton, Henry, 176
Middleton, Hugh, 178
Mildmay, Sir Henry, 384
Mildmay, Sir Walter, 172, 179, 455
Milič, John of Kroměříž, 3
Miller, Perry, 432, 451
Milton, John, 273
Mitchell, William, 181
Møller, Jens, 81
Modena, Mary of, 403
Mollet, Francis, 224
Monmouth, Henry, 77, 370
Montmorency, Constable, 116-117
More, Sir Thomas, 74-75, 79, 83-92, 98, 113, 377; Bugenhagen, 83-84; Cochlaeus, 86; Confutation of Tyndale's Answer (1532), 89-91; Coverdale, 113; Dialogue Against Heresies(1529), 83,85, 88-89; Erasmus, 86; John Foxe, 377; John Frith, 74; C. S. Lewis,91; Response to Luther (1523), 83; Roper, 86-87; St. German, 98; Tyndale, 79
Morgan, John, 308
Morgan, William, 267
Morison, Richard, 75, 113
Morison, Samuel Eliot, 286
Morone, Giovanni, Cardinal, 193
Morrey, Thomas, 181
Morton, Bishop, 280
Moulin, Pierre de, 265
Mozley, J. K., 101, 104, 106, 109, 122-123
Munster, Sebastian, 118,159,309
Musculus, Wolfgang, 220, 241

Napier, John, 216
Neale, Sir John, 230
Nero, Emperor, 144,152,161,187
Netter, Joyagaine, 263
Neville, Bishop, 51
New, J. F., 252, 308
Newbery, Ralph, 178
Newdygate, 369
Nicholas, bookseller, 73
Norfolk, Duke of, 117
Norfolk, Fourth Duke of (Thomas Howard), 194
Northumberland, Duke of, 140, 143-144, 191
Norton, John, 420
Norton, Thomas, 238
Nowell, Alexander, 236-237, 241, 329
Nuttall, Geoffrey, 263
Nycholson, James, English printer, 95, 99, 104-105, 107, 114, 116

O'Day, Rosemary, 222
Ochino, Bernardino, 176, 367
Octavius Caesar, 161
Oecolompadius, Johannes, 74, 80, 86, 220
Oldcastle, Sir John, 13, 47, 51, 75
Olsen, V. Norskov, 376
Origen of Alexandria, 85, 318, 371
Ormerud, Oliver, 219
Osiander, Andreas, 75, 95, 330-331, 341
Oswald, King of Northumbria, 19
Owen, H. G., 374
Owen, John, 403

Paget, Eusebius, 181
Pagninus, 101, 109
Palmer, Anna, 17
Parker, Matthew, Archbishop, 226, 238, 240-241, 245, 248, 267, 323, 374
Parker, Sir George, 369
Parker, T. H. L., 309
Parkhurst, John, Bishop, 225, 228, 235, 241, 324, 371
Parsons, Robert, S.J., 190, 192, 267, 275
Partridge, A. C., 164-165
Patience, Thomas, 400
Paul, G., 247
Payne, Peter, 13
Pearson, J. F. Scott, 245, 249
Pelham, Sir John, 179
Penry, John, 175, 177-179, 266
Pepin III, Frankish King, 188
Pepin the Short, 188
Percy, Henry, 16
Perkins, William, 178, 220, 271, 273, 345, 420, 425
Perna, Pietro, 313
Perrin, John, 178
Petre, William, 114
Petyt, 110
Philip II, French King, 187
Philip II, Spanish King, 152, 159, 181, 190, 267
Pierson, Thomas, 220
Pigge, Oliver, 177
Pilkington, James, Bishop, 225-226
Plato, 5, 404, 411
Plautus, 95
Pole, Reginald, Archbishop and Cardinal, 224
Pollard, A. F., 105
Pollard, A. W., 108-109
Polton, Thomas, Bishop, 51
Pomeranus [see Bugenhagen]
Ponet, John, 153, 148, 238
Porter, H. C., 273
Potmore, Thomas, 370
Poullain, Valerand, 142-143,152
Prescott, Anne, 180
Preston, John, 247,278,318,384
Pricke, Robert, 265
Pricke, Timothy, 265
Ptolemy, 161
Purfoot, Thomas, 178
Purvey, John, 17, 39-41, 45, 50
Pykas, John, 93, 368-369

Pythagoras, 5

Quentel, Peter, 99

Rahner, Karl, 451
Rainolds, William, 194
Rastell, John, 87
Rawlings, John, 368
Redman, Robert, 139
Regnault, Francois, Paris printer, 114-116
Reid, W. Stanford, 145
Reina, Casiodoro de, 238, 240
Reniger, Michael, 225
Repingdon, Philip, 16, 34, 50
Reynolds, John, 199
Rice, Mr., 277
Richard II, King, 34, 41, 49
Richardson, Samuel, 401
Ridley, Nicholas, Bishop, 75, 95, 141, 144, 149, 228, 239, 377, 399
Ridley, Robert, 76
Rigg, Chancellor, 34
Robinson, John, 389-390, 394-397
Rochepot, 117
Rogers, John, 106, 109
Rogers, Richard, 260, 271-276, 288, 310; Cambridge, 272-273; Commentary on Judges (1615), 175-176; Diary (1588), 274; Nicholas Wyeth, 288; Richard Greenham, 271; Seven Treatises, 275, 310; Wethersfield, 272
Rogers, Thomas, 180
Roper, John, 86, 91
Rough, John, 373
Roye, William, 74
Rupp, E. G., 87, 90

St. German, Christopher, 87-88, 97-98
St. Giles, John, 4
Salisbury, John, 224
Saltmarsh, John, 430
Sampson, Thomas, 154, 159-160, 180, 191
Sampson, Thomas, 374-375
Sander, Nicholas, 193
Sanderson, Robert, 336, 337
Sandys, Edwin, Bishop, 225, 237, 239, 242
Sarcerius, Erasmus, 105
Sater, Johannes, 99
Saxton, Bishop, 114
Scambler, Edmund, Bishop, 225, 373
Schildus, Richard, 178
Scotus, John Duns, 21
Sedgwick, Obediah, 287
Selby, Robert, 287
Seleucus, 161
Servetus, Michael, 240, 363-365, 367, 376, 426, 432
Seymour, Edward, Duke of Somerset, 140
Seymour, Jane, Tudor queen, 99, 104
Shelton, John, 70-72
Shepard, Margaret, 283

Shepard, Thomas, 260, 276-279, 280-287, 420, 422, 455; Antinomians, 283-284, 422; Cambridge, 277-279; <u>Confessions</u>, 287-290; English pastor, 280; Harvard, 284-285; Anne Hutchinson, 422; New England, 281-187; Newtown Church, 282; Pastoral profile, 286; Wives, 280, 285; Youth, 276-277
Shepard, William, 276-277
Sibbes, Richard, 264, 319
Singleton, Hugh, 178
Sixtus IV, Pope, 187
Sixtus V, Pope, 190, 192
Skelton, Samuel, 420
Slavin, Arthur J., 112
Sleidan, Johannes, 151
Smith, John, 373
Smith, Ralph, 430
Smith, William, 47
Smyth, John, 389, 397-398
Socinus, Lelio, 367, 454
Solomon, 382
Southern, Richard, 5
Sparkes, 387
Speed, John, 181
Spencer, Edmund, 267
Spenser, Benjamin, 333
Spiera, Francis, 409
Sprint, John, 400
Spufford, Margaret, 342, 344
Spurgeon, Charles Haddon, 7
Squier, John, 340
Stacey, John, 69
Stag, Sister, 431
Standish, John, 141
Stannard, David, 342
Stapleton, Thomas, 215, 230
Starkey, Thomas, 112
Staunton, Edmund, 336
Stephen II, Pope, 188
Sternhold, Thomas, 153
Stockwood, John, 173, 179, 331
Stokes, Peter, 33, 34
Strafford, Earl of, 405
Strickland, William, 254
Stroud, John, 262
Strype, John, 141
Stubbs, John, 179
Stubbs, Philip, 219
Sturm, John, 181
Sudbury, Simon, Archbishop, 15-16, 27
Swadlin, Thomas, 335
Swinderby, William, 16, 48-49
Sylvanus, John, 432

Talbert, Ernest William, 36-37
Tauteville, Mistress Margaret, 280-281
Taverner, Richard, 75, 104-106, 109-110, 113, 155
Taylor, Edward, 289, 454
Taylor, John, 377
Terence, 95
Tertullian, 220, 229, 371
Tewkesbury, John, 69
Theodoret, 233
Thomson, 372
Thomson, S. Harrison, 23, 25-26

Thoresby, John, Archbishop, 19
Thorpe, William, 17, 48-50, 75
Tiberius Caesar, 161
Tolmie, Murray, 400
Tolwyn, William, 75
Tombes, John, 401
Tomson, Laurence, 169-170, 173, 179, 182, 186, 397
Topley, Thomas, 93
Traske, John, 428
Travers, Walter, 258-259, 387
Trefnant, Bishop, 49
Tremellius, Emmanuel, 159, 185
Trevesa, John, 40-41
Trewe, John, 372
Trinterud, L. J., 80, 82
Trajan, Emperor, 186
Trumbull, John, 287
Tunstall, Cuthbert, Bishop, 122, 145, 225, 369
Turner, William, 368, 370-372
Tyacke, Nicholas, 221
Tyball, John, 76, 93, 369-370
Tymme, Thomas, 223
Tyndale, Edward, 77
Tyndale, John, 370
Tyndale, William, 50, 69,74-93, 94-96, 102, 106-107,109,113, 122-123, 148-149, 155-158, 163-166, 170, 180, 198, 200, 222, 228, 369-370, 374, 452; Covenant, 81-82, 148; Coverdale, 102; Robert Crowley, 374; Deuteronomy (32), 164; Enchiridion (1533), 78; Exodus (15), 163-164; Exposition of Matthew V-VII (1533-49), 148-149; Anthony Gilby, 158; Henry VIII, 113; Joshua-Chronicles, 106; Gregory Martin, 198; Thomas More, 88-92; N.T. (1525), 75-76; N.T. (1526), 76,85, 369-370; N.T. (1534), 123, 155-157, 165,222,228; Obedience of a Christen man (1528), 84-85, 92-93, 96, 200; Oxford, 77; Parable of Wicked Mammon (1528), 69,74, 83; Pater Noster (1526), 82-83; Pathway Into Holy Scripture, 81; Pentateuch (1530), 79-80; Preface to Romans (1526), 79-80; Sermon on the Mount (1532/23), 80; Wm. Thorpe, 50; Tutor, 77-78

Udall, John, 177-178, 180
Ullerston, Richard, 18-19
Urban VI, Pope, 40
Utie, Emmanuel, 326-327

Valera, Cipriano de, 240
Van Emmerson, Margaret, 94
Vane, Sir Henry, 423
Vaughn, Stephen, 113
Vautroullier, Thomas, English printer, 168, 176-177
Veale, Abraham, 178
Vergerio, Pier Paolo, Bishop, 409

Vermigli, Pietro Martire [Martyr, Peter], 144,159,176, 182,189,215,220-221,228-229, 231-232,238,241,276,308-318, 371,374,383; Beza, 182; Book of Common Prayer (1552), 383; Robert Cooche, 371; Commentaries, 310; Common Places, 221, 310-311; Robert Crowley, 374; John Day, 176; John Jewel, 215,228-229,231-232,238; Judges (1554), 159; Judges (1561), 276; Knox, 144; Oxford, 189, 232; "Prophesyings," 241; Romans, 231; Romans (8), 312-318
Villers, Pierre L'Oiseleur de, 169
Vingle, Pierre de, 106
Viret, Pierre, 173, 176-178
Virvliet, Daniel, 197
Vitells, Christopher, 372
Vives, Juan Louis, 371
Von Rohr, John, 389, 393

Wake, Arthur, 258
Wakefield, Bishop, 40, 48
Wakeham, William, 51
Waldegrave, Robert, English printer, 175-178
Waller, Lady Anne, 223
Walsh, Sir John, 77
Walsingham, Sir Francis, 169, 182, 322
Walsingham, Thomas, 15, 17
Ward, Samuel, 263
Warde, William, 332, 334
Warden, John, 47
Warwick, Earl of, Lord Robert Rich, 384
Watkins, Owen, 325
Watson, William, 193
Weld, Thomas, 278, 280
Wesley, Charles, 7
Westmorland, Earl of, 191
Weston, William, S.J., 344-345
Whitaker, William, 194, 199
Whitchurch, Edward, English printer, 106, 116-117, 123
White, B. R., 387, 389, 400
White, John, Bishop, 224
Whitgift, John, Archbishop, 172,185,242,246-247,250,252, 256-259,261,263,322,326,383
Whittingham, William, 143,152-157,160,165-166,170,173,179
Wilcox, Thomas, 179, 241, 254, 256, 369
Wilkins, John, 311
Wilks, Michael, 39-40
Williams, Alice, 420
Williams, James, 420
Williams, Robert, 81
Williams, Roger, 2,419-427,430-432, 451-452; Native Americans, 419-420, 422-423; Bloudy Tenent (1644), 423-425, 427; Bloody Tenent more Bloody (1652), 423-424; Charges against (1635), 421; John Cotton, 423, 425-426; George Fox, 426-427; Samuel

Gorton, 430; Hireling Ministry (1652), 419; John Mason, 431; Plymouth Bay, 419; Religious freedom, 424-425, 432; Rhode Island Charter, 423; Salem Church, 419; Governor Winthrop, 421-422; Youth, 419
Willoughby, Harold R., 109
Wilson, Edward, 328
Wilson, John, 402
Winthrop, John, 282, 285, 346, 420-421, 425, 428-431
Wither, George, 199, 337
Wodeford, William, 17
Woldhauser, Conrad, 3
Wolphius, 231
Wolsey, Thomas, Cardinal, 70, 73-74, 105, 112, 261
Wood, Thomas, 153
Woodcocke, Thomas, 178
Wren, Mathew, Bishop, 324
Wright, Mr., S.J., 244
Wyclif, John, 2, 4-6, 13-37, 39-42, 47, 50-55, 72, 74, 88, 109, 374, 451-452, 455; Alms, 14-15; Archbishop Arundel, 17-18; Augustinian theology, 25-31; Biblical scholar, 31-36; Archbishop Courteney, 16; Robert Crowley, 374; Doctor Evangelicus, 13, 53; English New Testament, 40; John of Gaunt, Duke, 15; Robert Grosseteste, 4-5; Thomas More, 74, 88; Pastoral Office (1378), 41; Postilla, 31-32; Realist Philosophy, 20-25; Sermons, 34-35; Skelton, 72; Archbishop Sudbury, 15-16; Wm. Thorp, 50
Wyeth, Nicolas, 287-288
Wykeham, William, Bishop, 15, 26
Wyllyms, Robert, 124

Yost, John, 105

Zanchi, Jerome, 159
Zbynek, Zajic of Hazmburk, Archbishop, 4
Zwingli, Huldrych, 74-75, 80, 86, 176

Akhtar, Shabbir

REASON AND THE RADICAL CRISIS OF FAITH

American University Studies: Series VII (Theology and Religion). Vol. 30
ISBN 0-8204-0451-9 281 pp. hardback US $ 40.20/sFr. 60.30

Recommended prices - alterations reserved

Is belief in the Christian God intellectually defensible? Is it even morally necessary? In this book, Dr. Shabir Akhtar, himself a Muslim, examines and rejects one fideist and two reductionist defences of the rationality of Christian conviction in modern industrial society. He identifies another defensive position - «theological revisionism» - which has recently gained popularity with secularized Christian thinkers. Rejecting this as merely a conservative version of reductionism, he emphazises the need for reviving the tradition of natural theology and, in doing so, a religious vision of the world.

Contents: Faith and reason - Fideism - The Christian tradition - Reductionism - Revisionism - Natural Theology - Presupposes some familiarity with philosophical reasoning - Philosophy of the Christian faith in the context of related religious rivals: Judaism and Islam.

«Akhtar undermines this central orthodoxy (among theists in analytical philosophy of religion), and, shows such revisionist views to be evasive and not providing the rational underpinning for religious belief in our secular age ... This is an important book running against the stream...» (Kais Nielsen, University of Calgary)
«Not only ... erudite and well-researched, but... eloquent and forceful... work of considerable public interest.» (Hugo Meynell, University of Calgary)
«Dr. Akhtar's book stands out from most recent work in the philosophy of religion in being intelligent, clear, direct and forceful.» (C.B. Martin, University of Calgary)

PETER LANG PUBLISHING, INC.
62 West 45th Street
USA - New York, NY 10036

Whittemore, Robert Clifton

THE TRANSFORMATION OF THE NEW ENGLAND THEOLOGY

American University Studies: Series VII (Theology and Religion). Vol. 23
ISBN 0-8204-0374-1 437 pp. hardback US $ 53.00/sFr. 79.50

Recommended prices - alterations reserved

Here is the first detailed textual and critical study in more than half a century of the New England theology of Jonathan Edwards, his disciples Bellamy, Hopkins, Emmons, and Dwight, and their nineteenth-century successors Taylor, Park, and Harris. Largely forgotten today, their quest for a consistent and coherent Calvinism over a period of two centuries is nevertheless of transforming significance for contemporary Protestant thought. Complete with annotated bibliographies and appendices.

Contents: The quest for a consistent and coherent Calvinist theology by Jonathan Edwards and his New England posterity, and what it portends for the present and future of American protestantism – College education.

PETER LANG PUBLISHING, INC.
62 West 45th Street
USA - New York, NY 10036